Nutrition and Feeding in Fish

Nutrition and Feeding in Fish

edited by

C. B. COWEY, A. M. MACKIE and J. G. BELL
Institute of Marine Biochemistry
Aberdeen, Scotland

1985

ACADEMIC PRESS
HARCOURT BRACE JOVANOVICH, PUBLISHER
LONDON ORLANDO SAN DIEGO NEW YORK
TORONTO MONTREAL SYDNEY TOKYO

ACADEMIC PRESS INC. (LONDON) LTD.
24/28 Oval Road,
London NW1 7DX

United States Edition published by
ACADEMIC PRESS INC.
Orlando, Florida 32887

ISBN 0 12 194055 1

Printed in Great Britain

CONTRIBUTORS

R. Ash, School of Biological Sciences, University of Bradford, Bradford, West Yorkshire, UK.

A. D. Beck, U.S. Environmental Protection Agency, Environmental Research Laboratory, Narragansett, Rhode Island 02882, USA.

J. G. Bell, N.E.R.C. Institute of Marine Biochemistry, St. Fittick's Road, Aberdeen AB1 3RA, UK

M. V. Bell, N.E.R.C. Institute of Marine Biochemistry, St. Fittick's Road, Aberdeen AB1 3RA, UK.

D. A. Bengtson, Department of Food Science and Technology, Nutrition and Dietetics, University of Rhode Island, Kingston, Rhode Island 02881, USA.

N. R. Bromage, Fish Culture Unit, Department of Biological Sciences, University of Aston, Gosta Green, Birmingham B4 7ET, UK.

P. J. Bromley, M.A.F.F. Directorate of Fisheries Research, Fisheries Laboratory, Lowestoft, Suffolk NR33 0HT, UK.

C. Y. Cho, Fish Nutrition Laboratory, Department of Nutrition, University of Guelph, Guelph, Ontario, Canada.

J. Clark, Department of Brewing and Biological Sciences, Heriot-Watt University, Chambers Street, Edinburgh, UK.

C. B. Cowey, N.E.R.C. Institute of Marine Biochemistry, St. Fittick's Road, Aberdeen AB1 3RA, UK.

V. O. Crampton, Ewos-Baker Ltd., Westfield, Bathgate, West Lothian EH48 3BP, UK.

P. R. T. Cumaranatunga, Fish Culture Unit, Department of Biological Sciences, University of Aston, Gosta Green, Birmingham B4 7ET, UK.

B. Fauconneau, Laboratoire de Nutrition et d'Elevage des Poissons, I.N.R.A., St. Pée-sur-Nivelle, 64310 Ascain, France.

J. E. Halver, School of Fisheries, University of Washington, Seattle, Washington 98195, USA.

R. J. Henderson, N.E.R.C. Institute of Marine Biochemistry, St. Fittick's Road, Aberdeen AB1 3RA, UK.

P. J. Higgins, Freshwater Fisheries Laboratory, Pitlochry PH16 5LB, UK.

R. Hofer, Institute of Zoology, University of Innsbruck, Austria.

A. J. Jackson, Tyrell, Byford and Pallett Ltd., Station Road, Attleborough, Norfolk NR17 2AX, UK.

A. Kanazawa, Faculty of Fisheries, Kagoshima University, 4-50-20 Shimoarata, Kagoshima 890, Japan.

S. J. Kaushik, Laboratoire de Nutrition des Poissons, I.N.R.A., St. Pée-sur-Nivelle, 64310 Ascain, France.

H. G. Ketola, Tunison Laboratory of Fish Nutrition, U.S. Fish and Wildlife Service, 28 Gracie Road, Cortland, New York 13045, USA.

B. Knights, Applied Ecology Research Group, Polytechnic of Central London, 115 New Cavendish Street, London W1M 8JS, UK.

G. Lambertsen, Institute of Nutrition, Directorate of Fisheries, P.O. Box 4285, N-5013 Nygaardstangen/Bergen, Norway.

C. Leger, Station de Recherches de Nutrition, I.N.R.A., 78350 Jouy-en-Josas, France.

O. Lie, Institute of Nutrition, Directorate of Fisheries, P.O. Box 4285, N-5013 Nygaardstangen/Bergen, Norway.

E. Lied, Institute of Nutrition, Directorate of Fisheries, P.O. Box 4285, N-5013 Nygaardstangen/Bergen, Norway.

K. P. Lone, Department of Zoology, Punjab University, New Campus, Lahore-20, Pakistan.

N. L. Macdonald, Department of Brewing and Biological Sciences, Heriot-Watt University, Chambers Street, Edinburgh, UK.

A. M. Mackie, N.E.R.C. Institute of Marine Biochemistry, St. Fittick's Road, Aberdeen AB1 3RA, UK.

A. J. Matty, Department of Biological Sciences, University of Aston, Gosta Green, Birmingham B4 7ET, UK.

A. I. Mitchell, N.E.R.C. Institute of Marine Biochemistry, St. Fittick's Road, Aberdeen AB1 3RA, UK.

K. T. O'Grady, Department of Zoology, Royal Holloway College, Englefield Green, Surrey TW20 9TY, UK.

B. J. S. Pirie, N.E.R.C. Institute of Marine Biochemistry, St. Fittick's Road, Aberdeen AB1 3RA, UK.

J. R. Sargent, N.E.R.C. Institute of Marine Biochemistry, St. Fittick's Road, Aberdeen AB1 3RA, UK.

K. L. Simpson, Department of Food Science and Technology, Nutrition and Dietetics, University of Rhode Island, Kingston, Rhode Island 02881, USA.

P. B. Spillett, Thames Water Authority, Denton House, Iffley Turn, Oxford OX4 4HT, UK.

J. R. C. Springate, Fish Culture Unit, Department of Biological Sciences, University of Aston, Gosta Green, Birmingham B4 7ET, UK.

J. R. Stark, Department of Brewing and Biological Sciences, Heriot-Watt University, Chambers Street, Edinburgh, UK.

Ch. Sturmbauer, Institute of Zoology, University of Innsbruck, Austria.

P. A. Sykes, M.A.F.F. Directorate of Fisheries Research, Fisheries Laboratory, Lowestoft, Suffolk NR33 0HT, UK.

A. G. J. Tacon, Aquaculture Department and Coordination Programme, Fisheries Department, F.A.O., Rome 00100, Italy.

C. Talbot, Freshwater Fisheries Laboratory, Pitlochry PH16 5LB, UK.

M. J. Walton, N.E.R.C. Institute of Marine Biochemistry, St. Fittick's Road, Aberdeen AB1 3RA, UK.

T. Watanabe, Laboratory of Fish Nutrition, Tokyo University of Fisheries, Konan 4-5-7, Minato-Ku, Tokyo 108, Japan.

R. P. Wilson, Department of Biochemistry, P.O. Drawer BB, Mississippi State University, MS 39762, USA.

PREFACE

Fish farming has been practised over a very long period, pond culture of carp being said to have proceeded in a primitive form 2000 years ago. Improvements in culture methods have occurred continuously but the advances which have transformed fish farming from an art to a science have gathered momentum over the past three decades. The increase in number of fish hatcheries and the general advance of commercial aquaculture in recent years has been dependent upon research findings, while at the same time they have given an impetus to a further mushrooming of research work.

The resulting increase in knowledge has been reflected, over recent years, in scientific meetings and reviews. These have evaluated and summarized the position as it stood at the time. The symposium on which this book is based was organized to provide a forum for the presentation and discussion of reviews and original contributions on all aspects of research in fish nutrition and feeding, authors being given considerable licence over the subject matter with which they dealt. Much new data was presented in poster form at the symposium and material from some of these posters has been included in the book, limitations of space unfortunately preventing this happening to a greater extent. No attempt was made to cover each area of fish nutrition exhaustively, and to a degree the book inevitably reflects the interests of the editors and symposium organizers.

The widespread interest in the subject was mirrored by the enthusiasm of people attending, the bulk of whom were from outside the UK, giving a truly international flavour to the meeting. They earned our thanks, especially those who gave posters, for the way in which they co-operated in meeting programme schedules.

Without the symposium there would, of course, have been no book. Planning and organizing were a considerable undertaking which the committee met with a blend of good humour and energy. Dr Peter Tytler of the University of Stirling, sometime Meetings Secretary of the Fisheries Society of the British Isles, provided much useful guidance. Especial mention should be made of the splendid contributions Sandy Mitchell and Margaret Maxwell made to the organization, somehow keeping track of things and knowing the answers to (most) questions.

Finally, we are especially grateful to Professor John Sargent for his unfailing encouragement and support and for making available facilities without which we would have been hard pressed to cope.

C. B. COWEY
A. M. MACKIE
J. G. BELL

ACKNOWLEDGEMENTS

The organizers thank the staff of the University of Aberdeen who contributed to the success of the meeting. The assistance of the following organizations is also gratefully acknowledged since without their help it would have been much more difficult to hold the meeting.

Bank of Scotland
EWOS International AB
Unilever Research

CONTENTS

AMINO ACID AND PROTEIN REQUIREMENTS OF FISH[1]

ROBERT P. WILSON

Department of Biochemistry, Mississippi State University,
Mississippi State, MS 39762, U.S.A.

I.   GROSS PROTEIN REQUIREMENTS

Fish, like other animals, do not have a true protein
requirement but have a requirement for a well balanced
mixture of essential and nonessential amino acids.
Numerous investigators have utilized various semipurified
and purified diets to estimate the protein requirements
for specific fish species. The dietary protein
requirements of several species of young fish have
recently been tabulated in other reviews (Millikin, 1982;
NRC, 1983). In general, the values range from about 30 to
55% crude protein for maximum growth. Many of these values
are probably overestimated due to one or more of the
following reasons: most requirement values are based on
levels of protein that result in maximum growth with
little or no index of protein utilization; many of the
requirement values have been determined with varying
protein to energy ratios; various investigators have used
different estimated metabolizable energy values in
formulating their test diets; and the protein source(s)
may not contain adequate amounts of each of the essential
amino acids.

[1]Mississippi Agricultural and Forestry Experiment
Station Publication Number 5841.

NUTRITION AND FEEDING IN FISH
ISBN: 0 12 194055 1

II.   QUALITATIVE AMINO ACID REQUIREMENTS

The essentiality of various amino acids for fish has been determined either by growth studies or by ^{14}C-labelling studies.   Most of these studies have involved feeding purified diets containing crystalline amino acids and determining the essentiality of each amino acid based on the growth response associated with the deletion of that amino acid from the diet.   On the basis of these types of studies, several fish species have been shown to require the following 10 amino acids: arginine, histidine,   isoleucine,   leucine,   lysine,   methionine, phenylalanine,   threonine,   tryptophan and valine.   The species that have been studied by this method include the chinook   salmon   (Halver   et al.,   1957),   sockeye salmon (Halver and Shanks, 1960), rainbow trout (Shanks et al., 1962), channel catfish (Dupree and Halver, 1970), Japanese eel and European eel (Arai et al., 1972), common carp (Nose et al., 1974), red sea bream (Yone, 1976) and Tilapia zillii (Mazid et al., 1978).   Additional studies have   indicated that   these   same   10   amino   acids   are essential for the plaice and sole (Cowey et al., 1970) and sea bass (Metailler et al., 1973) based on the lack of ^{14}C incorporation into these amino acids following intra-peritoneal injection of uniformly labelled ^{14}C-glucose.

III.   DETERMINATION OF AMINO ACID REQUIREMENTS

The complete quantitative amino acid requirements have been established for only four species, namely the chinook salmon, common carp, Japanese eel and channel catfish.   A limited number of requirement values have also been reported for the coho salmon, sockeye salmon, rainbow trout, lake trout, gilthead bream, sea bass, and one species of tilapia (Sarotherodon mossambicus).

Most investigators have used the basic method developed by Halver and coworkers (Mertz, 1972) to determine the quantitative amino acid requirements of fish.   This procedure involves feeding graded levels of one amino acid at a time in a test diet containing either all crystalline amino acids or a mixture of casein, gelatin and amino acids formulated so that the amino acid profile is identical to whole hen's egg protein except for the amino acid being tested. This procedure has been used successfully with chinook, coho and sockeye salmon, Japanese eel and rainbow trout. However, the amino acid test diets must be neutralized with sodium hydroxide for utilization by carp (Nose et al., 1974) and channel catfish (Wilson et al., 1977).

Most of the amino acid requirement values reported to date have been estimated based on the conventional growth response curve. A few investigators have also shown a high degree of correlation of serum free amino acid levels to dietary amino acid intake. For example, the serum content of certain amino acids remained very low until the requirement for that amino acid was obtained and then increased to very high levels when excessive amounts of the amino acid were fed.

Several investigators have had varying degrees of success by using semi-purified and practical type test diets to determine amino acid requirements for fish. The semipurified type diet involves using an imbalanced protein as the major source of intact amino acids such as zein or corn gluten which are quite deficient in certain esential amino acids. This type of diet only requires the use of a small amount of a limited number of crystalline amino acids in the test diets. The practical type diet involves using normal feedstuffs to furnish the bulk of the amino acids in the test diets. These may be formulated either to make up a fixed amount of the desired protein level with the remaining amount of the protein equivalent being made up of crystalline amino acids or to be deficient in only the amino acid being studied. Requirement values obtained by the use of these types of diets should only be used as estimated values because of the many inherent problems in this procedure. Some of these include: protein digestibility coefficients vary; amino acid availability within a protein may vary; the rate of passage and digestion of various proteins varies and may be slower than the rate for supplemental amino acids; the imbalanced proteins commonly used, i.e., zein and corn gluten, contain high levels of leucine which may depress the rate of absorption of other amino acids; and an accurate analysis of the total protein content of the test diets is necessary due to the relationship between the amino acid requirement and level of protein intake.

Cowey and Luquet (1983) have recently reviewed the various problems involved in the accurate determination of the amino acid requirements of fish. Therefore these problems will not be further discussed here.

IV.   QUANTITATIVE AMINO ACID REQUIREMENTS

A. Arginine

The arginine requirement values are summarized in Table I.   Salmon have the highest requirement of about 6% of dietary protein, whereas the other species require about 4 to 5% of protein.   The requirement value of about 4% of protein for rainbow trout appears to be the most reasonable however values ranging from 3.3 to 5.9 have been reported.   Additional studies are needed to confirm this requirement in rainbow trout.

Table 1. Arginine Requirements

Fish	Requirement	Type of Diet	Reference
Chinook salmon	6.0(2.4/40)	Purified[a]	Klein and Halver (1970)
Coho salmon	5.8(2.3/40)	Purified	Klein and Halver (1970)
Common carp	4.3(1.6/38.5)	Purified	Nose (1979)
Japanese eel	4.5(1.7/37.7)	Purified	Arai (Nose, 1979)
Channel catfish	4.3(1.03/24)	Purified	Robinson et al. (1981)
Rainbow trout	3.3(1.2/36)	Semipurified[b]	Kaushik (1979)
	4.0-4.9 (1.4-1.7/35)	Purified	Kim et al. (1983)
	3.5-4.0 (1.6-1.8/45)	Semipurified[c]	Walton et al.[g]
	<5.9(2.8/47)	Semipurified[ed]	Ketola (1983)
Gilthead bream	5.0 (1.7/34)	Semipurified[e]	Luquet and Sabaut (1974)
Tilapia	<4.0(1.59/40)	Practical[f]	Jackson and Capper (1982)

Requirements are expressed as percent of protein. In parenthesis, the numerators are requirements as percent of diet and the denominators are percent total protein in diet. [a] Contained either amino acids or casein, gelatin and amino acids. [b] Contained zein, fish meal and amino acids. [c] Contained white fish meal, zein and amino acids. [d] Contained corn gluten meal and amino acids. [e] Contained CPSP 80 and amino acids. [f] Contained fish meal, soya meal, groundnut and amino acids. [g] Unpublished data.

A dietary lysine–arginine antagonism has been well documented in certain animals. Based upon growth studies, this antagonism could not be demonstrated in channel catfish (Robinson et al., 1981) or rainbow trout (Kim et al., 1983).

Table II. Histidine and Threonine Requirements

Fish	Requirement	Type of Diet	Reference
		Histidine	
Chinook salmon	1.8(0.7/40)	Purified[a]	Klein and Halver (1970)
Coho salmon	1.8(0.7/40)	Purified	Klein and Halver (1970)
Common carp	2.1(0.8/38.5)	Purified	Nose (1979)
Japanese eel	2.1(0.8/37.7)	Purified	Arai (Nose, 1979)
Channel catfish	1.5(0.37/24)	Purified	Wilson et al. (1980)
		Threonine	
Chinook salmon	2.2(0.9/40)	Purified	DeLong et al. (1962)
Common carp	3.9(1.5/38.5)	Purified	Nose (1979)
Japanese eel	4.0(1.5/37.7)	Purified	Arai (Nose, 1979)
Channel catfish	2.0(0.53/24)	Purified	Wilson et al. (1978)

Requirements are expressed as percent of protein. In parenthesis, the numerators are requirements as percent of diet and the denominators are percent total protein in diet.

[a] Contained either amino acids or casein, gelatin and amino acids.

B. Histidine and threonine

The histidine requirements of fish are presented in Table II. Excellent agreement has been found among the species studied with a range of 1.5 to 2.1% of protein. Wilson et al. (1980) were able to confirm the requirement value by the serum free histidine pattern in channel catfish.

The threonine requirement values are also presented in Table II. The salmon and catfish require about 2% of protein, whereas the eel and carp require about 4% of protein. The requirement value in channel catfish was confirmed by the serum free threonine pattern (Wilson et al., 1978).

Table III. Branched chain Amino Acid Requirements

Fish	Requirement	Type of Diet	Reference
		Isoleucine	
Chinook salmon	2.2(0.9/41)	Purified[b]	Chance et al. (1964)
Common carp	2.5(0.9/38.5)	Purified	Nose (1979)
Japanese eel	4.0(1.5/37.7)	Purified	Arai (Nose, 1979)
Channel catfish	2.6(0.62/24)	Purified	Wilson et al. (1980)
Lake trout	2.0-2.6[a] (0.5-0.72/27.6)	Practical[c]	Hughes et al. (1983)
		Leucine	
Chinook salmon	3.9(1.6/41)	Purified	Chance et al. (1964)
Common carp	3.3(1.3/38.5)	Purified	Nose (1979)
Japanese eel	5.3(2.0/37.7)	Purified	Arai (Nose, 1979)
Channel catfish	3.5(0.84/24)	Purified	Wilson et al. (1980)
Lake trout	3.5-4.6[a] (0.96-1.28/27.6)	Practical	Hughes et al. (1983)
		Valine	
Chinook salmon	3.2(1.3/40)	Purified	Chance et al. (1964)
Common carp	3.6(1.4/38.5)	Purified	Nose (1979)
Japenese eel	4.0(1.5/37.7)	Purified	Arai (Nose, 1979)
Channel catfish	3.0(0.71/24)	Purified	Wilson et al. (1980)
Lake trout	2.6-3.3[a] (0.62-0.78/23.7)	Semipurified[d]	Hughes et al. (1983)

Requirements are expressed as percent of protein. In parenthesis, the numerators are requirements as percent of diet and the denominators are percent total protein in diet. [a] These values are recalculated based on the nitrogen content of the test diets. [b] Contained either amino acids or casein, gelatin and amino acids. [c] Contained fish meal, blood meal, cottonseed meal, wheat middlings and amino acids. [d] Contained fish meal and amino acids.

C. Branched-chain amino acids: isoleucine, leucine and
   valine

The requirement values for the branched-chain amino
acids are given in Table III.   The values for salmon,
carp and catfish are essentially the same for all three
amino acids, whereas the values for eel are consistently
higher.   The values originally reported for lake trout
were considerably lower than those observed in the above
group of fish (Hughes et al., 1983).   However, when the
requirement data is recalculated based on the apparent
protein content of the diets, the values fall within the
range as reported for other species.
   Wilson et al. (1980) recorded the changes in serum
concentrations of free isoleucine, leucine and valine as
influenced by increasing dietary levels of each
branched-chain amino acid.   Even though the circulating
levels of the branched-chain amino acids responded to
intake of each respective amino acid the serum patterns
did not confirm the requirement data as determined by
growth rate analysis.   Suboptimal intake of leucine had a
marked effect on serum free isoleucine and valine
levels.   This observation was interpreted to indicate
that leucine may facilitate the tissue uptake of
branched-chain amino acids and/or their intracellular
metabolism.   More recent studies of the channel catfish
have shown additional evidence to support this hypothesis
(Robinson et al., 1984).

D. Lysine

The lysine requirement values are presented in Table
IV.   Similar values have been reported for salmon, eel,
catfish and gilthead bream.   A slightly higher value was
found for carp.   The lower value for tilapia may be due
to low growth rates observed and/or to low digestibility
or utilization of the test diet.   The requirement for
rainbow trout may be lower than for other fishes.   Kim and
Kayes (1982) reported a value of 3.7% of protein based on
6-week growth studies.   Walton et al. (1984a) found the
value to be 4.2% of protein based on growth data.   They
obtained a similar requirement value from a dose-response
curve of expired $^{14}CO_2$ (following an intraperitoneal
injection of L-[U-^{14}C] lysine) against dietary lysine
concentration.   It is not clear why Ketola (1983)
obtained a much higher requirement value of 6.1% of

R. P. WILSON

protein for rainbow trout. His experimental conditions
were, however, quite different in that he used much
smaller fish (initial weight of 1.1g) and an imbalanced
protein source. He also observed very high mortality and
incidence of caudal fin erosion in fish fed the lysine
deficient diets.

Table IV. Lysine Requirements

Fish	Requirement	Type of Diet	Reference
Chinook salmon	5.0(2.0/40)	Semipurified[a]	Halver et al. (1958)
Common carp	5.7(2.2/38.5)	Purified[b]	Nose (1979)
Japanese eel	5.3(2.0/37.7)	Purified	Arai (Nose, 1979)
Channel catfish	5.1(1.23/24)	Purified	Wilson et al. (1977)
	5.0(1.5/30)	Purified	Robinson et al. (1980b)
Rainbow trout	3.7(1.3/35)	Purified	Kim and Kayes (1982)
	4.2(1.9/45)	Semipurified[c]	Walton et al. (1984a)
	6.1(2.9/47)	Semipurified[a]	Ketola (1983)
Gilthead bream	5.0(1.7/34)	Semipurified[ed]	Luquet and Sabaut (1974)
Tilapia	4.1(1.62/40)	Practical[e]	Jackson and Capper (1982)

Requirements are expressed as percent of protein. In parenthesis, the numerators are
requirements as percent of diet and the denominators are percent total protein in diet.
[a] Contained corn gluten meal and amino acids. [b] Contained either amino acids or casein,
gelatin and amino acids. [c] Contained white fish meal, gluten and amino acids.
[d] Contained CPSP 80 and amino acids. [e] Contained fish meal, soya meal, groundnut and
amino acids.

Serum free lysine levels were useful in confirming the
lysine requirement in channel catfish originally
determined at 24% crude protein (Wilson et al., 1977);
however, the serum free lysine levels provided little
indication of the lysine requirement when re-evaluated at
the 30% crude protein level (Robinson et al., 1980b).

E. Total sulfur amino acids: methionine and cystine

The requirement values for methionine and total sulfur amino acids are summarized in Table V. There appear to be some species differences with chinook salmon and gilthead bream requiring the highest level at about 4% of protein, channel catfish requiring the least at about 2.3% of protein and the other species about 3% of protein.

Table V. Methionine and Total Sulfur Amino Acid Requirement

Fish	Requirement	Type of Diet	Reference
Chinook salmon	4.0(1.6/40) Cys = 1% in diet	Purified[a]	Halver et al. (1959)
Common carp	3.1(1.2/38.5) Cys = 0% in diet	Purified	Nose (1979)
Japanese eel	3.2(1.2/37.7) Cys = 0% in diet	Purified	Arai (Nose, 1979)
Channel catfish	2.3(0.56/24) Cys = 0% in diet	Purified	Harding et al. (1977)
Rainbow trout	2.2(1.0/46.4) Cys = 0% in diet	Purified	Walton et al. (1982)
	3.0(1.1/35) Cys = 0.3% in diet	Purified	Rumsey et al. (1983)
	2.9(1.0/35) Cys = 0.5% in diet	Purified	Kim et al. (1984)
Gilthead bream	4.0(1.4/34) Cys not stated	Semipurified[b]	Luquet and Sabaut (1974)
Tilapia	3.2(1.27/40) Cys = 0.7% in diet	Practical[c]	Jackson and Capper (1982)
Sea bass	2.0(1.0/50) Cys not stated	Practical[d]	Thebault (1983)

Requirements are expressed as percent of protein. In parenthesis, the numerators are requirements as percent of diet and the denominators are percent total protein in diet. [a] Contained either amino acids or casein, gelatin and amino acids. [b] Contained CPSP 80 and amino acids. [c] Contained fish meal, soya meal, groundnut and amino acids. [d] Contained fish meal, soya meal, brewers' yeast and methionine.

Several studies have shown that the presence of dietary cystine reduces the amount of dietary methionine necessary for maximum growth. The cystine replacement value for methionine on an equivalent sulfur basis has been determined to be about 60% for channel catfish (Harding et al., 1977) and 42% for rainbow trout (Kim et al., 1984). Robinson et al. (1978) studied the utilization of several potential dietary sulfur compounds in channel catfish. These workers found that DL-methionine was as effective as L-methionine, methionine hydroxy analogue was only about 26% as effective as L-methionine in promoting growth, and no significant growth response was observed when either taurine or inorganic sulfate was added to the basal diet. D-methionine has been shown to replace L-methionine on an equal basis in rainbow trout (Kim et al., 1984).

Rainbow trout appear to be unique in that methionine deficiency results in bilateral cataracts (Poston et al., 1977; Walton et al., 1982; Rumsey et al., 1983). This deficiency sign has not been reported in any other species of fish.

Harding et al. (1977) were able to confirm the methionine requirement in channel catfish by correlating serum free methionine levels with dietary intake.

F. Total aromatic amino acids: phenylalanine and tyrosine

Table VI. Phenylalanine and Total Aromatic Amino Requirements

Fish	Requirement	Type of diet	Reference
Chinook salmon	5.1(2.1/41)[a] Tyr = 0.4% in diet	Purified[b]	Chance et al. (1964)
Common carp	6.5(2.5/38.5) Tyr = 0% in diet	Purified	Nose (1979)
Japanese eel	5.8(2.2/37.7) Tyr = 0% in diet	Purified	Arai (Nose, 1979)
Channel catfish	5.0(1.20/24)[a] Tyr = 0.3% in diet	Purified	Robinson et al. (1980a)

Requirements are expressed as percent of protein. In parenthesis, the numerators are requirements as percent of diet and the denominators are percent total protein in diet.

[a] Calculated to be the total aromatic amino acid requirements based on the phenylalanine plus tyrosine content of the test diets. [b] Contained either amino acids or casein, gelatin and amino acids.

The phenylalanine and total aromatic amino requirement values are presented in Table VI.   Similar values have been reported for salmon and catfish with higher levels being required by the eel and carp.   Growth studies with channel catfish indicated that tyrosine can replace or spare about 50% of the phenylalanine requirement (Robinson et al., 1980a).

G. Tryptophan

The tryptophan requirement values are summarized in Table VII.   It appears that tryptophan levels of about 0.5% of dietary protein are required by most fish with higher values being required by eel, carp and possibly the rainbow trout.   The low value of 0.3% of protein for carp was determined in very small fish (initial weight about 0.2g) fed a zein based test diet (Dabrowski, 1981).   The

Table VII.   Tryptophan Requirements

Fish	Requirement	Type of Diet	Reference
Chinook salmon	0.5(0.2/40)	Purified[a]	Halver (1965)
Coho salmon	0.5(0.2/40)	Purified	Halver (1965)
Sockeye salmon	0.5(0.2/40)	Purified	Halver (1965)
Common carp	0.8(0.3/38.5)	Purified	Nose (1979)
	0.3(0.13/42.5)	Semipurified[b]	Dabrowski (1981)
Japenese eel	1.1(0.4/37.7)	Purified	Arai (Nose, 1979)
Channel catfish	0.5(0.12/24)	Purified	Wilson et al. (1978)
Rainbow trout	0.5(0.25/55)	Semipurified[c]	Walton et al. (1984b)
	0.6(0.20/35)	Purified	Kim et al.[e]
	1.4(0.58/42)	Purified	Poston and Rumsey (1983)
Gilthead bream	0.6(0.2/34)	Semipurified[d]	Luquet and Sabaut (1974)

Requirements are expressed as percent of protein. In parenthesis, the numerators are requirements as percent of diet and the denominators are percent total protein in diet. [a] Contained either amino acids or casein, gelatin and amino acids. [b] Contained zein and amino acids. [c] Contained white fish meal, gelatin and amino acids. [d] Contained CPSP 80 and amino acids. [e] Unpublished data.

high value of 1.4% of protein for rainbow trout may be
overestimated because no dietary levels between 0.25 and
0.50% of diet were fed (Poston and Rumsey, 1983).   These
workers recommend a value of 1.4% of protein for maximum
growth and 1.5% of protein for optimum health scores.

Tryptophan deficiency has been reported to cause
scoliosis and lordosis in sockeye salmon but not in
chinook salmon (Halver and Shanks, 1960) and only
scoliosis in rainbow trout (Shanks et al., 1962; Kloppel
and Post, 1975).   This deficiency sign has not been
reported in other fishes.   Poston and Rumsey (1983) also
observed some incidence of caudal fin erosion, cataracts
and short gill opercula in tryptophan deficient rainbow
trout.

V. VARIOUS METHODS OF ESTIMATING AMINO ACID NEEDS

Since the quantitative amino acid requirements have
only been established for a limited number of fishes,
several investigators have used various methods to
estimate the amino acid needs of other fishes in order to
design and improve their test diets.   The amino acid
patterns of fish eggs and whole body protein have been
used for this purpose.   The results of this approach have
been encouraging and these methods show considerable
promise in the initial design of diets for various fish
until their quantitative requirements are established.

Rumsey and Ketola (1975) reported that improved growth
was observed when Atlantic salmon fry were fed casein in
diets supplemented with essential amino acids to levels in
isolated fish protein.   Similar improvements were
observed when rainbow trout fingerlings were fed soybean
diets supplemented with essential amino acids to simulate
those in either trout eggs or isolated fish protein.
Additional results presented by Ketola (1982) indicate
that both Atlantic salmon and rainbow trout respond well
to various diets supplemented with essential amino acids
to simulate the patterns found in either trout eggs,
salmon eggs or salmon carcass.

Arai (1981) introduced the concept of using A/E ratios
of whole body coho salmon fry to formulate test diets for
this fish.   The A/E ratios were calculated based on the
amino acid composition of whole body coho salmon fry by
dividing the weight of each essential amino acid present
by the total weight of all essential amino acids present,
including cystine and tyrosine and multiplying by 1000.

Fish fed casein diets plus amino acids to simulate the A/E ratios of whole body protein showed much improved growth and feed efficiency.   The same growth rates were observed with a 33% crude protein diet containing casein plus amino acids and a 40% crude protein diet containing casein alone.   Ogata et al. (1983) have also used the A/E ratio concept to design test diets for cherry and amago salmon fry.   A casein diet supplemented with amino acids to simulate the A/E ratio pattern of whole body protein of cherry salmon resulted in better growth in both species than diets containing casein alone, casein plus amino acids to simulate the A/E ratio pattern in eyed egg protein, or white fish meal.

The above experimental evidence supports the empirical relationship between the essential amino acid requirements as determined by growth studies and the pattern of the same amino acids in whole body protein in growing carp previously described by Cowey and Tacon (1983).   They observed a very good correlation when the essential amino acid requirement pattern was regressed against the essential amino acid composition of whole body protein. Cowey and Luquet (1983) also discussed the apparent relationship between dietary amino acid requirements of fish and the essential amino acid composition of fish muscle tissue.   We have also investigated this relationship in channel catfish (Wilson and Poe, 1985). The amino acid composition of channel catfish eggs and whole body protein for three different size groups of fish ranging from 30 g to 863 g was determined.   The amino acid composition of the whole body protein did not differ with size of fish; however, the amino acid pattern in the eggs did differ somewhat from the whole body protein.   A significant correlation (r=0.96) was observed when the requirement pattern was regressed against the whole body protein pattern.   A much poorer relationship (r=0.68) was found when the requirement pattern was regressed against the egg protein pattern.   A/E ratios for channel catfish whole body protein were also calculated by the method of Arai (1981) and found to be highly correlated (r=0.96) with the essential amino acid requirement pattern for channel catfish.   These data indicate that the whole body essential amino acid patterns can serve as a valuable index to confirm amino acid requirement data as determined by growth studies and to formulate test diets for those species where requirement data are not available.   The whole body amino acid pattern appears to be a better index than the fish egg amino acid pattern.   The lack of any significant difference in the amino acid composition of the whole body protein of channel catfish ranging from 30 g to 863 g indicates that the amino acid requirements when expressed as a percent of dietary protein should not change dramatically with increasing size of the fish.

Ogino (1980) has used a somewhat similar approach to actually estimate the amino acid requirements of carp and rainbow trout. He based these estimated values on nitrogen retention studies and the calculated increase in essential amino acid content of whole body protein. He found the requirement values to be quite similar for carp and rainbow trout by this method. Even though the values obtained by this method correlate quite well (r=0.96) with the requirement values reported by Nose (1979) for carp based upon growth studies, they should be treated only as estimates and not as quantitative requirements,

For example, this method underestimated the requirement values for 8 of the 10 essential amino acids, with the requirement value estimated for histidine being 33% less than the value determined by Nose (1979). This underestimation of the requirement values may indicate that a significant amount of certain essential amino acids is needed for maintenance and other metabolic or physiological needs. It also points out the limitations of the predictive nature of this index with respect to estimating requirement values.

REFERENCES

Arai, S. (1981). Bull. Jap. Soc. Sci. Fish. 47, 547–550.

Arai, S., Nose, T. and Hashimoto, Y. (1972). Bull. Jap. Soc. Sci. Fish. 38, 753–759.

Chance, R.E., Mertz, E.T. and Halver, J.E. (1964).J.Nutr. 83, 177–185.

Cowey, C.B. and Luquet, P. (1983). In "Protein Metabolism and Nutrition" (M. Arnal, R. Pion and D. Bonin, eds.) I, 365–384,, INRA, Paris.

Cowey, C.B. and Tacon, A.G.J. (1983). In "Proc. Second Int. Conf. Aquaculture Nutr.: Biochemical and Physiological Approaches to Shellfish Nutrition" (G.D. Pruder, C.J. Langdon and D.E. Conklin, eds.) 13–30, Louisiana State University, Baton Rouge.

Cowey, C.B., Adron, J.W. and Blair, A. (1970). J. Mar. Biol. Assoc. U.K. 50, 87–95.

Dabrowski, K.R. (1981). Z. Tierphysiol., Tierernahrg. u. Futtermittelkde. 46, 64–71.

DeLong, D.C., J.E. Halver, J.E. and Mertz, E.T. (1962).
   J. Nutr. 76, 174–178.
Dupree, H.K. and Halver, J.E. (1970).   Trans. Am. Fish.
   Soc. 99, 90–92.
Halver, J.E. (1965).   Fed. Proc. 24, 229 (abstr.)
Halver, J.E. and Shanks, W.E. (1960).   J. Nutr. 72,
   340–346.
Halver, J.E., DeLong, D.C. and Mertz, E.T. (1957). J.Nutr.
   63, 95–105.
Halver, J.E., DeLong, D.c. and Mertz, E.T. (1958).   Fed.
   Proc. 17: 1873. (abstr.)
Halver, J.E., DeLong, D.c. and Mertz, E.T. (1959).   Fed.
   Proc. 18, 2076. (abstr.)
Harding, D.E., Allen, O.W. and Wilson, R.P. (1977).J.Nutr.,
   107, 2031–2035.
Hughes, S.G., Rumsey, G.L. and Nesheim, M.C. (1983).
   Trans. Am. Fish Soc. 112, 812–817.
Jackson, A.J. and Capper, B.S. (1982).   Aquaculture 29,
   289–297.
Kaushik, S. (1979).   In "Finfish Nutrition and Fishfeed
   Technology" (J.E. Halver and K. Tiews, eds.) I,
   197–207. I.H. Heenemann GmbH and Co., Berlin.
Ketola, H.G. (1982). Comp. Biochem. Physiol. 73B, 17–24.
Ketola, H.G. (1983). J. Anim. Sci. 56, 101–107.
Kim, K.I. and Kayes, R.B. (1982). Fed. Proc. 41, 716.
   (abstr.)
Kim, K.I., T.B. Kayes, T.B. and Amundson, C.H. (1983).
   Fed. Proc. 42, 2198. (abstr.).
Kim, K.I., Kayes, T.B. and Amundson, C.H. (1984). Fed.
   Proc. 43, 3338. (abst.).
Klein, R.G. and Halver, J.E. (1970). J. Nutr. 100,
   1105–1109.
Kloppel, T.M. and Post, G. (1975).   J. Nutr. 105,
   861–866.
Luquet, P. and Sabaut, J.J. (1974).   Actes de colloques,
   Colloques Sur L'Aquaculture, Brest. 1, 243–253.
Mazid, M.A., Tanaka, Y., Katayama, T., Simpson, K.L. and
   Chichester, C.O. (1978).   Bull. Jap. Soc. Sci. Fish.
   44, 739–742.
Mertz, E.T. (1972). In "Fish Nutrition", (J.E. Halver,
   ed.), 105–143. Academic Press, New York.
Metailler, R., Febvre, A. and E. Alliot, E. (1973). Stud.
   Rev. GFCM 52, 91–96.
Millikin, M.R. (1982). Fishery Bulletin 80, 655–686.
N.R.C. (1983). Nutrient requirements of warmwater fishes
   and shellfishes. National Academy Press, Washington,
   D.C. 102 p.

Nose, T. (1979). In "Finfish Nutrition and Fishfeed Technology", (J.E. Halver and K. Tiews, eds.) 1, 145-156. Heenemann GmbH and Co., Berlin.

Nose, T., Arai, S., Lee, D.J. and Hashimoto, Y. (1974). Bull. Jap. Soc. Sci. Fish. 40, 903-908.

Ogata, H., Arai, S. and Nose, T. (1983). Bull. Jap. Soc. Sci. Fish. 49, 1381-1385.

Ogino, C. (1980). Bull. Jap. Soc. Sci. Fish. 46, 171-174.

Poston, H.A., Riis, R.C., Rumsey, G.L. and Ketola, H.G. (1977). Cornell Vet. 67, 472-509.

Poston, H.A. and Rumsey, G.I. (1983). J. Nutr. 113, 2568-2577.

Robinson, E.H., Allen, O.W., Poe, W.E. and Wilson, R.P. (1978). J. Nutr. 108, 1932-1936.

Robinson, E.H., Poe, W.E. and Wilson, R.P. (1984). Aquaculture 37, 51-62.

Robinson, E.H., Wilson, R.P. and Poe, W.E. (1980a). J. Nutr. 110, 1805-1812.

Robinson, E.H., Wilson, R.P. and Poe, W.E. (1980b). J. Nutr. 110, 2313-2316.

Robinson, E.H., Wilson, R.P. and Poe, W.E. (1981). J. Nutr. 111, 46-52.

Rumsey, G.L. and Ketola, H.G. (1975). J. Fish. Res. Board Can. 32, 422-426.

Rumsey, G.L., Page, J.W. and Scott, M.L. (1983). Prog. Fish-Cult. 45, 139-143.

Shanks, W.E., Gahimer, G.D., and Halver, J.E., (1962). Prog. Fish-Cult. 24, 68-73.

Thebault, H. (1983). These de Doctorat, Univ. D'Aux-Marseille, France.

Walton, M.J., Cowey, C.B. and Adron, J.W. (1982). J. Nutr. 112, 1525-1535.

Walton, M.J., Cowey, C.B. and Adron, J.W. (1984a). Br. J. Nutr. 52, 115-122.

Walton, M.J., Coloso, R.M., Cowey, C.B., Adron, J.W. and Knox, D. (1984b). Br. J. Nutr. 51, 279-287.

Wilson, R.P. and Poe, W.E. (1985). Comp. Biochem. Physiol. In press.

Wilson, R.P., Harding, D.E. and D.L. Garling, D.L. (1977). J. Nutr. 107, 166-170.

Wilson, R.P., Allen, O.W., Robinson, E.H. and Poe, W.E. (1978). J. Nutr. 108, 1595-1599.

Wilson, R.P., Poe, W.E. and Robinson, E.H. (1980). J. Nutr. 110, 627-633.

Yone, Y. (1976). In "Proceedings First Int. Conf. Aquaculture Nutr." (K.S. Price, W.N. Shaw and K.S. Danberg, eds.), 39-64. University of Delaware, Delaware, U.S.A.

PROTEIN SYNTHESIS AND PROTEIN DEPOSITION
IN FISH

B. FAUCONNEAU

Laboratoire de Nutrition et d'Elevage des Poissons,
I.N.R.A., St. Pee Sur Nivelle, 64310 Ascain, France.

I. INTRODUCTION

The dynamic state of body protein is achieved through
two processes: protein synthesis and protein breakdown.
In fish, the first qualitative studies tried to analyze
relative differences between protein synthesis and protein
breakdown in different tissues (Das and Prosser, 1967;
Somero and Doyle, 1973) or changes in protein synthesis
according to environmental changes (Haschemeyer, 1969a;
Dean and Berlin, 1969).   For the last few years
(Haschemeyer, 1973) studies have attempted to quantify
these differences and to measure protein synthesis rates,
using methods developed in mammals.   From a nutritional
point of view, measurement of protein synthesis and
breakdown rates make a budget of protein metabolism
feasible. In this budget, the input of amino acids coming
from protein breakdown and the output by incorporation of
amino acids into protein can be compared to classical
input through the diet and outputs by protein deposition
and degradation of amino acids (Millward et al., 1976).
The relative changes in components of this budget under
different nutritional states (Reeds and Lobley, 1980) as
well as the relative contribution of the different
tissues, in mammals, demonstrate that this is a new
investigative tool for the study of protein metabolism.
The resultant difference between protein synthesis and
protein breakdown is represented by protein deposition or

NUTRITION AND FEEDING IN FISH
ISBN: 0 12 194055 1

protein loss. Mechanism and regulation of protein deposition in whole body and muscle are analysed through measurement of the relative contributions of protein synthesis and breakdown during normal and induced growth (Waterlow et al., 1978; Millward et al., 1981; Millward et al., 1982). In fish during the major period of develoment, growth seems to proceed principally by hyperplasia (Stickland, 1983; Weatherley and Gill, 1984). It appears then that it would be interesting to analyse such a relation in fish.

The difference between protein synthesis and protein breakdown can be used as a measure of protein turnover. These equal amounts of synthesized and degraded proteins represent, at whole body level, a part of the minimal metabolism of an organism. In adult mammals, whole body protein turnover represents 15% of basal metabolic expenditure (Reeds et al., 1982). Fish have a low basal metabolic rate compared to mammals and the decrease in basal nitrogen loss, still compared to that of mammals, seems to be less important than for energy (Cho and Kaushik, this volume). Therefore, the relation between whole body protein turnover and other metabolic rates in fish require further analysis.

The literature on protein synthesis in fish is rarely directed towards such an analysis perhaps because of a greater interest in the consequences of poikilothermism. So in this review I will first deal with the available methods of measurement of protein synthesis and protein breakdown, then try to estimate the contribution of different tissues to protein synthesis (or breakdown). Finally, I will consider the influence of some abiotic (temperature, oxygen) and biotic factors (diet, growth, development) on protein synthesis and occasionally on protein turnover rates in different tissues.

II. REGULATION OF PROTEIN SYNTHESIS AND PROTEIN BREAKDOWN

Mechanisms of protein synthesis are similar in fish and in mammals. In response to changes in environmental temperature, some specific regulations are known.

One of these concerns the synthesis of specific proteins which appear in the serum of polar ·fish when environmental temperature falls below $0^{\circ}C$ (Hew et al., 1978). These proteins and particularly some glycoproteins increase the osmolarity of body fluids and so decrease their freezing-point.   The synthesis of serum antifreeze glycoprotein (SAGP) by liver seems to be regulated by the synthesis of the corresponding mRNA.   It has been demonstrated that there is a large amount of synthesized SAGP-mRNA in winter amounting to about 0.5 to 1% of RNA found in liver (Pickett et al., 1983).   But Pickett et al. (1983) also found measurable amounts of this mRNA in summer.   The synthesis of SAGP may thus be regulated by the transcription rate of its genes.   This could be one mechanism of regulation of protein synthesis with temperature changes.

Another control step of protein synthesis relating to temperature change is demonstrated at the translational level.   Rates of transport of free amino acids (Haschemeyer, 1968; Persell and Haschemeyer, 1976) as well as of protein synthesis measured by the elongation rate of the polypeptide chain (Mathews and Haschemeyer, 1978; Haschemeyer and Mathews, 1982) increase when environmental temperature increases.   But fish acclimatized to 'cold' temperature and transferred to 'warm' temperature show a higher protein synthesis rate than fish acclimatized to 'warm' temperature (Haschemeyer, 1969b).   This temperature compensation (Precht, 1967) for protein synthesis, is demonstrated in vitro (Haschemeyer, 1969a; Jankowsky et al., 1981; Kent and Prosser, 1980) as well as in vivo (Haschemeyer, 1968; Das and Prosser, 1967).   But temperature compensation cannot reliably be observed in vitro either in trout (Owen, 1975) and carp (Saez et al., 1982) or in vivo in toadfish (Pocrnjic et al., 1983). Preliminary studies on trout liver (Rosen et al., 1967) and on toadfish liver (Haschemeyer, 1969a) have proved that a cellular fraction containing amino-acyl transferases is responsible for temperature compensation. The specific factor, i.e. the elongation factor 1 (EF1), is now characterized (Plant et al., 1977).   The increase of protein synthesis in low-temperature acclimatized fish when compared to warm-temperature fish is correlated with tissue concentration of EF1 (Nielsen et al., 1977). Temperature compensation effect could take place through thyroid balance of fish as it has been shown that EF1 activities are affected by thyroxin treatment (Nielsen, 1977).   The difference between tissues in EF1 concentration is also consistent with differences in protein synthesis rates in these tissues (Nielsen, 1977).   Furthermore, tissue levels of EF1 in Antarctic fish (15-30 units/mg) are higher than those in tropical fish (2.5-10 units/mg).   This can be linked to the fact that protein synthesis rates in some Antarctic fish are higher than those obtained by extrapolation of results obtained in other species taking into account temperature differences and a Q_{10} of 2.5–3.0.

There is little information on mechanisms of protein breakdown in fish. Lysosomal proteinases are roughly similar to those of mammals such as the rat. The acid proteinase activity (particularly cathepsins B and D) have been measured in different tissues of carp. Activities in liver, kidney and spleen were higher than those in red and white muscle (Creach, 1973). Tissue distribution of exopeptidase activities (cathepsins A and C) in carp were also similar (Creach, 1973). However, specific activities of lysosomal enzymes in fish were found to be higher than those in mammals such as the rat when tested at the same temperature (Creach 1973, Dannevig and Berg, 1978). Alkaline protease which can be involved in an extralysosomal pathway of protein breakdown (Millward et al., 1981; Ballard and Gunn, 1982) has also been detected in many fish (Manikodan et al., 1982). But myofibrillar degradation by Ca-activated neutral protease remains to be measured in fish. The relative contribution of these different pathways to protein degradation (Millward et al., 1981) also remains to be analysed in fish.

III.   METHODS OF MEASURING PROTEIN SYNTHESIS AND PROTEIN
                         BREAKDOWN

Methods used in fish for the measurement of protein synthesis are adapted from those developed in mammals. The same model of amino acid metabolism can be applied to interpret results obtained with radioactive amino acids. This model is composed of two compartments. The first compartment represents the free pool from which amino acids are drawn for protein synthesis and the second compartment represents the protein pool. The origin of this model is found in the precursor/product model developed by Zilversmit (1960) for the analysis of isotopic tracer studies. It is necessary to assess if protein synthesis occurs from an homogeneous pool and if recycling of labelled amino acids derived from labelled protein degradation can be ignored (Waterlow et al., 1978). The specific activity of amino acids (SA) in the protein pool, is linked to specific activities in the free pool and in the protein pool by the equation:

$$dP/dt = ks.F - kd.P$$

where ks and kd are respectively fractional rates of protein synthesis and protein breakdown (in a steady state ks=kd).

The free pool in this model must be assimilated to the pool of aminoacyl-tRNA which is the direct precursor for protein synthesis. But measurement of the specific activity of an amino acid at the site of protein synthesis is not easy. Except for some studies on characterization of the tRNA pool (Araya and Krauskopf, 1976), nothing is known about tRNA in fish and especially on the relative levels of specific activity (SA) in the aminoacyl tRNA pool and in the other free pools (extracellular and intracellular). The only observation so far is that after a pulse injection in the portal vein, there is a rapid rise in total radioactivity collected in aminoacyl-tRNA so that it reaches a maximum level at 0.5% of the given dose 15 to 30 s after injection (Haschemeyer, 1973). Even though intracellular SA is commonly used as an estimate of precursor pool SA in fish, it is an empirical option only as we lack data affecting this choice.

Several methods, using different modes of marker administration, have been applied to fish to resolve this problem. The first method consists of a single pulse injection of a trace dose of marker. Kinetics of incorporation of labelled amino acids into proteins is analysed together with kinetics of amino acid SA in the free pool. A good description of these kinetics is not easy. The second method is the infusion method which was first applied in mullet (Haschemeyer and Smith, 1979). Infusion leads to a stabilization of amino acid SA of the free pool in a few hours. The rate constant of increase of SA to the 'plateau' value is lower in fish (13/d at -1.5°C to 24/d at 28°C) (Haschemeyer and Smith, 1979; Smith and Haschemeyer, 1980) than in mammals (80/d) (Garlick et al., 1976) with infusion of ^{14}C-tyrosine. The measurement of incorporation rate of amino acid into protein is easier than with the first method. But the choice between SA of extracellular pool and SA of intracellular pool to estimate SA of precursor pool has still to be made. The third method, injection of a large dose of an unlabelled amino acid along with the marker, also tends to stabilize free amino acid SA during a short period (McNurland and Garlick, 1980). But, the consequences of this injection are that it saturates the transport system of amino acids (Persell and Haschemeyer, 1980) and reduces differences between the SA of the different free pools (Haschemeyer, 1983). This method, first used in goldfish Carassius auratus (Lajtha and Sershen, 1976), gives accurate estimates of protein synthesis rate in tissues with high protein turnover rates (Pocrnjic et al., 1983).

The results obtained with these methods are roughly dependent on the amino acids used and on systematic errors linked to the method itself. In fish, the protein synthesis rate in liver is lower when measured with tyrosine than when measured with leucine (Smith and Haschemeyer, 1980). This is also the case for whole body protein synthesis in rat (Obled et al., 1983) but is not a general rule (Reeds and Lobley, 1980). Moreover, differences between estimation of protein synthesis rate in fish liver, with alanine, leucine and tyrosine, are correlated to the respective levels of these amino acids in the free pool (Smith and Haschemeyer, 1980) and not to their content in protein as in mammals (Obled et al., 1983). However, results obtained with pulse injection of leucine are higher than with infusion of tyrosine, in rainbow trout, Salmo gairdneri, (Fauconneau, 1980; Fauconneau et al., 1981; Smith, 1981). It is a general trend in mammals (Waterlow et al., 1978) but differences are too high to be explained only by a difference of method. Estimations of protein synthesis rate in toadfish (Opsanus tau) liver after a pulse injection of leucine (Mathews and Haschemeyer, 1978) and after injection of a large dose of phenylalanine (Pocrnjic et al., 1983) are similar.

There is no reliable method for the measurement of protein breakdown in fish. A first method largely used in mammals by Schimke (1970) is related to the analysis of half lives of specific protein from decay of pulse labelled protein radioactivity. This method, when used in fish (Castilla, 1974; Bouche, 1975; Sidell, 1977; Bahamondes-Rojas, 1981) overestimates protein half lives as radioactive amino acids in the free pool are not rapidly eliminated from the organism (Zak et al., 1979). Recycling of labelled amino acid coming from protein degradation is also a source of error. No significant decrease in radioactivity of pulse labelled muscle protein has been observed for two weeks in carp (Cyprinus carpio) when fasting (Bouche, 1975) or after hormonal treatment (Castilla, 1974). Finally, in trout, the decay curve of radioactivity in muscle protein implies a non-random turnover of protein (Millward et al., 1976). This probably explains the strange figure obtained in fed carp which have a muscle protein breakdown rate (Bouche, 1975) ten times as high as any known rate of muscle protein synthesis in fish.

Protein breakdown is generally estimated by the difference between protein synthesis rate and protein growth rate. But for the estimation of myofibrillar protein degradation rate, a method based on the measurement of excretion of 3-methyl histidine is currently used in mammals. 3-methyl histidine (3MH) is a specific component of myofibrillar protein (Haversberg et al., 1974) and, in some mammals, free 3MH coming from protein breakdown is not metabolized any further (Ward and Buttery, 1978; Young and Munro, 1978). If 3MH is rapidly and quantitatively eliminated, the excretion rate provides an estimate of muscle protein breakdown rate. In fish, a number of difficulties have arisen in the use of 3MH to measure muscle protein breakdown. Significant amounts of 3MH were detected in the muscle protein of rainbow

Table I. Radioactivity excreted by fish in water, urine and carbon dioxide (percent of dose given) after a pulse injection of [^{14}C]-3-methyl histidine (2μ Ci/100 g) in two groups of rainbow trout : a control group (mean body weight 159.9 g; n = 5) fed a casein diet (protein content 48.7% dry matter) and another group (mean body weight 131.2 g; n = 5) fasting for 3 weeks. (Fauconneau unpublished results).

Time after injection	Urine		Water		Carbon dioxide		Total	
	control	fasted	control	fasted	control	fasted	control	fasted
0-24 h	33.7 (31.0)	24.6 (15.4)	39.2 (30.9)	22.5 (16.7)	0.05 (0.0)	4.4 (3.2)	72.9 (5.4)	51.4 (5.8)
24-48 h	1.9 (2.3)	4.3 (3.7)	3.1 (1.2)	4.7 (2.2)	0.8 (1.0)	2.0 (0.8)	5.9 (1.7)	11.0 (1.8)
48-72 h	0.2 (0.4)	1.9 (1.3)	1.0 (0.6)	1.9 (0.6)	0.2 (0.1)	0.8 (0.6)	1.4 (0.9)	4.6 (1.3)
Total	35.8	30.8	43.3	29.1	1.0	7.2	80.2 (3.9)	67.0 (3.7)

trout (0.34 mg/100 mg protein) (Fauconneau unpublished results) but the free pool is very high, 4.92μ moles/g muscle (Gras et al., 1978) when compared to that of mammals, 10 to 20 nmoles/g muscle (Harris and Milne, 1977). Recoveries of radioactivity in water and urine after an intravenous injection of $3-[^{14}C$ methyl]-histidine in fed rainbow trout were not complete even after 3 days (Table I). Total recoveries in fasting fish (67% in 72h) were lower than in fed fish (80% in 72h). On the other hand, radioactivity seemed to be equally excreted in urine and in water, and a small but significant amount of radioactivity was detected in CO_2 excreted by fish. After a single injection of 'cold' 3MH (10μmoles/100g fish) in rainbow trout, we were never able to collect any significant amount of 3MH either in urine or in water even when it had been hydrolysed to take into account the possible transformation of 3MH into N-acetyl-methyl histidine. Finally, as in mammals (Rennie and Millward, 1983) 3MH excreted by fish may have other origins than the degradation of skeletal muscle protein and principally degradation of digestive tract proteins which have a very high turnover rate in fish (Fauconneau, 1980). On these grounds, it appears that 3 methyl histidine excretion can not be applied as an index of muscle protein breakdown in fish without further detailed studies.

IV. RELATIVE PROTEIN SYNTHESIS RATES IN DIFFERENT TISSUES

Protein synthesis rates are higher in liver, gill, digestive tract, kidney and spleen than in heart, red muscle and white muscle. This was first demonstrated by qualitative work (Das and Prosser, 1967; Dean and Berlin, 1969; Smith and Haschemeyer, 1974; Narayansingh and Eales, 1975) without any integration of variations in the size of free amino acid pools. Recent work quantified these differences in mullet (Mugil cephalus) (Haschemeyer and Smith, 1979) and rainbow trout (Smith, 1981) with the infusion method and in toadfish (Pocrnjic et al., 1983) and some Antarctic fish (Haschemeyer, 1983) with the large dose method (Table II). Disparity between tissues is consistent with results obtained in mammals (McNurlan and Garlick, 1980). Protein synthesis can be expressed in terms of RNA to give an estimate of the efficiency of protein synthesis. Differences between tissues in efficiency of protein synthesis are low but significant (Cowey and Luquet, 1983). Efficiency of protein synthesis is higher in liver than in muscle, in fish (Fauconneau, 1980; Smith, 1981) as in mammals such as pig (Garlick et al., 1976). However, in fish, protein synthesis rates seem to be lower than in mammals with similar tissue contents of RNA. This alteration in protein synthesis in fish may be principally a consequence of differences in temperature experienced by fish and mammals. For instance, a Q_{10} of 2.5 applied to protein synthetic rate of different tissues (Fauconneau, 1980) gives values similar to those obseved in mammals (Waterlow et al., 1978).

Interspecific variations of protein synthesis may be explained by differences in environmental temperature. In triggerfish (Sufflamen verres) at 30°C, fractional protein synthesis rates in liver and gill, 36 and 14%/d respectively (Haschemeyer et al., 1979) were considerably higher than in some Antarctic fish living at 2°C, 10 and 5%/d respectively (Haschemeyer, 1983). The contribution of plasma protein to total liver protein synthesis seems to be very constant in a number of different species at 20 to 35% (Smith et al., 1980; Smith and Haschemeyer, 1980) but is lower in rainbow trout at 11% (Smith, 1981). In liver, protein breakdown rates measured at 15°C in carp and trout (Bouche, 1974, Bahamondes-Rojas, 1982) are not different from protein synthesis rates observed at similar temperature in intrahepatic protein or total protein. This proves that protein synthesis in liver is principally directed towards the renewal of protein. This is also true for gill and digestive tract where protein deposition rate is low in comparison with protein synthesis rate. In digestive tract, protein synthesis rate measured in rainbow trout: 23 and 60%/d respectively at 10 and 18°C (Fauconneau, 1980) is higher than in Antarctic fish: 12 to 18%/d (Smith and Haschemeyer, 1980). The contribution of exported proteins in digestive lumen to total protein synthesis had been estimated between 5 and 10% in rainbow trout (Fauconneau and Arnal unpublished results).

In muscle, interspecific variations of protein synthesis rate may also be related to environmental temperature. But it is shown that in muscle, protein synthesis is mainly directed towards protein deposition (Fauconneau et al., 1981; Smith, 1981). In other words, in fish, muscle protein turnover represents only a small part of protein synthesis whereas in mammals, it may reach over 60% of protein synthesis (Reeds and Lobley, 1980).

Table II   Relative rate of protein synthesis in different tissues (basis 100 for liver)

	Tropical Fish (1) 28°C	Trigger fish (2) 26°C	Mullet (3) 25°C	Toadfish (fasted) (2) 20°C	Trout (5) 18°C	Trout (6) 12°C	Notothenia coriceps (7) 2°C	Icefish (7) 2°C	Antarctic fish (8) -15°C
Liver		100	100	100	100	100	100	100	100
Gill	72	60	115	56		27	15	9	95
Foregut					69				248
Head kidney				111			34	35	29
Trunk kidney							18	10	9
Spleen				36			20	7	48
Testis				10			25	7	
Brain							4	3	
Heart				17			13	4	
Red muscle	10	15.2							4.3
White Epaxial muscle	2.7	3.3	2.7	1.7	2.1	2.2	3.6	1.3	3.3
Pectoral muscle				1.5			10	13	

(1) Smith et al., 1980 (tropical and pelagic fish)

(2) Haschemeyer et al., 1979

(3) Haschemeyer and Smith, 1979

(4) Pocrnjic et al., 1983

(5) Fauconneau and Arnal (unpublished results)

(6) Smith, 1981

(7) Haschemeyer, 1983

(8) Smith and Haschemeyer, 1980

Characteristics of muscle growth in fish which mainly occurs through hyperplasia (Strickland, 1983; Weatherley and Gill, 1984) may explain this peculiarity. Therefore, interspecific variations in muscle protein synthesis may both be explained by differences in temperature and by differences in growth rate (Table III).

Table III. Fractional protein synthesis rate in muscle and growth rate of different species of fish.

	Specific growth rate (%/d)	Fractional protein synthesis rate (%/d)
Toadfish 22°C (1)	0.4	1.1
Trout 12°C (2)	0.25	0.38
Trout 10°C (3)	1.1	1.9
Trout 18°C	1.5	1.8
T. bernacchii −15°C (4)	0.1−0.15	0.23

(1)   Smith and Haschemeyer, 1974 (ks calculated from 190 mg protein synthesized/g muscle/d and 140 mg protein/g muscle)

(2)   Smith, 1981

(3)   Fauconneau et al., 1981

(4)   Smith and Haschemeyer, 1980

In fish muscle, it has been shown qualitatively that protein synthesis in myofibrillar protein is approximately half that in sarcoplamic proteins (Das and Krishnamoorthy, 1968). But total muscle protein breakdown is similar to that of fibrous protein (Somero and Doyle, 1973). Therefore, heterogeneity in muscle protein turnover is not very noticeable.

V. INFLUENCE OF EXTRINSIC FACTORS ON PROTEIN SYNTHESIS

Temperature is one of the most important factors governing protein synthesis in active tissues such as liver, gill, digestive tract and kidney in triggerfish (Haschemeyer et al., 1979) and in toadfish (Mathews and Haschemeyer, 1978; Pocrnjic et al., 1983). These changes occur with a Q_{10} of 2.5. As basal metabolic rate measured by oxygen consumption is temperature-dependent with a Q_{10} of 2.3 (Brett and Groves, 1979), it can be concluded that the relative contribution of protein turnover of active tissues to basal metabolic expenditure is almost constant. In muscle the pattern of changes according to temperature is not so clear. Fractional protein synthesis rate increased as incubation temperature was increased for triggerfish acclimatized to $28^{\circ}C$ (Haschemeyer et al., 1979) and for toadfish acclimatized to $22^{\circ}C$ (Pocrnjic et al., 1983). But in muscle of well fed rainbow trout, acclimatization temperature influence on muscle protein synthesis was evident (Fauconneau et al., 1981). An increase in muscle protein turnover with increase in temperature does occur as shown in fasted toadfish acclimatized to 10 and $20^{\circ}C$ (Pocrnjic et al., 1983). However the overall changes in muscle protein synthesis are rather dependent on relative changes in growth rate as affected by temperature. Finally as relative rates of protein synthesis in the different tissues (Table IV) are not altered by temperature changes, relative differences in requirement for amino acids would be difficult to detect whereas a large increase in absolute protein quantitative requirement in response to temperature increase, can be supposed from above results.

Oxygen is also a limiting factor for protein synthesis. The whole physiology of the fish can be organized around oxygen requirement of tissues and oxygen limiting factors (Holeton, 1980). Protein synthesis is linked to oxygen consumption when analysing interspecific variations in protein synthetic rates (Smith and Haschemeyer, 1980). Jackim and Laroche (1973) have found that muscle protein synthesis is dramatically altered when oxygen concentration in the water decreases below 2.5 mg/l in Fundulus heteroclitus. Above this threshold, muscle protein synthesis seems to be stimulated by a small decrease in oxygen level in the water with only small change in protein breakdown (Bahamondes-Rojas, 1982).

Table IV.   Influence of temperature on relative rate of protein synthesis in different tissues of fish (basis 100 in liver).

	Triggerfish 22°C acclimated (1)			Toadfish 22°C acclimated (2)				Trout acclimated to (3)	
22°C				fed		fasted			
	20°C	26°C	30°C	11°C	22°C	10°C	20°C	10°C	18°C
Liver	100	100	100	100	100	100	100	100	100
Gill	42	71	39			95	56		
Digestive tract								71	51
White muscle	3	3	3	14	13	2	3	5	2
Red muscle	8	15	8						

(1) Haschemeyer et al. (1979);   (2) Pocrnjic et al. (1983); (3) Fauconneau (1980).

But, protein turnover rates in liver proteins are similar in trout acclimatized to 50% oxygen in the water and in trout acclimatized to 100% oxygen (Bahamondes- Rojas, 1982).   This dependence of protein synthesis on oxygen level provides an additional source of error when analysing temperature influence on muscle protein synthesis.

Finally, salinity can directly affect specific tissues involved in ion exchange such as gill, kidney and digestive tract. Protein synthesis in gills of mullet measured in sea water, is very high when compared to that of other species. This may be due to salinity because the metabolic rate measured by oxygen uptake seems to be minimal, in mullet, when water salinity is the same as that of body fluids (Nordlie and Leffler, 1975).   The direct influence of salinity on protein synthesis in gill has been shown in eel by a qualitative study (Tondeur and Sargent, 1978).   Salinity can also apparently affect muscle protein synthesis (Jackim and Laroche, 1973), whether this action occurs through changes in growth rate has still to be explained.

In conclusion, abiotic factors have a significant influence on protein synthesis in active tissues such as liver, gill and digestive tract and consequently on their protein turnover rates. In muscle, as protein turnover is

very low and dependence of protein synthesis upon protein
deposition high, the specific influence of abiotic
factors, independently from alteration in growth rate, is
difficult to measure. Consequently, relative
distribution of protein synthesis among the different
tissues seems to be affected by oxygen and salinity but
not by temperature. Therefore, qualitative protein
requirements (amino acid balance) may be affected by these
two factors. The confrontation of quantitative changes
with simultaneous changes in energy requirements could
provide a basis for quantitative protein requirements (in
% of the diet).

VI. CHANGES IN PROTEIN SYNTHESIS AND PROTEIN DEPOSITION ASSOCIATED WITH FEEDING

Fasting has proved to have little influence on protein
synthesis in liver, gill and other regulatory tissues
(Smith and Haschemeyer, 1980; Smith, 1981; Pocrnjic et
al., 1983) except in nototheniids and icefish
(Chaenocephalus aceratus; Haschemeyer, 1983). On the
contrary, breakdown rates of liver and plasma proteins in
carp increase with long-term fasting along with a two-fold
decrease in protein content of liver and plasma (Bouche,
1975). There is also a fall in muscle protein synthesis
in fasted fish (Smith and Haschemeyer, 1980; Haschemeyer,
1983; Pocrnjic et al., 1983). In rainbow trout,
fasting is also associated with an increase in muscle
protein breakdown (from 0.13 to 0.61%/d) without any
changes in muscle protein turnover (0.09-0.13%/d) (Smith,
1981). Thus, in muscle there is a correlation between
protein synthesis and feeding level. With in vitro
measurement of muscle protein synthesis in saithe
(Pollachius virens), it has been shown that this relation
takes place through changes in muscle protein deposition
and consequently through growth rate (Rosenlund et al.,
1984).

Incorporation of labelled amino acids into liver and
carcass proteins are not affected by protein content of
the diet (Cowey, 1975). But as specific activity in the
free pool is not measured in this study, it is difficult
to draw any conclusion. In rainbow trout, muscle protein
synthesis is altered by qualitative changes in the diet
(Fig. 1). When increasing arginine in the diet,
deficiency in lysine was revealed by a decrease in growth

rate and a decrease in muscle protein synthesis. Muscle
protein synthesis was restored by increasing the lysine
content of the diet (Fauconneau and Kaushik, unpublished
results). Muscle protein synthesis is therefore altered
when fish are fed an unbalanced protein. This sensitivity
of muscle protein synthesis to dietary amino acid balance

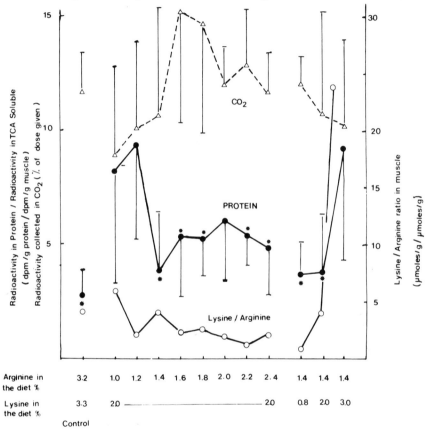

Fig. 1. Effect of dietary arginine and lysine on
incorporation of radioactivity into muscle protein, (dpm/g
protein/dpm in TCA soluble/g muscle). Carbon-dioxide
excreted by fish (% of dose given) and relative amount of
free lysine and free arginine in muscle 6 hours after a
pulse injection of L-[U-^{14}C]-arginine in rainbow trout.
Fish were fed either a commercial diet (control) or an
experimental diet composed of 12% fish meal-36% zein
supplemented with different levels of lysine and arginine.
*Data significantly different from the highest data
P < 0.05.

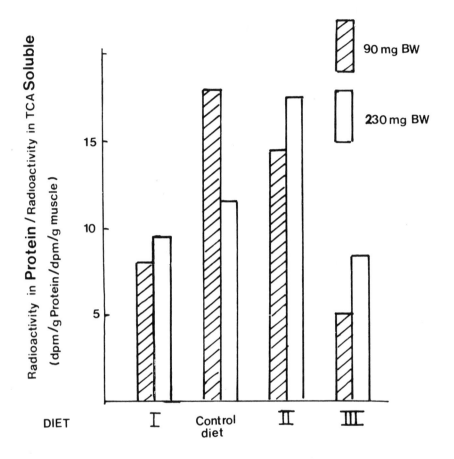

Fig. 2. Influence of the diet on whole body protein synthesis in juvenile whitefish (Coregonus schinzii pallea). Ratio of radioactivity in protein to radioactivity in the TCA soluble fraction of whole fish was measured 18 h. after immersion of fish in water containing L-[U-^{14}C]-arginine. (Fauconneau and Bergot, unpublished results).

has led some authors to use the in vitro muscle protein synthesis, as an index of growth rate under different feeding conditions (Lied et al., 1983; Rosenlund et al., 1983).

In the early development of fish, growth rate sensitivity to dietary changes is more marked. Whole fish protein synthesis measured in vivo decreases, in juvenile

Table V. Composition of the diet distributed to whitefish
(Coregonus shinzii pallea) larvae

| Components % of DM | Diet | | | |
	I	Control	II	III
Beef liver	33	35	35	41
Yeast	44	50	40	59
Cod liver oil	7	5	5	-
Mineral premix	7	5	5	-
Vitamin premix	7	5	5	-
Fat-enriched starch *	-	-	10	-
Protein (Nx6.25) % DM	45.7	47.0	43.9	55.5
Energy kJ/gDM	20.7	20.2	20.8	20.5

DM : dry matter
* : enriched with 30% fat

whitefish (Coregonus schinzii pallea), when feeding a
deficient diet or an unbalanced diet compared to a
'control' diet (Fig.2 and Table V) (Fauconneau unpublished
results). As long term measurement of growth rate in
juvenile fish is difficult, whole fish protein synthesis
can also be used as an index of sensitivity to diet
composition.
    The analysis of changes in protein synthesis either in
the whole body or in the muscle due to the quantity and
the quality of the food is a prospective way of estimating
protein quality and biological value.   These changes

analysed in conjunction with the measurement of amino acid oxidation rates, provide a basis for the estimation of absolute protein requirements in fish.

VII.   CHANGES IN PROTEIN SYNTHESIS THROUGHOUT DEVELOPMENT

The decrease in protein synthesis of different tissues and of whole body throughout development (from neonate to adult is a general trend in mammals (Waterlow et al., 1978; Arnal et al., 1983). Furthermore, in muscle, the decrease in protein deposition from young to adult mammals is associated with a decrease in protein turnover (Millward and Waterlow, 1978). In fish, changes in growth rate throughout development are very important. But few studies have analysed protein synthesis in immature fish because of technical limits of methods used. In rainbow trout, protein synthesis rate and protein turnover rate in liver and muscle are higher in fish of 100g body weight than in 200-300g fish (Fauconneau et al., 1981; Smith, 1981). During the same period of development protein synthesis in liver, measured by incorporation rate of labelled ^{14}C-leucine in vivo into plasma protein was lower in rainbow trout weighing 80g than in trout weighing 280g (Fig. 3). But in muscle, there was no significant change in amino acid incorporation rate between 80g trout and 380g trout (Fauconneau unpublished results). As the growth rate of these fish (half-sibling rainbow trout) did not decrease throughout this period of development, it is difficult to make inferences on changes in protein turnover rate of muscle, even if turnover rate of liver protein decreases in the same period.

During early development measurement of the protein synthesis rate in egg or in yolk sac larvae can provide an estimate of maximum efficiency of protein synthesis in fish. In eggs of the teleostean fish Oryzias latipex, loss of radioactivity in yolk protein labelled with ^{35}S-methionine and ^{14}C-leucine provided an estimate of yolk sac utilization: 9.7%/d in embryos showing complete establishment of circulation (Monroy et al., 1961). In carp weighing 50mg, whole body protein synthesis and growth rate were respectively estimated to be 300%/d and 18%/d (Fauconneau, 1983). When compared to whole body protein synthesis and growth rate in rainbow trout weighing 100g, respectively: 4-5%/d   and   1.5%/d

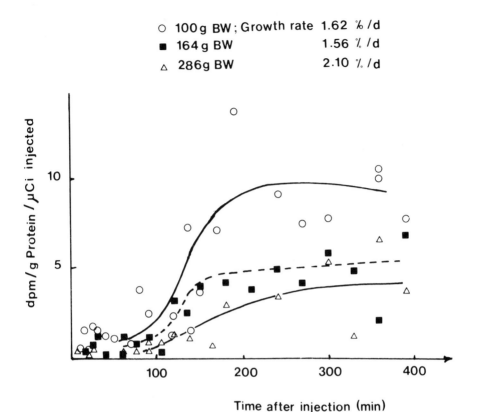

Fig. 3. Incorporation of radioactivity into plasma protein of rainbow trout after injection of L-[U-14C]-leucine (5 μCi/100 g body weight) (Fauconneau, unpublished results).

(Fauconneau, 1980), the decrease in whole body protein turnover from larvae to immature fish, associated with a decrease in growth rate, is very important.

Throughout early development of whitefish, there are also measurable changes in protein synthesis. Incorporation of radioactivity into TCA-soluble fraction after immersion of fish in a solution containing 14C-arginine (Table VI) is much greater in eggs and yolk sac larvae compared to that in free swimming larvae. Relative incorporation of radioactivity into whole fish protein decreases from yolk sac larvae to juvenile, fed

Table VI.   Whole fish protein synthesis throughout early
development of coregonid (Coregonus schinzii pallea).
Radioactivity in TCA soluble and protein were measured in
the different groups 18 h after immersion of fish in a
solution containing [U-^{14}C] arginine.

	Eggs	Yolk sac larvae	Fasted larvae	Fed larvae			Juvenile fed fish		
Temperature °C	9	9	9	8	12	16	13	13	13
Mean body weight (mg)	9.6	4.7	4.0	12.0	13.0	13.4	60	90	230
TCA soluble radioactivity (DPM/g/μCi x 10^3)	190	6.0	0.8	1.1	1.5	2.8	1.6	1.5	1.5
Protein/TCA soluble (DPM/g protein/DPM/g fish)	5.9	16.5	10.0	10.5	10.0	17.0	13.0	13.0	10.4

fish.   But it appears that the decrease of whole body
protein synthesis of fed free swimming larvae from 12 mg
BW to 230 mg BW is not very important.   The highest rate
of incorporation of amino acids in whole body protein is
observed in yolk sac larvae (Table VII).   Whole body
protein synthesis rates estimated from incorporation rates
of radioactivity are also very high : 100–400%/d when
compared to results obtained in many adult fish (Smith and
Haschemeyer, 1980; Smith et al., 1980).
    From these observations, it follows that the decrease
in growth rate throughout development is associated with a
large decrease in whole body protein synthesis and hence
with a decrease in whole body protein turnover.   Relative
changes in body protein composition and particularly
changes in muscle proportion are not large enough to
explain this decrease in whole body protein turnover.

Table VII. Change in protein synthesis of whole fish throughout early development of coregonid fish (Coregonus schinzii pallea) measured after immersion of fish in solution containing L-[U-^{14}C] arginine.

	Eggs	Yolk sac larvae	Fasted larvae	Juvenile fed fish		
	9°C	9°C	9°C	8°C	12°C	16°C
Mean body weight (mg)	9.6	4.7	4.0	12.0	13.0	13.4
Growth rate (%/d)				7.0	11.4	15.5
Ammonia excretion rate (mg N/g/d)	0.10	0.23	0.35	0.45	0.70	1.20
Rate of intake of radioactivity in the free pool (h^{-1}): $\lambda1$	0.34	0.22	0.12	0.21	0.18	0.15
Rate of incorporation of radioactivity from the free pool into protein (d^{-1}): $\lambda2$	1.8	4.4	3.6	-	1.0	3.9

$\lambda1$: calculated from the equation $X = X\,max\,(1 - e^{-\lambda1.t})$

$\lambda2$: calculated from the equation $Y = Y\,max\left[\dfrac{\lambda1}{\lambda1 - \lambda2}.\dfrac{1 - \exp(-\lambda2.t)}{1 - \exp(-\lambda1.t)} - \dfrac{\lambda2}{\lambda1 - \lambda2}\right]$

VIII.   CHANGES IN MUSCLE PROTEIN SYNTHESIS UNDER NORMAL AND STIMULATED GROWTH

In mammals, high rates of protein deposition, during rapid growth of immature mammals or during muscular hypertrophy, can be associated with high rates of protein degradation. But high rates of protein deposition induced by genetic selection, hormonal stimulation or dietary manipulation, are associated with a decrease in protein degradation (Millward et al., 1982). Rainbow trout with high growth potentials showed a slightly higher rate of muscle protein synthesis than trout with low growth (Fig. 4; families of half-sibling trout selected by growth performance in a progeny test, see Kaushik et al., 1984) even if these two groups showed similar growth during the

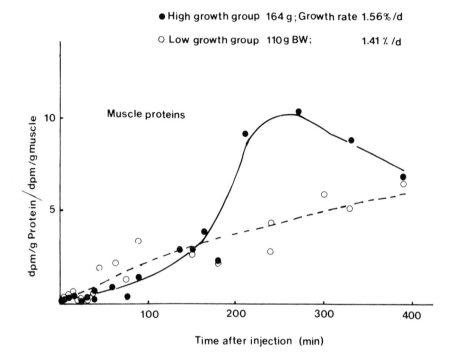

Fig. 4. Incorporation of radioactivity into protein of muscle relative to TCA soluble radioactivity in muscle of two groups of rainbow trout of potentially different growth. Trout received a pulse injection of L-[U-^{14}C]-leucine (5 μ Ci/100 g) (Fauconneau unpublished results).

measurement. Synthesis of plasma proteins seemed to be lower in the high growth group than in the low growth group (Fauconneau unpublished results). But, stimulated growth obtained by oral treatment with steroid hormone was associated with a small decrease in muscle protein synthesis (Fig. 5). Consequently, in this case, growth can be associated with a decrease in muscle protein breakdown. Results obtained in fish acclimatized at two temperatures led to similar conclusions (Somero and Doyle, 1969; Fauconneau et al., 1981).

Mechanisms of muscular growth associated either with an increase or a decrease in protein turnover rate are similar in fish and in mammals. But turnover rate of

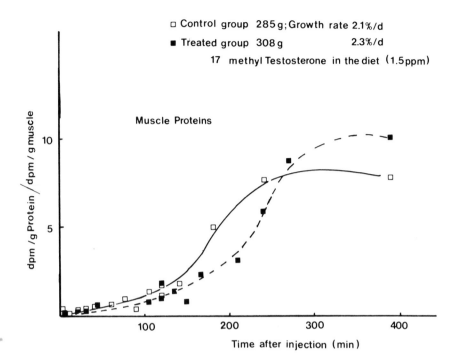

Fig. 5. Incorporation of radioactivity into protein of muscle (relative to radioactivity in TCA soluble fraction of muscle) in trout fed either a control diet or a diet containing 1.5 ppm of 17 -methyl testosterone for 10 weeks. Trout received a pulse injection of L-[U-^{14}C]-leucine (5 Ci/100 g) (Fauconneau, unpublished results).

resident protein in fish muscle is low when compared to that of other tissues and also when compared to muscle protein synthesis rate. So protein deposition in muscle appears to be equivalent to an accumulation process with a relative lability of so stored protein.

IX. PARTICIPATION OF TISSUES IN WHOLE BODY PROTEIN SYNTHESIS

The analysis of protein synthesis in whole fish shows that the overall quantity of protein synthesized by non-muscular tissues is more than twice as high as that synthesized by muscle which represents 40-60% of the body

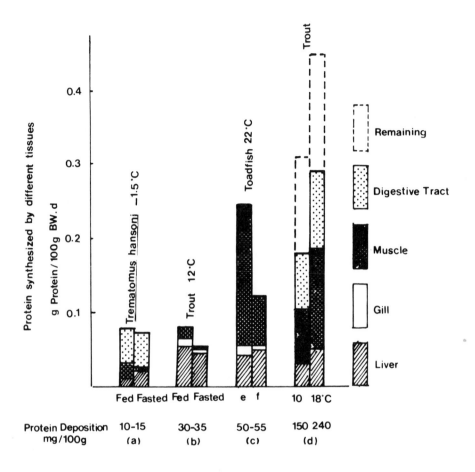

a   Smith and Haschemeyer, 1980

b   Smith, 1981

c   Smith and Haschemeyer, 1974 (e) recalculated with ks given
    by Pocrnjic et al., (1983) (f)

d   Fauconneau, 1981 (estimation based on extracellular specific
    activities)

Fig. 6. Relative contribution of different tissues to
total amount of protein synthesized by fish (mg
protein/100 g body weight/d)

(Fig. 6). Consequently, the greater part of dietary protein supply is used to ensure protein turnover in non-muscular tissues which may be called regulatory tissues for protein metabolism. Protein turnover in these tissues is altered by changes in environmental factors but is little affected by dietary changes.

Muscle, on the other hand, carries out the main part of protein deposition at whole body level with a very low protein turnover compared to other tissues. This picture is also observed in mammals (Waterlow et al., 1978) but is amplified in fish. Low muscle protein turnover rates were obtained first in genetically selected poultry with high muscle growth (Orcutt and Young, 1982) and also in rapidly growing rats (Millward and Waterlow, 1978) when compared to control animals. Therefore, it would be interesting to analyse changes in protein deposition rate in muscle together with muscle protein breakdown rate. Protein synthesis in muscle shows important variations with both dietary manipulation and developmental changes.

Dependence of protein synthesis upon dietary protein supply is greater in fish than in mammals. For example in rainbow trout weighing 100 g, acclimatized to $10^{\circ}C$, leucine used for whole fish protein synthesis (51 mg/100g.d) is similar to leucine ingested (47 mg/100g.d) whereas in mammals, amino acid uptake through the diet is two to three times lower than amino acid utilization for protein synthesis (Reeds and Lobley, 1980). Moreover, recycling of amino acids and exchange between tissues are not negligible as the total amounts of leucine metabolized through the plasma and by whole fish can be estimated respectively as 80-90 mg/100g. d and 450 mg/100g. d. (Fauconneau, 1983). When compared to the total amounts of leucine deposited, 11 mg/100g. d., it appears that protein synthesis and protein deposition are dependent both on dietary supply and reutilization of amino acids.

REFERENCES

Araya, A. and Krauskopf, M. (1976). Acta. Physiol. Lat. Amer. 26, 97-105.

Arnal, M., Obled, C. and Attaix, D. (1983). In "Protein Metabolism and Nutrition, (M. Arnal, R. Pion and D. Bonin, eds.). I, 117-136, INRA, Paris.

Bahamondes-Rojas, I. (1982).   Thèse 3ème cycle. Univ. P.
    Sabatier. Toulouse, 79 pp.
Ballard, F.J. and Gunn, J.M. (1982).   Nutr. Rev. 40,
    33-42.
Bouche, C. (1975). Thèse Doct. Sci., Univ. P. Sabatier.
    Toulouse, 188 pp.
Bouche, C. and Vellas, F.(1975).   Comp. Biochem Physiol.
    51A, 185-193.
Brett, J.R. and Groves, T.D.D. (1979).   In "Fish
    Physiology" (W.S. Hoar, D.J. Randall and J.R. Brett,
    eds.) 8, 279-352, Academic Press, New York.
Castilla, C. (1974). Thèse 3ème cycle. Univ. P. Sabatier,
    Toulouse, 71 pp.
Cheema, I.R. and Matty, A.J. (1977).   Proc. Soc.
    Endocrin., 72, 11p-12P.
Cowey, C.B. (1975).   Proc. Nutr. Soc. 34, 57-63.
Cowey, C.B. and Luquet, P. (1983).   In "Protein
    Metabolism and Nutrition", (M. Arnal, R. Pion and D.
    Bonin, eds.) I, 365-384, INRA, Paris.
Creach, Y. (1973). Thèse Doct. Sci., Univ. P. Sabatier,
    Tolouse.
Dannevig, B.H. and Berg, T. (1978).   Comp. Biochem.
    Physiol. 61B, 115-118.
Das, A.B. and Krishnamoorthy, R.V. (1968).   Experientia
    25, 594-595.
Das, A.B. and Prosser, C.L. (1967).   Comp. Biochem.
    Physiol. 21, 449-467.
Dean, J.M. and Berlin, J.D. 91969).   Comp. Biochem.
    Physiol. 29, 307-312.
Fauconneau, B. (1980). Thèse Doct. Ing. INA Paris. 110 pp.
Fauconneau, B. (1983).   Ichthyophysiologica Acta 7,
    34-75.
Fauconneau, B. (1984).   Comp. Biochem. Physiol. 78.   In
    press.
Garlick, P.J., Burk, T.L., and Swick, R.W. (1976).   Amer.
    J. Physiol. 23, 1108-1112.
Gras, J., Gudefin, Y. and Chagny, F. (1978).   Comp.
    Biochem. Physiol. 60B, 369-372.
Goolish, E.M. and Adelman, I.R. (1983).   Comp. Biochem.
    Physiol. 76A, 127-134.
Harris, C.I. and Milne, G. (1977).   Proc. Nutr. Soc. 36,
    138A.
Haschemeyer, A.E.V. (1968).   Biol. Bull. 135, 130-140.
Haschmeyer, A.E.V. (1969a).   Proc. Nat. Acad. Sci. 62,
    128-135.
Haschemeyer, A.E.V. (1969b).   Comp. Biochem. Physiol. 28,
    535-552.

Haschemeyer, A.E.V. (1973). J. Biol. Chem. 248, 1643-1649.
Haschemeyer, A.E.V. (1982). Amer. J. Physiol. 242,
    R280-R284.
Haschemeyer, A.E.V. (1983). Comp. Biochem. Physiol. 76B,
    541-543.
Haschemeyer, A.E.V. and Jannasch, H.W. (1983). Comp.
    Biochem. Physiol. 76B, 545-548.
Haschemeyer, A.E.V. and Mathews, R.W. (1980). Physiol.
    Zool. 53, 383-393.
Haschemeyer, A.E.V. and Mathews, R.W. (1982). Biol.
    Bull. 162, 18-27.
Haschemeyer, A.E.V. and Mathews, R.W. (1983). Physiol.
    Zool. 56, 78-87.
Haschemeyer, A.E.V. and Persell, R. (1973). Biol. Bull.
    145, 472-481.
Haschemeyer, A.E.V., Persell, R. and Smith, M.A.K.
    (1979). Comp. Biochem. Physiol. 64B, 91-95.
Haschemeyer, A.E.V. and Smith, M.A.K. (1979). Biol. Bull.
    156, 93-102.
Haschemeyer, A.E.V. and Williams, R.C. (1982). Mar. Biol.
    Lett. 3, 81-88.
Haverberg, L.N., Munro, H.N. and Young, V.R. (1974).
    Biochim. Biophys. Acta 371, 226-237.
Hew, C.L., Liunardo, N. and Fletcher, G.L. (1978).
    Biochem. Biophys. Res. Comm. 85, 421-427.
Holeton, G.F. (1980). In "Environmental physiology of
    fishes" (M.A. Ali, ed.) 7-32, Plenum Press, New York
    and London.
Jackim, E. and Laroche, C. (1973). Comp. Biochem.
    Physiol. 44A, 851-866.
Jankowsky, H.D., Hotopp, W. and Vsiansky, P. (1981). J.
    Therm. Biol. 6, 201-208.
Kaushik, S.J., Fauconneau, B. and Blanc, J.M. (1984).
    Reprod. Nutr. Develop. 24. In Press.
Kent, J. and Prosser, C.L. (1980). Physiol. Zool. 53,
    293-304.
Krauskopf, M., Araya, A. and Litvak, S. (1974). Comp.
    Biochem. Physiol. 48B, 619-628.
Lajtha, A. and Sershen, H. (1976). Life Sci. 17,
    1861-1868.
Lied, E., Rosenlund, G., Lund, B. and Von Der Decken, A.
    (1983). Comp. Biochem. Physiol. 76B, 777-781.
McNurlan, M.A. and Garlick, P.J. (1980). Biochem. J. 186,
    381-383.
Manikodan, Y., Kyaw, N.N. and Ikeda, S. (1982). Comp.
    Biochem. Physiol. 73B, 785-789.
Mathews, R. and Haschemeyer, A.E.V. (1978). Comp.
    Biochem. Physiol. 61B, 479-484.

Millward, D.J., Bates, P.C., Brown, J.B. and Cox, M.
(1982). In "Nitrogen metabolism in man". (J.C.
Waterlow and J.M. Stephen, eds.), 409-418. Applied
Science Publishers Ltd., London.

Millward, D.J., Bates, P.C. and Rosochacki, S. (1981).
Reprod. Nutr. Develop. 21, 265-277.

Millward, D.J., Garlick, P.J., James, W.P.T., Sender, P.M.
and Waterlow, J.C. (1976). In "Protein metabolism and
nutrition". (D.J.A. Cole, ed.) 446-491. Butterworths,
London.

Millward, D.J. and Waterlow, J.C. (1978). Fed. Proc. 37,
2283-2290.

Monroy, A., Ishida, M. and Nakano, E. (1961).
Embryologia, 6, 151-158.

Narayansingh, T. and Eales, J.G. (1975). Comp. Biochem.
Physiol. 52B, 399-405.

Nielsen, J.B.K. (1977). Biol. Bull. 153, 442-449.

Nielsen, J.B.K., Plant, P.W. and Haschemeyer, A.E.V.
(1977). Physiol. Zool. 50, 22-30.

Nordlie, F.C. and Leffler, C.W. (1975). Comp. Biochem.
Physiol. 51A, 125-131.

Obled, C., Arnal, M. and Fauconneau, G. (1983). In
"Protein Metabolism and Nutrition", (M. Arnal, R. Pion
and D. Bonin, eds.) II 23-27, INRA, Paris.

Orcutt, M.W. and Young, R.B. (1982). J. Anim. Sci., 54,
769-776.

Owen, T.G. (1975). Comp. Biochem. Physiol. 52B, 557-559.

Persell, R. and Haschemeyer, A.E.V. (1976). Amer. J.
Physiol. 231, 1817-1823.

Persell, R. and Haschemeyer, A.E.V. (1980). Biochim.
Biophys. Acta 602, 653-660.

Pickett, M.H., Hew, C. and Davies, P.L. (1983). Biochim.
Biophys. Acta 739, 97-104.

Plant, R.W., Nielsen, J.B.K. and Haschemeyer, A.E.V.
(1977). Physiol. Zool. 50, 11-21.

Pocrnjic, Z., Mathews, R.W., Rappaport, S. and
Haschemeyer, A.E.V. (1983). Comp. Biochem. Physiol.
74B, 735-738.

Precht, H. (1967). In "The cell and environmental
temperature", (A.S. Troshin, ed.), 307-321. Pergamon
Press, Oxford.

Rannels, D.E., Wartell, S.A. and Watkins, C.A. (1982).
Life Sci. 30, 1679-1690.

Reeds, P.J. and Harris, C.I. (1982). In "Nitrogen
metabolism in man", (J.C. Waterlow and J.M. Stephen,
eds.), 391-408. Applied Science Publishers Ltd.,
London.

Reeds, P.J. and Lobley, G.E. (1980). Proc. Nutr. Soc. 39, 43-52.

Reeds, P.J., Wahle, K.W.J. and Haggarty, P. (1982). Proc. Nutr. Soc. 41, 155-159.

Rennie, M.J. and Millward, D.J. (1983). Clin. Sci. 65, 217-225.

Rosen, L., Murray, E.L. and Novelli, G.D. (1967). Can. J. Biochem. 45, 2005-2014.

Rosenlund, G., Lund, B., Lied, E. and Von Der Decken, A. (1983). Comp. Biochem. Physiol. 74B, 389-397.

Rosenlund, G., Lund, B., Sandnes, K., Braekkan, O.R. and Von Der Decken, A. (1984). Comp. Biochem. Physiol. 77B, 7-13.

Saez, L., Giocoechea, O., Amthauer, R. and Krauskopf, M. (1982). Comp. Biochem. Physiol. 72B, 31-38.

Schimke, R.T. (1970). In "Mammalian protein metabolism", (H.N. Munro, ed.) 4, 178-228. Academic Press, New York.

Smith, M.A.K. (1981). J. Fish. Biol. 19, 213-220.

Smith, M.A.K. and Haschemeyer, A.E.V. (1974). Biol. Bull. 147, 500-508.

Smith, M.A.K. and Haschemeyer, A.E.V. (1980). Physiol. Zool. 53, 373-382.

Smith, M.A.K., Mathews, R.W., Hudson, A.P. and Haschemeyer, A.E.V. (1980). Comp. Biochem. Physiol. 65B, 415-418.

Somero, G.N. and Doyle, D. (1973). Comp. Biochem. Physiol. 46B, 463-474.

Strickland, N.C. (1983). J. Anat. 137, 323-333.

Tondeur, F. and Sargent, J.R. (1979). Comp. Biochem. Physiol. 62B, 13-16.

Waterlow, J.C., Garlick, P.J. and Millward, D.J. (1978). "Protein turnover in mammalian tissues and in the whole body", 804pp. Elsevier, North Holland Biochemical Press.

Weatherley, A.H. and Gill, H.S. (1984). Experientia. In press.

Ward, L.C. and Buttery, P.J. (1978). Life Sci. 23, 1103-1116.

Young, V.R., Meguid, M., Meredith, C., Matthews, D.E. and Bier, D.M. (1982). In "Nitrogen metabolism in man" (J.C. Waterlow and J.M.L. Stephen, eds.), 133-153. Applied Science Publishers Ltd., London.

Young, V.R. and Munro, H.N. (1978). Fed. Proc. 37, 2291-2300.

Zak, R., Martin, A.F. and Blough, R. (1979). Physiol. Rev. 59, 407-447.

Zilversmit, D.B. (1960). Amer. J. Med. 29, 832-848.

ASPECTS OF AMINO ACID METABOLISM IN TELEOST FISH

M.J. WALTON

NERC Institute of Marine Biochemistry,
Aberdeen, U.K.

I. INTRODUCTION

A knowledge of amino acid metabolism in fish is useful for several reasons. All species so far examined have relatively high dietary requirements for both protein and essential amino acids (see reviews by Ketola, 1982; Millikin, 1982). Amino acids are precursors for many biological compounds notably protein and are also substrates for energy production. Carbohydrates are relatively poorly utilized by fish (see Walton and Cowey, 1982) and the main sources of energy in fish appear to be protein and lipid in contrast to mammals in which carbohydrate and lipid are more important. From measurements of ammonia excretion and oxygen uptake it is possible to estimate the contribution of amino acid catabolism to energy production under aerobic conditions. Such studies have shown that the standard metabolic rate seems to be almost completely due to amino acid catabolism (Brett and Zala, 1975) but as the metabolic rate increases then lipid catabolism becomes increasingly more important. The relative contributions of lipids and amino acids to energy production are dependent on a number of factors including species involved, nutritional state, temperature, e.g. in fed salmonids performing routine activity more than 40% of energy production is due to amino acid catabolism. Also many fish can withstand long periods of starvation, during which they catabolise their

NUTRITION AND FEEDING IN FISH
ISBN: 0 12 194055 1

own body proteins (Créach and Serfaty, 1974; Moon and Johnston, 1981).

The main pathways of amino acid metabolism are probably basically similar in all vertebrates and are well described in standard text books. This paper cannot cover all aspects of this wide subject but will attempt to give an overview of amino acid metabolism as it applies to fish, noting any differences to the mammalian situation; it will also describe the effects of some nutritional factors. For more details on amino acid metabolism and ammonia formation and excretion in fish see the reviews by Walton and Cowey (1982) and van Waarde (1983).

II. AMINO ACID METABOLISM - AN OVERVIEW

As Fig. 1 shows, the body pool of amino acids arises from two main sources namely the diet and catabolism of body proteins which are in a state of constant turnover. Some interconversion of amino acids and synthesis of non-essential amino acids also occurs. Amino acids are primarily required for the synthesis of new body protein and (quantitatively less important) for other compounds

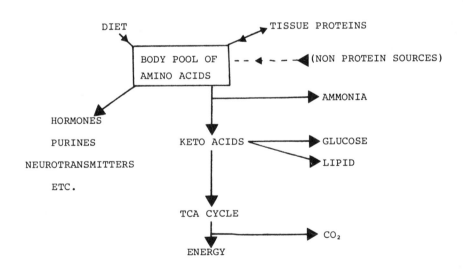

Fig. 1. Overview of amino acid metabolism in fish

with special properties, e.g. hormones, neurotransmitters. There are no known body stores of amino acids, although their existence cannot be entirely discounted (Driedzic and Hochachka, 1978), and excess amino acids are rapidly deaminated, the amino group being ultimately excreted as ammonia and the carbon skeleton being oxidised via the tricarboxylic acid (TCA) cycle for energy or in some cases converted to glucose or lipid.   These pathways will now be examined in more detail.

A. Synthesis of non-essential amino acids

Non-essential amino acids may be synthesised by transfer of amino groups to α-keto acids which can be derived from non-protein sources.   The evidence comes from several fish species, Pleuronectes platessa, Solea solea (Cowey et al., 1970;   Cyprinus carpio (Créach et al., 1973); Dicentrarchus labrax (Metailler et al., 1973) which were injected with $[U-^{14}C]$ glucose, left for several days, killed, the body proteins hydrolysed and the resulting amino acids separated and assayed for radioactivity.   High radioactivity levels were found in aspartic and glutamic acids, glycine, alanine and serine and lower but still significant levels were found in proline, which probably reflects the fact that the biosynthetic pathway from glutamate is not very rapid. Very low or no radioactivity was found associated with the essential amino acids arginine, histidine, isoleucine, leucine, lysine, methionine, phenylalanine, tyrosine, threonine and valine.   Tryptophan, glutamine and asparagine are destroyed by this technique but numerous feeding experiments have shown that tryptophan is an essential amino acid (see Ketola, 1982);   the enzymes for glutamine and asparagine biosynthesis have been detected in fish tissues (van Waarde, 1983; Webb and Brown, 1980) but at much lower activities than in mammalian tissues. Glutamine synthetase is predominantly located in brain tissue where it is thought to have a protective role in preventing the build up of toxic NH_3 concentrations. From nutritional experiments it can be inferred that tyrosine and cysteine may be synthesised from phenylalanine and methionine respectively.

B. Uptake and tissue distribution of amino acids

The uptake of amino acids derived from diets of complete proteins or crystalline amino acids is reviewed by Ash (this volume). In gut tissues of mammals and birds much glutamine is utilised for energy and much glutamate and aspartate are converted to alanine (Neame and Wiseman, 1957), but these occurrences have not been studied in fish. On leaving the gut amino acids enter the portal blood system and pass through the liver, which has an important role in amino acid metabolism, and thence to other tissues. The free amino acid concentrations of tissues in catfish (Wilson and Poe, 1974) and trout (Walton and Cowey, 1982; Cras et al., 1978, 1982) show that several amino acids notably glutamate and aspartate are present in tissues at concentrations much greater than in plasma (see Table I). Erythrocytes may play a role in the transport of some amino acids (Felig, 1975).

Table I. Ratio of concentrations of amino acids in certain tissues to that in plasma of rainbow trout.

Ratio	Tissue			
	RBC	Liver	Kidney	Muscle
>20		Glu, Asp, Gln	Glu, Asp	Gly
10-20	Asp	Gly, Ser, Ala	Gly	His, Ala, Glu
5-10	Glu, Gly	His, Asn, Pro, Met	Ala, Gln	–
<5	←	(Remaining amino acids)		→

RBC = red blood cells. Data is from Walton and Cowey (1982)

C. Protein synthesis

See the article by Fauconneau (this volume).

D. Amino acid deamination and N-excretion

The degradation of amino acids occurs in two major stages the first being the conversion to an intermediate which can enter the TCA cycle and the second is oxidation of the intermediate to CO_2 and H_2O. The first stage involves removal of the amino group which, since there is no functional urea cycle in adult teleosts (Dépêche et al., 1979) is ultimately excreted as ammonia. Nitrogen excretion has been widely studied in the fish (see reviews by Watts and Watts, 1974; Brett and Groves, 1979; van Waarde, 1983) and it has been shown that over 90% is excreted via the gills, urinary excretion being relatively unimportant.   60-90% of the excreted N is in the form of ammonia, and the gills extract preformed ammonia from the blood rather than having a major role in its formation (Walton and Cowey, 1977; Payan and Pic, 1977).   By analysis of blood from various sites within the carp, the liver (hepatopancreas) was found to be the major site of ammonia formation (Pequin and Serfaty, 1963).   Other tissues (i.e. kidney and muscle) also play a lesser but still significant role in NH_3 formation.   Eels with the liver surgically removed still excrete NH_3, but lose the ability to deaminate excess amino acids after feeding (Kenyon,   1967)   i.e.   a   post-prandial   rise   in NH_3 excretion is not observed.   In   salmon   the   ammonia excretion rate rose rapidly 4 hr after feeding (from 8 to 35 mg N/kg body wt/hr) whereas there was no change in urea excretion rate (Brett and Zala, 1975);   these figures show that dietary amino acids are rapidly utilised, ammonia excretion being related to protein catabolism.

However, what is still not absolutely clear is which of the many enzyme mechanisms which can produce NH3 from amino acids are quantitatively most important.   Generally speaking there is a specific enzyme responsible for the deamination of each amino acid.

Two main types of deaminating mechanisms exist 1) direct deamination and 2) transfer of the amino group to a common acceptor which is then deaminated.   Direct deamination of the primary amino group may be catalysed by a number of enzymes e.g. L- or D- amino acid oxidases, histidase, arginase, serine dehydratase and glutamate dehydrogenase.   Of these glutamate dehydrogenase is likely to have the most significant role (see van Waarde, 1983).   This enzyme has been investigated in several fish species (see Walton and Cowey, 1982 for refs.) and in all cases the enzyme is mitochondrial, but unlike its mammalian counterpart, which uses both NAD(H) and NADP(H) in fish it is specific for NAD(H). Deamination of the secondary amino group of glutamine by the enzyme glutaminase is thought to be quantitatively significant in carp (Vellas and Serfaty, 1974).

Deamination by transfer to a common acceptor may be carried out by two postulated pathways (see Fig. 2) - the

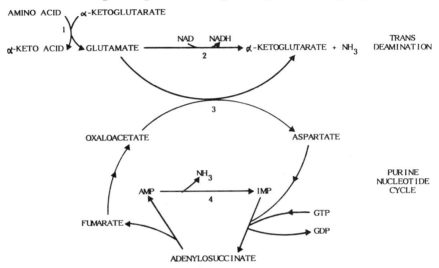

Fig. 2. Transdeamination and the purine nucleotide cycle; 1, amino acid aminotransferase; 2, glutamate dehydrogenase; 3, glutamate oxaloacetic aminotransferase; 4, adenosine monophosphate deaminase

transdeamination pathway of Braunstein (1957) or the purine nucleotide cycle of Lowenstein (1972). During recent years there has been much discussion on the relative merits of these two schemes in mammalian liver but, from enzymic studies and studies with ^{13}N several groups have concluded that the purine nucleotide cycle is unlikely to have a major role in fish livers (Walton and Cowey, 1977; van Waarde, 1983; Casey et al., 1983; Campbell et al., 1983), though it could play a role in muscle where ammoniogenesis is proportional to the work load. Transdeamination involves the transfer of the amino group to α ketoglutarate, forming glutamate and a keto acid. This reaction is catalysed by a transaminase and is followed by deamination of glutamate by glutamate dehydrogenase. Some transaminases are very specific while others react with several amino acids; they occur in most tissues, the most significant quantitatively being alanine and aspartate aminotransferases. Experiments with liver and kidney preparations (Steiber and Cvancara, 1977; Salvatore et al., 1965) and cod muscle (Siebert et al., 1965; Bell, 1968) showed the presence of many transaminases and also that liver had the capacity to deaminate all amino acids. However as yet not all the individual deaminating enzymes have been investigated in fish tissues. The branched chain amino acid aminotransferases appear to have a similar distribution as mammals with high activities in red muscle but lesser activities in white muscle and liver (Zébian and Créach, 1979; Hughes et al., 1983). Though most amino acids could take part in transamination reactions, not all would take place at a significant rate in vivo, and in these cases enzymes specific for a given amino acid, usually located in the liver, would be involved.

E. Control of deamination

Amino acids are preferentially required for protein synthesis, therefore animals must exercise some control over catabolic pathways especially when dietary supplies are restricted. Control of amino acid catabolism according to Krebs (1972) depends basically on coarse controls (presence and level of the relevant enzyme) and fine controls (substrate concentration in relation to Km i.e. the substrate level which produces half-maximal activity; cofactor concentrations; and allosteric factors). The enzymes responsible for initiating protein synthesis (amino acyl tRNA synthetases) are present in most tissues whereas the enzymes responsible for catabolism tend to be concentrated in the liver. Changes in enzyme level can occur as metabolic adaptations to dietary changes. In fish this coarse control sometimes appears to be lacking (see later). However, control by Km is likely to play an important role. Table II shows the Km values of some rainbow trout enzymes and liver concentrations of the amino acid (20hr after feeding).

Tissue concentrations of amino acids are generally greater than the Km values (typically of the order 0.01–0.1 mM) of the amino acyl tRNA synthetases which would, therefore, be saturated with substrate and hence be fully active. On the other hand Km values of the catabolizing enzymes are higher (typically of the order

1-10 mM) and these enzymes would not be saturated and any increase in substrate concentration e.g. after feeding would automatically lead to increased catabolism.

F. Reaction of the α-Keto acids

After removal of the amino group from an amino acid, the resultant α-keto acid can be oxidised via the TCA cycle for energy (probably the major fate), or in some cases converted to glucose or lipid, or even reconverted

Table II. Km values of amino acid catabolising enzymes and the corresponding amino acid concentrations in rainbow trout liver.

Enzyme	[Amino acid] mM	Km mM
Alanine aminotransferase	4.2	2.5
Arginase	0.1	4.9
Glutaminase	4.5	3.3
Glutamate dehydrogenase	7.2	3.7
Lysine αKG reductase	2.8	7.3
Serine pyruvate transaminase	2.6	8.1
Threonine dehydrogenase	1.1	7.8
Tryptophan pyrrolase	0.02	0.2
Tyrosine aminotransferase	0.07	3.2

Data is from Walton and Cowey (1982) and Walton, (unpublished results)

Amino acid concentrations were measured 20 hr after feeding

to the amino acid. Despite the poor utilisation and production of glucose by fish (Bever et al., 1981; Cowey et al., 1977a), glucose is required as a fuel for red blood cells, nervous tissue, gonads and production of mucopolysaccharides, glycogen etc.

Glucose is stored as glycogen and in mammals liver glycogen is almost completely depleted after 2 days starvation. However in fish the liver reserves are maintained even after many weeks of starvation (Dave et al., 1975; Hilton, 1982). However, elevated hepatic levels of glycogen caused by feeding high levels of dietary carbohydrate will decrease during periods of starvation. Gluconeogenesis is likely to occur mainly during starvation or if low carbohydrate diets are fed and the most probable precursors are amino acids.

Most amino acids can theoretically yield 1 mole glucose from 2 moles amino acid. However in vivo alanine is thought to be quantitatively the most important. During starvation or spawning migration of the salmon alanine was found to be the only amino acid released in quantity from muscle tissue (Mommsen et al., 1980). A number of studies have demonstrated the conversion of alanine to glucose in whole fish (e.g. Cowey et al., 1977a; Bever et al., 1981) and in liver preparations (e.g. Hayashi and Ooshiro, 1979; Walton and Cowey, 1979a,b). The distribution of enzymes required for gluconeogenesis has been investigated in several species and in all cases the liver was the only tissue containing significant levels of the requisite enzymes (Knox et al., 1980). Quantitatively gluconeogenesis is likely to be only a minor pathway of amino acid metabolism (Bever et al., 1981).

Henderson and Sargent (1981) demonstrated that in trout the liver is a more important site of triacylglycerol synthesis than adipose tissue and in addition much greater incoporation of radioactivity into the fatty acid component was noted from alanine than from glucose. In Japanese eel, amino acids were apparently more effective than glucose as precursors of lipid (Nagai and Ikeda, 1972; 1973).

G. Other reactions

A few of the many biochemically important compounds derived from amino acids are purines, pyrimidines, glutathione, polypeptide hormones, carnitine, serotonin and niacin though few of these pathways have been investigated in fish. [U-^{14}C] glucose was incorporated into purines and pyrimidines of plaice and sole (Cowey et al., 1970), but Dabrowski and Kaushik (1982) have recently speculated that pyrimidine biosynthesis may be insufficient in fish because of low levels of carbomyl

phosphate synthetase. In mammals tryptophan may be
converted to niacin, but this pathway is thought to be of
little significance in fish (Poston and Combs, 1980).
Methionine is important in the transfer of methyl groups
for biosynthesis of phospholipids, purines etc. Some
evidence that this occurs in fish was presented by Walton
et al. (1982) who injected groups of trout with either
[^{14}COOH-] or [^{14}CH$_3$] labelled methionine. About
100 times more radioactivity from the methyl group than
from the carboxyl group was found in the lipid fraction
whereas up to 3 times more of the carboxyl label was found
in the expired CO_2 and incorporated into protein. These
results are consistent with the metabolic pathways known
to occur in mammals.

IV. INFLUENCE OF NUTRITIONAL FACTORS ON AMINO ACID
    METABOLISM

A. Level of amino acid in the diet

When a series of diets, nutritionally complete except
for one essential amino acid and containing graded levels
of this amino acid are fed to fish several biochemical
effects are noted in addition to the effects on growth.
The concentration of the amino acid in plasma and tissues,
oxidation of it to CO_2 and enzyme activities (especially
those related to the catabolism of the amino acid
concerned) can all vary with the concentration of the
amino acid in the diet and it is sometimes possible to
determine the dietary requirement from these changes.
Studies, mainly with rainbow trout and channel catfish,
have been performed both to assess the suitability of
measuring these changes for determining dietary
requirements in fish and to investigate how fish adapt to
dietary changes.
    In the case of amino acid blood concentrations the
level of the amino acid ideally (i.e. if it is to be of
use for determining dietary requirement) remains low at
sub-requirement levels but rises markedly once the
requirement level has been surpassed. This procedure
(using serum concentrations) has been successfully used
with catfish to determine the requirements of methionine,
lysine and threonine but could not be applied to
histidine, arginine, phenylalanine, and branched chain

amino   acids   (Wilson,   this   volume).   It   was   also
unsuccessful for determining requirements of tryptophan,
lysine and arginine in rainbow trout (Walton et al., 1984
a,b,c) although Kaushik (1979) using the same species
found the method satisfactory for arginine.   In those
cases   when   the   method   was   unsuccessful,   the   plasma
concentrations either tended to rise and then level off
without a well-defined breakpoint or changed very little
as the dietary level increased (Table III).   Thus this

Table III.   Effect of dietary amino acid concentration on
plasma and liver concentration of the amino acid.

1] Tryptophan	(0.25)						
Dietary level	(%)	0.08	0.13	0.2	0.3	0.4	0.6
6 hr Blood	μM	2.9	4.1	16.5	22.1	27.6	38.5
20 hr Blood	μM	1.6	5.9	12.4	18.3	23.6	20.7
20 hr Liver	μM	6.5	9.5	15.5	17.1	21.2	20.7

2] Lysine	(1.9)							
Dietary level	(%)	1.0	1.2	1.4	1.7	2.0	2.3	2.6
Blood	μM	52	30	31	24	58	61	46

3] Arginine	(1.6-1.8)						
Dietary level	(%)	0.9	1.3	1.8	2.3	2.8	3.3
Blood	μM	10	16	46	36	61	69

Figure in brackets = dietary requirement level from growth data

method has only met with limited success in fish.
Sometimes changes in dietary level of one amino acid can
influence the plasma concentration of other amino acids,
e.g.   amongst   the   branched   chain   amino   acids   or
lysine-arginine interactions.
      Few studies have been performed on how liver (and other
tissue) enzymes are affected by the level of amino acid in

the diet.   In rainbow trout, variations in the dietary
levels   of   lysine,   tryptophan   and   arginine   had   no
significant effect on hepatic activities of lysine-α-keto-
glutarate   reductase,   tryptophan   pyrrolase   and   arginase
respectively (Walton et al., 1984a,b,c) (Table IV).   This
is   in   contrast   to   the   situation   in   rats   where   these
enzymes are induced by increasing levels of substrate.   It
may be that the trout differs from the rat by catabolising
these   amino   acids   by   routes   initiated   by   enzymes   other
than   the   ones   mentioned,   however   the   results   are
consistent with other findings which show that fish show
little adaptation of amino acid metabolism to changes in
protein content of the diet (Rumsey, 1981) i.e. the coarse
control appears to be lacking.   It is also worth noting
that   when   Brown   and   Dodgen   (1968)   repeatedly   injected
catfish with L-tryptophan they failed to induce tryptophan
pyrrolasae activity, and excess tryptophan proved to be
toxic to the fish.   It has since been discovered that
tryptophan   pyrrolase   can   exist   in   apo   and   holo   enzyme
forms   (Badawy   and   Evans,   1976).   The   enzyme   is   only
inducible in those species which possess both forms e.g.
rat,   pig,   whereas   in   some   species,   e.g.   cat,   rabbit   and
probably fish the apo enzyme is absent and the enzyme is
non-inducible.

The catabolism of an amino acid (oxidation to CO_2) is
affected   by   its   dietary   concentration   and   sometimes
follows a similar pattern to that described previously for
the changes in plasma concentration.   As Fig. 3 shows
when   [1-^{14}C]-tryptophan   was   injected   intraperitoneally
into   rainbow   trout   and   the   expired CO_2 collected   for
20 hr, little radioactivity was found in it when the fish
were fed subrequirement levels of tryptophan but when the
requirement level was surpassed radioactivity in expired
CO_2 increased markedly (Walton et al., 1984a).   However
the   breakpoint   in   the   dose   response   curve   gave   a
requirement level of 0.21% diet compared to a value of
0.25% from the growth data.

Similar   experiments,   using   [U-^{14}C]-lysine   and
[U-^{14}C]-arginine in fish fed diets relevant to the amino
acid under investigation, also revealed marked increases
in $^{14}CO_2$ production   once   the   requirement   level   had
been surpassed, but the changes were not sufficiently
precise for determination of the dietary requirement level
(Table V).   Hence, from these findings it seems that at
subrequirement levels the amino acid is presumably used
principally for protein synthesis and only when excess of
the amino acid is present is catabolism increased.

Table IV.   Effect of dietary amino acid concentration on the activity of its catabolising enzyme in rainbow trout liver

1] Tryptophan (0.25)

Dietary level %	0.08	0.13	0.2	0.3	0.4	0.6
TP (μmol/hr/g)	5.1	13.3	8.8	15.9	14.2	12.8

2] Lysine (1.9)

Dietary level %	1.0	1.2	1.4	1.7	2.0	2.3
L-KGR (μmol/min/g)	0.16	0.16	0.16	0.18	0.18	0.17

3] Arginine (1.6–1.8)

Dietary level %	0.9	1.3	1.8	2.3	2.8	3.3
Arginase (μmol/min/g)	69	61	67	55	72	79

TP = Tryptophan pyrrolase
L-KGR = Lysine αKetoglutarate reductase

Figure in brackets = Dietary requirement level from growth data

Table V.   Effect of dietary amino acid concentration on expiration of $[^{14}CO_2]$ from $[^{14}C]$ amino acids in rainbow trout

1] Tryptophan (0.25)

Dietary level	%	0.08	0.13	0.2	0.3	0.4	0.6
$[1-^{14}C]$Trp	% dose	3.1	3.3	4.5	13.4	22.4	32.0

2] Lysine (1.9)

Dietary level	%	1.0	1.2	1.4	1.7	2.0	2.3	2.6
$[U-^{14}C]$Lys	% dose	2.1	2.2	5.3	6.2	6.4	14.0	13.9

3] Arginine (1.6-1.8)

Dietary level	%	0.9	1.3	1.8	2.3	2.8	3.3
$[U-^{14}C]$Arg	% dose	10.1	13.1	13.0	19.9	20.5	19.9

$^{14}CO_2$ collected for 20 hr at 15°C

Figure in brackets = Dietary requirement level from growth data

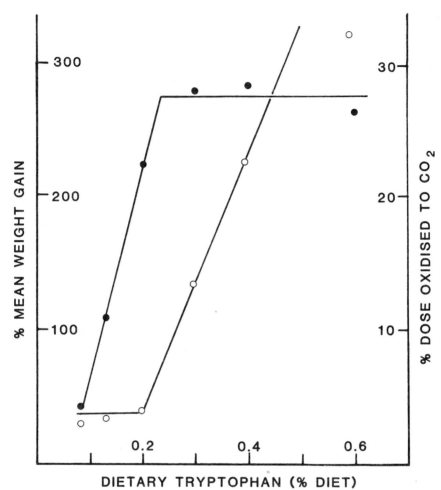

Fig. 3. Effect of dietary tryptophan level on % mean weight gain (●———●) and oxidation of injected [1 - ^{14}C] tryptophan to CO_2 over 20 hr (O———O).

However such changes, at least in these three instances, were unsatisfactory for accurate determination of amino acid requirements since, either they did not produce suitable dose-response curves or they produced a value different from that obtained from the growth data.   It is probably better to use [1-^{14}C] rather than [U-^{14}C] amino acids but often they are not commercially available or else very expensive. Also it must be noted that fractional rather than true oxidation rates are measured by this technique so different pool sizes could influence the results.

Sometimes amino acid deficiences cause certain pathological deficiency symptoms. Kloppel and Post (1975) noticed that tryptophan deficient rainbow trout suffered from scoliosis (lateral deformations of the spine) and histological examinations revealed calcium deposits in the kidney. These symptoms were not seen in tryptophan deficient catfish (Wilson et al., 1978). Walton et al. (1984a) extended these studies and measured the concentrations of several minerals in liver and kidney of trout fed diets varying in tryptophan content. In those fish fed deficient diets levels of several minerals were significantly increased (see Table VI). As yet no

Table VI. Mean concentration of several minerals (μmol/g dry wt) in kidneys of rainbow trout fed diets containing different levels of tryptophan.

	Dietary tryptophan (%)					
	0.08	0.13	0.20	0.30	0.40	0.60
Ca	64	25	14	15	17	16
Na	947	565	358	352	385	362
K	450	358	312	320	312	312
P	450	395	417	428	410	408
Mg	37	33	33	35	34	34
Zn	1.9	1.6	1.6	1.7	1.7	1.7

Mean values from 6 fish. (Walton et al., 1984a)

satisfactory explanation can be given to explain these effects, but it may be that certain tryptophan metabolites (e.g. serotonin) exert some influence on mineral balance in fish.

B. Level of protein in the diet

Plasma amino acid levels reflect the protein content of the diet, e.g. total plasma amino acids were 10.2mM in fish fed diets containing 60% crude protein compared to 3.05 mM in fish fed diets containing 10% crude protein (Cowey et al., 1977b). In mammals amino acid metabolism adapts to variations in protein intake whereas many fish have their metabolism apparently "permanently" adapted to deal with a high protein diet (Rumsey, 1981). McFarlane and Holt (1969) injected [^{14}C] labelled amino acids intraperitoneally into rats which had previously been given high or low protein diets and followed the expiration of [^{14}CO$_2$]. The non-essential amino acids glutamate and alanine were oxidised rapidly on both feeding regimes, whereas the essential amino acids leucine and phenylalanine were oxidised considerably less rapidly in rats fed the low protein diet. These results show that conservation of essential amino acids apparently occurs in rats fed low protein diets. More evidence is needed, however, to distinguish between an effect due to changes in enzyme level (coarse control) or an effect due to differences in substrate concentration (fine control). These experiments were repeated using turbot (Knox and Cowey, 1974) fed diets containing either 6 or 50% protein and carp (Zébian and Créach, 1979) fed diets of 0 or 32% protein. In turbot over 50% injected dose of glutamate and alanine was expired as CO$_2$ within 24 hr irrespective of diet, giving similar results to the rat. However appreciable quantities of leucine and phenylalanine (20-30% dose) were expired as CO$_2$ on both the high and low protein diets, showing no conservation mechanisms for at least 2 essential amino acids. In contrast in the carp less [^{14}CO$_2$] was produced from all 4 amino acids fed the protein-free compared to the protein-containing diet. Such experiments using a single pulse of [^{14}C]-amino acids are open to a number of criticisms e.g. they do not take into account different pool sizes and caution must be exercised in interpreting the results. Some of the differences observed between trout and carp may be due to the use of [1-^{14}C] compared to [U-^{14}C] amino acids. Obviously more work is needed to clarify these points.

Coarse control of amino acid metabolism implies that amino acid deaminating enzymes would be present in greater amounts in animals fed high compared to low protein diets in order to facilitate disposal of excess N. Few studies have been done with fish. Sakaguchi and Kawai (1970) found an increase of 4-10 fold in hepatic histidine deaminase activity in carp fed diets containing 80% casein compared to those fed diets containing 8% casein. However

levels of this enzyme were unaffected by diets containing
25-60% protein (Cowey et al., 1981), whereas levels of
serine pyruvate transaminase increased 2-3 fold. Also no
effects due to dietary protein level were found on
activities of glutamate dehydrogenase, aspartate
aminotransferase and alanine aminotransferase in plaice
(Cowey et al., 1974) or these aminotransferases in carp
(Nagai and Ikeda, 1973), or of arginase, glutamate
dehydrogenase and branched chain aminotransferase in
rainbow trout (Rumsey, 1981).   Leucine aminotransferase
in carp (Zébian and Créach, 1979) increased 2 fold in red
muscle but not liver when the dietary protein level rose
from 0 to 32%. Whiting and Wiggs (1977) detected a
1.5-fold increase in tyrosine aminotransferase activity
when the dietary protein level increased from 30 to 55%.
Hence, whereas conservation mechanisms appear to exist in
some species for certain amino acids, they are lacking for
others; once again more research is needed to clarify the
situation.

Feeding diets containing high protein/low carbohydrate
compared to low protein/high carbohydrate leads to marked
changes in the hepatic activities of the regulatory
enzymes of glycolysis (pyruvate kinase, phosphofructo-
kinase) and gluconeogenesis (fructose diphosphatase, PEP-
carboxykinase).   Cowey et al. (1981) found that the
activities of the glycolytic enzymes decreased and those
of the gluconeogenic enzymes increased as the dietary
protein level increased and carbohydrate level decreased.

V. SUMMARY OF DIETARY EFFECTS ON AMINO ACID METABOLISM

As yet, too few experiments have been performed to
allow definite conclusions to be drawn on the ability of
fish to adapt to dietary changes.   Although some of the
available evidence is conflicting much of it suggests that
the amino acid catabolising pathways are permanently set
to deal with high protein diets and show little, if any,
adaption (i.e. variation in enzymes levels) to changes in
dietary protein or amino acid level.   However some
control of catabolism is still exercised to conserve
essential amino acids when the dietary supply is
limiting. This is probably mainly due to the lowering of
enzyme substrate (amino acid) concentrations caused by
dietary restrictions.

REFERENCES

Badawy, A.A.B. and Evans, M. (1976). Biochem. J. 158, 79–88.

Bell, G.R. (1968). J. Fish. Res. Bd. Canada 25, 1247–1268.

Bever, K., Chenoweth, M. and Dunn, A. (1981). Am. J. Physiol. 240, R246–252.

Braunstein, A.E. (1957). Adv. Enzymol. 19, 335–377.

Brett, J.R. and Groves, T.D.D. (1979). In "Fish Physiology" (W.S. Hoar, D.J. Randall and J.R. Brett, eds.) 8, 279–352. Academic Press, New York.

Brett, J.R. and Zala, C.A. (1975). J. Fish. Res. Bd., Canada 32, 2479–2486.

Brown, J.N. and Dodgen, C.L. (1968). Biochim. biophys. Acta 165, 463–469.

Campbell, J.W., Aster, P.L. and Vorhaben, J.E. (1983). Am. J. Physiol. 244, R709–717.

Casey, C.A., Perlman, D.F., Vorhaben, J.E. and Campbell, J.W. (1983). Mol Physiol. 3, 107–126.

Cowey, C.B., Brown, D.A., Adron, J.W. and Shanks, A.M. (1974). Mar. Biol. 28, 207–213.

Cowey, C.B., Adron, J.W. and Blair, A. (1970). J. Mar. Biol. Ass. U.K. 50, 87–95.

Cowey, C.B., de la Higuera, M. and Adron, J.W. (1977a). Br. J. Nutr. 38, 385–395.

Cowey, C.B., Knox, D., Walton, M.J. and Adron, J.W. (1977b). Br. J. Nutr. 38, 463–470.

Cowey, C.B., Cooke, D.J., Matty, A.J. and Adron, J.W. (1981). J. Nutr. 111, 336–345.

Créach, Y. and Serfaty, A. (1974). J. Physiol. (Paris) 68, 245–260.

Créach, Y., Bouche, G. and Vellas, F. (1973). C.R. Acad. Sci. Paris 276, 2569–2572.

Dabrowski, K. and Kaushik, S.J. (1982). Speculation in Sci. Tech. 5, 447–454.

Dave, G., Johansson-Sjöbeck, M., Larsson, A., Lewander, K. and Lidman, U. (1975). Comp. Biochem. Physiol. 52A, 423–430.

Dépêche, J., Gilles, R., Daufresne, S. and Chiapello, H. (1979). Comp. Biochem. Physiol. 63A, 51–56.

Driedzic, W.R. and Hochachka, P.W. (1978). In "Fish Physiology" (W.S. Hoar and D.J. Randall, eds.) 7, 503–543. Academic Press, New York.

Felig, P. (1975). Ann. Rev. Biochem. 44, 933–955.

Gras, J., Gudefin, Y. and Chagny, F. (1978). Comp. Biochem. Physiol. 60B, 369–372.

Gras, J., Gudefin, Y., Chagny, F. and Perrier, H. (1982). Comp. Biochem. Physiol. 73B, 845–847.

Hayashi, S. and Ooshiro, Z. (1979). J. Comp. Physiol. B. 132, 343–350.

Henderson, R.J. and Sargent, J.R. (1981). Comp. Biochem. Physiol. 69C, 31–37.

Hilton, J. W. (1982). J. Fish Biol. 20, 69–78.

Hughes, S.G., Rumsey, G.L. and Nesheim, M.C. (1983). Comp. Biochem. Physiol. 76B, 429–431.

Kaushik, S.J. (1979). In "Finfish Nutrition and Fishfeed Technology" (J.E. Halver and K. Tiews, eds.) 1, 209–220. Heeneman, Berlin.

Kenyon, A.J. (1967). Comp. Biochem. Physiol. 22, 169–175.

Ketola, H.G. (1982). Comp. Biochem. Physiol. 73B, 17–24.

Kloppel, T.M. and Post, G. (1975). J. Nutr. 105, 861–866.

Knox, D. and Cowey, C.B. (1974). data cited by Cowey, C.B. and Sargent, J.R. (1979). In "Fish Physiology" (W.S. Hoar and D.J. Randall, eds.) 8, 1–69. Academic Press, New York.

Knox, D., Walton, M.J. and Cowey, C.B. (1980). Mar. Biol. 56, 7–10.

Krebs, H.A. (1972). Adv. Enzyme Regul. 10, 397–420.

Lowenstein, J.M. (1972). Physiol. Rev. 52, 383–414.

McFarlane, I.G. and Holt, C. (1969). Biochem. J. 111, 557–563.

Metailler, R., Febvre, A. and Alliot, E. (1973). Stud. Rev. CFCM, 52, 91–96.

Millikin, M.R. (1982). Fisheries Bull. 80, 655–686.

Mommsen, T.P., French, C.J. and Hochachka, P.W. (1980). Can. J. Zool. 58, 1785–1799.

Moon, T.W. and Johnston, I.A. (1981). J. Fish Biol. 19, 653–663.

Nagai, M. and Ikeda, S. (1972). Bull. Jap. Soc. Sci. Fish. 38, 137–143.

Nagai, M. and Ikeda, S. (1973). Bull. Jap. Soc. Sci. Fish. 39, 633–643.

Neame, K.D. and Wiseman, G. (1957). J. Physiol. 135, 442–450.

Payan, P. and Pic, P.P. (1977). C.R. Acad. Sci. Ser. D. 284, 2519–2521.

Pequin, L. and Serfaty, A. (1963). Comp. Biochem. Physiol. 10, 315–324.

Poston, H.A. and Combs, G.F. (1980). Proc. Soc. Exp. Biol. Med. 163, 452–454.

Rumsey, G.L. (1981). Salmonid 5, 20–24.

Sakaguchi, M. and Kawai, A. (1970). Bull. Jap. Soc. Sci. Fish. 36, 783–787.

Salvatore, F., Zappia, V. and Costa, C. (1965). Comp. Biochem. Physiol. 16, 303–310.

Siebert, G., Schmitt, A. and Bottke, I. (1965). Arch. Fisch. Wiss. 15, 233.

Stieber, S.T. and Cvancara, V.A. (1977). Comp. Biochem. Physiol. 56B, 285–287.

van Waarde, A. (1983). Comp. Biochem. Physiol. 74B, 675–684.

Vellas, F. and Serfaty, A. (1974). J. Physiol. (Paris). 68, 591–614.

Walton, M.J. and Cowey, C.B. (1977). Comp. Biochem. Physiol. 57B, 143–149.

Walton, M.J. and Cowey, C.B. (1979a). Comp. Biochem. Physiol. 62B, 75–79.

Walton, M.J. and Cowey, C.B. (1979b). Comp. Biochem. Physiol. 62B, 497–499.

Walton, M.J. and Cowey, C.B. (1982). Comp. Biochem. Physiol. 73B, 59–79.

Walton, M.J., Cowey, C.B. and Adron, J.W. (1982). J. Nutr. 112, 1525–1535.

Walton, M.J., Coloso, R.M., Cowey, C.B., Adron, J.W. and Knox, D. (1984a). Br. J. Nutr. 51, 279–287.

Walton, M.J., Cowey, C.B. and Adron, J.W. (1984b). Br. J. Nutr. 52, 115–122.

Walton, M.J., Cowey, C.B. and Adron, J.W. (1984c). (unpublished results).

Watts, R.L. and Watts, D.C. (1974). In "Chemical Zoology. VIII, Deuterostomians, Cyclostomes and Fishes". (M. Florkin and B.T. Scheer, eds.). 369–446. Academic Press, New York.

Webb, J.T. and Brown, G.W. (1980). Science 208, 293–295.

Whiting, S.J. and Wiggs, A.J. (1977). Comp. Biochem. Physiol. 58B, 189–193.

Wilson, R.P. and Poe, W.E. (1974). Comp. Biochem. Physiol. 48B, 545–556.

Wilson, R.P., Allen, O.W., Robinson, E.H. and Poe, W.E. (1978). J. Nutr. 108, 1595–1599.

Zébian, M.F. and Créach, Y. (1979). In "Finfish Nutrition and Fishfeed Technology" (J.E. Halver and K. Tiews, eds.), II 531–544. Heeneman, Berlin.

PROTEIN DIGESTION AND ABSORPTION

R. ASH

School of Biological Sciences, University of Bradford,
Bradford, West Yorkshire, U.K.

I. INTRODUCTION

Although many factors, both biotic and abiotic, no
doubt affect protein requirements in fish (Austreng and
Refstie, 1979; Cowey and Luquet, 1983), it must be
remembered that protein is only useful to the animal if it
can be digested and the degradation products (peptides and
amino acids) absorbed. This statement presupposes that
intact protein absorption is nutritionally unimportant to
the fish (see later). Thus, the high dietary protein
levels required to achieve optimal growth in most fish
species (Cowey, 1979) might simply reflect either, a low
percentage efficiency of hydrolysis coupled with
inefficient absorption of degradation products, or, either
one of these individual components acting alone.
Information regarding these physiological processes and
factors which might affect their overall efficiency are
therefore of considerable interest to all concerned with
the science of aquaculture.

II. PROTEIN DIGESTION AND ABSORPTION

A considerable amount of attention has been focused on
the question of protein digestibility in fish and such
work (see Table I) demonstrates that, with few exceptions,

NUTRITION AND FEEDING IN FISH
ISBN: 0 12 194055 1

most dietary proteins exhibit high true and, or, apparent digestibility coefficients (absorption efficiency). Furthermore, where low digestibilities have been recorded these can generally be explained by reference to factors other than those relating to inefficient potential for hydrolysis and absorption, viz: inadequate processing (presence of inhibitors); inappropriate diet formulation; inefficient trituration (physical unavailability), etc.

Table I. True Digestibility (Absorption) Coefficients

Species	*Protein	Coeff. of true digestibility	Reference source
Carp (C. carpio)	Casein White fish meal Dried egg yolk Gelatin Trout pelleted ration	0.98 0.95 0.95 0.97 0.93	Ogino and Chen (1973)
	Corngluten meal Soybean meal Wheatgerm Petroleum yeast	0.91 0.96 0.97 0.87-0.94	
	Whitefish meal Silk-worm pupae Wheatgerm Brownfish meal Soybean meal	0.89-0.90 0.66 0.90 0.78 0.92	Kim (1974)
Rainbow trout (S. gairdneri)	Casein Egg albumin White fish meal Soybean meal	0.99-1.00 0.84 0.92 0.92	Nose (1967)
	Casein-gelatin	0.97-0.99	Rychly and Spannhof (1979)
Tilapia (S. mossambicus)	White fish meal	0.89-0.92	Jauncey (1982)

* Fed at various levels (see references for details).

It should be stressed that although percentage digestibility values do provide some indication of the efficiency of protein assimilation (particularly so with true digestibility values), they do not provide any information on the form(s) in which amino-nitrogen is absorbed.

Experiments in which dietary protein was provided at various levels, ranging from well below, to equivalent, or in excess of, that generally considered necessary to obtain optimal growth have demonstrated that, although the metabolic fate of absorbed amino acids may differ at the higher protein intakes (Ogino and Saito, 1970; Cho et al., 1976), digestibilities remain consistently high and unaffected by the level of protein fed (Nose, 1967; Kim, 1974; Cho et al., 1976; Windell et al., 1978; Austreng and Refstie, 1979; Rychly and Spannhof, 1979; Jauncey, 1982). As stated by Cho et al. (1976), these experiments do indicate that, although the higher protein levels used are certainly not the most rational from a fish culturist's point of view, they do confirm that limitations are not imposed by any inability to assimilate the presented protein. Such experiments are important since they indicate that the processes of protein digestion and absorption are normally efficient and non-limiting. It therefore seems reasonable to conclude that the high dietary protein levels required for optimal growth in fish do not arise from any inherent insufficiency in the capacity to digest and/or absorb this nutrient. Knowledge relating to those elements (digestive enzymes, transport mechanisms etc.) and other factors (water quality, feeding rate, etc.) which either confer or compromise the efficiency of protein digestion and absorption are therefore pertinent to any study of fish productivity.

A. Digestive Enzymes

For the purpose of this review, fish will be divided into two classes on the basis of whether or not they possess a morphologically and physiologically definable stomach. In the latter situation these fish have become familiarly known as 'stomachless' or 'agastric' species, and all indications are that in such fish (e.g. Cyprinidae) protein hydrolysis is a totally alkaline event (see later), there being no preliminary acidic or peptic secretions.

B. Gastric Phase of Digestion

In those species of fish possessing a stomach, proteolysis is initiated by the combined action of pepsins initially secreted in zymogen form (Kapoor et al., 1975; Twining et al., 1983), and gastric acid (HCl). The rate of acid-mediated activation (optimum pH 2.0) of a specific rainbow trout (Salmo gairdneri) pepsinogen and the proteolytic activity (pH optimum 3.0) of the so-derived pepsin have been shown to be both rapid and, at equivalent temperatures (between 0-37°C), greater than those of either porcine or canine counterparts (Twining et al., 1983). However, remarkably similar rates obtain when comparisons are made at the respective temperatures at which these processes occur in vivo. Further evidence that differences exist between piscine and mammalian or avian pepsins was provided by the demonstration that the synthetic peptides carbobenzoxy-L-glutamyl-L-tyrosine and glycyl-L-glutamyl-L-tyrosine were effective substrates for pig, cattle, sheep, chicken but not for salmon pepsins (Fruton and Bergmann, 1940). In addition, Twining et al. (1983) reported differences in the relative activities of pig and trout pepsins with respect to a haemoglobin substrate (trout > pig), and in a milk clotting assay (pig > trout). Norris and Mathies (1953), using crystalline preparations obtained from tuna species (Thunnus sp.), found their activity/mg protein-nitrogen to be greater than that of any other higher vertebrate pepsin reported. They also reported that tuna pepsins, in contrast to those of the pig, had little activity against zein. Differences have also been noted between pepsins from various fish and warm-blooded animals when comparisons have been made of specific chemical and physical characterics, e.g. crystalline form; amino acid composition; temperature and pH optima; solubility etc. (Norris and Elam, 1940; Norris and Mathies, 1953; Twining et al., 1983).

Synchronisation of peptic and acid secretion is presumably under neuronal and hormonal control but discussion of this important aspect of fish digestive physiology lies outside the scope of this review, (see Fish, 1960; Nilsson and Fange, 1969; Holstein and Haux, 1982). The extent of proteolysis within the stomach depends upon a number of factors, e.g. secretory rate of acid and pepsin; specific activity of pepsin(s); retention time; feed intake etc., many of which are interactive events. Feed intake (see Barrington, 1957), and presumably therefore retention time, is affected by temperature: a lower environmental temperature decreasing feed intake and increasing retention time. The net effect of these responses with respect to the contribution of gastric proteolysis to total proteolysis is difficult to predict particularly since the output of gastric juice, acid and pepsin (Smit, 1967) are all affected by environmental temperature. A further complicating factor is that relating to the degree of penetration of the food by gastric secretions. The role of the gastric phase may simply be one of preparing, by acid denaturation and limited proteolysis, susceptible peptide linkages for subsequent hydrolysis within the small intestine. Such would seem to be the situation in man where only large polypeptides and negligible amounts of free amino acids enter the duodenum (Silk et al., 1984). The possibility therefore exists that any contribution the stomach makes to the overall efficiency of protein assimilation is more related to it functioning as a reservoir and hence in the control of nutrient flow into the small intestine (see later). Nevertheless, the results of Austreng (1978) and Dabrowski and Dabrowska (1981) do indicate that to some extent protein digestion and even amino acid absorption occurs within the stomach of the rainbow trout. It must also be remembered that the possession of a morphologically and physiologically definable stomach is not a characteristic of all species of fish. Most notable in this latter category are members of the Cyprinidae in which it is well documented that, despite the 'stomachless' condition, the ability to digest protein is not impaired (see Table I).

C. Small Intestinal Phase of Protein Digestion

For the purpose of this discussion the pyloric caecae, where present, will be considered as functional extensions of the small intestine performing a role qualitatively similar to that organ with respect to protein digestion. Such a classification would seem acceptable since Bogé et al. (1979) referred to the pyloric caecae in rainbow trout as being histologically identical to the midgut (see also Bergot, 1979). The endo- and ecto-peptidases of the pyloric caecae are considered to be pancreatic in origin (Croston, 1965; Bergot, 1979) and there is no doubt that these appendages, together with the associated pancreatic mesentry provide a rich source of such enzymes (Bishop and Odense, 1966; Overnell, 1973). Few teleostean fishes possess a compact pancreas: see Yoshinaka et al., 1983a. The presence of digestive enzymes within the pyloric caecae in vivo is generally considered to arise by reflux

from the small intestine.   Such a situation is in accord
with the statement (Bergot, 1979), that no secretory gland
or cell has ever been described within the pyloric caecae
(see however Zendzian and Barnard, 1967a).

(a) Luminal enzymes: information collated from many
     sources and therefore encompassing a large number of
     different species of fish employing different feeding
     strategies and dietary habits collectively indicate
     that the spectrum of enzymes contributing to the
     luminal hydrolysis of dietary proteins in fish is
     qualitatively similar to that reported for higher
     vertebrates.   These enzymes include: trypsins,
     chymotrypsins, carboxypeptidases (both A and B) and
     elastases (see, for example, Sundaram and Sarma,
     1960; Croston, 1960; Prahl and Neurath, 1966; Nilsson
     and Fänge, 1969; Reeck et al., 1970; Jany, 1976;
     Cohen et al., 1981a; McLeese and Stevens, 1982;
     Yoshinaka et al., 1981, 1982, 1983a, b, 1984) which
     are generally considered to be predominantly, if not
     totally, of pancreatic origin (Bishop and Odense,
     1966; Jany, 1976; Fraisse et al., 1981).   The
     secretion of these enzymes in zymogen form and their
     subsequent   activation   is   considered   to be by
     mechanisms analogous to those described for higher
     vertebrates (Nilsson and Fänge, 1969; Cohen et al.,
     1981a; Yoshinaka et al., 1981, 1982).

     Comparison   of   the   characteristics   of   fish
     endopeptidases with those of higher vertebrates
     reveals a high degree of structural and functional
     homogeneity.   Differences appear to be relatively
     minor and largely relate to chromatographic and
     electrophoretic mobility (Croston, 1965, Nilsson and
     Fänge, 1969; Reeck et al., 1970; Cohen et al., 1981b;
     Yoshinaka et al., 1982, 1983a).   Interestingly, when
     compared to those of higher vertebrates, fish trypsin
     and chymotrypsin (particularly so the latter) were
     consistently observed to be most sensitive to
     soya-bean   trypsin   inhibitors   (Croston,   1960;
     Overnell, 1973; Combs and Poston, 1978; Krogdahl and
     Holm, 1983), a factor which may have important
     implications for the compounding industry.

(b) Enterocyte associated enzymes;   Although much less
     information is available it would appear that, in
     general,   the   organisation   and   distribution   of

enterocyte-associated enzymes involved in protein digestion, i.e. adsorbed pancreatic (Kuz'mina, 1978; Ugolev et al., 1983) and both extracellular (intrinsic, brush border-bound) and cytoplasmic di- and tri-peptidases (Nilsson and Fänge, 1969; Ash, 1980; Kuz'mina, 1978; Fraisse et al., 1981) are similar to those described for higher vertebrates (Radhakrishnan, 1976; Ugolev et al., 1983).

D. Protein Digestion and Feeding Strategy

In a comparative study of proteolytic activity in the digestive tracts of several species of fish, Hofer (Hofer and Schiemer, 1981; Hofer, 1982) noted that the average proteolytic activity of the total gut contents was highest in carnivorous and lowest in herbivorous species. Furthermore, they observed that the relative length of the gut was negatively correlated with average proteolytic activity and, in order to compare the relative efficiencies of the different digestive strategies, they introduced the concept of 'daily proteolytic duration', in which due note was taken, not only of specific proteolytic activity, but also of volume of gut fluid, number of gut fillings per day, and retention time. Thus, although average proteolytic activity in herbivorous (and omnivorous) species is low relative to that of carnivores, the non-carnivores can, due to relatively larger gut volumes and number of gut fillings per day, achieve a proteolytic duration (effective food exposure to proteolytic enzymes) in excess of that observed in carnivores.

In the above studies, it was observed that proteolytic activity in the intestinal segments generally decreased from foregut to hindgut and since proteolytic enzymes were considered resistant to autolysis within the small intestine (see Jany, 1972; cited by Hofer et al., 1975; Hofer, 1982), it was inferred that these enzymes were reabsorbed intact in posterior sections of the gastro-intestinal tract. Hofer (1982), also calculated that the daily production of proteolytic (luminal) enzymes in roach feeding on grass was higher than in those fed mealworms and concluded that herbivorous fish attempt to compensate for the low nutrient-density of their diet by increasing consumption rate and enzyme production. It was suggested that the elongated intestinal tract commonly found in herbivores and the disappearance of proteases in

the posterior portions of the intestine of the fish were
adaptive features associated with the requirements for
both an economical use of digestive enzymes and effective
exposure of food to such enzymes. This information, as
stated by the authors "offers new insight into the
function of a long intestine in herbivorous animals" and
indicates how such species may attempt to maximise their
ability to assimilate nutrients.

Kuz'mina (1978) referred to the greater development of
the mechanism of membrane (external-surface) digestion and
the apparently greater strength of fixation of adsorbed
enzymes in predatory fish by comparison with non-predatory
(phytophagous) fish. He suggests that this may be
related to the greater height and complexity of (mucosal)
folds and the greater length of the microvilli observed in
predatory fish. Such interesting work, although
indicating possible mechanisms by which proteolytic
efficiency within the relatively short alimentary tract of
a carnivorous species may be optimised, nevertheless
highlights the limitations of enzyme studies with respect
to describing, or quantifying, dynamic aspects of nutrient
assimilation in vivo. Thus, although quantitative
measurements of enzyme activities within luminal and/or
tissue extracts have provided valuable information
concerning aspects of enzyme distribution and development
with respect to diet (Kawai and Ikeda, 1972; Hofer, 1979),
time after feeding (Onishi et al., 1973a, b Fal'ge and
Shpannkhof, 1976), age (Kawai and Ikeda, 1973a, b; Alliot
et al., 1977; Vu, 1983), etc. such data is necessarily
limited with respect to its applicability to any
quantitative (dynamic) assessment of changes in overall
proteolytic efficiency.

E. Amino Acid and Peptide Absorption

Prior to considering any aspects of amino acid
absorption in vivo it must be stressed that, during the
second half of this century, opinion has shifted away from
the previously held belief that protein must necessarily
be hydrolysed to its constituent free amino acids as a
prerequisite for absorption. It is currently accepted
that, in higher vertebrates, peptides (di- and possibly
tri-peptides) can be absorbed intact across the mucosal
brush border by mechanisms entirely separate to, and
unaffected by, those relating to free amino acid
absorption (Matthews, 1977; Silk et al., 1982, 1984).

Thus, the contribution of free amino acids to total α-amino-nitrogen absorption has shifted from a position of absolute to one of joint (shared) status.

Characterisation of the free amino acid transport systems in higher vertebrates indicates the probable existence of several (see below) group-specific, Na$^+$-dependent, carrier-mediated mechanisms for amino acid transport which are separate and independent from the di- (and possibly tri-) peptide transport system(s). Results of competition studies have revealed the existence of at least three major group-specific active transport systems (Matthews, 1971; Silk et al., 1984), within each of which the amino acids display different affinities for the carrier mechanism (Adibi, 1969). The three major systems are characterised according to whether they transport either neutral, dibasic (+ cystine) or acidic amino acids respectively. Such a classification may indeed be too simplistic since some amino acids may be transported by more than one mechanism and species differences may exist. The transport systems for dipeptides are less well characterised but have been shown to be saturable (Adibi, 1971; Silk, 1976), and competition between peptides demonstrated (Matthews, 1975). For a comprehensive and critical appraisal of the current state of knowledge concerning aspects of amino acid and peptide transport across ther mammalian small intestine reference to the recent review of Smith (1983) is recommended.

The characteristics of amino acid absorption across the small intestine of fish, both marine and freshwater, are less well researched than those of higher vertebrates. Nevertheless, most studies indicate that differences are likely to be of a quantitative rather than qualitative nature (see Cartier et al., 1979). Thus, Smith (1970) demonstrated that everted sacs of the goldfish (Carassius auratus) intestine possessed the facility to actively transport eighteen different amino acids against their respective (mucosal-serosal) concentration gradients. Other studies employing a variety of in vitro and in vivo techniques have, with a limited number of amino acids, confirmed the energy dependency (active nature) of the process (Rout et al., 1965; Smith, 1969; Ingham and Arme, 1977; Cartier et al., 1979; Garg, 1981); its stereospecificity (Rout et al., 1965; Ingham and Arme, 1977) and sodium-dependency (Rout et al., 1965; Smith, 1969; Ingham and Arme, 1977; Cartier et al., 1979). Smith and Ellory (1971), from a study of alanine absorption in the goldfish intestine concluded that the presence of

Na$^+$ can be said to increase the apparent affinity of the carrier for alanine but not to alter the maximal rate of uptake attainable.   Interestingly, Bogé et al., (1983) recently demonstrated that, in addition to being energised by a Na$^+$-gradient (out > in), amino acid transport by brush-border membrane vesicles prepared from enterocytes of the sea bass (Dicentrarchus labrax) was dependent upon the presence of Cl$^-$ ions in the extravesicular medium. In the presence of Cl$^-$ ions the K$_m$ of 2-aminoisobutyric acid was reduced and its V$_{max}$ enhanced.   The Cl$^-$ requirement was however influenced by pH, a change from pH 6.5 to 8.4 markedly reducing its efficacy.   A dependence on external Cl$^-$ ions for amino acid transport has previously been described (Bogé and Rigal, 1981) for the marine herbivore (Boops salpa) and, as yet, has not been shown to be a characteristic of intestinal absorption of amino acids in mammals.   The results of Bogé et al. (1977) can be interpreted as evidence   for   competition   between   methionine   and phenylalanine for transport, (see also Ingham and Arme, 1977), whilst those of Buclon (1974), derived from a study of bioelectric potentials across the digestive epithelium of tench (Tinca tinca) provided evidence for the existence of two separate amino acid transport systems: one for neutral,   acyclic   L-amino   acids,   and   the   second   for diamine-L-amino acids.   No transfer potential, and hence no evidence for a separate transport system, was obtained with the dicarboxylic-L-amino acids.   However, Buclon did not preclude the possibility that further mechanisms might exist   and   indeed   interpreted   his   results   as   providing evidence that, in addition to their separate transfer mechanisms, sugars and amino acids were capable of sharing a   common   transport   pathway   in   the   fish   intestine. Although sodium ions were shown to be essential for the evolution of a transfer potential, Buclon (1974) in contrast to others (see above), was of the opinion that his results were not supportive of mechanisms of transport 'energised' via a maintained sodium-gradient.

Pérès et al. (1964) suggested that the kinetics of glycine absorption by the small intestine of the tench could be described by the existence of two components viz: a saturable component associated with absorption at lowest substrate concentrations and a second component, also closely   related   to   amino   acid   concentration,   which accounted   for   the   passage   of   higher   substrate concentrations.   Bogé et al. (1979) also demonstrated that absorption of glycine in the midgut of rainbow trout

in vivo was nearly proportional to its concentration with
no evidence for rate limiting kinetics over the
physiological concentration range (0.5-10mM). However,
in this study saturation kinetics were observed associated
with the hindgut over the same concentration range. In
contrast, in vitro studies reported by the same group
(Bogé et al., 1979) showed glycine absorption to be a
saturable phenomenon obeying classical Michaelis-Menten
kinetics in both mid- and hind-gut of the rainbow trout.
The transport kinetics, maximum transport rate and net
liquid fluxes were all higher in the mid portion rather
than the hind portion of the gut. Garg (1978, 1981)
similarly noted the existence of regional variations in
the ability of intact intestinal sacs (maintained in situ)
to absorb amino acids. In general it was noted that with
both the species studied [Heteropneustes fossilis and
Ophiocephalus (Channa) punctatus] the anterior intestine
was the most active region. Interestingly, despite the
high proteolytic activity characteristic of pyloric caecae
(see above), these studies demonstrated that, in the
carnivore O. punctatus, these organs possessed the lowest
capacity for amino acid transport.

There exists a paucity of information relating to the
characteristics of peptide absorption in fish. However,
the limited data available on the distribution and
organisation of specific dipeptidases (Ash, 1980) and the
absorption of dipeptides (Bogé et al., 1981) indicate that
these systems are likely to parallel those described for
higher vertebrates (Matthews, 1975; Silk et al., 1982).
The relative contribution and hence importance of peptide
absorption to total α-amino-nitrogen absorption remains,
as in higher animals, an unknown factor. However,
Dabrowski (1983b) presented data which suggests that
liberated amino acids constitute a significant proportion
of the total amino acids (free and peptide-bound) present
within the fish gut. Furthermore, Dabrowski (1983b)
indicated that the concentration of free amino acids
within the intestinal contents of fish might be several
fold higher than that of other animals and that amino acid
absorption into fish enterocytes might be a largely
passive event.

F. Dynamic Aspects of Protein Digestion and Absorption

It should be appreciated that the majority of in vitro
studies concerned with aspects of amino acid absorption

across the fish intestine involve the application of conditions which, with respect to either substrate availability or tissue status, can be considered to be highly unphysiological. Many problems (see Smith, 1983) therefore ensue in the interpretation of results so gained and their extrapolation to the in vivo situation. From a nutritional point of view the real interest lies in obtaining an understanding of what might actually be taking place in vivo under normal conditions.

Valuable insight into aspects of protein digestion and absorption in vivo can be obtained from measurements of the apparent (or true) absorption of individual amino acids from commericial or experimental diets. In particular, such determinations, although not without technical and interpretive difficulties (Dabrowski and Dabrowska, 1981; Dabrowski, 1983a, b) do provide a composite picture which reflects the integrated absorption of all forms of α-amino-nitrogen, i.e. amino acids, peptides, etc., and the sites at which absorption predominates. To date, only a limited number of such studies have been completed. Thus, with both young and adult grass carp (C. idella) fed a commercial ration, Stroband and Van der Veen (1981) demonstrated that protein digestion and absorption predominantly took place from the anterior 40-50% of the gut. Furthermore, they showed that the essential amino acids appeared to be preferentially absorbed within the more anterior regions of the gut. Thus, whilst methionine, lysine, histidine and arginine were largely absorbed in the anterior 10% of the gut, other amino acids such as glycine and proline were absorbed more caudally. However, despite these regional differences, the overall absorption of individual amino acids at the level of the posterior intestine was similar and ranged from between 75% for glycine to 97% for methionine. A similar pattern of results was obtained with adult carp (C. carpio) by Shcherbina and Sorvatchev (1969) and Plakas and Katayama (1981), whilst for juvenile carp (200 mg) fed a casein-based diet, Kaushik and Dabrowski (1983) reported that the apparent digestibilities of most amino acids were more than 95% (true digestibility values were very high and even exceeded 100%).

For rainbow trout fed an experimental diet based on capelin and soyabean meal, Austreng (1978), reported that 72.2% of the protein had been absorbed at the level of the posterior half (post-caecal) of the small intestine. This value rose to 84.5% in the posterior half of the

rectum.   Dabrowski   and   Dabrowska   (1981)   presented
apparent digestibility values for individual amino acids
from   three   diets   (fishmeal-based;   poultry   by-product
meal-based;   poultry   by-product   meal-based   plus
supplemental   essential   amino   acids;   respectively)   fed
rainbow trout of 80 g weight.   These results confirmed
that   the   extent   to   which   individual   amino   acids   were
absorbed from any given section of the gut and their total
apparent   absorption   in vivo   depended   on   the   type   of
protein   fed.   Such   results   presumably   reflect   the
considerable   differences   which   exist   between   the
composition   and   primary   structure   of   the   proteins
concerned.   Thus, under comparable conditions within the
gut,   these   characteristics   will   influence   the   rate   of
release   (number,   susceptibility   and   accessibility   of
appropriate bonds for hydrolytic cleavage), and hence the
absolute amount of each individual amino acid and peptide
initially available for absorption.   The actual extent of
absorption of the available amino acids at any particular
site would then be determined by the relative affinities
for the available transport systems and the concentrations
of individual amino acids present.

Interesting interspecies differences have been noted in
both the time and pattern of appearance of essential amino
acids   in   the   plasma   of   carp   and   trout   following   the
provision of whole-protein or equivalent diets containing
free amino acids.   Thus, in a study involving rainbow
trout (190-220 g), Yamada et al. (1981) observed that,
although   the   free   essential   amino   acid   levels   did   not
appreciably   change   during   a   12 h   period   immediately
following   force-feeding   of   casein,   they   increased
thereafter to attain maximum levels between 24-36 h and
thence declined to the fasting (reference) level 72-96 h
post-feeding.   In contrast, most of the plasma free
essential   amino   acids   increased   immediately   after
force-feeding an equivalent amino acid mixture, reached a
mean peak at 12 h, and returned to the fasting levels at
48 h post-feeding (see also Schlisio and Nicolai, 1978).
Higher   maximum   levels   of   essential   amino   acids   were
observed with fish force-fed the amino acid diet rather
than that containing casein.   Significantly, although
Yamada et al. (1981) noted that the stomach contents of
fish fed the amino acid mixture emptied more rapidly than
when fed the whole protein diet, it was nevertheless
apparent that with both treatments considerable amounts of
the diet (dry weight basis) remained within the stomach
6-12 h after force-feeding (the amino acid content of the

dry matter was unfortunately not published). Yamada et
al. (1981) concluded that the 12 h lag period prior to the
increase in free essential amino acids in the plasma of
fish force-fed the casein diet was probably related to the
"digestive processes of the stomach and small intestine".
In the absence of such constraints, force-feeding an amino
acid mixture would create a situation in which amino acids
could more rapidly exit from the stomach and become
available for immediate absorption.   Such a situation
combined with a rapid and efficient absorption of the free
amino acids would explain the observed decrease in time
for the plasma essential amino acids to reach maximum
levels (and the higher maximum levels attained) when free
amino acids rather than whole protein feeds were force-fed
to rainbow trout.   An alternative explanation for the
12 h lag period (see above) observed by Yamada et al.
(1981) might conceivably reside in stress effects on
digestive physiology induced by the imposed force-feeding
protocol.   Indeed, no such lag period was recorded in
experiments conducted by Nose (1972) in which rainbow
trout (150 g) were offered commercial trout pellets.   In
these experiments the plasma free essential amino acids
were observed to increase in concentration immediately
after feeding and to attain their maximum values between
12-24 h before gradually declining to fasting levels.
Despite these differences with respect to the chronology
of response it is noteworthy that, in all experiments
involving rainbow trout fed either whole protein or free
amino acid containing diets, comparison of the ensuing
plasma essential amino acid profiles reveals an
essentially synchronous pattern of response.

In contrast to these results, Plakas et al. (1980)
observed that in yearling carp (87-106 g) fed a casein-
based diet all essential amino acids had, with the
exception of arginine, attained their maximum levels at
4 h after feeding and had returned to basal (fasting)
level by 8-16 h post-feeding.   Arginine peaked after 2 h
and declined slowly thereafter to reach basal level after
8 h.   With a corresponding amino acid diet Plakas et al.
(1980) noted that, whereas lysine and arginine were
present in plasma at their highest level 2 h after feeding
and returned to pre-feeding levels at 4 h, leucine,
valine, isoleucine and threonine were at peak levels at
4 h.   All other essential amino acids peaked at 2 h and
declined somewhat between 2-4 h after feeding before
returning to basal levels by times in excess of 4 h.
Again, in contrast to the results obtained with rainbow

trout, all plasma amino acids (with the exception of alanine) achieved high plasma concentrations in carp fed the whole protein diet rather than that containing free amino acids. From a study of fingerling carp (35 g) fed either a casein-gelatin (control) diet or an isonitrogenous gelatin diet containing casein-coated or uncoated supplemental crystalline amino acids, Murai et al. (1982) obtained plasma profiles which essentially support the observations and conclusions of Plakas et al. (1980). Thus, in carp, plasma essential amino acids appear to reach peak values later and thence decrease to basal values more slowly in fish fed whole protein rather than free amino acid-containing diets. Furthermore, in carp fed synthetic amino acid mixtures there appears to be no synchronous pattern to the ensuing plasma essential amino acid profiles (cf. trout). Such a response may provide some explanation for the observation that young carp but not young trout (Aoe et al., 1970) fail to thrive when fed with an amino acid-containing diet formulated to mimic the composition of a conventional casein-gelatin based feed.

Murai et al. (1982) noted that casein-coating supplemental amino acids did not significantly decrease their rate of absorption and concluded that the markedly improved growth characteristics previously reported (Murai et al., 1981) for fish fed coated rather than uncoated free amino acids was a result of an improvement in the balance of essential amino acids available in plasma. A mathematical consideration of the essential amino acid profiles (Murai et al., 1982) was presented as evidence that casein-coating did indeed improve 'plasma balance' largely, it was suggested, by alterations in the level of available tryptophan and leucine. These results demonstrate that the balance of absorbed essential amino acids and not simply their overall availability as estimated by apparent digestibility at the level of the distal gut is important to sustain efficient growth (protein synthesis).

It should be noted that the sampling sites employed in the previously described studies do not provide direct access to blood draining the gastro-intestinal tract and thus selective extraction, interconversions, or catabolism, of the absorbed amino acids may have occurred within the intervening tissues (including enterocytes). Nevertheless, the plasma values do represent that profile of amino acids available to the peripheral tissues for protein synthesis and hence highlight the differences in

the way in which various fish species respond to a given
dietary input. Thus, compared with the rainbow trout,
digestion of casein is very rapid in the carp. Such a
situation most likely reflects the control exerted by the
stomach on nutrient supply to the small intestine of the
former species. Interestingly, Holstein and Haux (1982)
have demonstrated that in the Atlantic cod (Gadus morhua),
basal acid secretion is depressed by the administration of
a mixture of L-amino acids and that the degree of
inhibition observed is related to the attained level of
plasma amino-nitrogen. Whether the inhibition was direct
or mediated by hormone(s) of pancreatic or mucosal origin
could not be ascertained but, by analogy to higher
animals, it is possible that peptide hormone(s) may be
involved in this control mechanism. Gastric motility, and
hence evacuation rate, may be similarly controlled and
thus provide for the gradual release of protein
degradation products to the small intestine. With
rainbow trout fed free amino acid-containing diets it must
be assumed that the stomach retains some measure of
control of the flow of digesta (including the aqueous
phase) to the small intestine.

In 'agastric' species ingested protein or the
corresponding free amino acids will become immediately
available, en masse, to the proteolytic enzymes and
transport systems present within the anterior small
intestine. However, due to the requirements for
hydrolysis of the ingested protein, differences will exist
between the two diets concerning the profile and
concentration of amino acids (and peptides) available for
absorption at any one time or site. Thus, as is
evidenced from the ensuing plasma profile, the ingestion
of whole protein provides for the gradual and 'even'
release of amino acids into the portal vasculature. In
contrast, when crystalline amino acid-containing diets are
fed to the carp the immediately available constitutent
amino acids will compete for carrier uptake and hence the
plasma profile of absorbed amino acids will initially
reflect the relative concentrations of ingested amino
acids and their carrier affinities. Since the relative
concentrations of amino acids present within the gut will
change with time the absorption profile will likewise
alter. Such a situation existing within the small
intestine of the carp would explain the imbalanced and
disparate nature of the ensuing plasma essential amino
acid profiles. Mechanisms which might allow a more
gradual and, or, proportional release of amino acids to

the available carrier mechanisms (see Tanaka et al., 1977;
Yamada et al., 1981) might thus be expected to improve the
growth response of carp (or similar species) to free- or
supplemental-amino acid containing diets.   In a recent
publication Viola et al., 1981 (cited by Dabrowski, 1983a)
reported on aspects of growth improvements achieved in
carp by feeding soyabean meal diets supplemented with free
methionine and lysine.   Such results would thus indicate
that, under certain conditions, supplemental free amino
acids can be of value to the carp. Murai et al. (1981)
also   demonstrated   that   although   casein   diets
isonitrogenously supplemented with arginine did not match
the casein-gelatin control diet for growth potential and
feed conversion in carp they nevertheless proved superior
to isonitrogenous casein-only inclusions.

G. Intact Protein Absorption

The phenomenon of intact protein absorption constitutes
an aspect of fish digestive physiology which, despite
considerable reference and some speculation (see later),
remains   unconfirmed   as   being   of   any   quantitative
nutritional significicnce.   Nevertheless, discrete sections
of the alimentary tract of many fish species have been
shown to possess those attributes generally considered to
be characteristic of the potential for intact protein
absorption and described by Gauthier and Landis (1972) as
"extensive invaginations of the luminal surface membrane
and massive accumulation of vesicles and vacuoles in the
apical   cytoplasm.   In   addition,   a   conspicuous
PAS-positive supranuclear 'body' is visible with the light
microscope".   Such ultrastructral features are typical of
that process, namely pinocytosis, by which intact protein
is considered to be absorbed.   Protein thereby enters the
enterocyte   enclosed   within   the   membranes   which,   as
cytoplasmic vacuoles, ultimately fuse with the supranuclear   body   within   which   intracellular   (lysosomal)
proteolysis   occurs.   Cytological   and   histochemical
techniques have confirmed that absorption of specific
proteins, namely horseradish peroxidase (Noaillac-Depeyre
and Gas, 1973, 1976) and ferritin (Stroband and Van der
Veen, 1981) can occur within caudal sections of the gut of
adult cyprinids (carp, tench and grasscarp).   The hydrolytic capacity of the enterocyte may not be total since
intact protein of luminal origin has been shown to
penetrate both intercellular spaces and subepithelial

connective tissue (Noaillac-Depeyre and Gas, 1976) and plasma (Ash et al., unpublished observations) of the tench and carp respectively. However, the exact mode of intact protein transference across the enterocyte remains a contentious issue (Walker and Isselbacher, 1974; Hemmings, 1980).

The suggestion (Yamamoto, 1966; Iwai, 1969; Tanaka, 1971; Gauthier and Landis, 1972; Noaillac-Depeyre and Gas, 1976) that the potential for intact protein absorption was associated with the absence of a gastric (peptic) phase of proteolysis and therefore peculiar to fish larvae and post-larval stages of the so-called "stomachless" fish has required revision with the demonstration that caudal sections of the gastro-intestinal tract of juvenile and, or, adult trout (Bergot, 1976; Ezeasor and Stokoe, 1981), perch (Noaillac-Depeyre and Gas, 1979), and catfish (Stroband and Kroon, 1981; Naoillac-Depeyre and Gas, 1983), all "gastric" species, similarly display pinocytic manifestation. Sufficient experimental evidence now exists (Kayanja, Maloiy and Reite, 1975; Watanabe, 1981; Teshima and Hara, 1983) to support the statement that, irrespective of stage of development, the potential for absorption of intact protein appears to be a common feature of the fish gut. However, the physiological significance of this potential within post-larval forms must remain in doubt particularly since several authors have clearly indicated that ingested protein is mainly assimilated within sections of the gut more cranially disposed than those in which pinocytotic potential has been confirmed (Shcherbina and Sorvatchev, 1969; Shcherbina et al., 1976; Stroband and Van der Veen, 1981; Dabrowski, 1983a, b). However, such experiments (see Austreng, 1978; Dabrowski and Dabrowska, 1981) do indicate that some absorption of amino nitrogen may occur in the more distal (rectal) areas of the gut. The form in which this amino-nitrogen was absorbed was not however ascertained.

The possibility that intact protein absorption is more relevant to larval stages exists because, in the absence of a stomach, food may reach the posterior gut within a very short time and absorption of intact protein or other nutrients in macromolecular form would, by avoiding excretion within the faeces confer nutritional advantage. For the adult, Stroband and Van der Veen (1981) hypothesised that the facility for intact protein absorption might provide a "standby" function. Thus, it was suggested that, after a period of starvation where the

Table II. Levels of Horseradish Peroxidase in Plasma of
Common Carp and Rainbow Trout

Peroral treatment	Carp plasma HRP	Trout plasma HRP
Time after intubation	μg/ml	
0	+ negligible	+ negligible
0.5	14.30	0.08*
1.0	7.45	0.08
2.0	0.90	0.07
2.0	0.80	-
2.0	0.81	-
2.0	0.80	-
3.0	0.87	0.07
3.0	0.85	-
24.0	1.28	-

* cf: Intra-rectal value: 1.72

+ <0.5 ng

Dose: 10 mg/ml as a 2 ml per-oral loading to
      non-starved fish.

secretion of digestive enzymes would be low, the
subsequent sudden ingestion of food might compromise the
normal efficiency for luminal proteolysis and intact
protein absorption would therefore assume temporary
importance. An alternative and physiologically relevant

explanation for the pinocytotic manifestations observed within the gut of herbivorous species was contained within the proposal of Hofer (Hofer and Schiemer, 1981; Hofer, 1982), in which it was suggested that, due to the requirement for maximal exposure of ingested food to proteolytic activity and relative resistance of proteolytic enzymes to autolysis (see II D   ), significant amounts of such enzymes were present and subsequently absorbed intact from caudal sections of the intestine. That such a suggestion is not supported by the results of Stroband and Van der Veen (1981) relating to the grass carp may, in part, be due to the nature of the commercial pelleted ration employed by these authors. Thus, Dabrowski (1983b) indicated that the digestion of protein may be displaced in a more caudal direction when, as might more closely reflect the "wild" non-intensive rearing situation, less readily digestible food was ingested. Employing the enzyme-linked-immuno specific antibody technique described by Ambler and Peters (1984), Ash et al. (unpublished observations) have detected significant (see Table II) horseradish peroxidase activity in the plasma (caudal peduncle source) of fed carp within minutes of intubating this protein (20 mg in solution) directly into the anterior small intestine. Comparative studies revealed no such elevation within the plasma of rainbow trout after intubation into the stomach. Indeed, no significant elevation was observed in this species throughout a 4h experimental period. Interestingly however, the level of horseradish peroxidase in trout plasma rose significantly when the proteolytic activity of the stomach and anterior small intestine was bypassed by the introduction of 20 mg of this protein intra-rectally. However, since neither blood draining the gut nor blood flow measurements were obtained in this preliminary study, the extent of horseradish peroxidase absorption could not be quantified. The immunological implications of such results are, if applicable to natural food proteins, quite considerable and must imply a high degree of immunological tolerance in such species. A discussion of the immunological implications relating to the phenomenon of intact protein absorption in fish is however beyond the scope of this article but surely presents considerable challenge for future research.

REFERENCES

Adibi, S.A. (1969). Gastroent. 56, 903–913.

Adibi, S.A. (1971). J. Clin. Invest. 50, 2266–2275.

Alliot, E., Pastoureaud, A. and Trellu, J. (1977). Actes du Colloq. C.N.E.X.O., France. 4, 85–91.

Ambler, L. and Peters, G.E. (1984). Anal. Biochem. 137, 66–68.

Aoe, H., Masuda, I., Abe, I., Saito, T., Toyoda, T. and Kitamura, S. (1970). Bull. Jap. Soc. Sci. Fish. 36, 407–413.

Ash, R. (1980). Comp. Biochem. Physiol. 65B, 173–176.

Austreng, E., (1978). Aquaculture 13, 265–272.

Austreng, E. and Refstie, T. (1979). Aquaculture 18, 145–156.

Barrington, E.J.W., (1957). In "The Physiology of Fishes" (M.E. Brown, ed.), 1, 109–161. Academic Press, New York.

Bergot, P., (1976). Ann. Biol. Anim. Biochem. Biophys. 16, 37–42.

Bergot, P. (1979). In "Nutrition des Poissons". Actes du Colloq. C.N.E.R.N.A., Paris. 45–53.

Bishop, C. and Odense, P.H. (1966). J. Fish. Res. Bd. Canada, 23, 1607–1615.

Bogé, G. and Rigal, A. (1981). Biochim. Biophys. Acta. 649, 455–461.

Bogé, G. Rigal, A. and Pérès, G. (1979). Comp. Biochem. Physiol. 62A, 831–836.

Bogé, G., Rigal, A. and Pérès, G. (1981). Comp. Biochem. Physiol. 69A, 455–459.

Bogé, G., Rigal, A. and Pérès, G. (1983). Biochim. Biophys. Acta. 729, 209–218.

Buclon, M. (1974). J. Physiol. Paris 68, 157–180.

Cartier, M., Buclon, M. and Robinson, J.W.L. (1979). Comp. Biochem. Physiol. 62A, 363–370.

Cho, C.Y., Slinger, S.J. and Bayley, H.S. (1976). J. Nutr. 106, 1547–1556.

Cohen, T., Gertler, A. and Birk, Y. (1981a). Comp. Biochem. Physiol. 69B, 639–646.

Cohen, T., Gertler, A. and Birk, Y. (1981b). Comp. Biochem. Physiol. 69B, 647–653.

Combs, G.F. and Poston, H.A. (1978). Poult. Sci. 57, 1130.

Cowey, C.B. (1979). In "Finfish Nutrition and Fishfeed Technology", (K. Tiews and J.E. Halver, eds.) 1, 17–29. Heenemann and Co., GmbH, Berlin.

Cowey, C.B. and Luquet, P. (1983). In, "Protein metabolism and nutrition". (R. Pion, M. Arnal and D. Bonin, eds.), 1, 365-384. I.N.R.A., Paris.

Croston, C.B. (1960). Arch. Biochem. Biophys. 89, 202-206.

Croston, C.B. (1965). Arch. Biochem. Biophys. 112, 218-223.

Dabrowski, K. (1983a). Comp. Biochem. Physiol. 74A, 409-415.

Dabrowski, K. (1983b). Comp. Biochem. Physiol. 74A, 417-425.

Dabrowski, K. and Dabrowska, H. (1981). Comp. Biochem. Physiol. 69A, 99-111.

Ezeasor, D.N. and Stokoe, W.M. (1981). J. Fish. Biol. 18, 527-544.

Fal'ge,. R. and Shpannkhof, L. (1976). J. Ichthyol. 16, 672-677.

Fish, G.R. (1960). Hydrobiologia 15, 161-178.

Fraisse, M., Woo, N.Y.S., Noaillac-Depeyre, J. and Murat, J.C. (1981). Comp. Biochem. Physiol. 70A, 443-446.

Fruton, J.S. and Bergmann, M. (1940). J. Biol. Chem. 136, 559-560.

Garg, V.K. (1978). Indian J.Exp. Biol. 16, 1095-1098.

Garg, V.K. (1979). Revista Espanoch de Fisiologia 35, 111-114.

Garg, V.K. (1981). Acta Physiol Academiae Scientiarum Hung. 58, 299-305.

Gauthier, G.F. and Landis, S.C. (1972). Anatomical Record 172, 675-702.

Hemmings, W.A. (1980). Med. Hypotheses 6, 1215-1216.

Holstein, B. and Haux, C. (1982). Acta Physiol. Scand. 116, 141-145.

Hofer, R., Ladurner, H., Gattringer, A. and Wieser, W. (1975). J. Comp. Physiol. 99, 345-355.

Hofer, R. (1979). J. Fish Biol. 15, 373-379.

Hofer, R. (1982). Comp. Biochem. Physiol. 72A, 55-63.

Hofer, R. Schiemer, (1981). Oecologia (Berl). 48, 342-345.

Ingham, I. and Arme, C. (1977). J. Comp. Physiol. 117, 323-334.

Iwai, T. (1969). Arch. histol. Jap. 30, 183-199.

Jany, K-D (1976). Comp. Biochem. Physiol. 53B, 31-38.

Jauncey, K. (1982). Aquaculture 27, 43-54.

Jonas, E. Ragyanszki, M., Olah, J. and Boross, L. (1983). Aquaculture 30, 145-154.

Kapoor, B.G., Smit, H. and Verighina, I.A. (1975). Adv. mar. Biol. 13, 109-239.

Kaushik, S.J. and Dabrowski, K. (1983). Reprod. Nutr. Dévelop. 23, 741-754.

Kawai, S-i and Ikeda, S. (1972). Bull. Jap. Soc. Sci. Fish. 38, 265-270.

Kawai, S-i and Ikeda, S. (1973a). Bull. Jap. Soc. Sci. Fish. 39, 819-823.

Kawai, S-i and Ikeda, S. (1973b). Bull. Jap. Soc. Sci. Fish. 39, 877-881.

Kayanja, F.I.B., Maloiy, G.M.O. and Reite, O.B. (1975). Anat. Anz. Bd. 138, 451-462.

Kim, Y.K. (1974). Bull. Jap. Soc. Sci. Fish. 40, 651-653.

Krogdahl, A. and Holm, H. (1983). Comp. Biochem. Physiol. 74B, 403-409.

Kuz'mina, V.V. (1978). J. Ichthyol. 18, 599-611.

Matthews, D.M. (1971). J. Clin. Pathol. 5 (Suppl. 24: Royal Coll. Pathol), 29-40.

Mathews, D.M. (1975). Physiol. Rev. 55, 537-608.

Matthews, D.M. (1977). Gastroent. 73, 1267-1279.

McLeese, J.M. and Stevens, E.D. (1982). Comp. Biochem. Physiol. 73B, 631-634.

Murai, T., Akiyama, T. and Nose, T. (1981). Bull. Jap. Soc. Sci. Fish. 47, 523-527.

Murai, T., Akiyama, T., Ogata, H., Hirasawa, Y. and Nose, T. (1982). Bull. Jap. Soc. Sci. Fish. 48, 703-710.

Nilsson, A. and Fänge, R. (1969). Comp. Biochem. Physiol. 31, 147-163.

Nilsson, A. and Fänge, R. (1970). Comp. Biochem. Physiol. 32, 237-250.

Noaillac-Depeyre, J. and Gas, N. (1973). Z. Zellforsch. 146, 525-541.

Noaillac-Depeyre, J. and Gas, N. (1976). Tissue and Cell 8, 511-530.

Noaillac-Depeyre, J. and Gas, N. (1979). Anat. Rec. 195, 621-639.

Noaillac-Depeyre, J. and Gas, N. (1983). Can. J. Zool. 61, 2556-2573.

Norris, E.R. and Elam, D.W. (1940). J. Biol. Chem. 134, 443-454.

Norris, E.R. and Mathies, J.C. (1953). J. Biol. Chem. 204, 673-680.

Nose, T. (1967). Bull. Freshwater Fish Res. Lab. 17, 97-105.

Nose, T. (1972). Bull. Freshwater Fish. Res. Lab. 22, 137-144.

Ogino, C. and Chen, M-S (1973). Bull. Jap. Soc. Sci. Fish. 39, 649-651.

Ogino, C. and Saito, K. (1970). Bull. Jap. Soc. Sci.
    Fish, 36, 250–254.
Onishi, T., Murayama, S. and Takeuchi, M. (1973a). Bull.
    Tokai Reg. Fish. Res. Lab. 75, 23–31.
Onishi, T., Murayam, S. and Takeuchi, M. (1973b) Bull.
    Tokai Reg. Fish. Lab. 75, 33–38.
Overnell, J. (1973). Comp. Biochem. Physiol. 46B, 519–531.
Pérès, GF., Buclon, M. and Conthier, B. (1964). Bull Soc.
    Sci. Vet. Med. Comp. Lyon 4, 299–302.
Plakas, S.M. and Katayama, T. (1981). Aquaculture 24,
    309–314.
Plakas, S.M., Katayama, T., Tanaka, Y. and Deshimaru, O.
    (1980). Aquaculture 21, 307–322.
Prahl, J.W. and Neurath, H. (1966). Biochemistry 5,
    2131–2146.
Radhakrishan, A.N. (1976). In "Peptide Transport and
    Hydrolysis", (K. Elliott and M. O'Connor, eds.).
    37–52. Ciba Fdn. Symp. 50, New Series. Elsevier,
    North Holland, Amsterdam.
Reeck, G.R., Winter, W.P. and Neurath, H. (1970).
    Biochemistry 9, 1398–1403.
Rout, W.R., Lin, D.S.T. and Huang, K.C. (1965). Proc.
    Soc. Exp. Biol. Med. 118, 933–938.
Rychly, J. and Spannhof, L. (1979). Aquaculture 16,
    39–46.
Schlisio, W. and Nicolai, B. (1978). Comp. Biochem.
    Physiol. 59B, 373–379.
Shcherbina, M.A. and Sorvatchev, K.F. (1969). VOPR Prod.
    Rubov 16, 315–322. (English abstract).
Shcherbina, M.A., Trofimova, L.N. and Kazlauskene, O.P.
    (1976). J. Ichthyol. 16, 632–36.
Silk, D.B.A. (1976). In "Peptide Transport and
    Hydrolysis", (K. Elliott and M. O'Connor, eds.),
    15–36. Ciba Fdn. Symp. 50, New Series. Elsevier,
    North-Holland, Amsterdam.
Silk, D.B.A., Hegarty, J.E., Fairclough, P.D. and Clark,
    M.L. (1982). Ann. Nutr. Metab. 26, 337–352.
Silk, D.B.A., Crimble, G.K. and Rees, R.G. (1984). Proc.
    Nutr. Soc. In press.
Smit, H. (1967). Comp. Biochem. Physiol. 21, 125–132.
Smith, M.W. (1970). Comp. Biochem. Physiol. 35, 387–401.
Smith, M.W. and Ellory, J.C. (1971). Phil. Trans. Roy.
    Soc. Lond. B. 262, 131–140.
Smith, M.W. (1983). In, "Protein Metabolism and
    Nutrition". (R. Pion, M. Arnal and D. Bonin, eds.), 1,
    211–232. I.N.R.A., Paris.

Smith, R.L. (1969). Comp. Biochem. Physiol. 30, 1115–1123.
Stroband, H.W.J. and Kroon, A.G. (1981). Cell Tissue Res. 215, 397–415.
Stroband, H.W.J. and Van der Veen, F.H. (1981). J. Exptl. Zool. 218, 149–156.
Sundaram, S. and Sarma, P.S. (1960). Biochem. J. 77, 465–471.
Tanaka, M. (1971). Jap. J. Ichthyol. 18, 164–174.
Tanaka, Y., Hokazono, S., Katayama, T., Simpson, K.L. and Chichester, C.O. (1977). Mem. Fac. Fish., Kagoshima Univ. 26, 39–43.
Teshima, K. and Hara, M. (1983). Bull. Jap. Soc. Sci. Fish. 49, 1665–1668.
Twining, S.S., Alexander, P.A., Huibregtse, K. and Glick, D.M. (1983). Comp. Biochem. Physiol. 75B, 109–112.
Ugolev, A.M. Egorova, V.V., Kuz'mina, V.V. and Grusdkov, A.A. (1983). Comp. Biochem. Physiol. 76B, 627–635.
Vu, T.T. (1983). Aquaculture 32, 57–69.
Walker, W.A. and Isselbacher, K.J. (1974). Gastroent. 66, 987–992.
Watanabe, Y. (1981). Bull. Jap. Soc. Sci. Fish. 47, 1299–1307.
Watanabe, Y. (1982). Bull. Jap. Soc. Sci. Fish 48, 37–42.
Windell, J.T., Foltz, J.W. and Sarokon, J.A. (1978). Trans. Am. Fish. Soc. 107, 613–616.
Yamada, S., Simpson, K.L., Tanaka, Y. and Katayama, T. (1981). Bull. Jap. Soc. Sci. Fish. 47, 1035–1040.
Yamamoto, T. (1966). Z. Zellforschung 72, 66–87.
Yoshinaka, R., Sato, M. and Ikeda, S. (1981). Bull. Jap. Soc. Sci. Fish. 47, 1615–1618.
Yoshinaka, R., Sato, M., Suzuki, T. and Ikeda, S. (1984). Comp. Biochem. Physiol. 77B, 1–6.
Yoshinaka, R., Suzuki, T., Sato, M. and Ikeda, S. (1983a). Bull. Jap. Soc. Sci. Fish 49, 207–212.
Yoshinaka, R., Tanaka, H., Sato, M. and Ikeda, S. (1982). Bull. Jap. Soc. Sci. Fish. 48, 573–579.
Yoshinaka, R., Tanaka, H., Sato, M. and Ikeda, S. (1983b). Bull. Jap. Soc. Sci. Fish. 49, 637–642.
Zendzian, E.N. and Barnard, E.A. (1967a). Arch. Biochem. Biophys. 122, 699–713.
Zendzian, E.N. and Barnard, E.A. (1967b). Arch. Biochem. Biophys. 122, 714–720.

EFFECTS OF PROTEIN INTAKE ON METABOLIZABLE AND
NET ENERGY VALUES OF FISH DIETS

C.Y. CHO[1] AND S.J. KAUSHIK[2]

[1] Fish Nutrition Laboratory, Fisheries Branch,
Ontario Ministry of Natural Resources and Dept. of
Nutrition, University of Guelph, Guelph,
Ontario, Canada.

and

[2] Laboratoire de Nutrition de Poissons,
Institut National de la Recherche Agronomique,
St. Pee-Sur-Nivelle, France.

I.   INTRODUCTION

The high requirement for dietary protein in fish has
been subject to much critical analysis in recent years
(Luquet and Kaushik, 1980; Cowey and Luquet, 1983). As
efficiency of protein utilization falls with increasing
protein intake in fish as in other animals, and as current
fish diets contain high amounts of protein, the overall
protein retention efficiencies can be lower in fish than
in higher animals. Nevertheless, protein deposition per
unit energy intake is potentially greater in ammoniotelic
fish than in uricotelic birds or ureotelic mammals
(Pfeffer and Potthast 1977; Smith et al., 1978).
The maintenance energy needs of fish are considerably
lower than those of homeothermic animals (Table I).
However, compared to higher vertebrates, usually a higher
proportion of heat production is derived from dietary
protein. Although the utilization of proteins for basal

NUTRITION AND FEEDING IN FISH
ISBN: 0 12 194055 1

Table I.   Maintenance energy expenditures in fish, chick and rat.

Species	Body weight (g)	Temp. (°C)	Energy $(kJ/kg^{0.75}.day)$
Rainbow trout*	50 - 150	7.5	11
		10	24
		15	29
		20	33
Carp	40 - 90	23	54
Chicken	1500	Thermoneutral	355
Rat	130	22	552
	80 - 120	30	380

* Cho and Slinger (1980)

energy metabolism is a well-established phenomenon, conventional "energy-yielding" nutrients like fats and carbohydrates can reduce the oxidation of protein to satisfy the energy needs of fish and thus improve the utilization of dietary protein (Cowey, 1975; Watanabe, 1977). The beneficial effects of the incorporation of such protein-sparing nutrients have been widely studied (Takeuchi et al., 1979; Bromley, 1980) and optimal ratios between protein and energy have been proposed for many species of fish (Table II). It appears from these data that there are considerable differences between species and, in general, the requirements of the fish for protein per unit energy (digestible or metabolizable) intake is greater than those of higher animals (14-18 for chick, 10-16 for swine and 6-10 g protein/MJ for cattle). Many of these studies have considered the ratio in terms of energy per unit protein level of the diet (calorie to protein ratio). This would imply that feed intake is regulated to satisfy protein requirements rather than to meet energy needs.

Table II. Recommendation for protein:energy ratio
(g protein/MJ) in the diets of different fishes*

Species	Temp. (°C)	B.W. (g)	P/E ratio	Energy	Reference
Brook trout	6-17	3-6	32	DE	Ringrose 1971
Rainbow trout			19-24	ME	Lee and Putnam 1973
	7-15	1-90	20-25	DE	Cho 1983
	11-14	15	19	DE	Takeuchi et al., 1978
	18	40-200	15	**	Kaushik and Luquet 1984
Carp	25	40-300	12-13	DE	Eckhardt et al., 1983
	24	160	21-23	DE	Schwartz et al., 1983
	23	4	21-23	DE	Takeuchi et al., 1979
Catfish	27	200	21	ME	Garling and Wilson 1976
Tilapia	31	2.5	29	DE	Winfree and Stickney 1981
	31	7.5	26	DE	
Yellow tail	25-29	65	26-35	ME	Takeda et al., 1975
	23	105	35	ME	Shimeno et al., 1980

* Protein:Energy ratio may vary depending upon the criterion (retention efficiency of
protein or energy)

** Measured under conditions of 'separate feeding' of protein and non-protein energy

However, fish like other animals, eat to satisfy their
energy requirements. The control mechanisms involved in
the regulation of feed intake are varied (Overmann, 1976;
Anderson, 1979). Under separate feeding conditions, an
adjustment of the voluntary non-protein energy intake in
response to graded amounts of protein intake seems to
operate in rainbow trout (Kaushik et al., 1980; Kaushik
and Luquet, 1984) similar to higher animals (Calet et al.,
1961). Under such voluntary energy intake conditions, the
protein/energy ratio (P/E) appears to be much lower,
probably indicating a physiological requirement level.
Bowen (1982) distinguished the maintenance and growth
needs of Tilapia in terms of P/E ratios and provided
figures of 4 and 25 mg protein/kJ DE for maintenance and
growth respectively. As both intake and utilization are
affected by dietary manipulations of protein and energy
(Adron et al., 1976; Garling and Wilson, 1976; Takeuchi et
al., 1978), the effects of "protein-yielding" and
"energy-yielding" nutrients on energy flow (Fig. 1)

UTILIZATION OF DIETARY ENERGY IN FISH

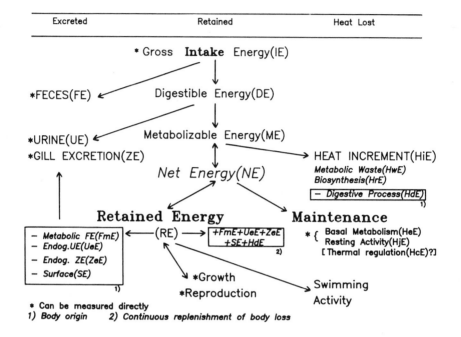

Fig. 1. Schematic presentation of the fate of dietary energy for fish categorizing the losses of energy which occur as food is digested, and metabolized leaving a fraction of the dietary energy to be retained as new tissue (Cho, 1981).

require serious attention. This becomes all the more important in light of prevalent difficulties in the interpretation of currently available data on energy requirements presented either in the context of ecological energetics or that of nutritional physiology.

II. AVAILABLE DIETARY ENERGY

A. Digestible Energy

The nutrient content of a diet can be determined by chemical analysis. Such analyses measure the total amount of the nutrient in a feed. However, they yield no information on whether or not the nutrients are made "available" to fish through the digestive process.

Ingested dietary nutrients such as protein, fat and carbohydrate in feedstuffs must be hydrolyzed prior to utilization by the fish. Digested protein, fat and carbohydrate provide such essential nutrients as amino acids, fatty acids, and glucose and also fulfill a major dietary function in supplying digestible energy (DE) which is fuel for metabolic activity. Dietary protein is both a "protein-yielding" and "energy-yielding" nutrient and its digestibility determines the "potentially available" amount of amino acids and energy for utilization by the animal. In contrast to carbohydrates which are poorly digested by carnivorous fish, protein and fat are very well digested. The apparent digestibility coefficients of many protein ingredients are very high (80-95%) (Cho and Slinger, 1979; Cho et al., 1982). It is a necessity to determine ingredient digestibilities prior to any attempt to formulate diets for fish as the digestibility coefficients of nutrients in the individual dietary ingredients solely determine "potentially available" nutrients and energy values of the diets. Digestibility coefficients are little affected by biotic and abiotic factors and these coefficient values of individual ingredients can be assumed to be additive so that the final content of digestible protein and energy in the diets can be predicted. However, these values of digestible nutrients and energy only indicate the contribution of available nutrients and energy from each ingredient, not necessarily the measure of utilizable dietary nutrients or energy nor the productivity of the complete diet.

Feces are a mixture of undigested food components and unreabsorbed residues of body origin. These residues are the remains of mucosal cells, digestive enzymes and other secretions released into the digestive tract by the animal. The heat of combustion of these residues represents a loss of energy due to the process of digestion, which is not derived from the food. This energy loss is designated as fecal energy of metabolic origin (FmE) (Fig. 1) and is to some extent influenced by the characteristics of the food and the level of feed intake. Metabolic fecal nitrogen loss has been measured in a few species of fish (Nose, 1967; Ogino et al., 1973). This FmE would represent only 2-3% of fecal energy (FE) loss or 0.6-0.7% of gross intake energy (IE). Therefore at normal feeding levels, the proportion of FmE in feces is negligible. It is therefore not necessary to calculate so called "corrected" or "true" digestibility by subtracting FmE from FE as "apparent" digestibility coefficients are accurate enough for the formulation of diets. But, application of normal feeding levels at which the fish perform to their growth potential should always be employed in digestibility studies.

Too often the gross intake energy (IE) and digestible energy (DE) values of feedstuffs are estimated indirectly using the Weende's proximate analyses and caloric conversion values of each of the components. However, with inaccuracy in the proximate analyses, and caloric conversion factors, these estimations may not be appropriate for fish diets. The caloric conversion factors (see below) served a convenient purpose in earlier days, however, they have since created much confusion and been misused. Therefore, it is very important to measure the heat of combustion of feed ingredients using a bomb calorimeter and the apparent digestibility coefficients of individual feedstuffs using one of several methods currently available (Cho and Slinger 1979; Cho et al., 1982; Choubert et al., 1982; Nose 1960; Ogino et al., 1973). It is very essential to estimate accurate values of biologically available energy (digestible energy) for all ingredients prior to the formulation of diets for fish production. Measurements of digestibility coefficients of feed ingredients are relatively simple compared with those of metabolizable energy coefficients of the diets.

III.   UTILIZABLE DIETARY ENERGIES

A. Metabolizable and Net Energy

The major portion of digestible energy (DE) is utilized for the maintenance (HeE + HjE + HcE) of the fish and retained as growth (RE). Generally, 15-25% of digested energy in a balanced diet is lost as nitrogen excretion through the gills (ZE) and kidney (UE) and as the heat increment of feeding (HiE). These losses are very important to nutritional energetics and diet formulation, because the amounts of nitrogen and heat lost are largely dependent on the balance of digestible protein and energy in the diet. The more protein that is utilized as an energy source, the more nitrogen that is lost as ammonia through the branchial system. Heat energy is also lost in the deamination of amino acids to ammonia. Accordingly the proportion of utilizable energies, metabolizable energy (ME) and net energy (NE), in diets is reduced. Therefore minimizing losses of non-fecal nitrogen and the heat increment of feeding of the diets is a major part of nutritional manipulation and can be achieved by optimization of the protein to energy ratio in formulating diets. [The amount of feed consumed is determined by the animal, however, the protein to energy ratio in the diet should be optimized for production by nutritionists.] There are also other factors which influence the metabolizable and net energy values of the diets. Among these are: balance of amino acids, water temperature and metabolic rate, physiological state and feeding levels above maintenance requirement.

Endogenous urinary energy loss (UeE) is energy contained in nitrogenous excretion which is of body origin and is 70–90 mg N/kg/day as reported by Ogino et al. (1973) and Kaushik (1980). This amount of UeE may represent over 20% of non-fecal loss (ZE + UE). However, this is a negligible proportion of total energy loss, representing approximately 1% of the metabolizable energy. Therefore at normal feeding levels and growth rates, correction for FmE and UeE is a futile exercise in the view of practical application.

There is no doubt that a large portion of a fish's maintenance requirement is met by energy from protein (see Table VIII), possibly because most fish, like homeotherms, may preferentially (or inevitably) use proteins as an energy source. But the portion of dietary protein which is utilized as an energy source can be reduced by manipulating the ratio of digestible protein and energy in the diets.

B. Protein Intake and Metabolizable Energy

Metabolizable energy (ME) is that portion of digestible energy (DE) which is capable of undergoing transformation within the body and represents the amount of energy that is effectively utilizable for heat production and growth by the organism. The estimation of ME necessitates the quantitative assessment of the non-fecal energy losses: branchial (ZE) and urinary nitrogen excretion (UE). Of the three major metabolic fuels (amino acids, fatty acids and sugars), the end products of amino acid catabolism are of main concern in measuring the metabolizable energy.

The ME value of a diet is determined by measuring catabolized amino acids or nitrogenous losses through the gills and kidney. Once across the gut wall, the dietary nitrogen absorbed is transported through the circulatory system to the target organs. Any excess of dietary amino acids above that required for protein synthesis is deaminated. The ammonia (plus heat) which is produced through the different metabolic pathways (Walton and Cowey, 1982) accounts for 55 to 85% of the total nitrogen excreted by fish. Of the many other catabolic end products, urea appears to be the second major nitrogenous catabolite (5 to 15% of total N), at least in freshwater teleosts.

Correlating non-fecal nitrogen loss to a given N-intake is extremely difficult in practice. Some of the difficulties are overcome by continuous measurement of the excretory losses in a flow-through system (Kaushik, 1980). The post-prandial excretion rates and patterns are affected by intake, fish size or temperature. The amplitude and duration of such feeding impulse should also be known in order to quantitate ME.

Metabolizable energy values have been widely used with avian species for practical reasons, but with fish species there has been considerable misuse. Further confusion resulted from the use of physiological fuel values (PFV) (Atwater and Bryant, 1899) which were designed strictly for human foods whose digestibility coefficients are over 92%. Phillips (1969) proposed modified PFVs for fish in which digestibility coefficients for raw starch were reduced to 40%, and 1.3 kcal were subtracted for non-fecal nitrogen loss from protein intake. These new PFVs for fish (protein 3.9 kcal, fat 8 kcal and carbohydrates 1.6 kcal) have been unfortunately misunderstood and used as DE or ME values by many workers (Jobling 1983).

Jobling (1983) suggested that once digestible energy and protein digestibility are known, a rough estimate of ME can be obtained by using the "compromise solution": ME (kJ/g) = DE - 3.98 x g digestible protein. However, it is not possible to estimate ME in this way because the amount of catabolized digestible protein is not known without actually measuring non-fecal nitrogen losses or/and carcass nitrogen. Besides, the eventual effects of other factors are totally disregarded.

Relevant data on the effect of biotic factors such as age on ME are relatively scarce. However, some information can be drawn from recent work on post-prandial nitrogen excretion in larval and juvenile fish. In

juvenile pike fed natural or artificial diets, the ZE + UE
losses represent 2 to 6% of GE intake.   In juvenile
whitefish and carp, the range of ZE + UE was found to vary
between 0.9 to 5% of GE (Kaushik and Dabrowski, 1983).

Table III.   Daily nitrogen intake and non-fecal excretion
by carp (Watanabe et al., 1983).

Diets	G.E. intake	N intake	Nonfecal N	Endog. excret.
	(MJ)	(mg)	(mg)	(mg)
35%/ 0% casein/gelatin	82	203	107	40
25%/10%	77	207	130	39
15%/20%	77	219	122	40
5%/30%	72	218	153	37

Body weight: 500-600 g/fish; 3 feedings/day
Water temperature: 20C

The   effects   of   feed   intake   levels   and   feeding
frequencies when high protein diets (712 g/kg DM) were fed
to   rainbow   trout   and   carp   were   studied   by   Kaushik
(1980).   Feeding to satiation twice each day led to a
non-fecal loss of 5.7% of IE, compared to 6.3-6.9% when
fed   fixed   rations.   In   carp   (300g   BW),   a   linear
relationship   was   found   between   non-fecal   losses   and
intake.   With a normal level of protein in the diet, this
non-fecal loss was relatively low (3% of IE) and was not
affected by the water temperature (Kaushik, 1981).
The effect of amino acid imbalance (protein quality) on
non-fecal   nitrogen   loss   in   carp   is   shown   in   Table   III
(Watanabe et al., 1983).   A higher proportion of gelatin
to casein in the diet increased nitrogen loss from 107
mg/day to 153 mg/day.   This indicates that the poor amino
acid balance of gelatin caused higher oxidation of amino
acids which the fish was unable to utilize for protein
synthesis.   The interaction of protein quality and feeding
levels is shown in Table IV (Watanabe et al., 1983).
When rainbow trout were fed amino acid imbalanced diets,
non-fecal losses were high (4-7% of IE) and were inversely
related to feed intake levels.   With a well-balanced

diet, non-fecal losses were lower and not influenced by feed intake.

Kaushik (1981) found that a rise in temperature from 10° to $18^{\circ}C$ did not affect fecal and non-fecal losses (% of intake) by rainbow trout. The beneficial effect of a rise in temperature on growth was mediated only through an increase in feed intake. An interaction between temperature and protein quality (Table V) was also found to affect the non-fecal losses in trout (Watanabe et al., 1983).

Table IV. Daily feed intake and non-fecal energy loss in rainbow trout (Watanabe, et al., 1983).

Diets	Feed Intake	G.E. Intake	Non-fecal Energy loss
	(%BW)	(MJ)	(% of GE)
25%/10% casein/gelatin	0.5	12	3.5
	1.0	60	3.4
	1.5	70	3.2
15%/20%	0.5	21	6.1
	1.0	62	3.4
	1.5	69	3.5
5%/30%	0.5	11	6.8
	0.75	34	5.0
	1.0	56	4.4
	1.5	65	4.4

Body weight: 200-400 g/fish
Non-fecal energy = 25 kJ/g N

These results clearly indicate that branchial and urinary nitrogen excretion were influenced by the quality of dietary protein, the level of feed intake and water temperature. For these reasons the ME of complete diets is not a measure of the availability of dietary nutrients, but a good measure of the utilization of the diet under given husbandry conditions.

Since ammonia is the dominant end product of protein metabolism in most fish species, the abundant literature to date on N-excretion has mostly been restricted to the measurement of this portion of the metabolic loss in response to a given intake. Few studies have been devoted to the estimation of total N-excretion. According to Solomon and Brafield (1972), the assumption

Table V. Effect of water temperatures on non-fecal energy loss in rainbow trout (Watanabe, et al., 1983).

Water temperature	Diets	G.E. intake	Non-fecal energy loss
		(MJ/day)	(% of GE)
7°C	35%/ 0% casein/gelatin	37	1.1
	25%/10%	44	1.8
	15%/20%	40	1.6
	5%/30%	45	1.3
16°C	35%/ 0%	97	2.3
	25%/10%	60	3.4
	15%/20%	62	3.4
	5%/30%	56	4.4

Body weight: 200-400 g/fish
Non-fecal energy = 25 kJ/g N

that all nitrogen is excreted as ammonia would lead to an overall error of less than 0.5%. However, from many nitrogen balance studies it appears that this assumption is not valid and that significant information is lost when ammonia and/or urea alone are measured (Kaushik, 1980; Kaushik and Dabrowski, 1983).

Therefore it is clear that balance studies should be corroborated by carcass composition analyses. In many studies on nutrient balance, agreement between expected and measured retention values are difficult to obtain either because both are not simultaneously measured or because portions of non-fecal losses are left out. As measurement of nitrogen losses in a flow-through system necessitates fine control of flow rate and volume besides the use of precise analytical procedures, errors involved would accumulate and lead to spurious values. Measurement of only a few nitrogenous catabolites could underestimate ZE + UE and overestimate ME.

The ME/DE ratios which were calculated from the data of NRC-NAS (1981) and Smith et al. (1980) for different feedstuffs used in salmonid rations range from 0.72 to 0.93 (see Cho et al., 1982). Many of the ratios are considered to be too low and this may be attributed to increased metabolic losses due to stress and possible negative nitrogen balance of fish receiving a single dietary ingredient in the confinement of metabolism chambers.

As shown in Fig. 2 the same lot of fish meal can be used in different rations which can be fed under different husbandry conditions. In the case of diet A the protein from the fish meal is utilized to a minimum for energy purposes since the diet contains enough non-protein "energy-yielding" nutrient (fat). Hence the reduction in catabolism of protein and in non-fecal nitrogen loss increase the ME in fish meal. But in the case of diet B

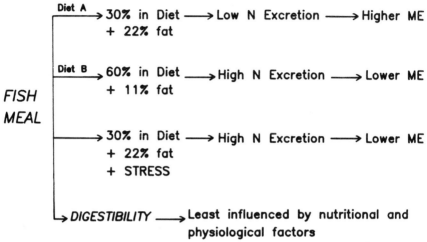

Fig. 2.   Schematic illustration of the factors affecting metabolism of fish meal.

a high level of fish meal (protein) with low energy (fat) content in the diet increases the oxidation of protein to satisfy the energy needs of the fish and therefore a high excretion of non-fecal nitrogen results.   Accordingly the amount of ME in the fish meal is underestimated because of a poor balance of protein/energy in the diet even though the fish meal is the same as that used in diet A.   This demonstrates that ME values should not be used for the evaluation of individual ingredients and should be used as a measure of the balance of protein and energy in fish diets.

ME has significance only as long as it has been measured with respect to an animal's response to a complete diet in a given set of biological and environmental conditions. It has long been known that "Feedstuffs express their characteristic net energy values only as they are of components of nutritionally complete rations, and the same must be applied to metabolizable energy" (Forbes 1933, cited by Maynard et al., 1979).

C. Net Energy and Heat Increment of Feeding

The ingestion of food by an animal which has been fasting results in an increase in heat production. This heat production or energy expenditure due to nutrient intake or feeding is referred to as the heat increment of feeding (HiE) or the so called "specific dynamic action (SDA)". This HiE can be measured using either indirect calorimetry (oxygen consumption) or direct calorimetry (heat production).

This energy loss of HiE is deducted from metabolizable energy, the remainder of utilizable dietary energy is net energy (NE = ME - HiE). The NE is the total amount of energy for maintenance (NEm) and for production (NEp) and is a realistic measure of the dietary value because all the losses associated with feeding are excluded from the ingested energy. The factors contributing to the HiE are the digestion and absorption processes (HdE), transformation and interconversion of the substrates and their retention in tissues (HrE) and formation and excretion of metabolic wastes (HwE) (Kleiber, 1975). The energy expenditure associated with food ingestion (mechanical) and digestion is very small compared to that associated with the metabolic work (Brody, 1945). This conclusion was reinforced by the observation that feeding bone meal to dogs did not increase heat production (Rubner, 1902), however, intravenous infusion of amino acids increased heat production to the same extent as oral administration of the amino acids (Benedict and Emmes, 1912; Borsook, 1936). Tandler and Beamish (1979) partitioned heat increment into biochemical and mechanical components. In this study with largemouth bass they attributed up to 30% of the heat increment to the "Mechanical SDA" which is much higher than observed by Smith et al. (1978), Jobling and Davies (1980) and Cho et al. (1982). Since an increase in muscular activity is required for any increase in all physiological processes, it is meaningless to attempt to partition heat increment of feeding into biochemical component and a negligible quantity of physical component.

As with non-fecal nitrogen loss, the HiE is mainly influenced by the protein intake of the fish (Table VI) (Cho, 1982). The diet containing a high level of digestible protein (47%) resulted in high HiE regardless of fat levels (6, 11 and 16% fat) in the diets. However, increasing the fat level in the lower protein diet (36%) resulted in a substantial reduction in HiE which indicates

Table VI.   Energy utilization by rainbow trout (Cho, 1982).

Digestible Protein(%)	36			47		
Lipid(%)	6	11	16	6	11	16
			(% of DE)			
Retained energy (RE)	49	55	61	57	57	61
Heat increment of feeding (HiE)	14	11	7	15	14	13

that the amount of protein oxidized is decreased with an increased amount of dietary non-protein energy (fat). The higher heat increment of feeding with 47% digestible protein diets is presumably because of the metabolic work associated with the higher influx of amino acids provided by the high protein level in the diets and also suggests that these diets contain excessive dietary protein. Accordingly, the NE (also ME) is reduced with the diets containing excessive protein or a less optimal ratio of protein and energy.

Table VII.   Influence of water temperature upon the utilization of digestible energy by rainbow trout for gain, heat increment and maintenance (Cho and Slinger, 1980).

Water Temp.(C)	7.5	10	15	20
Energy retained (% of DE intake)	44	49	53	58
Heat increment (% of DE intake) (kJ/g N intake)	20 50	14 34	11 27	15 38
Maintenance (kJ/kg BW $^{0.824}$/day)	12	19	35	38

Diet contains 38% digestible protein and 9% digestible fat
1 g oxygen = 13.6 kJ

The water temperature also affects the HiE (Cho and Slinger, 1980) and this is shown in Table VII.   The HiE was increased from 27 kJ/g digestible N intake to 50 kJ when the water temperature was decreased from 15°C to 7.5°C.   There is also evidence that cold exposure of mammals does result in increased urinary nitrogen excretion and heat production (Oldham and Lindsay, 1983). Even though the fish are poikilothermic animals, higher heat production at lower temperatures may be used as a compensating mechanism (e.g. to maintain fluidity of biomembranes) in a colder environment.

Under most dietary regimes the HiE loss (9-14% of D.E.) of fish is greater than non-fecal energy loss (ZE + UE) (4-8% of DE), therefore NE is more appropriate than ME as measure of the productive value of a diet.

D. Estimation of Utilizable Dietary Energies

The measurement of non-fecal energy loss (ZE + UE) and heat increment of feeding (HiE) requires the collection of ammonia from the gills and urea from urine. Furthermore, it also requires a respirometer to measure oxygen consumption to estimate fasting and feeding heat production. However, for applied purposes the "apparent" ME and NE can be estimated in a rather simple manner by measuring proximate compositions of feed and carcass and apparent digestibility coefficients of feedstuffs in the following way:

1. Measure digestibility coefficients (DC) of ingredients or diet.

2. Analyse feed and initial and final carcass samples.

3. Calculate digestible N (DN) and energy (DE) consumed by fish.

4. Calculate retained N (RN) and energy (RE) in carcass.

5. DN - RN = non-fecal nitrogen loss.
   (DN - RN) x 25 kJ/g N* = non-fecal energy loss (ZE + UE)
   DE - (ZE + UE) = ME

6. DN x 28 kJ/g N = HiE (15°C)**
   or ME - RE - Maintenance (=55 kJ/kg.day x days) = HiE (15°C)**
   ME - HiE = NE

7. DE - RE - ZE - UE - HiE = Maintenance Energy
   (HeE + HjE + HcE) - see Figure 1

 *Elliot and Davison (1975)
**Cho et al. (1982)

The above can be carried out at any laboratory with minimal equipment resulting in a more accurate estimation than the methods reviewed by Jobling (1983). Determination of the ME and NE of single dietary ingredients must not be performed since these values are dependent on the proportion of protein and energy employed in the complete diets. However, apparent digestibility of the ingredients is crucial for the formulation of the diet. Estimation of the ME, preferably NE of diets is important as an indicator of their productive value to fish and nutritional utilization of the diets. The HiE loss (9-14% of DE) must be considered along with ZE + UE (4- 8% of DE). A factual example (Cho et al., 1976 and 1982) is shown in Table VIII using the above method of estimating the ME and NE.

Overall more than half of the ingested digestible nitrogen (48-63%) was excreted through branchial and urinary systems and these losses of ammonia and urea represent 8-11% of energy derived from dietary protein (Table VIII). The range of nutrient retention efficiency (NRE) was 0.38-0.52 for the protein and 0.73-0.88 for the non-protein constituents (mainly fat). Oxidation of dietary protein accounted for the major portion of heat produced by rainbow trout. For diet A, containing 34% digestible protein and 22% fat, 57% of total heat production came from protein, while for diet B, containing 55% digestible protein and 13% fat, this value was 90%. This indicates the inevitability of protein being catabolized as an energy source for fish. However, the protein utilized as an energy source can be spared by balancing protein and energy in the diets as shown in Table VIII.

IV. EFFICIENCY OF PROTEIN AND ENERGY RETENTION BY FISH AND POULTRY

A schematic partitioning of protein and energy flow in fish is presented in Fig. 3. On the basis of feed/gain ratio (dry feed intake/live weight gain), fish are generally considered more efficient feed converters than other farm animals. By means of a comparison of the protein and energy utilization, a critical evaluation is presented herein of the feed utilization by the salmonids and poultry.

Table VIII. Estimation of dietary nitrogen and energy utilization by rainbow trout[1] (calculated from Cho et al., 1976 and 1982).

	Nitrogen (N)	Energy Sources			
		N	Non-N	Diet	%
	g	kJ	kJ	kJ	
Diet A (34% dig. prot/22% dig. fat):					
Intake, digestible	5.6	837	923	1760	100
Retained, carcass	2.9	435	670	1105	63
(NRE) (2)	(0.52	0.52	0.73	0.63)	
Losses: Ammonia + Urea(3)	2.7	68	–	68	4
Heat increment (4)	–	–	–	157	9
Maintenance(5)	–	–	–	430	24
Total heat production	–	334	253	587	–
(% of heat produced)		(57%	43%)		
Metabolizable energy	–	–	–	1692	96
Net energy (maint.+ prod.)	–	–	–	1535	87
Diet B (55% dig. prot/13% dig. fat):					
Intake, digestible	9.0	1277	593	1870	100
Retained, carcass	3.3	483	520	1003	53
(NRE) (2)	(0.38	0.38	0.88	0.53)	
Losses: Ammonia + Urea (3)	5.7	143	–	143	8
Heat increment (4)	–	–	–	252	14
Maintenance (5)	–	–	–	472	25
Total heat production	–	651	73	724	
(% of heat produced)		(90%	10%)		
Metabolizable energy	–	–	–	1727	92
Net energy (maint. + prod.)	–	–	–	1475	78

1. Body weight: 1-100g/fish
2. Nutrient Retention Efficiency (NRE) = Gain/Digestible intake
3. Elliott and Davison, 1975 (25 kJ/g Ammonia-N; 23 kJ/g Urea-N)
4. Cho et al., 1982 (28 kJ DE/g digestible N intake) at 15°C
5. Cho et al., 1982 (55 kJ DE/kg.day or 170mg oxygen/kg.h) at 15°C

Table IX presents a comparison of efficiencies of protein and energy retention between rainbow trout and broiler chicken. With 55% digestible protein and 13% fat in the diet (diet B), rainbow trout retain a smaller proportion of ingested protein (34%) than chickens (37%). This is because almost three-quarters (74%) of the total energy loss by rainbow trout fed high protein diets (more than 30g protein/MJ DE) is derived from dietary protein. By contrast, only 39% of the total energy loss by broiler chicken is derived from dietary protein. The situation for the rainbow trout is improved if the diet contains a higher proportion of non-protein energy as fat. With a protein-to-fat ratio of 34%/22% (diet A, 20g protein/MJ DE), the proportion of ingested protein retained (47%) is greater than that of the broiler

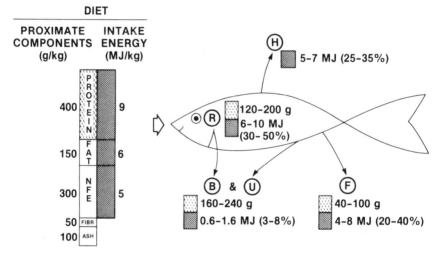

Fig. 3. Schematic budgeting of protein and energy flow in fish. B and U, branchial and urinary losses; F, fecal loss; H heat loss; R, retention in body. The vertical bars on the left depict proximate and energy components of a fish diet. All values shown are absolute values. Numbers in parentheses are % of total energy intake.

chicken. In trout fed the "low" protein diet a greater proportion of the total energy loss (55%) is derived from non-protein energy constituents of the diet than is the case for trout fed the "high" protein diet.

The present practice of formulating high protein salmonid diets, therefore, does not permit optimal retention of dietary protein or total energy by the fish.

Moreover, present information suggests that, even with improved diet formulations, retention of dietary protein and energy by the rainbow trout will be only moderately superior to that of the broiler chickens.

This is not apparent if comparisons are made only on the basis of feed/gain ratios which by themselves are misleading because they do not take into account the critical factors of dietary protein and energy density.

Table IX. Estimation of dietary nitrogen and energy utilization by broiler chicken and rainbow trout.

	Nitrogen (N)	Energy Sources		
		N	Non-N	Diet
Broiler Chicken diet (20% crude protein/6% fat)*:				
Intake, gross	225 g	33 MJ	61 MJ	94 MJ
Retained, carcass (% of intake)	37	37	46	43
(% of retained)		30	70	
Excretion & heat (% of intake)	63	63	54	57
(% of losses)		39	61	
Trout diet A (34% dig. prot/22% dig. fat):				
Intake, gross	6.2 g	0.9 MJ	1.3 MJ	2.2 MJ
Retained, carcass (% of intake)	47	47	52	50
(% of retained)		39	61	
Excretion & heat (% of intake)	53	53	48	50
(% of losses)		45	55	
Trout diet B (55% dig. prot/13% dig. fat):				
Intake, gross	10.0 g	1.5 MJ	0.9 MJ	2.4 MJ
Retained, carcass (% of intake)	34	34	59	43
(% of retained)		49	51	
Excretion & heat (% of intake)	66	66	41	57
(% of losses)		74	26	

Body weight: 50-3500 g/bird in 70 days
              1- 100 g/fish in 140 days

* Leeson and Summers (1980)

V. CONCLUSIONS

1. Metabolizable energy and net energy of fish diets are influenced mainly by protein intake and by dietary digestible protein and energy balance.

2. Apparent digestibility should be used to evaluate the nutritional quality of individual feed ingredients for fish diets.

3. By contrast, metabolizable energy, or preferably net energy, should be used to evaluate the productivity of complete diets.

4. Utilization of dietary protein and energy by rainbow trout is not as efficient as is generally believed or as it could be, at least as far as total carcass production (Fig. 3) is concerned and considerable improvement can be achieved provided more attention is drawn to the interrelationships between dietary protein- and energy-yielding nutrients.

5. The quality of the edible portion of the final product will to some extent depend on the gustatory, socio-cultural needs of the immediate consumers and standardization of quality criteria can be of only limited geographical significance.

REFERENCES

Adron, J.W., Blair, A., Cowey, C.B. and Shanks, A.M. (1976). Aquaculture 7, 125-132.

Anderson, G.H. (1979). Can. J. Physiol. Pharmacol. 57, 1043-1057.

Atwater, W.O. and Bryant, A.P. (1899). The availability and fuel value of food materials. 12th Ann. Report, p. 73-110.

Benedict, F.G. and Emmes, L.E. (1912). Am. J. Physiol. 30, 197-204.

Borsook, H. (1936). Biol. Rev. 11, 147-180.

Bowen, S.H. (1982). In "The biology and culture of tilapias", (R.S.V. Pullin and R.H. McConnell, eds.), 7, 141-156. ICLARM, Manila, Philippines.

Brody, S. (1945). "Bioenergetics and growth". Reinhold, reprinted 1974 by Hafner Press, New York 1023pp.

Bromley, P.J. (1980).   Aquaculture 20, 359–369.

Calet, C., Jouandet, C. and Baratou, J. (1961).   Ann.
Biol. Anim. Bioch. Biophys. 1, 5–9.

Cho, C.Y. (1982).   Proc. 9th Symp. on Energy Met. Farm
Animals.   European Assoc. Anim. Prod. Pub. No. 29,
250–254.

Cho, C.Y. (1983).   "A guide to integrated fish health
management in Great Lakes basin", (F.P. Meyer, J.W.
Warren and T.G. Carey, eds.)   Great Lakes Fishery
Commission, Ann Arbor, Michigan.   Spec. pub. 83–2:272
pp.

Cho, C.Y. and Slinger, S.J. (1979).   In "Finfish Nutrition
and Fishfeed Technology", (J.E. Halver and K. Tiews,
ed.), 2, 239–247.   H. Heenemann GmbH and Co., Berlin.

Cho, C.Y. and Slinger, S.J. (1980).   Proc. 8th Symp. on
Energy Metabolism Farm Animals.   European Assoc. Animal
Prod. Pub. No. 26, 287–291.

Cho, C.Y., Bayley, H.S. and Slinger, S.J. (1976). European
Assoc. for Animal Production, Pub. No. 19, 299–302.

Cho, C.Y., Slinger, S.J. and Bayley, H.S. (1982).   Comp.
Biochem. Physiol. 73B, 25–41.

Choubert, G. Jr., De la Noue, J. and Luquet, P. (1979).
Prog. Fish Cult. 41, 64–67.

Cowey, C.B. (1975).   Proc. Nutr. Soc. 34, 57–63.

Cowey, C.B. and Luquet, P. (1983). In "Protein Metabolism
and Nutrition", (M. Arnal, R. Pion and D. Bonin, eds.)
1, 365–384, INRA, Paris.

Eckhardt, O., Becker, K. and Gunther, K.-D. (1983).   Z.
Tierphysiol. Tierernahr. u. Futtermittlekde.,   49,
260–265.

Elliott, J.M. and Davison, W. (1975).   Oecologia 19,
195–201.

Garling, D.L. and Wilson, R.P. (1976).   J. Nutr. 106,
1368–1375.

Jobling, M. (1983).   J. Fish. Biol. 23, 685–703.

Jobling, M. and Davis, P.S. (1980).   J. Fish Biol. 16,
629–638.

Kaushik, S.J. (1980).   Reprod. Nutr. Develop. 20,
1751–1765.

Kaushik, S.J. (1981).   In "Aquaculture in Heated Effluents
and Recirculation Systems", (K. Tiews, ed.) 1, 77–89.
H. Heenemann GmbH and Co., Berlin.

Kaushik, S.J. and Dabrowski, K. (1983).   Reprod. Nutr.
Develop., 23, 223–234.

Kaushik, S.J. and Luquet, P. (1984). 2. Tierphysiol.
Tierernahr. Futtermittlekde. 51, 57–69.

Kaushik, S.J., Luquet, P. and Blanc, D. (1980). Ann. Zootech. 30, 3-11.

Kleiber, M. (1975). "The Fire of Life", 453 pp. Robert E. Krieger, New York.

Lee, D.J. and Putnam, G.B. (1973). J. Nutr. 103, 916-922.

Leeson, S. and Summers, J.D. (1980). Poultry Sci. 59, 786-798.

Luquet, P. and Kaushik, S.J. (1980). In "Nutrition des Poissons" (M. Fontaione ed), pp. 171-184 Actes due colloque. C.N.E.R.N.A., C.N.R.S., Paris.

Maynard, L.A., Loosli, J.K., Hintz, H.F. and Warner, R.G. (1979). "Animal Nutrition". 602 pp. McGraw-Hill, New York.

Nose, T. (1960). Bull. Freshwater Fish Res. Lab. 10, 23-28.

Nose, T. (1967). Bull. Freshwater Fish Res. Lab. 17, 97-106.

NRC-NAS (1981). Nutrient Requirements of Domestic Animals. No. 16. National Academy Press, Washington, D.C.

Ogino, C., Kakino, J. and Chen, M.S. (1973). Bull. Jap. Soc. Sci. Fish. 39, 519-523.

Oldham, J.D. and Lindsay, D.B. (1983). In "Protein Metabolism and Nutrition", (M. Arnal, R. Pion and D. Bonin, eds.) 1, 183-209, INRA, Paris.

Overmann, S.R. (1976). Psychological Bull. 83, 218-235.

Phillips, A.M. (1969). In "Fish Physiology" (W.S. Hoar and D.J. Randall, eds.) 1, 391-342. Academic Press, New York.

Pfeffer, E. and Potthast, V. (1977). Fortschr. Tierphysiol. Tierernahr. 8, 32-55.

Ringrose, R.C. (1971). The Progressive Fish Culturist 32, 36-38.

Rubner, M. (1902). Die Gesetze des Energieverbrauchs bei der Ernahrung. Deutiche, Leipzig und Wien.

Schwartz, F.J., Zeitler, M.H. and Kirchgessner, M. (1983).Z. Tierphysiol. Tierernahr. u. Futtermittlekde. 49, 88-98.

Shimeno, S., Hosokawa, H., Takeda, M. and Kajiyama, H. (1980). Bull. Jap. Soc. Sci. Fish. 46, 1083-1087.

Smith, R., Peterson, M. and Allred, A. (1980). The Progressive Fish-Culturist 42, 195-199.

Smith, R.R., Rumsey, G.L. and Scott, M.L. (1978). J. Nutr. 108, 1025-1032.

Solomon, D.J. and Brafield, A.E. (1972). J. Anim. Ecol. 41, 699-718.

Takeda, M., Shimeno, S., Hosokawa, H., Kajiyama, H. and
    Kaisyo, T. (1975). Bull. Jap. Soc. Scient. Fish. 41,
    443–447.
Takeuchi, T., Yokoyama, M. and Watanabe, T. (1978). Bull.
    Jap. Soc. Sci. Fish. 44, 729–732.
Takeuchi, T., Watanabe, T. and Ogino, C. (1979). Bull.
    Jap. Soc. Sci. Fish, 45, 983–987.
Tandler, A. and Beamish, F.W.H. (1979). J. Fish. Biol.
    14, 343–350.
Walton, M.J. and Cowey, C.B. (1982). Comp. Biochem.
    Physiol. 73B, 59–72.
Watanabe, T. (1977). Technocrat. 10, 34–39.
Watanabe, T., Takeuchi, T., Chang, Y.F., Satoh, S. and
    Nose, T. (1983). Proc. Jap. Soc. Sci. Fish. October
    1983 p. 91.
Winfree, F.A. and Stickney, R.R. (1981). J. Nutr. 111,
    1001–1012.

UTILISATION OF CONVENTIONAL AND UNCONVENTIONAL PROTEIN SOURCES IN PRACTICAL FISH FEEDS

ALBERT G.J. TACON[1]* AND ANDREW J. JACKSON[2]**

[1]Institute of Aquaculture, University of Stirling, Stirling FK9 4LA, Scotland.

[2]Dunstaffnage Marine Research Laboratory, P.O. Box 3, Oban, Argyll PA34 4AD, Scotland.

I. INTRODUCTION

Unlike most domesticated farm animals the majority of fish species currently farmed in intensive culture systems are carnivorous or omnivorous in habit and consequently have a high dietary requirement for protein. At present high quality fish meals supply the major portion of the protein in commercial rations formulated for coldwater fish in intensive culture systems. For example, in commercial salmonid rations fish meal commonly varies between 25 and 65% by weight (mean value 30-40%), with higher levels being used in starter and fingerling rations. In view of the high cost of good quality fish meals of relatively constant chemical composition, it is not surprising that feed costs amount to 40-60% of total

*   Present address – Aquaculture, Development and Coordination Programme, Fisheries Department, Food and Agriculture Organisation of the United Nations, Rome 00100, Italy.

**   Present address – Tyrell, Byford and Pallett Ltd., Station Road, Attleborough, Norfolk NR17 2AX, England.

NUTRITION AND FEEDING IN FISH
ISBN: 0 12 194055 1

operating costs in intensive aquaculture enterprises (FAO, 1983). Clearly, alternative and, ideally, less expensive sources of good quality protein must be found.

Unfortunately, attempts by feed compounders and nutritionists alike to replace the fish meal component of practical fish feeds with alternative protein sources have met with only variable success, and have generally led to reduced feed efficiency and growth. Protein sources which have been considered in this category include meat and bone meal, blood meal, soybean meal, poultry by-product meal, dried brewers yeast, hydrolysed feather meal and corn gluten meal. These proteins have generally been termed secondary protein sources and as such are commonly incorporated at low levels in practical fish feeds (5-15% individual inclusion level). Collectively these secondary protein sources may account for up to half the total protein in a commercial feed (the remainder being fish meal).

Approaches employed for the partial or total replacement of fish meal in commercial fish feeds fall into two broad categories, namely the use of conventional feed ingredients but maximising their nutritional value in one of several ways; and the use of a new generation of unconventional feed ingredients.

II.   USE OF CONVENTIONAL FEED INGREDIENTS AND
MAXIMISING THEIR NUTRITIONAL VALUE

i. Use of new processing technology

Until recently the processing of feed ingredients such as cereals, pulses and oilseeds consisted merely of grinding, crushing, flaking or soaking. Only limited heat processing or cooking, if any, was used prior to animal feeding. Now, for a multititude of reasons, heat processing of cereals, pulses and oilseeds has become almost universally accepted. In essence, with the aid of various heat processing techniques it has been possible to greatly enhance the nutritional characteristics and consequent feed value of feeding stuffs which would otherwise have only limited value to the animal.

Before considering the relative merits of individual heat treatment techniques it should be emphasised that their effectiveness is dependent upon the initial grinding, and consequent particle size, of the material concerned. Grinding is usually performed prior to heat processing by using hammer mills, plate mills or roller mills. The advantages of grinding are two fold: to the nutritionist it facilitates the destruction of the heat labile anti-nutritional factors invariably present and it improves nutrient digestibility by increasing the surface area of the feed particles; to the animal feed compounder grinding improves feed acceptability and pelletability (it prolongs die life, facilitates the penetration of steam within the feed particles, and increases the horsepower efficiency), it improves the mixing property of individual feed ingredients, and also increases the bulk density of the feed stuff.

Heat treatment processes which have been successfully applied to oilseeds, pulses and cereals are as follows;

A. Micronisation

This is a dry heat treatment process whereby the cereal or feed grain is exposed to infra-red radiation (produced by heating ceramic tiles positioned above the moving steel belt) for a 20-50 second period. Cereals and feed grains absorbing this radiation are rapidly heated (ca 150°C) resulting in an increased internal water vapour pressure. After micronisation the material is flaked (roller mill) while still hot, resulting in a limited amount of gelatinisation and rupture of the starch granules in the case of cereals, and a slight loss of moisture. Compared with other heat treatment processes micronisation is relatively inexpensive, improves starch availability and digestibility, and imparts enhanced storage and handling properties to the feed stuff. However, micronisation can be somewhat erratic in the degree of cooking achieved (depending on the particle size of the feed stuff treated and the duration of the heat treatment).

B. Extrusion

In this heat treatment process the appropriately sized particles are forced by a tapering screw or rolls through a single or a series of die holes under high pressure. Cooking is achieved either by dry heat (individual grains have retained moisture contained within them, and frictional pressure on the individual plasticised grains causes moisture within to be superheated) or by additional steam.   In the case of oilseeds frictional pressures may be such that the cells containing oil rupture.   During this heat treatment process the starch granules present are ruptured and the starch gelatinised (depending on the length and degree of the cooking process).   Gelatinisation not only enhances the ability of starch to absorb water, but also facilitates enzyme digestion, with consequent improved feed digestibility.

C. Expansion

This moist heat treatment process involves the cooking of the material under high pressure with steam and/or water in a pressurised vessel and extruding the feed via a tapering screw through a die plate from the pressure vessel to the exterior with consequent expansion of the intracellular material.   During this process the material emerges with a lower bulk density and having a moisture content of 28–30%, which then requires further drying. This processing technique requires a certain amount of carbohydrate (as starch) to be present within the feed mixture for expansion to take place (starch on gelatinising becomes plastic, absorbs water and on superheating vapourises with consequent expansion).

These heat treatment processes have a considerable effect on the degree of disclosure and gelatinisation of the starch grains present: ranging from a limited rupture of the starch granules within micronised maize, gelatinisation within extruded maize, to almost complete disclosure and rupture of the starch granules within expanded maize.

The beneficial effect of these heat treatment processes on the nutritive value of plant oilseeds, pulses and cereals can be summarised as follows:

(a) Heat processing facilitates the rupture of the indigestible cellulose membrane surrounding the plant cell and the individual starch granules contained within.   By releasing the cell contents nutrients such as proteins are made more bioavailable (Kies, 1981) and carbohydrates cooked with consequent improvement in digestibility (Hilton et al., 1981; Tiews et al., 1976).   However, particular care must be given during heat processing to ensure that the protein fraction is not subjected to excessive heat damage with consequent loss in availability through denaturation or combination with other nutrients (i.e. sugars).

Table 1.   Anti-nutritional   factors   present   in   plants commonly used for animal feeding.

		Anti-nutritional factors[*]
Cereals	Barley, Hordeum vulgare	1,2,5,8,25
	Rice, Oryza sativum	1,2,5,8,13,25
	Sorghum, Sorghum bicolor	1,4,5,7,18,25
	Wheat, Triticum vulgare	1,2,5,8,11,18,22,25
	Corn, Zea mays	1,5,8,19,25
Root tubers	Sweet potato, Ipomoea batata	1,19
	Cassava, Minihot utilissima	1,4,25
	Potato, Solanum tuberosum	1,2,4,8,18,19,21
Legumes	Broad bean, Vicia faber	1,2,5,7,22
	Chick pea, Cicer arietinum	1,4,5,8,11,25
	Cow pea, Vigna unguiculata	1,2,5,11,25
	Grass pea, Lathyrus sativus	1,9
	Haricot bean, Phaseolus vulgaris	1,2,4,5,6,11,12,18,25
	Horse gram, Macrotyloma uniflorum	1,2
	Field bean, Dolichus lablab	1,2,4
	Lentil, Lens culinaris	1,2,6,25
	Lima bean, Phaseolus lunatus	1,2,4,5,7
	Lupin, Lupinus albus	1
	Mung bean, Phaseolus aureus	1,5,6,11,13,25
	Field pea, Pisum sativum	1,2,4,5,6,12
	Pigeon pea, Cajanus cajan	1,2,4,5,25
	Rice bean, Vigna umbellata	2
	Runner bean, Phaseolus coccineus	1,2
	Jack bean, Canavalia gladiata	1,2,4,6
	Velvet bean, Stizobolium deeringianuum	1,22
	Winged bean, Psophocarpus tetragonolobus	1,2
	Guinea bean, Abrus precatorius	1,2
	Carob bean, Ceratonia siliqua	1,7
	Guav bean, Cyamopsis psoraloides	1
	Alfalfa, Medicago sativa	1,6,8,12
	Blackgram, Phaseolus mungo	1,5
	Ipil, Leucaena leucocephala	23
Oilseeds	Groundnut, Arachis hypogaea	1,2,5,6,8,25
	Rapeseed, Brassica campestris	1,3,5,7,25
	Indian mustard, Brassica juncea	1,3,13,25
	Soybean, Glycine max	1,2,3,5,6,8,11,12,14,16,17,25
	Sunflower, Hellianthus annuus	1,7,20,25
	Cottonseed, Gossypium spp.	5,8,10,12,24,25
	Linseed, Linum usitatissimum	4,8,13,15
	Sesame, Sesamum indicum	5,25
	Crambe, Crambe abyssinica	3

[*]   1, Protease   inhibitors;   2, Phytohaemaglutinins;   3, Glucosinolates;   4, Cyanogens;   5, Phytic acid;   6, Saponins;   7, Tanins;   8, Ostrogenic factors;   9, :athyyogens;   10, Gossypol;   11, Flatulence factor;   12, Anti-vitamin E;   13, Anti-thiamin;   14, Anti-vitamin A;   15, Anti-pyridoxin;   16, Anti-vitamin D;   17, Anti-vitamin B_{12};   18, Amylase inhibitor;   19, Invertase inhibitor;   20, Arginase inhibitor;   21, Cholinesterase inhibitor;   22, Dihydroxy-phenylalanine;   23, Mimosine;   24, Cyclopropenoic fatty acids;   25, Possible mycotoxin (aflatoxin) contamination.

Compiled from Kay (1979) and Liener (1980).

(b) Heat processing facilitates the inactivation and/or destruction of the heat labile endogenous anti-nutritional factors present within the majority of plant proteins (Table I) and to a lesser extent exogenous contaminants within animal by-products (i.e. Salmonella).

Apart from amino acid profiles that are often imbalanced, endogenous anti-nutritional factors are the main factor limiting the use of plant feedstuffs in animal and fish feeds at high levels. Although these endogenous factors vary in their individual toxicity to farm animals (Liener, 1980) and differ widely in chemical complexity, many of them can be inactivated by moist heat treatment (depending on feed particle size, duration of heat treatment and moisture conditions employed). These include (Liener, 1980) protease inhibitors; phytohemagglutinins; glucosinolates, cyanogens and lathyrogens (in conjunction with hot water extraction); anti-vitamin factors; anti-enzyme factors (hot water extraction in the case of the potato cholinesterase inhibitor); estrogenic factors, cyclopropenoic fatty acids and gossypol (in conjunction with lipid removal by solvent extraction); flatulence factors and saponins (in conjunction with alcohol extraction, although factors are relatively heat stable); phytic acid (by autoclaving); mimosine (in conjunction with soaking in hot water) and mycotoxins (only by limiting further mould growth).

Coupled with the development by plant breeders of strains low in particular anti-nutritional factors (for example the development of 'canola' meal varieties of rapeseed meal containing low levels of glucosinolates and erucic acid; Hardy and Sullivan, 1983), the recent developments in heat processing have enabled the feed compounder to utilise plant oilseeds and pulses which previously had only been ascribed a limited or secondary protein value in animal feeding.

Table II presents a summary of those oilseeds and pulses which have been evaluated as a partial or complete dietary replacement for fish meal within compounded fish feeds. The fact that many laboratories have met with variable success with individual oilseeds clearly illustrates the wide variation which is possible in their nutritive value to fish, and shows the importance of controlled processing and treatment of the meal prior to feeding.

Table II. Use of plant oilseeds and pulses in complete diets for fish.

Oilseed/pulse	Species	Percent in diet	Reference
Cottonseed, glanded solvent extracted or glandless solvent extracted or glandless full fat meal	Oreochromis mossambicus, Oreochromis aureus, Oreochromis niloticus, Oncorhynchus tshawytscha, Oncorhynchus tshawytscha, Cyprinus carpio	17-35	Jackson et al. (1982), Robinson et al. (1984), Fowler (1980), Dorsa et al. (1982), Viola and Zohar (1984)
Rapeseed, solvent extracted -standard, toasted or canola meal	Oreochromis mossambicus, Cyprinus carpio, Salmo gairdneri Oncorhynchus tshawytscha	16-42	Jackson et al. (1982), Dabrowska and Kozlowska (1981), Yurkowski, et al. (1981), Higgs et al. (1982), Hardy and Sullivan (1983)
Sunflower, solvent extracted, standard	Oreochromis mossambicus Salmo gairdneri	36-70%	Jackson et al. (1982), Tacon et al. (1984a)
Indian mustard, seed cake	Cyprinus carpio	20%	Capper et al. (1982)
Broad bean meal, standard	Salmo gairdneri	20%	Gropp et al. (1979)
Sweet lupin meal, standard	Salmo gairdneri	20%	Gropp et al. (1979)
Groundnut, expeller cake	Oreochromis mossambicus, Ictalurus punctatus	17-25%	Jackson et al. (1982) Robinson et al. (1980)
Soybean, solvent extracted, standard or solvent extracted toasted or full fat expanded or full fat extruded or full fat toasted or full fat micronised or soy protein concentrate	Oreochromis mossambicus Oreochromis niloticus, Oreochromis aureus, Ictalurus punctatus Cyprinus carpio, Salmo gairdneri, Oncorhynchus tshawytscha	10-73	Jackson et al. (1982), Tacon et al. (1984b), Viola and Arieli (1983), Lovell (1980), Viola et al. (1981,1983), Fowler (1980) Gropp et al. (1976), Reinitz et al. (1978) Tacon et al. (1983a).
Leucaena leucocephala, dried leaf meal	Oreochromis mossambicus	10	Jackson et al. (1982)

ii. Enzyme digestion techniques

During recent years there has been increased interest in the use of enzymatic stabilisation techniques for the preservation and utilisation of feed materials for animal

Table III. Quantities (% by weight) of various acids added to differing raw materials to produce stable silages of given pH.

Acid[*]	Ratio	Raw material	% acid	pH	Reference
Formic (85%) Formic (85%)	-- --	Herring offal Herring	1.62 2	4.4 4	Olsson (1942) Jensen and Schmidtsdorff (1977)
Formic:propionic	1:1	Gadoid viscera	1.65	4.5	Johnsen and Skrede (1981); Strom and Eggum (1981); Gildberg and Raa (1977)
Formic:propionic HCl:propionic H_2SO_4:propionic	5:1 5:1 5:1	40% coal fish and 60% capelin	3	4.1 4:4 3:3	Rungruangsak and Utne (1981)
H_2SO_4:formic	1:1	Sprats	3	3.8:4.2	Jackson et al. (1984a)
H_2SO_4:formic H_2SO_4	2.5:0.85 --	White fish offal	5.6 7.3	1.2 2.2	Atkinson et al. (1974)
H_2SO_4 H_2SO_4	-- --	Bony fish Oily fish	6.3 2.8	2 2	Edin (1940)
H_2SO_4:propionic	2:0.75	Pacific Whiting	2.75	-	Hardy et al. (1984)

* Conc., unless otherwise stated

feeding. In particular, a great deal of attention has been concentrated on the utilisation of fishery by-products, including low grade industrial fish species, filleting waste and by-catch. Although it has also been possible to treat plant proteins and terrestrial animal by-products using ensiling techniques (Norman et al., 1979), the concentration of research effort on fishery by-products has arisen because of the high level of wastage within the industry due to its often seasonal nature and cost of storing (freezing) and transporting these materials over long distances to the nearest fish meal plant. Since many marine fish farms are situated near fish landing sites ensiling techniques may offer an alternative and inexpensive route for the direct utilisation of these materials rather than via dry pelleted feeds from remote feed mills.

The two techniques which have received most attention are ensiling through chemical acidification (acid preserved silage) or bacterial fermentation (fermented silage) and protein hydrolysis under controlled conditions employing selected exogenous enzymes. Both procedures rely on producing unfavourable conditions for the development of spoilage bacteria but advantageous conditions for protease enzymes (a low pH in the silage and a high temperature in the controlled hydrolysis).

A. Acid preserved silages

Fish silage produced by the addition of external acids has received most attention with regard to its use in fish diets. Various acids, both organic and inorganic, have been used. Inorganic acids, typically sulphuric acid and hydrochloric acid, have the advantage of being strong acids, relatively cheap and widely available but they require the pH of the final silage to be 2 or below to prevent bacterial spoilage (Edin, 1940). In addition, before such a silage is fed (by mixing with an appropriate dry binder premix) it is usually recommended that it be neutralised with chalk (Petersen, 1953). In contrast, organic acids although more expensive have much better anti-bacterial properties (Woolford, 1975) and stable silages of pH 4 and pH 4.5 respectively can be obtained with formic acid and propionic acid (Gildberg and Raa, 1977). It is possible to use a mixture of inorganic and organic acids to obtain the strength and economy of the former with the preservative properties of the latter. Table III provides a summary of acids and acid mixtures used to produce stable silage from differing materials.

Propionic acid is often used not only for its anti-bacterial properties but also because it prevents mould growth. Mould growths, in particular Aspergillus flavus, have been reported in formic acid silages stored in tropical conditions even at pH less than 4 (Kompiang et al., 1980a). Strom et al. (1980) demonstrated that 0.2% propionic acid inhibited A. flavus growth at pH 4.5. However diets containing silage to which 0.5% propionic acid had been added were unpalatable to Atlantic salmon (Austreng, 1982). Such an aversion was not present if formic acid was used or if the diets were fed to rainbow trout.

Rungruangsak and Utne (1981) fed fish silages prepared using different acids to rainbow trout and examined changes in protease activity in the digestive tracts. They reported that of the acids tested (formic, hydrochloric and sulphuric) only hydrochloric acid had no effect on protease activity in any region of the intestine, while formic and sulphuric acids caused reduction in protease activity at high dietary silage levels. The trials with the formic and sulphuric acid silages were, however, conducted at higher water temperatures than was the trial with hydrochloric acid silage and the authors state that there was greatly reduced dietary feed intake at high silage inclusion levels (97% silage). The lower protease activity in the fish fed high levels of sulphuric or formic acid silage when compared to the control would therefore be due to the difference in dietary intake at $10^{\circ}C$ between the palatable control and the less palatable high inclusion silage diets. This is supported by the fact that they were unable to find any effect of the acidified feeds on the pH in the digestive tract.

During long term storage of silage various chemical changes occur and have been described by various authors (Backhoff, 1976; Tatterson and Windsor, 1974; Kompiang et al., 1980a; Jackson et al., 1984a). Two nutritionally undesirable changes that may occur are the loss of tryptophan and the oxidation of unsaturated lipids.

Tryptophan, although stable at low pH when present in proteins is labile under acid conditions in the free form; a situation that occurs during ensilage. The extent of degradation varies according to temperature and length of storage but experiments have shown that even after storage at high temperatures ($30^{\circ}C$) for prolonged periods (55 days) loss of tryptophan, rarely exceeded 50%. Assuming the silage is mixed with another protein source rich in tryptophan before feeding, a silage based fish diet, should meet the essential amino acid requirements of most fish.

The oil of fish silages is rich in unsaturated lipids susceptible to oxidation and the consequent formation of hydroperoxides and secondary breakdown products. However, the addition of 250 ppm of the lipid antioxidant ethoxyquin to a sprat silage containing 15% oil inhibited the formation of oxidation products for at least 6 months at room temperature (Jackson et al., 1984a).

The presence of the enzyme thiaminase in fish that are fed raw to other animals can result in vitamin B_1 deficiency and thiaminase activity has been reported in a wide range of fish species both marine and freshwater (Greig and Gnaedinger, 1971). Recent measurements by Anglesea and Jackson (unpublished) have shown thiaminase activity in herring silage to be 5 x 10^{-3}ug thiamin destroyed/min/g sample, immediately following acid addition, the activity decreased slowly to one-fifth of this value after 56 days. It should also be considered that when the water content of the silage is reduced as when it is mixed with other ingredients including thiamin to form a moist pellet, the enzyme activity will also fall and the rate of thiamin destruction may be very low.

Good results have generally been obtained with diets containing fish silage. Rungruangsak and Utne (1981) using diets containing 60% HCl silage produced growth in rainbow trout equivalent to that obtained with a fresh, waste fish, control diet. Similar results were reported by Asgard and Austreng (1981) using salmonids and by Jackson et al. (1984b) using Atlantic salmon.

Co-dried sulphuric/propionic fish silage has been used successfully as a replacement for fish meal in rainbow trout diets (Hardy et al., 1984). This contrasts with the normal use of fish silage as a liquid to which is added a binder meal (containing considerable amounts of good quality protein, usually fish meal, together with oils, vitamins, minerals and binder) before feeding as a moist feed pellet. Fish silage is therefore only a less expensive form of fish meal, and as such only of use within those areas remote from the major fishing ports and fish meal factories where such waste fish products can be obtained at a relatively low cost.

B. Fermented silages

Silage production is also possible by lactic acid bacterial fermentation. To undergo proper fermentation the raw material must contain lactic acid bacteria, a suitable nutritional substrate for the bacteria and a temperature compatible with rapid growth (Raa and Gildberg, 1982). Although lactic acid bacteria are invariably present in the raw material and a starter culture is not required (Kompiang et al., 1980b) the innoculation of the material with a fermented starter culture is recommended (James et al., 1977; Lindgren and Pleje, 1983). To favour the growth of lactic acid bacteria as opposed to spoilage bacteria a specific fermentable substrate is mixed with the minced raw material to be ensiled. Molasses added at a ratio of at least 1:10 (w/w) molasses to fish are particularly effective (Kompiang et al., 1980b; Raa and Gildberg, 1982). Under favourable conditions the lactic acid produced reduces the pH of the silage, preserving it from spoilage and encouraging autolysis by naturally occurring protease enzymes. Preliminary feeding trials with fish indicate that fermented silages are nutritonally equivalent to fishmeal (FAO, 1983). In view of the enhanced storage properties of these acid preservation techniques animal/carbohydrate silages hold particular promise for use within the subtropical/tropical regions where conventional freezing techniques are expensive or not available.

C. Protein hydrolysis under controlled conditions.

Controlled hydrolysis of fishery wastes by the addition of certain enzymes has been used for the production of fish protein hydrolysates. Mackie (1982) discusses the various techniques and products formed. The process receiving most interest is the addition of papain to minced fish or fishing waste. Papain has pH and temperature optima of 6.5 and 70°C respectively the latter being well above the survival temperature of spoilage bacterial. Following the addition of the enzyme the mixture is held at 65-70°C for about one hour during which time the level of soluble nitrogen (soluble in trichloroacetic acid) increases to about 70%. The mixture is then rapidly heated to 100°C to inactivate the enzymes, and the resulting liquid is sieved,

concentrated and spray dried.   The exact composition of
the final product will depend on the raw material used.

Commercially produced fish protein hydrolysates are at
present considerably more expensive than conventional fish
meals and are therefore rarely used as a major protein
source in fish diets.   However, their high level of
digestibility and the presence of free amino acids to act
as dietary feeding attractants means that they could prove
useful in diets for larvae and fry where price is less
critical than performance.

iii.   Ingredient supplementation with limiting essential
       amino acids

Apart from fishmeal there are no animal or plant feed
proteins available to the fish feed compounder with an
essential amino acid (EAA) profile approximating the
dietary EAA requirements of farmed fish.   Consequently, it
is not surprising that attempts to totally replace the
fishmeal component of practical fish feeds with
alternative individual protein sources has met with little
success.   Table IV presents the chemical score and
limiting EAAs of some food proteins available to the fish
feed compounder.   For the sake of comparison chemical
scores have been calculated for individual protein sources
with reference to the mean dietary EAA requirements of
rainbow trout and common carp (Ogino, 1980).   Compared to
fish meal, which has a well balanced amino acid profile,
the majority of the protein sources presented are either
deficient in a specific amino acid or suffer from an
imbalance of amino acids.

Imbalances   arising   from   the   presence   of
disproportionate levels of specific amino acids may
include leucine/isoleucine antagonism, and arginine/lysine
antagonism.   For example, blood meal is a rich source of
valine, leucine and histidine, but is a very poor source
of methionine and isoleucine;   because of the antagonistic
effect of excess leucine on isoleucine, animals fed high
dietary levels of blood meal suffer from an isoleucine
deficiency caused by an excess of dietary leucine (Taylor
et al., 1977).   Although similar antagonisms have also
been reported for cystine/methionine (hydrolysed feather
meal; Ichhponani and Lodhi, 1976) and arginine/lysine
(Harper et al., 1970) in terrestrial farm animals, they
have not been found to occur in fish fed synthetic amino
acid diet combinations (Robinson et al., 1981).

Table IV. Chemical score and limiting essential amino acids of selected, commonly used feed proteins.

Feedstuff	Reference	Chemical[*] score	First limiting amino acid
Chick pea	Kay (1979)	63	Methionine
Mung bean	Kay (1979)	54	Methionine
Cow pea	Kay (1979)	65	Methionine
Yellow lupin	Gohl (1980)	20	Methionine
Lima bean	Gohl (1980)	57	Methionine
Broad bean	Bolton and Blair (1977)	30	Methionine
Haricot bean	Kay (1979)	43	Methionine
Safflower	Gohl (1980)	43	Lysine
Crambe	Gohl (1980)	66	Lysine
Palm kernel	Gohl (1980)	41	Lysine
Cottonseed	Gohl (1980)	52	Met. and Lys.
Sunflower	Gohl (1980)	42	Lysine
Linseed	Gohl (1980)	43	Lysine
Sesame	Gohl (1980)	33	Lysine
Coconut	NRC (1983)	37	Lysine
Groundnut	NRC (1983)	39	Methionine
Rapeseed	NRC (1983)	74	Lysine
Soybean	NRC (1983)	46	Methionine
Potato protein concentrate	Tacon et al. (1983b)	63	Methionine
Leaf protein concentrate	Cowey et al. (1971)	57	Methionine
Spirulina maxima	Gohl (1980)	52	Methionine
Saccharomyces cerevisiae	NRC (1983)	63	Methionine
Methylophilus methylotrophus	Unpublished data	71	Lysine
Whole hen's egg	Cowey and Sargent (1972)	77	Threonine
Fish muscle	Connell and Howgate (1959)	83	Threonine
Fish meal (herring)	NRC (1983)	76	Threonine
Fish meal (white)	NRC (1983)	81	Threonine
Fish protein concentrate	Gohl (1980)	83	Threonine
Fish silage	Jackson et al. (1984a)	59	Tryptophan
Whole shrimp meal	Gohl (1980)	73	Histidine
Meat and bone meal	NRC (1983)	59	Methionine
Blood meal	NRC (1983)	24	Isoleucine
Liver meal	Gohl (1980)	71	Lysine
Poultry byproduct meal	NRC (1983)	71	Lysine
Hydrolysed feather meal	NRC (1983)	33	Lysine
Worm meal	Tacon et al. (1983b)	79	Lysine
House fly larvae	Spinelli (1980)	72	Methionine

[*] Scores based on comparison with the mean essential amino acid (EAA) requirements of rainbow trout and carp (Ogino, 1980). Mean EAA requirement (expressed as % of total EAA) being: threonine 10.6; valine 9.5; methionine 5.4; (cystine 2.7); isoleucine 7.5; leucine 13.5; phenylalanine 9.5; lysine 16.8; histidine 4.8; arginine 11.6; tryptophan 1.7.

Despite these inherent amino acid imbalances some researchers have had particular success in utilising these feed proteins simply by complementing them with other protein sources (generally having a low biological value) so as to obtain the required EAA profile for fish. For example, a dietary combination of poultry by-product meal and hydrolysed feather meal (1.3-1.5:1 by weight) has been employed with success to replace up to 75% of the fish meal protein in a practical ration for rainbow trout (Gropp et al., 1976; Higgs et al., 1979; Tiews et al., 1979) and coho salmon (O. kisutch; Higgs et al., 1979). Similarly, a dietary combination of hexane extracted meat and bone meal and spray dried blood meal (4:1, with exogenous methionine supplementation) has been successfully employed to replace up to 50% of the fish meal protein in a compounded diet for rainbow trout (unpublished data). This dietary combination has also been fed to tilapia (O. niloticus) with similar success (Tacon et al., 1984b).

Supplementation of amino acid-deficient feed proteins with exogenous crystalline amino acids has also been used to obtain the desired dietary EAA profile (Ketola, 1982; Tacon and Cowey, 1984). The beneficial effect of single or multiple amino acid supplements on amino acid-deficient feed proteins has been demonstrated in numerous fish species, including rainbow trout (Rumsey and Ketola, 1975; Dabrowska and Wojno, 1977; Tiews et al., 1979; Nose, 1974, 1975; Mahnken et al., 1980); Atlantic salmon (Ketola, 1982; Bergstrom, 1979); coho salmon (Mahnken et al., 1980; Spinelli et al., 1979); channel catfish (Murai et al., 1982; Robinson et al., 1980); common carp (Viola et al., 1982; Murai et al., 1982).

III.   USE OF A NEW GENERATION OF UNCONVENTIONAL FEED INGREDIENTS

i. Single cell proteins (SCP)

Single cell-protein is a term applied to a wide range of algae, fungi (including yeasts), and bacteria which are produced by fermentation processes for use as an animal feed. Compared with conventional plant and animal feed proteins these micro-organisms offer the following advantages as protein producers;

a) Their production can be based on raw carbon substrates which are available in large quantities (coal, petro-chemicals, natural gas) or on agricultural or cellulosic waste products which would otherwise cause an environmental hazard.

b) The majority of micro-organisms cultured are highly proteinaceous (40-70% crude protein, dry weight; depending on species).

c) They have a very short generation time; under optimum culture conditions bacteria can double their cell mass within 0.5-2h, yeasts within 1-3h and algae within a 2-6h period.

d) They can be cultivated in a limited land space and produced continuously with good control independently of climate.

e) To a certain degree their nutritional composition can be controlled by genetic manipulation.

By far the greatest research effort has centred on the use of yeast SCP, and in particular the alkane/petro-chemical yeast Candida lipolytica (i.e. 'Toprina'). Despite the encouraging results of Tiews et al. (1979) with rainbow trout in which DL-methionine supplemented alkane yeast was found to produce equivalent growth to a fish meal based ration, most studies to date involving the use of alkane yeast as the sole or principal source of dietary protein have resulted in reduced weight gain and feed efficiency compared to fishmeal protein (Matty and Smith, 1978; Atack and Matty, 1979; Atack et al., 1979; Nose, 1974, 1975; Beck et al., 1979; Cowey et al., 1971). Nevertheless, in practice alkane yeast has been successfully incorporated in production salmonid rations, replacing up to 25-50% of the fish meal component (equivalent to a dietary yeast SCP inclusion level of 15-30% by weight) with no loss in growth or feed efficiency (Gropp et al., 1976; Tiews et al., 1979; Beck et al., 1979; Mahnken et al., 1980; Spinelli et al., 1979). A combination of Torulopsis utilis and Endomycopsis fibuliger (symba-yeast) and the mould Pekilomyces varioti (pekiloprotein) have also been successfully used to replace 50% of the fish meal protein (36% dietary SCP by weight) in a diet for Atlantic salmon (Bergström, 1979).

Similar results have also been obtained with bacterial SCP, and in particular the bacterium Methylophilus methylotrophus (i.e. "Pruteen", "Hoechst AG") grown from a methanol substrate; the majority of studies indicating that methanol bacterial SCP can replace up to 75% of the fish meal protein (equivalent to 20-30% bacterial SCP by weight) in a salmonid production diet (Kaushik and Luquet, 1980; Bergström, 1979; Tiews et al., 1979; Beck et al., 1979; Spinelli et al., 1979; Tacon et al., 1983a), and up to 50% of the fish meal protein (10% "Pruteen") in a tilapia production diet (Viola and Zohar, 1984). In contrast to the studies of Matty and Smith (1978) and Atack and Matty (1979) with rainbow trout, bacterial SCP ("Pruteen") was found to have a higher nutritive value for common carp than alkane yeast SCP ("Toprina") when used as the sole source of dietary protein (Atack et al., 1979).

Despite the common use of unicellular algae and yeast SCP as a live food organism for a variety of fish and crustacean larvae (Appelbaum, 1979; Watanabe et al., 1983), relatively few studies have been reported on the direct use of dried algae meal within compounded fish feeds (Stanley and Jones, 1976). In general dried algae SCP has been found to have a lower feed value for fish than either yeast SCP, bacterial SCP or fish meal (Spirulina maxima - Matty and Smith, 1978; Atack and Matty, 1979; Atack et al., 1979). However, the studies of Appler and Jauncey (1983) with Oreochromis niloticus and of Hepher et al. (1979) and Meske and Pfeffer (1978) with common carp, indicate that certain dried algae meals (Cladophera glomerata, Scenedesmus obliqus, Chlorella spp., Oocystis spp., Euglena spp.) may offer particular promise as a partial dietary replacement for fish meal within practical fish rations at relatively low dietary inclusion levels (20% algae SCP).

In addition to the use of relatively pure SCP cultures, several studies have indicated the potential of using mixed SCP cultures (activated sludges - mixed suspension of bacteria, algae, Protozoa and rotifers) resulting from the biological oxidation of specific waste water streams as a supplementary dietary protein source for fish; these have included activated sludges arising from the treatment of paper processing waste (rainbow trout - Orme and Lemm, 1973); brewery effluent waste water (rainbow trout - Windell et al., 1974) and domestic sewage (rainbow trout - Tacon and Ferns, 1976; Tacon, 1979). Despite the promising results obtained during these preliminary feeding trials, further research is needed before activated sludge-SCP can be commercially used in production formulations.

In comparison with conventional feed proteins, a significant proportion of the nitrogen (N) present in SCP is in some form other than amino acid N. Nucleic acids and nucleotides are particularly prominent and, to a lesser extent, polymeric (N-acetyl) hexosamines. Thus, Kihlberg (1972) reported total nucleic acid values of 5-12% for yeasts and 8-16% by weight for bacteria, as a percentage of dry matter.   It has been suggested by some workers that the high nucleic acid content of SCP may be deleterious to fish at high dietary inclusion levels (Sanchez Muniz et al., 1978).   For example, in rainbow trout low and intermediate nucleic acid intakes (equivalent to 25% bacterial SCP inclusion level) were found to have no deleterious effect on the growth and food conversion efficiency of fish, although at a high nucleic acid inclusion level (equivalent to a bacterial SCP intake of 50%) feed intake, growth and food conversion efficiency were found to be adversely affected (Tacon and Cooke, 1980).   However,   although   these   authors   found   a significant increase in serum urea concentration and liver uricase activity in fish fed the highest level of nucleic acid tested, there was no indication of a nitrogen "sparing" action in fish fed nucleic acid supplemented rations. On the basis of this preliminary feeding trial it would appear that nucleic acid N is of no nutritive value to fish provided with an adequate supply of amino acid N, and as such should not be included within estimations of dietary crude protein content (N x 6.25) or calculations of net protein utilisation (NPU) based on total N intake. Clearly the exact role of nucleic acids and polymeric (N-acetyl) hexosamines in the nitrogen economy of fish warrants full investigation.

Provided that SCP remains stable in composition and competitively priced with respect to other animal protein sources it will always remain a much needed fish meal replacer for use within fish feeds.

ii. Plant protein concentrates

Only two plant protein concentrates will be considered here, potato protein concentrate (PPC) and leaf protein concentrate (LPC).

Potato protein concentrate (PPC) is a high grade protein isolate obtained, by a thermal coagulation process, from the treatment of waste potato juice (a by-product of the potato starch manufacturing industry). At present the use of PPC within the animal feed industry is almost entirely restricted to the dairy industry, as a 'milk-replacer' for calves. However, in view of its high crude protein content (75-80%) by weight), well balanced

EAA profile (with the possible exception of methionine; Table IV) and ideally suited particle size distribution (98% less than 40 microns) PPC may prove to be a valuable protein source for fish, particularly within larval and starter feed rations.

Although there is no published information on the nutritive value of PPC for fish, preliminary laboratory feeding trials have been conducted with rainbow trout using a commercial brand of PPC ("Protamyl MF") as a direct dietary substitute for white fish meal within a semi-synthetic test diet (Tacon - unpublished). These trials demonstrated that an anti-nutritional factor (later shown to be the heat stable glycoalkaloid solanine) was present in the PPC (1.6g solanine/kg PPC). When fish were fed a low solanine PPC (137 mg solanine/kg PPC) at dietary inclusion levels of 10, 20 or 30% growth was comparable to that obtained with a fishmeal control ration. Clearly long term feeding trials are required with PPC products of low solanine content (not more than 200 mg solanine/kg PPC) before the true nutritive value and potential of PPC can be assessed.

Leaf protein concentrate (LPC) is a protein isolate obtained from the mechanically extracted juices of a wide variety of pulses, legumes and grasses (Pirie, 1971). Although LPC is similar to PPC in that it is precipitated from an aqueous suspension by a thermal coagulation process, it differs from PPC by generally having a lower protein content (35-60%, depending on the level of sophistication of the LPC process). However, the EAA profile of LPC is similar to that of other plant proteins, with methionine and cystine being the first limiting amino acids present (Table IV).

As with all major plant proteins, LPC may contain a wide variety of endogenous anti-nutritional factors and therefore particular care must be given to the choice of plant material to be processed prior to feeding (FAO, 1983). Preliminary studies with plaice (Pleuronectes platessa) (Cowey et al., 1971) rainbow trout and carp (Ogino et al., 1978) indicate that LPC (prepared from rye grass) can provide a proportion of the protein in fish diets.

The success of PPC and LPC within compounded fish feeds will depend to a large extent upon the degree of sophistication and cost of the processing method employed. At present processing costs are high, and consequently LPC is not competitively priced with more conventional food proteins.

iii. Whole food organisms

In numerous aquaculture systems the feeding of live zooplankton (rotifers, copepods) is an essential part of the mass propagation of certain larval and exotic fish species (particularly for those fish species where the dietary nutrient requirements are still poorly understood, or where it has not been possible to use an effective dry diet). The use of live zooplankton as a larval food has been excellently reviewed by Watanabe et al. (1983).

Considerable interest has recently been focused on the use of selected macro-invertebrates (mainly insect larvae and oligochaetes) as a means of breaking down and utilising 'waste streams' (animal manures, domestic sewage, agricultural wastes) which would otherwise have little or no direct feed value within a compounded diet. By virtue of their ability to utilise and upgrade waste nutrients into a 'palatable' nutrient rich package, these food organisms may constitute a potential (although limited) feed source for fish. At present macro-invertebrates play a very minor role within integrated aquaculture systems, with available waste streams being used directly for pond fertilization.

iv. Animal and food processing wastes

The utilization of waste products as feedstuffs can be viewed at three levels of refinement.

A. Direct utilization

At its lowest level, utilization involves merely avoidance of the disposal costs with the possible benefit of an additional income. Waste products directly utilized in compounded fish feeds have included egg processing waste (Davis et al., 1976) rendered hide fleshings (Cowey et al., 1979) carrot waste (Wong and Cheung, 1980) activated sewage sludge (Wong and Cheung, 1980; Anwar et al., 1982; Lu and Kevern, 1975; Tacon, 1979a; Lu and Kevern, 1975) dried poultry manure (Lu and Kevern, 1975; Summerfelt and Yin, 1974; Kerns and Roelofs, 1977; Shiloh and Viola, 1973; Stickney et al., 1977) rumen/paunch contents (Summfelt and Yin, 1974) rumen contents/blood (Reece et al., 1975) dried cattle manure (Shiloh and Viola, 1973) dried coffee pulp (Christensen, 1981) brewery and distillery wastes (Tacon - unpublished data; FAO, 1983).

B. Substrate for protein production

Specific waste streams may be utilised as substrates for the production of single-cell protein (SCP), zooplankton, or macro-invertebrates (through pond fertilization or waste management techniques). This has been discussed above and is reviewed by Wohlfarth and Schroeder (1979), Edwards (1980) and Tortell (1979).

C. Direct nutrient extraction

The third and most refined method of waste utilization has been the direct recovery of specific nutrients of feed value from a normally heterogeneous waste. This category includes the extraction of potato protein concentrate (PPC) and leaf protein concentrate (LPC) from potato waste and plant juice extracts respectively.

Although there are a wide variety of hazards and difficulties associated with the utilization of animal and food processing wastes as feed for fish (Spinelli, 1980; Tacon, 1979), there can be little doubt that the increasing demand for more stringent waste disposal legislation, together with the shortages and rise in cost of more conventional protein sources, will have a considerable influence on the future value of these products.

IV.   CONCLUDING REMARKS

Despite the wide variety of animal and plant feeds which have been nutritionally evaluated for fish, the selection of foodstuffs by the commercial fish feed compounder is based on their market cost, nutritive value, availability, and the ultimate market value of the farmed fish.

As attempts are made to use greater amounts of novel or foreign (plant) proteins within compounded fish feeds, the problem of feed acceptability or palatability becomes greater. Exogenous dietary feeding stimulants or attractants are therefore necessary with certain fish species (see Mackie and Mitchell - this volume). Supplements which have been found to enhance the palatability of a soybean based trout diet include marine fish oil (sprayed onto the outside of the pellet), liver meal, vinasse (derived from beet-molasses), and a variety of animal and plant concentrates (branded under such titles as 'fish aroma', 'meat aroma' and 'soup aroma') Tacon - unpublished data. Much further research is required in this subject area.

The development of a whole series of high quality protein sources, in addition to fish meal, will not necesarily reduce the cost of the finished feed to the fish farmer, but will, it is hoped, reduce the reliance of the fish feed manufacturing industry upon fish meal. By so doing, the feed manufacturer in the next decade will be able to ensure that the fish farmer receives a relatively stable and high quality ration, not subject to the shortcomings in the supply, quality and fluctuating cost of a single commodity - fish meal.

V.   ACKNOWLEDGEMENTS

The authors acknowledge the financial support given by the Chief Scientist's Group, Ministry of Agriculture, Fisheries and Food, London and the support of the staff at the Institute of Aquaculture, University of Stirling, and N.E.R.C. Dunstaffnage Marine Research Laboratory, Oban, Scotland.

REFERENCES

Anwar, A., Ishak, M.M., El-Zeiny, M. and Hassanen, G.D.I. (1982). Aquaculture, 28, 321-325.
Appelbaum, S. (1979). In "Finfish Nutrition and Fishfeed Technology", (J.E. Halver and K. Tiews, eds.) Vol. II., 515-524. H. Heenemann GmbH., Berlin.
Appler, H.N. and Jauncey, K. (1983). Aquaculture 30, 21-30.
Asgard, T. and Austreng, E. (1981). Feedstuffs 53, 22-24.
Atack, T.H. and Matty, A.J. 91979). In "Finfish Nutrition and Fishfeed Technology", (J.E. Halver and K. Tiews, eds.). Vol. II, 261-273. H. Heenemann GmbH., Berlin.
Atack, T.H., Jauncey, K. and Matty, A.J. (1979). Aquaculture 18, 337-348.

Atkinson, A., Lamprech, E. and Misplon, D. 91974). 28th Annu. Rep. of the Dir. Fishing Industry Res. Inst., Cape Town, South Africa. 44 pp.

Austreng, E. (1982). Aktuelt fra Statens fagtjeneste i landbruket (Husdyrforsoksmotet 1982), Norwegian Agricultural University, 525 pp.

Backhoff, H.P. (1976). J. Food Technol. 11, 253-363.

Beck, H., Gropp, J., Koops, H. and Tiews, K. (1979). In "Finfish Nutrition and Fishfeed Technology", (J.E. Halver and K. Tiews, eds.), Vol. II: pp. 269-280. H. Heenemann GmbH., Berlin.

Bergstrom, E. 91979). In "Finfish Nutrition and Fishfeed Technology" (J.E. Halver and K. Tiews eds.), Vol. II pp. 105-116. H. Heenemann GmbH., Berlin.

Bolton, W. and Blair, R. (1977). Poultry Nutrition. Ministry of Agriculture Fisheries and Food Bulletin 174, H.M.S.O., London, 134pp.

Capper, B.S., Wood, J.F. and Jackson, A.J. (1982). Aquaculture 29, 373-377.

Christensen, M.S. (1981). Aquaculture 25, 235-242.

Connell, J.J. and Howgate, P.F. (1959). J. Sci. Food Agric. 10, 241-244.

Cowey, C.B. and Sargent, J.R. (1972). Fish Nutrition. Adv. Mar. Biol. 10, 383-492.

Cowey, C.B., Pope, J.A., Adron, J.W. and Blair, A. (1971). Mar. Biol. 10, 145-153.

Cowey, C.B., Adron, J.W., Hardy, R., Smith, J.G.M. and Walton, M.J. (1979). Aquaculture 16, 199-209.

Dabrowska, H. and Wojno, U. (1977). Aquaculture 10, 297-310.

Dabrowski, K. and Kozlowska, H. (1981). In "Heated Effluents and Recirculation Systems", (K. Tiews, ed.) Vol. II, 263-274. H. Heenemann GmbH and Co.,, Berlin.

Davis, E.M., Rumsey, G.L. and Nickum, J.G. (1976). Prog. Fish-Cult. 38, 20-22.

Dorsa, W.J., Robinette, H.R., Robinson, E.H. and Poe, W.E. (1982). Trans. Am. Fish. Soc. 3, 651-655.

Edin, H. (1940). Nord. Jordbr. Forsk. 22, 142.

Edwards, P. (1980). Aquculture 21, 261-279.

FAO. (1983). Fish Feeds and Feeding in Developing Countries - UNDPL/FAO, ADCP/REP/83/18, 97pp.

Fowler, L.G. (1980). Prog. Fish-Cult. 42, 87-91.

Gilberg, A. and Raa, J. (1977). J. Sci. Food Agric. 28, 647-653.

Gohl, B. (1980). Tropical Feeds. FAO Anim. Prod. Health Ser. 12, 529pp.

Creig, R.A. and Cnaedinger, R.H. (1971). U.S. Fish. Wildl. Ser. Spec. Scient. Rep. Fish. No. 631.

Gropp, J., Koops, H., Tiews, K. and Beck, H. (1976). FAO Technical Conference on Aquaculture. 1976. FAO-FIR; AQ/Conf/76.E.24, pp. 596–601.

Gropp, J., Beck, H., Koops, H. and Tiews, K. (1979). Coun. Meet. ICES, Mariculture Committee. F4, 1–17.

Hardy, R.W. and Sullivan, C.V. (1983). Can. J. Fish. and Aquat. Sci. 40, 281–286.

Hardy, R.W., Shearer, K.D. and Spinelli, J. (1984). Aquaculture 38, 35–44.

Harper, A.E., Benevanga, N.J. and Wohlhueter, R.M. (1970). Physiol. Rev. 50, 428–558.

Hepher, B., Sandbank, E. and Shelef, G. (1979). In "Finfish Nutrition and Fishfeed Technology", (J.E. Halver and K. Tiews, eds.), Vol. I, pp. 327–342. H. Heenemann GmbH., Berlin.

Higgs, D.A. Markert, J.R., MacQuarrie, D.W., McBride, J.R., Dosanjh, B.S., Nichols, C. and Hoskins, G. (1979). In, "Finfish Nutrition and Fishfeed Technology", (J.E. Halver and K. Tiews, eds.), Vol. II. pp. 191–218. H. Heenemann GmbH., Berlin.

Higgs, D.A., McBride, J.R., Markert, J.R., Dosanjh, B.S., Plotnikoff, M.D., and Clarke, W.C. (1982). Aquaculture 29, 1–31.

Hilton, J.W., Cho, C.Y. and Slinger, S.J. (1981). Aquaculture 25, 185–194.

Ichhponani, J.s. and Lodhi, G.N. (1976). Indian J. Anim. Sci. 46, 234–243.

Jackson, A.J., Capper, B.S. and Matty, A.J. (1982). Aquaculture 27, 97–109.

Jackson, A.J., Kerr, A.K. and Cowey, C.B. (1984a). Aquaculture 38, 211–220.

Jackson, A.J., Kerr, A.K. and Bullock, A.M. (1984b). Aquaculture 40, In press.

James, M.A., Lyer, K.M. and Nair, M.R. (1977). Proc. Conf. Handling Process. Mark. Trop. Fish, Tropical Products Institute, London. pp. 273–275.

Jensen, J. and Schmidtsdorff, W. (1977). In "Symposium on the production of fishmeal" pp. 23–26. International Assoc. Fishmeal Manufacturers, Hertfordshire, U.K.

Johnsen, F. and Skrede, A. (1981). Acta. Agric. Scand. 31, 22–27.

Kaushik, S.J. and Luquet, P. (1980). Aquaculture 19, 163–175.

Kay, D.E. (1979). Crop and Product Digest No. 3 – Food Legumes. London: Tropical Products Institute, 435pp.

Kerns, C.L. and Roelofs, E.W. (1977). Bamidgeh 29, 125–135.

Ketola, H.G. (1982). Comp. Biochem. Physiol. 73B, 17–24.

Kies, C. (1981). J. Agric. Fd Chem. 29, 435–440.

Kihlberg, R. (1972). Ann. Rev. Microbiol. 26, 427–466.

Kompiang, I.P., Arifudin, R. and Raa, J. (1980a). In, "Advances in Fish Science and Technology", (J.J. Connell, ed.), pp. 349–352. Fishing News Books Ltd., London.

Kompiang, I.P., Yushadi, T. and Cresswell, D.C. (1980b). In "Fish Silage Production and its use". (J.G. Disney and D. James, eds.), pp. 38–43. FAO Fish. Rep. No. 230.

Liener, I.E. (1980). "Toxic constituents of plant foodstuffs". Academic Press, New York. 2nd Edition, 502pp.

Lindgren, S. and Pleje, M. (1983). J. Sci. Food Agric. 34, 1057–1067.

Lovell, T. (1980). Aquacult. magz. 6, 39.

Lu, J.D. and Kevern, N.R. (1975). Prog. Fish–Cult. 37, 241–244.

Mackie, I.M. (1982). Anim. Feed Sci. Technol. 7, 113–124.

Mahnken, C.V.W., Spinelli, J. and Waknitz, F.W. (1980). Aquaculture 20, 41–56.

Matty, A.J. and Smith, P. (1978). Aquaculture 14, 235–246.

Meske, C. and Pfeffer, E. (1978). Animal research and development. Tubingen, Institute for Scientific Co-operation. 7, 112–121.

Murai, T., Ogata, H. and Nose, T. (1982). Bull. Jpn. Soc. Sci. Fish. 48, 85–88.

National Research Council. (1983). Nutrient requirements of warmwater fishes and shellfishes. National Academy Press, Washington, D.C.

Norman, G.A., Silverside, D., Hector, D.A. and Francis, S. (1979). Trop. Sci. 21, 221–230.

Nose, T. (1974). Bull. Freshwater Fish. Res. Lab. Tokyo 21, 57–63.

Nose, T. (1975). Bull. Freshwater Fish. Res. Lab. Tokyo 24, 101–109.

Ogino, C. (1980). Bull. Jap. Soc. Sci. Fish. 46, 171–174.

Ogino, C., Cowey, C.B. and Chiou, J.Y. (1978). Bull Jap. Soc. Sci. Fish. 44, 49–52.

Olsson, N. (1942). Lantbrukshogskolan Hnsdjurforsoksan- stalten Sweden, Report No. 7, pp. 55.

Orme, L.E. and Lemm, C.A. (1973). Feedstuffs 1973, 28–29.

Petersen, H. (1953). FAO Fish. Bull. 6, 18pp.

Pirie, N.W. (1971). "Leaf Protein: its agronomy, preparation, quality and use". IBP Handbook No. 20, Blackwell Scientific Publications, Oxford and Edinburgh, 192pp.

Raa, J. and Gildberg, A. (1982). Fish Silage: A Review.
    CRC Critical Reviews in Food Science and Nutrition,
    1982, 383–419.
Reece, D.L., Wesley, D.E., Jackson, G.A. and Dupree, H.K.
    (1975). Prog. Fish–Cult. 37, 15–19.
Reinitz, G.L., Orme, L.E., Lemm, C.A. and Hitzel, F.N.
    (1978). Feedstuffs 50, 23–24.
Robinson, E.H., Wilson, R.P. and Poe, W.E. (1980).J. Nutr.
    110, 2313–2316.
Robinson, E.H., Wilson, R.P. and Poe, W.E. (1981). J.
    Nutr. 111, 46–52.
Robinson, E.H., Rawless, S.D., Oldenburg, P.W. and
    Stickney, R.R. (1984). Aquaculture 38, 145–154.
Rumsey, G.L. and Ketola, H.G. (1975). J. Fish. Res. Bd.
    Can. 32, 422–426.
Rungruangsak, K. and Utne, F. (1981). Aquaculture 22,
    67–79.
Sanchez Muniz, F.J., Higuera, M., Mataix, F.J. and Varela,
    G. (1978). Proc. Nutr. Soc. 37, 81A.
Shiloh, S. and Viola, S. (1973). Bamidgeh 25, 17–31.
Spinelli, J. (1980). Fish Feed Technology. Rome,
    UNDP/FAO, ADCP/REP/80/11:187–214.
Spinelli, J., Mahnken, C.V.W., and Steinberg, M. (1979).
    In "Finfish Nutrition and Fishfeed Technology", (J.E.
    Halver and K. Tiews, eds.), Vol. II pp. 131–142.
    H. Heenemann GmbH., Berlin.
Stanley, J.G. and Jones, J.B. (1976). Aquaculture 7,
    219–223.
Stickney, R.R., Simmons, H.B. and Rowland, L.O. (1977).
    Texas J. Sci. 29, 93–99.
Strom, T., Gildberg, A., Stormo, B. and Raa, J. (1980).
    In "Advances in Fish Science and Technology" (J.J.
    Connell, ed.), pp. 352–355. Fishing News Books.
Strom, T. and Eggam, B.O. (1981). J. Sci. Food Agric.
    32, 115–120.
Summerfelt, R.C. and Yin, S.C. (1974). Paunch manure as a
    feed   supplement   in   channel   catfish   farming.
    Environmental Protection Series EPA 660/2-74-046,
    Washington, DC, 114pp.
Tacon, A.G.J. (1979). In, "Finfish Nutrition and Fishfeed
    Technology", (J.E. Halver and K. Tiews, eds.), Vol. II,
    pp. 249–267. H. Heeneman GmbH., Berlin.
Tacon, A.G.J. and Ferns, P.N. (1976). Nutr. Rep. Int.
    13, 549–562.
Tacon, A.G.J. and Cooke, D.J. (1980). Nutr. Rep. Int. 22,
    631–640.

Tacon, A.G.J. and Cowey, C.B. (1984). In, "Fish Energetics - a new look", (P. Tytler and P. Calow, eds.), Croom Helm Press Ltd., London (In Press).

Tacon, A.G.J., Haaster, J.V., Featherstone, P.B., Kerr, K. and Jackson, A.J. (1983a). Bull. Jap. Soc. Sci. Fish. 49, 1437-1443.

Tacon, A.G.J., Stafford, E.A. and Edwards, C.A. (1983b). Aquaculture 35, 187-199.

Tacon, A.G.J., Webster, J.L. and Martinez, C.A. (1984a). Aquaculture (In Press).

Tacon, A.G.J., Jauncey, K., Falaye, A., Pantha, M., MacGowan, I. and Stafford, E.A. (1984b). In, "Proceedings of First International Symposium on Tilapia in Aquaculture" (L. Fishelson and Z. Yaron eds.) pp. 356-365. Tel Aviv University Press, Israel.

Tatterson, I.N. and Windsor, M.L. (1974). J. Sci. Food Agric. 25, 369-379.

Taylor, S.J., Cole, D.J.A. and Lewis, D. (1977). Proc. Nutr. Soc. 36, 36A.

Tiews, K., Gropp, J. and Koops, H. (1976). Archiv. Fischereiwiss. Beih. 27, 1-29.

Tiews, K., Gropp, J., Beck, H. and Koops, K. (1979). In "Finfish Nutrition and Fishfeed Technology", (J.E. Halver and K. Tiews, eds.), Vol. II pp. 219-228. H. Heenemann GmbH, Berlin.

Tortell, P. (1979). Prog. Water Tech 11. 483-498.

Viola, S., Arieli, J., Rappaport, U. and Mokady, S. (1981). Bamidgeh 33, 35-49.

Viola, S., Mokady, S., Rappaport, U. and Arieli, Y. (1982). Aquaculture 26, 223-236.

Viola, S. and Arieli, Y. (1983). Bamidgeh 35, 9-17.

Viola, S., Mokady, s. and Arieli, Y. (1983). Aquaculture 32, 27-38.

Viola, S. and Zohar, G. (1984). Bamidgeh 37, 3-15.

Watanabe, T., Kitajima, C. and Fujita, S. (1983). Aquaculture 34, 115-143.

Windell, J.T., Armstrong, R. and Clinebell, J.R. (1974). Feedstuffs, May 20, 1974, 22-23.

Wohlfarth, G.W. and Schroeder, G.L. (1979). Agric. Wastes 1, 279-299.

Wong, M.H. and Cheung, S.P. (1980). Environm. Pollut., Series A 23, 29-39.

Woolford, M.K. (1975). J. Sci. Food Agric. 26, 219-228.

Yurkowski, M., Bailey, J.K., Evans, R.E., Tabachek, J.L., Ayles, G.B. and Eales, J.G. (1978). J. Fish Res. Board Can. 35, 951-962.

HORMONAL CONTROL OF PROTEIN DEPOSITION

ALLEN J. MATTY[1] and KHALID P. LONE[2]

[1]Department of Biological Sciences, University of Aston,
Gosta Green, Birmingham B47ET.

[2]Department of Zoology, Punjab University,
New Campus, Lahore-20, Pakistan.

I.   INTRODUCTION

Any symposium dealing with nutrition and feeding must at some point mention hormones, whether they be the hormones of the digestive tract or other hormones which may in turn affect the central nervous system and therefore, feeding behaviour. Also from the practical nutritional point of view it has now become a truism to say that major savings in the cost of farming fish would accrue if the efficiency of food conversion could be improved and if faster growth rates could be achieved. This has also been long recognised in animal husbandry – for nearly 50 years – and anabolic hormones or hormone like substances used to this end.   In fish nutrition, it is only during the last decade that hormones, nutrition and growth have received attention.   This review takes but one aspect of hormones and nutrition namely that of hormones and protein metabolism particularly the anabolic process.

II.   ANABOLIC – ANDROGENIC STEROIDS

The first clear cut demonstration of the anabolic effects of these compounds was provided by Kochakian

NUTRITION AND FEEDING IN FISH
ISBN: 0 12 194055 1

(1935). After these studies were published, different compounds with preponderant anabolic properties were synthesized and used in clinical practice and livestock (meat) production. Based on these studies work was first initiated about a decade ago on the effect of feeding anabolic–androgenic steroids on the growth, protein deposition and food conversion in fish.

Donaldson et al. (1979) listed details of the effects of androgenic–anabolic steroids on the growth and growth related processes of fish. Since the publication of their review, a number of studies have appeared on different aspects of anabolic–androgenic steroids and, in all, around 22 compounds with either androgenic or anabolic–androgenic properties have been tried and administered, through different routes, in 19 different species. As the oral route is the easiest and most economical and feasible way of treating fish with growth promotants, the majority of the recent studies used this route in various fish species (salmon, trout, carp, tilapia and estuary grouper). In the present discussion we will describe these studies in detail as they have appeared in the past 5 years only. For details of other routes the reader is referred to Donaldson et al. (1979) and Higgs et al. (1982).

Out of the 19 species studied so far three species i.e. carp (Cyprinus carpio), rainbow trout (Salmo gairdneri) and coho salmon (Oncorhynchus kisutch) have been studied extensively for effect on overall growth. Apart from this overall growth, some detailed studies on the protein and nucleic acid metabolism in muscle and other different body organs, for example liver, kidney, brain and spleen, have been reported in carp and trout from the laboratory of the present authors (Matty and Lone, 1979; Lone and Matty, 1980a,b; 1982a,b; 1983; 1984a,b; Lone and Ince, 1983). The interrelationship of dietary proteins and anabolic steroid has also been studied in rainbow trout and salmon (Ince et al., 1982; Lone et al., 1982; Fagerlund et al., 1983).

The Vancouver group started publishing their results on the effects of anabolic–androgenic steroids on different species of Pacific salmon in 1973 (for details see Donaldson et al., 1979; Higgs et al., 1982). Their studies clearly demonstrated the role of androgens as dietary additives for the Pacific salmons, particularly for coho salmon. The most important results were obtained with 17–methyltestosterone. This steroid increased growth and food conversion efficiency (protein deposition) and also food consumption (appetite) (Higgs et al., 1982).

There is an acute scarcity of studies on the role of cell size and number in the growth (protein deposition) of fish. Only on carp and rainbow trout have detailed studies been undertaken on these aspects after feeding anabolic androgenic steroids (Lone and Matty, 1980a; 1982 a, b). The parameters which are used in the studies on the role of cellular events in protein deposition are a) the concentrations of DNA in the said tissue (used as a measure of cell number of the tissue; b) protein/DNA is used as index of cell size; c) RNA/DNA is used to evaluate the role of RNA during growth. The studies undertaken on carp clearly show that cellular ratios and muscle protein contents at any time in life can be good indicators of growth (protein deposition). Another advantage of using this method in fish growth studies is that these ratios also tell us about the role of hypertrophy or hyperplasia in the growth. For example, in carp it appears that hypertrophy claimed a major share in growth during the period of studies (Lone and Matty, 1980a, 1983, 1984a).

Some experiments were also carried out on rainbow trout. Trout were given three isocaloric diets containing 35, 45 and 55% protein. Apart from these, diets were also prepared with 35, 45 and 55% proteins with ethylestrenol (3.5 mg/kg) added. The fish receiving lower protein with anabolic steroid had significantly higher weights than the respective controls. The steroid had no effects when given with the highest dietary protein, probably showing that the anabolic steroid was activating protein synthetic machinery at lower dietary protein than at higher. It appears that with the increase in the dietary proteins, muscle proteins and RNA increased to a certain level (45%) and then decreased. On the other hand DNA showed a parallel response with the increase in dietary proteins. Inclusion of the steroid further enhanced these parameters in the muscle. Increase in protein desposition/synthesis in response to anabolic steroid feeding has also been seen by direct measurement of incorporation of amino acids into proteins (Matty and Cheema, 1978).

Up to 30 days of feeding of the diets containing different protein concentration, all the parameters RNA/DNA, RNA/protein and protein/DNA showed an inverse relationship with dietary protein content. This clearly means that at lower dietary protein levels the efficiency of protein deposition is higher than at higher concentrations, and that at higher dietary protein concentrations DNA synthesis is faster than at the low dietary protein concentrations. The result is that higher dietary protein levels cause hyperplasia while at lower concentrations cell size contributes comparatively more to growth. After 60 days of the same dietary regime RNA/DNA and protein/DNA showed the same response described above, but RNA/protein was higher in the 45% protein group. It may be mentioned here that this dietary protein level is near the optimum dietary requirement level for this fish (Cowey and Sargent, 1979). This response of growth or protein deposition in trout is different from mammals, basically because of the fact that fish growth is largely due to protein deposition and is quite indeterminate. Although studies of this kind are very limited in fish, the effect of growth on nucleic acid content of trout muscle has been investigated by Luquet and Durand (1970) and Luquet (1971). The results of these studies suggest that the cellular growth responses of trout are fundamentally different (indeterminate growth) to mammals. In trout, cell multiplication (hyperplasia) appears to continue throughout life, whereas cell size increases up to a stage beyond which no further increase occurs. Furthermore, the muscle DNA content always keeps pace with the increase in muscle weight. In our studies on trout reported above we have seen that fish receiving 45% dietary protein increased in weight from an initial weight of 28g to an average weight of 85g after 60 days (a factor of 3.04), the muscle mass increased from 16.80 to 53.59g (X 3.20). The number of cells (proportional to DNA content) increased by a factor of 3.01, RNA by 6.76, and protein only by 2.34. (Lone and Ince, 1983). This parallelism between growth parameters and total body growth of trout points to the fact that like mammals, the molecular ratios can also be safely used in fish growth studies.

When ethylestrenol was added to diets with different protein levels, comparatively more RNA was synthesized in the muscle as compared to groups receiving diets without the steroid. This can be seen better in the RNA/DNA and RNA/protein ratios. Addition of ethylestrenol also increased the protein synthesized per unit weight of DNA and this was observed as increase in protein/DNA ratios in the experimental trouts. This means that growth (protein deposition) is more pronounced under steroid influence and that steroid preferentially causes cellular hypertrophy apart from causing normal hyperplasia. These results in rainbow trout are in line with the results obtained with carp, where it was seen repeatedly that under the influence of steroids, hypertrophy contributes more in growth than hyperplasia.   Studies in other species will help in generalizing the statements made above.

Not much is known about the mechanisms underlying these changes in fish in response to normal growth and growth under steroid feeding. However, it has consistently been seen that feeding of anabolic-androgenic steroids causes increases in the food conversion efficiency, and increase in appetite has also been referred to, particularly in pacific salmon (Higgs et al., 1982).   We have seen increases in the food conversion efficiency in carp and have also reported increased proteolytic activity of the gut of this fish under the influence of natural steroid hormones (Lone and Matty, 1981a,b).   Also our results with trout, which were given different dietary proteins, show that although the experimental fish were eating more than the control groups, nevertheless, when calculated on the percentage of body weight/day, the experimental fish were consuming less food than controls but had higher digestibility and assimilation (Ince et al., 1982).   This attribute together with higher food conversion and growth rate has obvious commercial implications.   Recently, Habibi and Ince (1983) and Habibi et al. (1983) studied the intestinal absorption of $[^{14}C-]$-leucine in rainbow trout both in vivo and in vitro. The results of these studies show that methyltestosterone significantly increases the transport of this essential amino acid. These results clearly support our hypothesis regarding the intestine as a target for anabolic-androgenic steroids (Lone and Matty, 1980a, 1981a).   Studies performed on the feeding of radioactive testosterone and 17-methyltestosterone also point in this direction (Lone and Matty, 1981b; Higgs et al., 1982).

III.   OESTROGENS

Studies investigating the use of diethylstilbestrol (DES) as a growth stimulant in meat animals began in early 1950.   During these experiments, it was seen that estrogens in general and DES in particular are toxic in human and laboratory animals (as far as growth is concerned), but show anabolic response in ruminants.   In ruminants, DES increased daily weight gain, feed consumption and improved the efficiency of food utilization. These effects are brought about by changes in the other endogenous anabolic hormones, such as increased androgens from adrenal cortex, increased thyroid activity, increased growth hormone secretion and direct effects at the tissue level.

Extrapolating the results from ruminants, the application of estrogens to fish therefore was investigated. In all, around 4 different estrogenic compounds have been used in 10 different species. The studies include work carried out on gonadal physiology and sex-reversal etc. Ashby (1957) showed that brown trout alevins treated with estradiol ($300\mu g/l$) had retarded growth, ceased feeding and showed high mortality. Hoar (1958) reported the protein catabolic effects of diethylstilbestrol in goldfish by studying the ammonia excretion which increased after 7, 14 and 21 days of treatment. Ghittino (1970) fed DES with diet at a rate of $50\mu g$–5.0 mg DES/100g live weight/day to rainbow trout. Growth of the fish receiving the drug was lower than the control group. Cowey et al. (1973) fed DES to plaice (Pleuronectes platessa) and found a positive growth response at 1.2 and 2.4 ppm dose level. Higher doses did not induce any growth. Bulkley (1972) used channel catfish (Ictalurus punctatus) in his studies of DES on fish growth. A statistically significant drop in growth rate with side effects was seen. Matty and Cheema (1978) used DES as food additive for rainbow trout and at a concentration of 1.2 mg/kg food, negative growth was observed. Yu et al. (1979) reported positive growth response in coho salmon (Oncorhynchus kisutch) receiving estradiol (2.5 mg/kg dry diet) in the food.

The above review clearly shows that there is controversy as to the role of estrogens in the fish growth. These equivocal results might have been obtained because of different experimental conditions, doses, species and size of the fish. A need for more systematic studies is acute. Apart from the growth studies, very little is known about the effects of estrogens on the protein and nucleic acid metabolism in fish, although their effects on lipid and carbohydrate metabolism are established (see Matty and Lone, 1984). In a recent study, Medda et al. (1980) have shown that estradiol dipropionate (0.5–$4\mu g/g$ intraperitoneal, for 7 consecutive days) increased the liver protein and RNA while no effect was seen in muscle in this regard. Very recently, Habibi

et al. (1983) and Habibi and Ince (1983) have shown that
estradiol has no effect on the intestinal transport of
[^{14}C]-leucine both in vitro and in vivo, while in the
same experiments methyltestosterone significantly enhanced
the absorption of the amino acid.

IV. CORTICOIDS

   Mammals deficient in corticoids (mainly glucocorticoid)
are   similar   in   many   responses   to   those   of
hypophysectomized animals.   These animals are unable to
maintain their blood sugar and liver glycogen levels
during fasting.   Further, they excrete less nitrogen as
compared   to   normal   animals.   This   means   that
glucocorticoids   promote   gluconeogenesis   by   bringing
catabolic   action   on   muscle   proteins.   It   has   been
repeatedly established that administration of the large
doses   of   corticosteroids   causes   loss   of   protein   from
skeletal musculature and degrowth, whereas liver protein
content increases.   The effects on the protein metabolism
have recently been confirmed by the estimation of urinary
3-methylhistidine (Odedra and Millward, 1982).
   The presence of corticoids in the blood of teleosts has
been confirmed and reviewed (Fontaine, 1975).   Cortisol
and cortisone are the major glucocorticoids present.   The
role of these steroids in the growth of fish has not been
worked   out   directly.   Some   studies   dealing   with   the
protein and carbohydrate metabolism have been published
and it appears that these steroids have the same effects
in   teleosts   as   in   the   mammals.   Corticoids   promote
gluconeogenesis and have a general catabolic action in
fish.   The protein catabolic property of these steroids
is very important and becomes useful to the animal in the
natural   non-feeding   phase   of   some   species,   where
mobilization of the protein from the muscles (mainly from
parietal muscle) provides energy and raw materials for the
development of certain organs (gonads) of the body.   Thus
in Oncorhynchus sp. a six fold increase in the plasma
corticoids   during   spawning   migration   brings   about
catabolism of 60% of the body proteins and an elevation of
liver glycogen (Fontaine, 1975).
   The injection of ACTH or cortisol into teleosts induces
protein catabolism and growth inhibition.   In hypophysectomized Poecilia latipinna, cortisol or ACTH increased

weight loss, exaggerated the shrinkage of fish in length and retarded the regeneration of the amputated caudal fin (Ball and Baker, 1969).

The mobilization of proteins from the muscle under the influence of corticoids does not seem to be an isolated process as changes in the muscle overall proximate composition are not seen. This has been seen both in mammals and fish. Further starvation also induced effects similar to the one induced by corticoids. Stimpson (1965) and Storer (1967) have reported that eight-day starved goldfish lost about 15% of their body weight, caused mainly by the loss of parietal muscle with no change in the muscle proximate composition. Cortisol injections for 4 days induced exactly the same results as the starvation. This may be due to the fact that starvation stress induced release of cortisol which had catabolic effects. Stress-induced changes in cortisol and tyrosine amino-transferase (an enzyme indicator of protein catabolism) have recently been described in brook trout (Salvelinus fontinalis) and Fundulus heteroclitus (Whiting and Wiggs, 1977, 1978; Leach and Taylor, 1980).

In mammals, apart from muscle, two other major targets for corticoids are lymphoid tissue and liver. Corticoids are catabolic to lymphoid tissue and some evidence towards this is also available in fish (Pickford et al., 1971). In contrast, corticoids increase liver weight in mammals. This increase in the liver weight is due to the increase in proteins, RNA and DNA; in the beginning the hypertrophy contributes more, but later on hyperplastic growth can also be seen. In fish, corticoid-liver interaction is confusing and different to what is seen in mammals. Liver increased in size after hypophysectomy in Fundulus heteroclitus, Poecilia formosa and Poecilia latipinna and remained increased till 9 days of starvation of P. latipinna (Ball and Baker, 1969). Injections of ACTH or cortisol reduce the weight of the liver, but growth hormone or thyroid stimulating hormone had no effect. There are indications that in Tilapia mossambica and Poecilia, ACTH has more stronger actions on glycogenolysis than gluconeogenesis. But on the other hand liver transaminases and other enzymes of carbohydrate metabolism increase after cortisol injections into rainbow trout, brook trout and eel Anguilla japonica (Freeman and Idler, 1973; Chan and Woo, 1978).

V.   THYROID HORMONES

Thyroid hormones (T_4 and T_3) are essential for growth of mammals including human beings.   Although they may not be required by the embryos, their absence during neonatal stages causes severe and irreversible nervous damage, and a euthyroid state is necessary for the normal growth and development.

Although the thyroid is ubiquitous in fish, the location and morphology may vary.   Detailed accounts of the thyroid gland, its hormones, metabolism and physiological effects have been described (Donaldson et al., 1979; Eales, 1979; Higgs et al., 1982; Leatherland, 1982).   Like mammals both T_4 and T_3 are present in the peripheral blood of fish.   The major route of excretion of the hormones is the biliary-fecal pathway.   Marked seasonal variations are found in the blood titers of both T_4 and T_3 in different species of fish (see Eales, 1979; Higgs et al., 1982).

There is considerable controversy in the literature as to whether the fish thyroid is essential for growth or not.   Growth and morphogenetic processes are slowed down when thiourea or other antithyroid drugs are administered to fish while thyroid hormones increased growth (for earlier studies see Donaldson et al.,1979). Administration of different doses of T_4 (1 and $10\mu g/g$ body weight/week) either intramuscularly, intraperitoneally or by cholesterol pellets implanted into the muscle of the coho salmon (Oncorhynchus kisutch) clearly spelled out the role of thyroxine in fish growth.   Later on, the effects of oral administration of T_4 and T_3 to coho salmon were reported.   In these studies T_3 at lower doses (20, 100 ppm) significantly increased the weight, length and food conversion efficiency. T_4 had no effect in this regard.   Higher doses brought changes in the skull and fins.   Lower doses of T_3 (4 or 20 ppm) as dietary additive to coho salmon held in freshwater till their transfer to sea water induced improved growth, appetite and food utilization both in fresh and sea-water (Higgs et al., 1982).   Growth rate of Salmo salar was shown to be best when receiving T_3.   The hormone-treated fish also showed better salt-water tolerance (Refstie, 1982).   Lam (1980) studied the effect of T_4 treatment (0.1 ppm) by immersion on the development and survival of the Sarotherodon mossambicus. T_4 treatment resulted in the accelerated development and enhanced survival rate as compared to normal developing larvae.

Studies in the laboratory of the present authors were also undertaken on the thyroid physiology in Sarotherodon mossambicus and Cyprinus carpio. Feeding experiments with tilapia and carp showed that T_4 (20, 50 and 100 mg/kg food) fed for 75 days was without any effect in tilapia while T_3 induced a positive growth response at the lower dose (20 ppm). Carp did not respond to either T_3 or T_4 (10 and 50 mg/kg food) as far as overall growth in terms of weight or length was concerned (Lone, Chaudhary and Matty, in preparation).

In mammals and birds, thyroidectomy or hypothyroidism decreases the protein and RNA content of skeletal muscle and thyroid hormones activate the protein synthesis in this tissue (Brown et al., 1981). It is now clearly known that these actions are mediated through transcriptional and translational changes. Very few studies by comparison on the effect of thyroid hormones on the protein and amino acid metabolism in fish are available.

Ammonia excretion increased when goldfish were immersed in thyroxine solution (Hoar, 1958; Thornburn and Matty, 1963). Ammonia production was temperature sensitive, higher temperature induced higher excretion rates while no effect was seen at low (14^OC) temperature. Further, T_4 and T_3 have been reported to stimulate protein synthesis in goldfish and rainbow trout studied through the incorporation of labelled amino acids (Thornburn and Matty, 1963; Narayansingh and Eales, 1975) but in Fundulus, these hormones had little effect in this respect (Jackim and LaRoche, 1973). Smith and Thorpe (1977) showed that T_4 (0.25–5 mg/day/kg) decreased the nitrogen excretion of fed Salmo gairdneri.

In a more systematic study, Ray and Medda (1976) and Medda and Ray (1979) investigated the effects of T_3, T_4 and thyroid hormonal analogues on the ammonia and urea excretion and on the protein and nucleic acid contents of liver and muscle of Ophicephalus punctatus. Ammonia and urea excretion was shown to be directly proportional to the environmental temperature ($10–30^O$C). Lower doses of the hormones induced anabolic effects characterized by lower ammonia and urea excretion and higher protein and RNA levels in liver and muscle. Higher doses at all temperatures (and lower, anabolic doses at higher temperatures) were catabolic as there was increase in the nitrogen excretion coupled with a decrease in protein and RNA contents of the tissues studied. This dual effect of the same hormone in the same animal species and body organ at two different doses or temperatures has also been seen in mammals and has been termed as a "bi-phasic" response.   It must be made clear here that other factors like nutritional state, age and sexual status can modify these responses.   Similar   results   were   achieved   when Channa   punctatus   were   immersed   in T_4 solution   (Lone, unpublished).

Recently, Matty et al. (1982) described the effects of thyroid   hormones   and   temperature   on   the   protein   and nucleic   acid   metabolism   in   tilapia   liver   and   muscle. Single injections of both T_3 and T_4 (0.25-2.0μg/g body weight)   induced   an   increase   in   the   protein   and   RNA contents   of   liver   and   muscle.   No   effect   on   DNA   was observed.   The effect of the hormones was dose dependent (biphasic response).   Ambient temperature influenced the effect of thyroid hormones in both tissues.   With the increase in temperature from 15-30°C, a parallel linear response both in protein and RNA was observed in both tissues. T_4 however,   became   toxic   at   high   (30°C) temperature.   Further,   thyroid   hormones   required   to increase the weight gain and protein and RNA synthesis in tilapia fry increased with age.   The increase of protein and   nucleic   acid   of   liver   and   muscle   following   single intraperitoneal injections of thyroid hormones to starved tilapia was observed only in fish up to 40g.   Fish of 230g showed no response.   Similarly in another study, feeding of T_3 induced increase in muscle protein and RNA contents   of   the   tilapia   and   decreased   the   muscle   total lipids (Lone, Chaudhary and Matty, in preparation).

Studies undertaken on carp Cyprinus carpio confirmed the   effects   seen   in   tilapia.   During   all   the   studies reported above it was seen that T_3 is more potent than T_4 in inducing changes in the protein and RNA contents of   liver   and   muscle.   Further   studies   in   carp   showed   that changes   in   liver   and   muscle   proteins   and   RNA   can   be blocked   by   a   single   injection   of   actinomycin-D   (150 ng/g).   In   fact   actinomycin   actually   decreased   these substances   both   in   liver   and   muscle.   Injections   of T_4 and   actinomycin-D   together   did   not   bring   any   change   in these parameters when compared with control values.   Tata (1963) showed that actinomycin-D injection made the rat system refractory to further injections of the inhibitor. Our results with carp are contrary to Tata's observations. After an injection of actinomycin-D, the carp system can still   be   activated   or   inhibited.   These   experiments (Lone, Chaudhary and Matty, in preparation) show that the changes in the cellular proteins and RNA after thyroid hormones injections were induced at transcription level. It is known that in mammals actinomycin-D inhibits all types of RNA synthesis in muscle, but the sensitivity of the various RNA types to inhibition is different. Further, it has been found that actinomycin-D in higher doses inhibits the polypeptide chain initiation at ribosome level, thus preventing expression of mRNA already present in the cell (Pain and Clemens, 1980). The actinomycin-D used in the carp system was nearly double the amount used by Tata (1963) in his experiments. This may explain why actinomycin-D treatment resulted in a decrease of liver and muscle protein content apart from total RNA.

It was reported above (Matty et al., 1982) that temperature seems to mediate the effects of thyroid hormones on protein and RNA in liver and muscle. Neither T_3 nor T_4 induced any change in these cellular parameters at lower temperature (15°C). In order to determine if the inability of thyroxine to induce cellular effects at low temperature is mediated through a temperature sensitive system for the translocation of T_4 into the nucleus to induce its effects at transcriptional level, the effect of temperature on the uptake of T_4 by body tissues and sub-cellular fractions of carp liver and muscle was studied in vivo. A single injection of $^{125}I-T_4$ ($1\mu Ci/10g$ body weight) was given intraperitoneally to juvenile carp maintained at 15 and 25°C. Uptake from the peritoneal cavity was quite rapid, maximum radioactivity being observed in tissues after 2 hours. Fish kept at 25°C showed another peak at 8 hours, and those at 15°C at 48 hours after the single injection. Low temperature acclimated fish had higher counts in all the tissues sampled than the higher temperature acclimated fish (Lone et al., 1983). Transfer of label (T_4) from the cytoplasm to nuclei was not blocked at lower temperatures. For example, both in liver and muscle at 8 hours, nuclei from carp tissues kept at lower or higher temperatures had comparable amounts of radioactivity.

Muscle nuclei had 15% more radioactivity than liver nuclei when expressed as radioactivity/g tissue. These studies point to the fact that temperature apparently does not block the translocation of T_4 from cytoplasm to nucleus and some mechanism/s other than a simple block in transport from cytoplasm to nuclei is operating. Perhaps coupling of T_4 (T_3) with chromatin is dependent upon a temperature sensitive nuclear enzyme system. Further, there are indications that the nutritional status of the fish might also play a vital role in this respect (Lone et al., 1983).

VI. GROWTH HORMONE

Growth hormone or somatotrophin (GH) is located in the mesoadenohypophysis of the different fish studied so far. As in mammals, this hormone is quite important in the growth and growth related processes in fish. Hypophysectomy arrests growth in Fundulus heteroclitus, Poecilia latipinna, Poecilia formosa, Ictalurus melas, Salmo gairdneri and Salmo trutta, while replacement therapy restores growth (Ball and Baker, 1969; Kays, 1978, 1979; Komourdjian et al., 1978).

Apart from the above studies the majority of workers treated intact fish with GH and obtained variable growth depending upon the environmental conditions and nutritional status of the fish in question. Even in such studies a dose-response relationship is discernable (Adelman, 1977, 1978. For earlier studies see Donaldson et al., 1979).

The majority of the studies reported above dealt with the effect of GH on the overall body growth (increase in weight and length) of fish. Very few studies are available on the mechanism involved in this growth promotion. In mammals among other effects, GH has been shown to cause an increase in the movement of amino acids into the cells, a decrease in extracellular amino acids, an increase in RNA and DNA synthesis and a decrease in urea excretion. In fish, studies of this type are very few by comparison. The major reason for this can be the difficulties in obtaining pure piscian hormone for metabolic studies. Although the hormone from the tilapia pituitaries has been purified (Farmer et al., 1976), no study on the level of GH in the plasma using homologous assay has been described to date. Studies which have been reported have used the mammalian (bovine or ovine) hormone.

Matty (1962) reported the protein-anabolic effects of bGH in Cottus scorpius. Plasma protein and urea decreased in the treated fish. Venugopalan (1967) investigated the effect on mammalian GH-injected Ophicephalus striatus.

Liver RNA and DNA were estimated after one to 7 days of injections of 10 rat units. Significant increase in liver RNA was observed even after 24 hours (10 rat unit) but the peak was seen after 5 days. After this peak the RNA levels started coming down. No effect was seen on DNA content of the liver.

Kays (1978) studied the relationship between food availability and pituitary gland in hypophysectomized Ictalurus melas given bovine growth hormone (bGH). Hypophysectomy decreased weight and length and this effect was shown to be due to the decreased food intake and food conversion. bGH given to hypophysectomized fish (1 g/g body weight every second day) increased the food intake and a 100% increase was shown in food conversion. GH did increase the growth in starved fish also but these fish never came comparable to sham-operated ones. Further, a positive correlation was seen in total muscle RNA and changes observed in the body size of Ictalurus melas. Hypophysectomy decreased the RNA and RNA/DNA ratios in muscle and liver. bGH increased the body weight and RNA and RNA/DNA in both organs (Kays, 1979). These studies clearly indicate that the GH controls the growth and also brings changes in the cellular machinery associated with protein deposition. Further, control over nutrient supply is also exercised by the hormone through increasing the appetite and food conversion efficiency. Another aspect which is worth mentioning here is the lipid mobilisation effects of GH seen in fish (Donaldson et al., 1979). It may be possible that this effect of GH helps the fish to use fat as energy fuel while sparing amino acids to be deposited as body proteins.

VII. INSULIN

Insulin, a polypeptide of 51 amino acids, is synthesized and secreted by ß-cells of the pancreas. Its presence and immunological characteristics in cyclostomes, elasmobranchs and teleosts have been reviewed (Cahill et al., 1972; Brinn, 1973; Plisetskaya et al., 1976; Ince, 1983). Although the role of insulin in carbohydrate metabolism is quite well known, studies performed in fish point to the fact that, unlike mammals, the role of insulin is more important in protein metabolism as compared with carbohydrate metabolism. It appears that in fish and mammalian foetus the insulin has a central role in modulating nitrogen metabolism and that protein anabolic effects of insulin appear to have come early in evolution.   It is interesting to note that fishes evolved in an energy deficient but protein rich environment.

In carnivore fish, Opsanus tau insulin increased the incorporation of glycine into the muscle proteins (Tashima and Cahill, 1968).   Similar results were reported in Fundulus heteroclitus, and goldfish (Jackim and LaRoche, 1973; Ahmad and Matty, 1975).   Injections of exogenous insulin decreased the plasma amino acids in Esox lucius (Thorpe and Ince, 1974), Anguilla anguilla (Ince and Thorpe, 1974) and Anguilla japonica (Inui et al., 1975).

In all the species studied so far, a clear relationship between dietary amino acids and insulin level in the blood is discernable.   It has been shown many times that a high protein diet increases, while starvation decreases the insulin levels.   Direct evidence that amino acids are better secretogogues than carbohydrates (glucose) has been presented by elegant experiments of Ince (for details see Ince, 1983).   Further, islectomy in rainbow trout caused the elevation of several plasma amino acids (Matty and Kumar, unpublished).

Very little is known about the role of insulin on the general growth of fish. Ahmad and Matty (1976) showed that insulin and tolbutamide treatment of goldfish (23°C) increased the muscle RNA, 48 hour post-injection. Alloxan treatment decreased the RNA levels. DNA was not changed by either of the two treatments. Intraperitoneal injections of bovine insulin (0.32-10 IU/kg body weight) either once or twice a week for 70 days did not induce any growth in the coho salmon (Ludwig et al., 1977).   Recent studies by Ablett et al. (1981a,b) on rainbow trout has shown that insulin in higher doses (0.5-5 IU/kg) significantly increased growth both in terms of weight and length when given for 56 days. Insulin increased the incorporation of [^{14}C]-leucine in the muscle both in fed and starved fish while specific activity of leucine decreased in the plasma and liver pointing to the fact that a net movement of this amino acid has occurred from these tissues to the muscle. Apart from the increase in the muscle proteins, muscle lipids also increased significantly while a decrease in the liver lipids was also noted. No effect on liver or muscle glycogen was observed.   Further, insulin caused hypoglycemia, but liver glycogen was not increased, in fact insulin promoted oxidative clearance of glucose. Also in rainbow trout,

insulin inhibited gluconeogenesis from alanine both in fed
and starved fish (Cowey et al., 1977). The results
discussed above clearly point to the fact that insulin
decreases the gluconeogenesis from amino acids and that
the amino acids spared are moved from extracellular space
and from peripheral organs towards the muscle, where
preferential influx of these amino acids takes place,
providing the raw material for protein synthesis and
deposition.

VIII. HORMONAL INTERRELATIONS AND INTERACTIONS IN PROTEIN DEPOSITION

Many studies are available on the hormone interaction
and interrelations on growth or metabolism in general in
mammals. Very few studies by comparison are available for
fish. Pickford (1957) showed that hypophysectomised
Fundulus heteroclitus exhibited a synergistic response
both in weight and length when hake GH and TSH were
injected together. Earlier, of these two hormones, only
hake GH was anabolic, TSH did not induce any significant
change. If GH is considered basic for growth then it
appears that TSH (or T_4 or T_3) had a permissive role
in growth. Enomoto's (1964) studies on the interaction
of GH, prolactin and TSH in different combinations did not
show any clear response in rainbow trout of 6-10g body
weight. A combination of ovine luteinizing hormone (oLH)
and bovine GH induced a synergistic effect on the weight
and length of hypophysectomized Fundulus. In the same
study oLH was shown to be thyrotrophic (Pickford et al.,
1972). The effect of combinations of bGH,
17-methyltestosterone (MT) and L-thyroxine (T_4) on
Oncorhynchus kitutch has been studied. The GH ($10\mu g/g$
body weight per week) and T_4 ($1\mu g/g$ body weight per
week) were administered by intramuscular injections while
methyl- testosterone was given orally at a rate of 1 mg/kg
diet. Each individual hormone and these hormones in
combination significantly enhanced the growth. The
sequence of growth promotion for different combinations of
hormones given for 59 days can be summarized as follows:

$$(GH+MT+T_4)>(GH+MT)>(GH+T_4)>GH>(MT+T_4)>MT>T_4>controls$$

These results show that additive and synergistic effects

were seen in different combinations as far as growth is concerned. The fact that 3 hormones were most effective when given together shows that probably a natural endogenous condition was mimicked. In a recent study the same group gave T_3 and MT both by oral route and gained significant growth in coho salmon in freshwater. Maximum response was seen when a combination of 4 ppm T_3 and 1 ppm MT was used (Higgs et al., 1982, Donaldson et al., 1979).

These studies clearly show that combination of hormones can give better results than the single hormone treatments as far as the protein deposition is concerned, but in order that these studies are applied in practical fisheries and aquaculture, detailed studies must be undertaken in order to include more fish of economical value and the best hormone combinations and their interactions with nutrition and the organoleptic properties of the muscle. The need for these studies is now acute in third world or developing countries where protein shortage is serious and where fish can provide a sizeable amount of human dietary animal protein requirements.

REFERENCES

Ablett, R.F., Sinnhuber, R.O., Holmes, R.M. and
    Selivonchick, D.P. (1981a). Gen. Comp. Endocrinol. 43,
    211-217.
Ablett, R.F., Sinnhuber, R.O., and Selivonchick, D.P.
    (1981b). Gen. Comp. Enocrinol. 44, 418-427.
Adelman, I.R. (1977). J. Fish. Res. Bd Can. 34, 509-515.
Adelman, I.R. (1978). Trans. Amer. Fish. Soc. 107,
    747-750.
Ahmad, M.M. and Matty, A.J. (1975). Pakistan J. Zool. 7,
    1-6.
Ahmad, M.M. and Matty, A.J. (1976). Islamabad J. Sci. 3,
    4-8.
Ashby, K.R. (1957). J. Embryol. Exp. Morphol. 5, 225-249.
Ball, J.N. and Baker, B.I. (1969). In "Fish Physiology"
    (W.S. Hoar and D.J. Randall), eds., 2, 1-111. Academic
    Press, New York.
Brinn, J.E. Jr. (1973). Amer. Zool. 13, 653-665.
Brown, J.G., Bates, P.C., Holliday, M.A. and Millward,
    D.J. (1981). Biochem. J.. 194, 771-782.

Bulkley, R.V. (1972). Trans. Am. Fish. Soc. 101, 537-539.

Cahill, A.F., Acki, T.T. and Marliss, E.B. (1972). In "Handbook of Physiology" (D.F. Sleiner and N. Fremkel, eds.), 1, 563-577. Amer. Physiol. Soc., Washington, D.C.

Chan, D.K.O. and Woo, N.Y.S. (1978).Gen. Comp. Endocrinol. 35, 205-215.

Cowey, C.B. and Sargent, J.R. (1979).In "Fish Physiology", (W.S. Hoar, D.J. Randall and J.R. Brett, eds.), 8, 1-69. Academic Press, New York.

Cowey, C.B., Pope, J.A., Adron, J.W. and Blair, A. (1973). Mar. Biol. 19, 1-6.

Cowey, C.B., Knox, D., Walton, M.J. and Adron, J.W. (1977). Brit. J. Nutr. 38, 463-470.

Donaldson, E.M., Fagerlund, U.H.M., Higgs, D.A. and McBride, J.R. (1979). In "Fish Physiology" (W.S. Hoar, D.J. Randall and J.R. Brett, eds.), 8, 455-597. Academic Press, New York.

Eales, J.G. (1979). In "Hormones and Evolution" (E.J.W. Barrington, ed.), 1, 341-436. Academic Press, London.

Enomoto, Y. (1964). Bull. Jap. Soc. Sci. Fish. 30, 537-541.

Fagerlund, U.H.M., Higgs, D.A., McBride, J.R., Plontikoff, B.C., Dosanjh, B.S. and Markert, J.R. (1983). Aquaculture 30, 109-124.

Farmer, S.W., Papkoff, H., Hayshida, T., Bewley, T.A., Bern, H.A. and Li, C.H. (1976). Gen. Comp. Endocrinol. 30, 91-100.

Fontaine, Y.A. (1975). In "Biochemical and Biophysical Perspectives in Marine Biology" (D.C. Malins and J.R. Sargent, eds.), 2, 139-212. Academic Press, London.

Freeman, H.C. and Idler, D.R. (1973). Gen. Comp. Endocrinol. 20, 69-75.

Ghittino, P. (1970). Riv. Ital. Piscic. Ittiopatol. 5, 9-11.

Habibi, H.R. and Ince, B.W. (1983). Gen. Comp. Endocrinol. 52, 438-446.

Habibi, H.R., Ince, B.W. and Matty, A.J. (1983). J. Comp. Physiol. 151, 247-252.

Higgs, D.A., Fagerlund, U.H.M., Eales, J.G. and McBride, J.R. (1982). Comp. Biochem. Physiol. 73B, 143-176.

Hoar, W.S. (1958). Can. J. Zool. 36, 113-121.

Ince, B.W., (1983). In "Control Processes in Fish Physiology" (J.C. Rankin, T.J. Pitcher and R. Duggan, eds.), 89-102. Croom Helm, London.

Ince, B.W. and Thorpe, A. (1974). Gen. Comp. Endocrinol. 23, 460-471.

Ince, B.W., Lone, K.P. and Matty, A.J. (1982). Brit. J.
  Nutr. 47, 615–624.
Inui, Y., Arai, S. and Yokote, M. (1975). Bull. Jap.
  Soc. Sci. Fish. 41, 1105–1111.
Jackim, E. and La Roche, G. (1973). Comp. Biochem.
  Physiol 44A, 851–866.
Kays, T. (1978). Gen. Comp. Endocrinol. 35, 419–431.
Kays, T. (1979). Gen. Comp. Endocrinol. 37, 321–332.
Kochakian, C.D. (1935). Proc. Soc. Exp. Biol. (N.Y.) 32,
  1064–1065.
Komourdjian, M.P., Burton, M.P. and Idler, D.R. (1978).
  Gen. Comp. Endocrinol. 34, 158–162.
Lam, T.J. (1980). Aquaculture 21, 287–292.
Leach, G.J. and Taylor, M.H. (1980).Gen. Comp. Endocrinol.
  42, 219–227.
Leatherland, J.F. (1982). Environ. Biol. Fish 7, 83–110.
Lone, K.P. and Ince, B.W. (1983). Gen. Comp. Endocrinol.
  49, 32–49.
Lone, K.P. and Matty, A.J. (1980a). Gen. Comp.
  Endocrinol. 40, 409–424.
Lone, K.P. and Matty, A.J. (1980b). Pakistan J. Zool.
  12, 47–56.
Lone, K.P. and Matty, A.J. (1981a). J. Fish Biol. 18,
  353–358.
Lone, K.P. and Matty, A.J. (1981b). Aquaculture 24,
  315–326.
Lone, K.P. and Matty, A.J. (1982a). J. Fish Biol. 20,
  93–104.
Lone, K.P. and Matty, A.J. (1982b). J. Fish Biol. 21,
  33–45.
Lone, K.P. and Matty, A.J. (1983). Aquaculture 32, 39–55.
Lone, K.P. and Matty, A.J. (1984a). Nutr. Rep. Int. 29,
  621–638.
Lone, K.P. and Matty, A.J. (1984b). Pakistan J. Zool. 16
  (In press).
Lone, K.P., Ince, B.W. and Matty, A.J. (1982). J. Fish
  Biol. 20, 597–606.
Lone, K.P., Chaudhary, M.A. and Matty, A.J. (1983). Acta
  Physiol. Latinoam. 33, 149–160.
Ludwig, B., Higgs, D.A., Fagerlund, U.H.M. and McBride,
  J.R. (1977). Can. J. Zool. 55, 1756–1758.
Luquet, P. (1971). Ann. Biol. Anim. Biochim. Biophys. 11,
  657–668.
Luquet, P. and Durand, G. (1970). Ann. Biol. Anim.
  Biochim. Biophys. 10, 481–492.
Matty, A.J. (1962). Nature (London) 195, 506–507.
Matty, A.J. and Cheema, I.R. (1978). Aquaculture 14,
  163–178.

Matty, A.J. and Lone, K.P. (1979). Proc. World Maricult. Soc. 10, 735-745.

Matty, A.J. and Lone, K.P. (1984). In "Fish Bioenergetics, a New Look", (P. Calow and P. Tytler, eds.). Croom Helm, London (In press.

Matty, A.J., Chaudhary, M.A. and Lone, K.P. (1982). Gen. Comp. Endocrinol. 47, 497-507.

Medda, A.K. and Ray, A.K. (1979). Gen. Comp. Endocrinol. 37, 74-80.

Medda, A.K., Dasmhapatra, A.K. and Ray, A.K. (1980). Gen. Comp. Endocrinol. 42, 427-437.

Narayansingh, T. and Eales, J.G. (1975). Comp. Biochem. Physiol. 52B, 399-405.

Odedra, B.R. and Millward, D.J. (1982). Biochem J. 204, 663-672.

Pain, V.M. anjd Clemens, M.J. (1980). Comprehensive Biochem. 19B, 1-76.

Pickford, G.E. (1957). In "The Physiology of the Pituitary Gland of Fishes" (G.E. Pickford and J.W. Atz, eds.), 4, 84-98. New York Zool. Soc., N.Y.

Pickford, G.E., Srivastava, A.K., Slicher, A.M. and Pang, P.K.T. (1971). J. exp. Zool. 177, 109-117.

Pickford, G.E., Lofts, B., Bara, C. and Aty, J.W. (1972). Biol. Reprod. 7, 370-386.

Plisetskaya, E., Leibush, B.N. and Bondareva, V. (1976). In "The Evolution of the Pancreatic Islets" (T.A.I. Grillo, B.N. Leibson and A. Epple, eds.), 251-269. Pergamon Press, Oxford.

Ray, A.K. and Medda, A.K. (1976). Gen. Comp. Endocrinol. 29, 190-197.

Refstie, T. (1982). Can. J. Zool. 60, 2706-2712.

Smith, M.A.K. and Thorpe, A. (1977). Gen. Comp. Endocrinol. 32, 400-406.

Stimpson, J.H. (1965). Comp. Biochem. Physiol. 15, 187-197.

Storer, J.H. (1967). Comp. Biochem. Physiol. 20, 939-948.

Tashima, L. and Cahill, G.F. (1968).Gen. Comp. Endocrinol. 11, 262-271.

Tata, J.R. (1963). Nature (London) 197, 1167-1168.

Thornburn, C.C. and Matty, A.J. (1963) Comp. Biochem. Physiol. 8, 1-12.

Thorpe, A. and Ince, B.W. (1974). Gen. Comp. Endocrinol. 23, 29-44.

Venugopalan, V.K. (1967). Gen. Comp. Endocrinol. 8, 332-336.

Whiting, S.J. and Wiggs, A.J. (1977). Comp. Biochem. Physiol. 58B, 189-193.

Whiting, S.J. and Wiggs, A.J. (1978). Comp. Biochem. Physiol. 60B, 463–465.
Yu, T.C., Sinnhuber, R.O. and Hendricks, J.D. (1979). Aquaculture 16, 351–359.

NUTRITIONAL EVALUATION IN FISH BY MEASUREMENT OF IN VITRO PROTEIN SYNTHESIS IN WHITE TRUNK MUSCLE TISSUE

EINAR LIED, OIVIND LIE AND GEORG LAMBERTSEN

Institute of Nutrition, Directorate of Fisheries,
P.O. Box 4285, N-5013 Nygaardstangen/Bergen, Norway.

I.   INTRODUCTION

Growth and cellular functions in tissues are closely related to protein synthesis and breakdown. For optimal protein synthesis food must be available in adequate amounts and its nutrient content balanced relative to the specific animal requirement.

Protein synthesis can be followed in vitro using active cell-free systems containing ribosomes of the tissues to be studied. Such studies have shown that protein synthesis activity in skeletal muscle is highly sensitive to alterations in dietary composition and food intake (von der Decken, 1983). Recent studies with cod (Gadus morhua) (Lied et al., 1982) and rainbow trout (Salmo gairdneri), saithe (Pollachius virens) and herring (Clupea harengus) (Rosenlund et al., 1983) have demonstrated that ribosomes from these fish species actively incorporate amino acids into protein in vitro. In this paper an in vitro assay for protein synthesis in white skeletal muscle tissue and its application to nutritional studies in fish is described.

NUTRITION AND FEEDING IN FISH
ISBN: 0 12 194055 1

II.   EXPERIMENTAL PROCEDURES

A detailed description of the method has been given previously (Lied et al., 1982; Rosenlund et al., 1983). Briefly, the epaxial muscle and (depending on fish size) part of the hypaxial muscle are dissected out, skinned and split lengthwise into several thin slices.   The muscle tissue is either used fresh or wrapped in aluminium foil and immediately placed between two blocks of solid CO_2 and stored at $-80^\circ C$ for not more than 14 days (Lund and von der Decken, 1980).

Ribosomes are isolated from 2.5 gram of minced and homogenised tissue by centrifugation in an angle rotor for 2 hrs at 165,000 x g_{av} using a discontinuous sucrose gradient.   The ribosome pellet is suspended in a final volume of 1.3 ml.   Soluble enzymes to be used in the incubation mixture of ribosomes are prepared from rainbow trout acclimatised to the same salinity and temperature as the experimental fish, and fed a commercial dry pellet diet.   In general, livers from 4–6 trout averaging 300–400 gram are homogenised and centrifuged for 2 hrs at 165,000 x g_{av}.   The supernatant is passed through a short column of Sephadex G–25 to remove low molecular weight components (von der Decken, 1968).

The ribosomes are incubated in a mixture containing phosphocreatine 25 mM, creatine phosphokinase 0.80 units, ATP 1 mM, GTP 0.1 mM, a mixture of amino acids excluding the radioactive one 0.1 mM, L-[1-^{14}C]-phenylalanine (57 mCi/mmol) 0.006 mM, sucrose 250 mM, Tris–HCl (pH 7.6 at $25^\circ C$) 35 mM, KCl 80 mM, $MgSO_4$ 5 mM, liver cell sap corresponding to 0.5 mg protein and increasing amounts of ribosomes in the range of 0.01 to 0.03 mg of RNA.   The final incubation volume is 0.13 ml.   The mixture is incubated for 4 min at $28^\circ C$.   After incubation 0.1 ml is transferred to filter–paper discs which are kept for 10 min in ice-cold 10% trichloroacetic acid, extracted twice for 10 min at $90^\circ C$ in 5% trichloroacetic acid followed by washing 3 times in ethanol, dried and radioactivity measured in a scintillation spectrometer.

The capacity for muscle protein synthesis is expressed as the amount of amino acid incorporated into protein per min and per g wet weight of tissue, per mg of ribosomal RNA and per mg of DNA.

III. DISCUSSION

In fish species such as salmonids, cod and saithe, the homogeneous cell-type of white skeletal muscle tissue accounts for approximately 50% of the body weight. Defining growth as the synthesis and accumulation of proteins, the production of myofibrillar proteins contributes significantly to the increase in size of the fish. As in the rat (von der Decken and Omstedt, 1970, 1972; Omstedt and von der Decken, 1972, 1974), protein synthesis in skeletal muscle of fish is highly sensitive to changes in food availability and composition. Thus, in cod starved for 10 days the in vitro capacity for protein synthesis of muscle ribosomes was reduced by 87% as compared with that of fish feeding normally (Lied et al., 1982). Further studies of the acute effects of food deprivation on cellular functions in muscle of cod showed a 50% reduction in the amino acid incorporating activity within 3 days of starvation, and a decrease to about 40% and 10% in fish starved for 5 and 8 days, respectively. On refeeding a marked increase in the amino acid incorporating activity was observed at 4 hrs post feeding, and at 12 hrs post feeding the activity per gram wet weight was restored close to the level of fish fed ad libitum.

The ratio of ribosomal RNA/DNA has been suggested as an indicator of recent growth and feeding condition (Haines, 1973; Bulow et al., 1981). The capacity for protein synthesis in white muscle tissue of fish is highly correlated to its content of ribosomal RNA and its ratio of rRNA/DNA (Lied and Rosenlund, 1984). Measurements of the in vitro amino acid incorporating activity in fish muscle ribosomes is, however, a far more sensitive and immediate indicator of recent feeding history than the ratio of rRNA/DNA (Lied et al., 1984).

The influence of dietary protein concentration on muscle protein synthesis was studied by Lied and Rosenlund (1984). Levels of protein energy to total energy (PE/TE %) in the diets of less than 48% reduced the ribosomal capacity for protein synthesis per gram wet weight as well as per mg DNA. The effect of increasing levels of PE/TE (%) was less pronounced when expressed in terms of specific activity of rRNA. An increase of protein concentration in excess of 48% PE/TE did not affect the incorporating activity in vitro.

Table I. The effect of feeding graded levels of lysine on the content of ribosomal RNA and DNA in muscle and on the in vitro amino acid incorporating activity of ribosomes isolated from white trunk muscle of cod.

Group No	Feed[1] lysine	mg RNA	mg DNA	RNA/DNA	pmoles 14-c-Phe inc. per min and		
					g.w.wt	mg RNA	mg DNA
1	2.4	0.680±0.045	0.818±0.070	0.831±0.077	25.40±2.31	37.35±3.27	31.05±1.64
2	3.4	0.791±0.023	0.792±0.019	1.016±0.035	49.11±2.79	62.08±3.68	62.00±4.96
3	4.4	0.818±0.026	0.804±0.015	1.017±0.041	56.44±3.98	69.00±5.44	70.20±7.33
4	6.4	0.838±0.054	0.807±0.017	1.009±0.074	60.04±5.55	71.64±4.15	74.39±6.98
5	8.4	0.869±0.060	0.801±0.016	1.075±0.064	58.31±4.54	67.10±3.71	72.79±6.18
6	10.4	0.783±0.050	0.797±0.017	0.997±0.092	54.36±4.55	69.42±4.05	68.20±5.87

[1] Percent lysine of feed protein

Initial fish weight: 34.3 ± 0.8 g

Values are given as mean ± SEM

Table II. Effects of ration size on growth, muscle content of ribosomal RNA and DNA, and on the *in vitro* amino acid incorporating activity of ribosomes isolated from white trunk muscle of cod.

	GROUP NO			
	1	2	3	4
Ration size (% of ad lib)	25	50	75	100
Mg/g w.wt muscle of				
RNA	0.549 ± 0.035	0.776 ± 0.040	0.948 ± 0.058	0.912 ± 0.064
DNA	0.538 ± 0.038	0.523 ± 0.041	0.564 ± 0.020	0.574 ± 0.021
RNA/DNA-ratio	1.020 ± 0.068	1.483 ± 0.080	1.680 ± 0.146	1.589 ± 0.129
pmoles 14-c-Phe inc./min and				
G w.wt of muscle	13.64 ± 4.11	39.09 ± 6.47	68.37 ± 6.65	64.39 ± 6.93
Mg RNA in muscle	24.84 ± 5.68	50.37 ± 8.02	72.12 ± 4.94	70.60 ± 7.04
Mg DNA in muscle	25.35 ± 5.46	74.74 ± 13.75	121.22 ± 14.69	112.17 ± 10.61
Average body weights (g)				
Initial	79.5 ± 2.1	78.9 ± 2.2	74.5 ± 2.1	81.5 ± 2.2
Final	87.2 ± 2.6	112.5 ± 3.3	123.2 ± 4.0	147.2 ± 5.4
Weight gain (%)	9.7	42.6	65.4	80.6
Liver, %	6.2 ± 0.3	8.4 ± 0.3	10.6 ± 0.4	11.5 ± 0.5
Energy conversion				
Kcal/g wt gain	9.1	4.1	4.3	4.3

Values are given as mean ± SEM
Initial per cent liver: 7.0 ± 0.4

Table III. Effects of feeding regime on growth, on muscle content of ribosomal RNA and DNA, and on the _in vitro_ amino acid incorporating activity of ribosomes isolated from white trunk muscle of cod.

	GROUP NO			
	1	2	3	4
Feeding intervals	2 x day	1 x day	2nd day	4th day
Mg/g w.wt muscle of				
RNA	0.881 ± 0.074	0.878 ± 0.041	0.983 ± 0.047	0.970 ± 0.068
DNA	0.554 ± 0.014	0.561 ± 0.020	0.563 ± 0.024	0.569 ± 0.015
RNA/DNA-ratio	1.590 ± 0.120	1.566 ± 0.108	1.745 ± 0.150	1.704 ± 0.133
pmoles 14-c-Phe inc./min and				
G w.wt of muscle	35.70 ± 8.27	48.82 ± 7.48	52.95 ± 4.17	64.79 ± 4.60
Mg RNA in muscle	40.52 ± 5.37	55.60 ± 7.48	53.86 ± 2.63	66.79 ± 2.20
Mg DNA in muscle	64.44 ± 13.43	87.02 ± 11.99	94.04 ± 10.50	113.86 ± 7.57
Average body weights (g)				
Initial	109.5 ± 2.5	111.9 ± 3.0	108.7 ± 3.2	107.1 ± 2.8
Final	170.7 ± 5.0	173.1 ± 5.4	163.9 ± 6.0	149.4 ± 4.0
Weight gain (%)	55.9	54.7	50.8	39.5
Liver, %	11.9 ± 0.3	12.7 ± 0.7	11.3 ± 0.4	9.5 ± 0.3
Energy conversion				
Kcal/g weight gain	6.4	5.1	5.0	4.7

Values are given as mean ± SEM
Initial percent liver: 9.1 ± 0.5

Similarly, as shown in Table I, levels of lysine less than 4.4% of dietary protein reduce the amino acid incorporationg activity in cod skeletal muscle tissue. This indicates a dietary requirement for lysine of approximately 4.5% of the feed protein for maximal protein synthesis in the white skeletal muscle of cod.

The effects of ration size and feeding intervals on growth, muscle content of ribosomal RNA and DNA, and on the in vitro amino acid incorporating activity of ribosomes isolated from white trunk muscle of cod are shown in Tables II and III. Groups of 40 fish were fed moist pellets, in which 45% of the total energy in the feed was derived from protein, while 45% and 10% of the feed energy was supplied by fat and carbohydrate, respectively. The experiments lasted for 70 days. A ration size of 25% of ad libitim feeding is close to the maintenance level of cod while a ration size of 50% is marginal for growth in cod. Feeding cod ad libitum is not necessary to obtain optimal growth of the muscle tissue. A feeding interval of twice a day seems to exceed the ability of the cod to convert the food effectively. Further, a feeding interval of every 4th day gives a lower total growth, but a maximal utilisation of the feed for muscle protein synthesis.

To conclude, the capacity for muscle protein synthesis is a significant and sensitive parameter of qualitative and quantitative changes of feeding and feed utilization in fish nutrition studies. Measurements of the in vitro protein synthesis in white skeletal muscle tissue may be used to study nutrient inadequacy in fish diets and to estimate the dietary nutrient levels required for optimal protein metabolism and maximal growth of the skeletal muscle tissue. The technique has the advantage of measuring the total effectiveness of a feed in meeting energy and nutrient demand for growth-related intracellular functions.

REFERENCES

Bulow, F.J., Zenman, M.E., Winningham, J.R. and Hudson, W.F. (1981). J. Fish. Biol. 18, 237-244.
Haines, T.A. (1973). J. Fish. Res. Bd. Can. 30, 195-199.
Lied, E., Lund, B. and von der Decken, A. (1982). Comp. Biochem. Physiol. 72B, 187-193.

Lied, E. and Rosenlund, G. (1984). Comp. Biochem. Physiol. 77A, 489–494.

Lied, E., Rosenlund, G., Lund, B. and von der Decken, A. (1984). Comp. Biochem. Physiol. 76B, 777–781.

Lund, B. and von der Decken, A. (1980). Z. Tierphysiol. Tierernährg. u. Futtermittelkde. 44, 255–266.

Omstedt, P.T. and von der Decken, A. (1972). Br. J. Nutr. 27, 467–474.

Omstedt, P.T. and von der Decken, A. (1974). Br. J. Nutr. 31, 67–76.

Rosenlund, G., Lund, B., Lied, E. and von der Decken, A. (1983). Comp. Biochem. Physiol. 74B, 389–397.

von der Decken, A. (1968). Eur. J. Biochem. 4, 87–90.

von der Decken, A. and Omstedt, P.T. (1970). J. Nutr. 100, 623–670.

von der Decken, A. and Omstedt, P.T. (1972). J. Nutr. 102, 1555–1562.

von der Decken, A. (1983). Comp. Biochem. Physiol. 74B, 213–219.

IDENTIFICATION OF GUSTATORY FEEDING STIMULANTS FOR
FISH-APPLICATIONS IN AQUACULTURE

A.M. MACKIE and A.I. MITCHELL

N.E.R.C. Institute of Marine Biochemistry,
Aberdeen, AB1 3RA, U.K.

I.   INTRODUCTION

The aim of the fish farmer is to convert diet into live
fish with the maximum efficiency and minimum cost.
Assuming a diet containing the ideal mix of protein,
vitamins and minerals, this requires that all the food
offered to the fish is in fact consumed. In practice this
is rarely if ever accomplished - a proportion of the diet
generally remains uneaten, thus reducing the "commercial"
food conversion ratio (weight gain over weight of diet
offered) as well as causing fouling of the water. Clearly
any way of increasing the acceptability or palatability of
fish diet will be advantageous.

II.   FACTORS INFLUENCING FEEDING BEHAVIOUR

To be acceptable, a diet must satisfy several criteria:-

a)   Appearance: size, shape and colour. Does the
     material in fact look like food?   This will
     depend on what the fish have been accustomed to
     eating.

NUTRITION AND FEEDING IN FISH
ISBN: 0 12 194055 1

b)   Smell: which in the case of fish should be
      termed long-range chemical attraction, since fish
      can use both smell and taste to detect food at a
      distance.

c)   Feel: is the material hard or soft, moist or
      dry, rough or smooth?

d)   Taste: taste buds in the mouth monitor the taste
      of the material.

Which are the most important features of a food,
depends on whether the particular fish is predominantly a
visual feeder such as the rainbow trout or turbot, or a
chemosensory feeder such as the Dover sole.

The terminology of chemical feeding activators proposed
by Lindstedt (1971) will be used in this review (Table
I). In a generalized feeding response, the animal must
first approach the food source, guided by an attractant.
Close to the food, an arrestant may cause the animal to
cease locomotion and an incitant invoke initiation of
feeding (biting and tasting). The ingestion of food and
continuation of feeding is stimulated by a feeding stimulant. Equivalent negative factors (repellent, suppressant
and deterrent) may also be present.

Table I. Responses to seven types of chemical stimuli

	Stimulus	
Response	+	−
Orientation (distant)	Attractant	Repellent
Orientation (near)	Arrestant	Repellent
Initiation of feeding (tasting)	Incitant	Suppressant
Continuation of feeding	Stimulant	Deterrent

After Lindstedt (1971)

One or more of these factors have been identified in
several species of fish. Irrespective of whether the fish
is a visual or chemosensory feeder, the taste buds in the
mouth and pharynx determine whether the food is swallowed,
and for this reason feeding stimulants have been studied
in greatest detail at the Institute of Marine Biochemistry
(IMB).

Other factors also have an effect on feeding behaviour. The appetite of the fish will be influenced by when it last ate and on its well-being, which in turn depends on internal and external factors. Problems have been encountered during the farming of eels, where uneven growth was observed.

Experiments at IMB confirmed this, and it would appear that hierarchical and stress effects were involved: uneven growth and cannibalism were both observed to increase with increasing crowding (Mackie, unpublished results; Degani and Levanon, 1983). Knights deals with this subject in greater detail in another chapter.

III. IDENTIFICATION OF GUSTATORY FEEDING STIMULANTS

The majority of fish farmed in the U.K. are carnivores, requiring high levels of protein in their diets. Commercial diets are mainly fish or fishmeal-based, although small amounts of soya protein may also be present. Salmon, trout and turbot generally find these diets acceptable, although batches of diet are occasionally found to be less palatable to the turbot. The biggest problem, however, was encountered in the farming of Dover sole, which were unwilling to eat fishmeal-based diets without the addition of Nethrops or scallop waste. A knowledge of the chemical nature of feeding stimulants for various species would therefore be useful in the formulation of diets, particularly for fastidious feeders such as sole.

The studies at IMB are dependent upon two materials - a bland casein diet (Table II) and a synthetic mixture of chemicals, based upon the analysis of an extract of squid mantle tissue (Mackie, 1973) (Table III). With the exception of the rainbow trout, none of the fish investigated found the unflavoured casein diet palatable, but the same diet was eaten voraciously after the addition of squid extract or "synthetic squid mixture", proving that the feeding stimulants for all species were present in the latter mixture.

With rainbow trout, a demand feeder system was used in conjunction with freeze-dried pellets to compare diet acceptability, but with the other species the percentage of dry pellets swallowed or the quantity of moist diet eaten was used as a measure of feeding stimulant

Table II. Composition of casein diet base

	(g/kg)
Vitamin-free casein	550
Dextrin	100
α-Cellulose	126
D-glucose	50
Cod liver oil	30
Capelin oil	60
Carboxymethylcellulose	50
Vitamin mixture	28
Mineral mixture	5
Edicol Sunset Yellow	1.25

For moist diet preparation, 100 g dry base mixed with 160 ml solution

activity. In addition to feeding stimulants, attractants and incitants may also have been monitored in the studies of Carr et al. (1977) and Goh and Tamura (1980). The method used to identify feeding stimulants was based on the "omission test" developed by Hashimoto et al., (1968), where the activity of the complete mixture was compared to that of its components, all at equivalent concentrations.

Tabulation of the fish under Order and Family indicated that if there is any taxonomic relationship with the feeding stimulants it exists at or below the Family level,

Table III. Composition of synthetic squid mixture

% Composition

L-aspartic acid	0.31	taurine	5.67
L-threonine	0.73	L-proline	24.69
L-serine	0.55	glycine	15.03
L-glutamic acid	0.89	L-alanine	4.60
L-valine	0.61	L-arginine	3.84
L-methionine	0.61	glycine betaine HCl	15.34
L-isoleucine	0.49	TMAO[1] HCl	19.17
L-leucine	0.92	TMA[2] HCl	1.53
L-tyrosine	0.37	hypoxanthine	0.80
L-phenylalanine	0.49	inosine	0.43
L-lysine HCl	0.49	AMP	0.67
L-histidine HCl	0.24	lactic acid	1.53

1   Trimethylamine oxide hydrochloride

2   Trimethylamine hydrochloride

Based on an analysis of squid mantle tissue (Mackie, 1973)

although an insufficient number of species has been studied for any really firm conclusions to be drawn (Table IV).

Another possible factor in the "choice" of feeding stimulant is the feeding habits of the wild fish under natural conditions. Free L-amino acids, the feeding stimulant for rainbow trout (Adron and Mackie, 1978), sea bass (Mackie and Mitchell, 1982a), European eel (Mackie and Mitchell, 1983) and Japanese eel (Takeda et al., 1984), are present in all animal tissues, both vertebrate and invertebrate. Different amino acid mixtures acted as feeding stimulants for the various species, and in all cases the corresponding D-amino acids were ineffective. In both the European and Japanese eel, the mixture glycine, L-proline and L-alanine was an effective feeding stimulant. ·

Table IV. Survey of food organisms and feeding stimulants

Order	Natural food organisms	Feeding stimulant
Clupeiformes Rainbow trout, Salmo gairdneri	Various invertebrates	Mixtures of L-amino acids (Adron and Mackie, 1978)
Anguilliformes European eel, Anguilla anguilla Japanese eel, A. japonica	Crustacea, molluscs, worms, small fish	Mixtures of L-amino acids (Mackie and Mitchell, 1983) Mixtures of L-amino acids (Takeda et al., 1984)
Perciformes Family Serranidae Sea bass, Dicentrarchus labrax	Juvenile: Crustacea, amphipods, small fish Adults: fish	Mixtures of L-amino acids (Mackie and Mitchell, 1982a)
Family Carangidae Yellowtail, Seriola quinqueradiata	Juveniles: cephalopods, fish Adults: fish	Inosine 5'-monophosphate (plus amino acids) (Hosokawa et al.; cited by Takeda et al., 1984)
Family Pomadasyidae Pigfish, Orthopristis chrysopterus	Various invertebrates, small fish	Glycine betaine plus L-amino acids (Carr et al., 1977)
Family Sparidae Red sea bream, Chrysophyrys major	Crustacea, worms	Glycine betaine plus L-amino acids (Goh and Tamura, 1980)
Pleuronectiformes Family Bothidae Turbot, Scophthalmus maximus	Juveniles: molluscs and worms Adults : fish	Inosine or inosine 5'-monophosphate (Mackie and Adron, 1978)
Brill, S. rhombus	Juveniles: molluscs and worms Adults : fish, squid, Crustacea	Inosine or inosine 5'-monophosphate (Mitchell, unpublished results)
Family Pleuronectidae Plaice, Pleuronectes platessa Dab, Limanda limanda	Worms, molluscs, Crustacea Crustacea mainly	Complex mixture of chemicals (Mackie, 1982)
Family Soleidae Dover sole, Solea solea	Worms, molluscs, Crustacea	Glycine betaine plus L-amino acids (Mackie et al., 1980)
Tetraodontiformes Puffer, Fugu pardalis	Worms, molluscs, Crustacea	Glycine betaine plus L-amino acids (Ohsugi et al., 1978)

Inosine and inosine 5'-monophosphate are the specific feeding stimulants for the turbot (Mackie and Adron, 1978) and the brill (Mitchell, unpublished results). Juveniles of both species eat molluscs and worms, while adult turbot eat fish and adult brill eat fish, squid and Crustacea, all these prey organisms containing free inosine 5'-monophosphate. Inosine 5'-monophosphate has also been reported to act as feeding stimulant for ·juvenile yellow-tail, the effect being potentiated by amino acids (Hosokawa et al., cited by Takeda et al., 1984). In this connection it is interesting that Takeda et al. (1984) found that uridine 5'-monophosphate potentiated the feeding stimulant activity of amino-acids for the Japanese eel, while inosine 5'-monophosphate did not.

The puffer, red sea bream and Dover sole each eat worms, molluscs and crustacea which all contain glycine betaine and free L-amino acids, the feeding stimulants. The situation is rather more complicated in the case of the pigfish, whose feeding stimulant is again a mixture of glycine betaine and L-amino acids (Carr et al., 1977). In addition to consuming a variety of invertebrates the pigfish is also reported to eat small fish. It is generally considered that teleost fish contain little or no glycine betaine (Love, 1970), while invertebrates and elasmobranchs are rich in this chemical. However, Carr et al. (1977) have reported fairly high levels of glycine betaine in extracts of mullet tissue. Relatively few species of teleost have in fact been analysed for glycine betaine, so it may simply be that there is a large interspecies variation in glycine betaine content.

Our studies involved fairly short-term feeding experiments. To check that the feeding stimulants were equally effective over a longer period, a study was made with the Dover sole in which a casein diet was compared with a fishmeal diet, both containing added glycine betaine and glycine. Initially both diets were consumed to the same extent, but the amount of casein diet eaten gradually decreased with time (Table V), resulting in a corresponding decrease in growth rate (Fig. 1). This decrease in food consumption could be due to a change in the palatability of the casein diet with time - the sole may gradually lose their liking for the taste of glycine betaine plus glycine, requiring another factor present in the fishmeal. Another explanation is, however, possible. Casein is low in sulphur amino acids, so the decrease in food consumption could be due to a loss of appetite arising from a nutritional imbalance. Dose-response

Table V. Consumption of fishmeal and casein diets

Time (days)	Moist diet eaten/100 g fish/day (g)	
	White fish meal diet	Casein diet
0	1.3	1.2
20	1.3	0.9
42	1.4	0.9
63	1.3	0.8
83	1.4	0.8

Both diets contained added glycine betaine (10^{-5} mole/g) plus glycine (2 x 10^{-5} mole/g)

curves were determined with casein diets for squid ethanol extract, "synthetic squid mixture" and glycine betaine plus glycine, to ascertain whether these stimulants were equally effective.

The squid extract and synthetic mixture had equal feeding stimulant activity at the concentrations tested (Fig. 2). However, the glycine betaine plus glycine was only about 60% as active, indicating that some as yet unidentified chemical enhances the feeding stimulant activity. Metailler et al. (1983) have found that inosine enhances the feeding stimulant activity of a mixture of glycine betaine and amino acids for baby sole. It had already been shown (Mackie et al., 1980) that glycine betaine alone could act as a feeding stimulant for adult sole, while the presence of amino acids was also required for juveniles. In addition to acting as a feeding stimulant glycine betaine is also a food attractant for sole. Glycine betaine has also been reported to reinforce the attractive effect of mixtures of L-amino acids for juvenile yellowtail (Harada and Matsuda, 1984).

In the plaice and dab, both the L-amino acid mixture and the non-amino acid components were moderately effective as feeding stimulants, but neither fraction was as active as the complete mixture. A decision as to whether there are synergistic interactions between, for example, glycine betaine and amino acids would require the

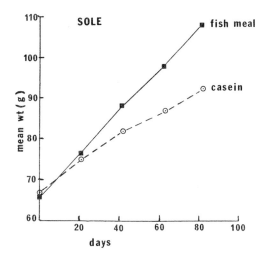

Fig. 1. Growth of Dover sole on moist fish meal and casein diets, both containing added glycine betaine (10^{-5}mole/g) and glycine $(2 \times 10^{-5}\text{mole/g})$.

determination of dose–response curves for the various constituents. Glycine betaine alone was without effect, but omission of this chemical from the non–amino acid fraction abolished feeding stimulant activity (Mackie, 1982).

IV. APPLICATIONS IN AQUACULTURE

The results help to explain some of the problems encountered in the farming of sole and turbot. Thus, with the sole, fishmeal prepared from mainly teleost waste will be low in glycine betaine, which can be supplied by adding Nephrops or scallop waste to the diets. Identification of inosine and inosine 5'-monophosphate as the feeding stimulants for turbot is consistent with the finding that some fishmeal diets are less palatable than others; if the fish waste used in the manufacture of the fishmeal was spoiled, inosine will have decomposed to the inactive hypoxanthine. Addition of crystalline inosine or inosine 5'-monophosphate restored palatability to such diets.

As plant and other novel proteins are substituted for fishmeal in commerical diets, a knowledge of feeding stimulants and deterrents will have increasing

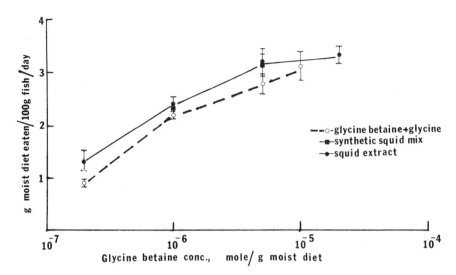

Fig. 2. Comparison of feeding stimulant activities of squid extract, synthetic squid mixture and glycine betaine plus glycine for Dover sole, initial mean weight 45 g.

importance. Unpalatability may be due to two factors – absence of feeding stimulant or presence of feeding deterrent. Thus, it has been reported that substituting leaf protein concentrate for some of the fishmeal resulted in a diet with reduced palatability for rainbow trout (Gwiazda et al., 1983). Chlorogenic acid, a phenolic germination inhibitor, would appear to be the feeding deterrent present in the leaf material.

A large number of feeding deterrents are produced by terrestrial plants against herbivores (Rosenthal and Janzen, 1979). If plant materials are incorporated into fish diets, these compounds may be present and act as feeding deterrents for the fish. It does appear that substances tasting bitter or astringent to the human tongue act as feeding deterrents for the puffer (Hidaka et al., 1978), the turbot (Mackie, 1982) and the Dover sole (Mackie and Mitchell, 1982b).

Terrestrial and aquatic oligochaete worms are being used in waste management and are a valuable source of protein for animal feed. One of the most successful species is the earthworm Eisenia foetida, used in the poultry and pig industries. Experiments with rainbow trout, however, indicate that this worm is totally unpalatable (Tacon et al., 1983). Whether the feeding deterrent is present in the mucous secretions or in the coelomic fluid remains to be determined.

It might be possible in some cases to overcome the effects of feeding deterrents by increasing the level of feeding stimulant, but this may not be advisable since many feeding deterrents are toxic.

Another aspect of fish farming where feeding stimulants may have a useful role to play is in the development of compounded diets for fish larvae, this subject being discussed by Bromley in this volume. Factors other than smell and taste may be important since some larvae detect live food visually or via vibrations set up in the water by prey. Four-day-old Dover sole larvae feed on Artemia nauplii only under illumination, while the settled stage, 7 to 16 days old, feed both in darkness and in light (Appelbaum et al., 1983).

Dover sole larvae, initial mean weight 120 mg, have been successfully weaned on to a crumble diet by the incorporation of a mixture of glycine betaine, glycine and inosine, survival over a 40 day period being over 70% (Metailler et al., 1983). A similar experiment with turbot larvae, initial mean weight 160 mg, incorporating large amounts of inosine, resulted in a survival of 93% after 45 days (Person-LeRuyet et al., 1983).

V.   CONCLUSIONS AND PROSPECTS

The feeding stimulants identified so far belong to a fairly small group of chemicals - L-amino acids, glycine betaine and inosine or inosine 5'-monophosphate. Many more species will have to be studied before it can be determined how general this is, but with the present knowledge, a mixture of these chemicals can be termed the "universal feeding stimulant".

One species being investigated in Europe for its potential for farming is the halibut, which belong to the same Family as the plaice and dab but which more resembles the brill in its food organisms. It will therefore be interesting to determine the nature of the feeding stimulant, to ascertain which factor is more important, the taxonomic position of the fish, or its food organism. Unfortunately, difficulties encountered at the larval stage have seriously hampered progress with the halibut. There is also a possibility of the cod being farmed or ranched and a start has been made on the characterization of the feeding stimulant (Johnstone et al., in preparation).

The main use for feeding stimulants so far has been in the field of experimental nutrition and larval food development. When studying the vitamin, mineral or lipid requirements of fish, it is often necessary to use vitamin-free casein diets which are generally unpalatable to fish without the addition of the appropriate feeding stimulant. The food consumption, and therefore growth or survival, of larval fish can be increased by increasing the concentration of the feeding stimulants of the adult forms (Metailler et al., 1983; Person-LeRuyet et al., 1983). In the future, however, greater use will be made of feeding stimulants for fish of all ages, particularly as other proteins are substituted for the presently ubiquitous fishmeal. Problems of acceptability and palatability have until now been relatively rare, but this has been more luck than good management and it is unlikely that this luck will last forever.

REFERENCES

Adron, J.W. and Mackie, A.M. (1978). J. Fish Biol. 12, 303–310.
Appelbaum, S., Adron, J.W., George, S.G., Mackie, A.M. and Pirie, B.J.S. (1983). J. mar. biol. Ass. U.K. 63, 97–108.
Carr, W.E.S., Blumethal, K.M. and Netherton, J.C. III. (1977). Comp. Biochem. Physiol., 58A, 69–73.
Degani, G. and Levanon, D. (1983). Bamidgeh 35, 53–60.
Goh, Y. and Tamura, T. (1980). Comp. Biochem. Physiol. 66C, 225–229.
Gwiazda, S., Noguchi, A., Kitamura, S. and Saio, K. (1983). Agric. Biol. Chem. 47, 623–625.
Harada, K. and Matsuda, H. (1984). Bull. Jap. Soc.scient. Fish. 50, 623–626.
Hashimoto, Y., Konosu, S., Fusetani, N. and Nose, T. (1968). Bull. Jap. Soc. scient. Fish. 34, 78–83.
Hidaka, I., Ohsugi, T. and Kubomatsu, T. (1978). Chem. Senses Flavour 3, 341–354.
Lindstedt, K.J. (1971). Comp. Biochem. Physiol. 39A, 553–581.

Love, R.M. (1970). The Chemical Biology of Fishes. Academic Press, London and New York.

Mackie, A.M. (1973). Mar. Biol. 21, 103-108.

Mackie, A.M. (1982). In "Chemoreception in Fishes" (T.J. Hara, ed.), 275-291. Elsevier Scientific Publishing Co., Amsterdam.

Mackie, A.M. and Adron, J.W. (1978). Comp. Biochem. Physiol. 60A, 79-83.

Mackie, A.M. and Mitchell, A.I. (1982b). Comp. Biochem. Physiol. 73A, 89-93.

Mackie, A.M. and Mitchell, A.I. (1983). J. Fish Biol. 22, 425-430.

Mackie, A.M., Adron, J.W. and Grant, P.T. (1980). J. Fish Biol. 16, 701-708.

Metailler, R., Cadena-Roa, M. and Person-LeRuyet, J. (1983). J. World Maricult.Soc. 14, 679-684.

Ohsugi, T., Hidaka, I. and Ikeda, M. (1978). Chem. Senses Flavour 3, 555-568.

Person-LeRuyet, J., Menu, B., Cadena-Roa, M. and Metailler, R. (1983). J. World Maricult. Soc. 14, 676-678.

Rosenthal, G.A. and Janzen, D.H. (1979). Herbivores. Their Interaction with Secondary Plant Metabolites. Academic Press, New York and London.

Tacon, A.G.J., Stafford, E.A. and Edwards, C.A. (1983). Aquaculture 35, 187-199.

Takeda, M., Takii, K. and Matsui, K. (1984). Bull. Jap. Soc. scient. Fish. 59, 645-651.

WEANING DIETS FOR TURBOT (SCOPHTHALMUS MAXIMUS L.), SOLE (SOLEA SOLEA) (L.) AND COD (GADUS MORHUA L.)

P.J. BROMLEY and P.A. SYKES

Ministry of Agriculture, Fisheries and Food,
Directorate of Fisheries Research,
Fisheries Laboratory,
Lowestoft, Suffolk, NR33 OHT, U.K.

I. INTRODUCTION

The pelagic, early larval stages of marine fish are primarily visual feeders and have otherwise poorly developed sensory and digestive systems (Iwai, 1980; Govoni, 1981). They are generally difficult to rear on artificial food (Adron et al., 1974; Girin, 1979; Limborgh, 1979; Meyers, 1979) and live food is at present the best practical solution to the early feeding problem.

The prolonged use of live food can be costly and variations in quality can adversely affect survival and growth of the fish (Lee and Hirano, 1981; Dabrowski and Rusiecki, 1983; Watanabe et al ., 1978 and 1982). An early change to an artificial food is therefore desirable (Bromley, 1979a; Jones, 1981). This has led to the development of a wide variety of methods for weaning fish from live foods to artificial foods. This is usually attempted during the larval or early juvenile phase, depending on which is the most practical.

Turbot and sole are potentially two of the most valuable species for cultivation (Purdom, 1973; Jones, 1972) and practical weaning methods have been developed for both species (Bromley, 1977; Bromley and Howell, 1983; Fuchs, 1982; Métailler et al., 1981). Turbot which are farmed commercially are currently weaned at a length of about 2 cm (Jones et al., 1981).

It is important to identify the major factors which govern the acceptance of artificial food, in order to improve the reliability of weaning methods.   Recent work with juvenile sole shows the importance of taste attractants in aiding the acceptance of extruded pellets (Cadena Roa et al., 1982).   Recent studies on turbot (Bromley and Howell, 1983) indicate that the quality of the live food used to rear turbot larvae can have a marked influence on the acceptance of weaning foods.

This paper concentrates on the weaning of turbot and sole. Advances in the technique for the early weaning of turbot are presented and preliminary studies on cod are also included.   The main areas of study include the effects of food type, particle size and live food quality on weaning. Performance during weaning was assessed in terms of the feeding response, survival and growth rate of the fish.

II. MATERIALS AND METHODS

A. Egg and larval supply

Eggs were obtained from broodstocks maintained at the Laboratory.   Egg incubation and larval rearing were based on the methods of Howell (1979) for turbot, Howell (1984) for cod, and Bromley (1977) for sole.   Sole were fed on Artemia salina nauplii.   Turbot and cod were fed first on rotifers (Brachionus plicatilis) and then on Artemia. Some turbot were reared entirely on rotifers, with Isochrysis sp. added to the tanks as food for the rotifers.

B. Weaning tanks

The sole were weaned in blue circular tanks (Fig. 1A) based on the design used by Bromley (1977).   Turbot and cod were weaned in black circular tanks (Fig. 1B) similar to those used by Bromley (1978).   In two instances, turbot were weaned in 60 x 30 x 60 cm deep rectangular tanks.

Sea water was supplied to each tank at the rate of 30-40 l h^{-1}.   Temperature was maintained at 16-18°C for turbot and sole, and at 10-12°C for cod. The water was aerated with a diffuser stone, and constant illumination from fluorescent tubes gave surface light levels of 200-400 lux.   The tanks were cleaned daily with a siphon.

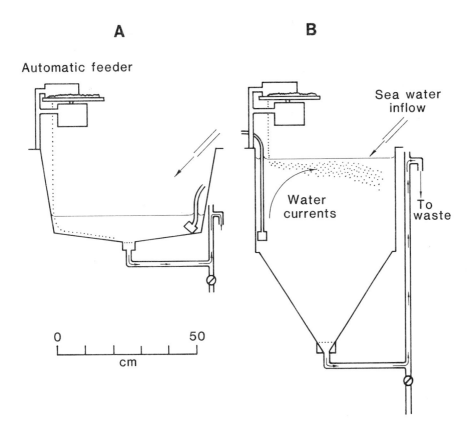

Fig. 1. Vertical sections of the tanks used to wean sole (1,A), turbot larvae and cod (1,B) with automatic feeders.

C. Weaning foods

The weaning foods included a standard weaning food (A); fish powder (B); mussel powder (C); salmon starter food (D); trout starter food (E); microcapsules with nylon/protein coat (F).

Foods A, B and C were prepared from the ingredients listed in Table I. The wet ingredients were homogenised and then mixed with the finely milled, dry ingredients. The foods were dried at 80°C before being milled and sieved to the requisite particle size, in the range 0.15-1.0 mm.

Table I. The composition of turbot weaning diets.

Contents	Diet and % composition		
	A (Standard weaning food)	B	C
White fish meal	30.4	–	–
Trout starter food	30.4	–	–
Vitamin mix[1]	1	1	1
Mineral mix[1]	1	–	–
Cod liver oil	2.4	–	–
Lugworm (Arenicola marina)	16.2	–	–
Shucked mussel (Mytilus edulis)	16.2	–	99
Black treacle	2.4	–	–
Sandeel (Ammodytes sp.)	–	60	–
Herring (Clupea harengus)	–	39	–

[1] After Castell and Tiews 1980, but without α-cellulose.

D. Weaning strategies

All experimental treatments were duplicated.

Feeding was to excess, either by hand 6-8 times a day or by automatic feeders of the revolving disc type which dispensed a continuous trickle of food. The change from live food to weaning food was made abruptly, except that supplements of Artemia were used in one experiment with sole.

Juvenile sole take food off the bottom. Cod and turbot larvae feed in the pelagic phase and aeration was used to generate water currents to disperse the food (Fig. 1). The methods used were described by Bromley (1979a).

E. Sampling

Mortalities were recorded daily and dead fish removed. The incidence of feeding in turbot larvae was estimated in situ from counts of the larvae which had food visible as an orange mass through the translucent body wall, or by the numbers of larvae with swollen stomachs after feeding.

Sole were removed from the tanks and the level of

Table II Details of larvae, foods and the duration of the series of weaning experiments

Treatment	Experiment							
	Sole		Turbot larvae					Cod
	1	2	3	4[1]	5[1]	6[2]	7[3]	8
Live foods prior to weaning[4]	Braz.	SF	SF	Various	SF on rotifers	Rotifers	Rotifers	Braz.
Number of larvae (duplicated)	50	50	30	11-32	20	50	30	25
Body length mm (± S.E.)	16(0.3)	23(0.5)	7.2(0.2) 10.8(0.2) 12.7(0.2)[5]	26-29	16-26	7-8	3.6(0.1)	25-30
Weaning foods	D	D+ Artemia supplement	A,B,C,F and mixture	E	E	A	A	D
Daily ration (g)	1.5	4	4	1.5	2	3	0.5	3
Particle size range (mm)	0.15-0.25 0.25-0.5 0.5-1.0	0.15-1.0	0.25-0.35	0.35-1.0	0.5-1.0	0.15-0.35	< 0.35	0.5-1.0
Foods for the controls	-	D only	Artemia	E fed to weaned fish	E	Rotifers	Live and frozen rotifers	Artemia
Duration of weaning experiment (d)	7	51	5-13	13	15	11	1 h	14

1 using rectangular tanks
2 results for three batches of larvae pooled
3 results for two batches of larvae pooled, using 10 l tanks
4 Braz. = Brazilian Artemia, SF = San Franciscan Artemia
5 fed on rotifers for the week before weaning

Table III. The influence of food particle size on the
stomach contents of sole one week after the start of
weaning (Food D, Experiment 2).

Stomach contents	Food particle size in mm		
	0.15–0.25	0.25–0.5	0.5–1
I Empty (%)	9	5	4
II Up to half-full (%)	51	60	54
III half-full to full (%)	40	35	42

(χ^2 = 3.69 with 6 d.f. Not significant at the P = 0.05 leve

stomach fullness was estimated on a scale I = empty, II =
up to half full, III = from half-full to full.

Samples of larvae were measured at the start and at
intervals to determine growth.

III. EXPERIMENTAL AND RESULTS

A series of experiments was conducted and the results
were pooled when applicable. Details of the fish, foods,
controls and the duration of weaning are shown in Table II.

A. Sole
Experiments 1 and 2. The influence of food particle size
and Artemia supplements during weaning.

Weaning was conducted with and without live food
supplements. Batches of 100,000 Artemia nauplii were
added at 1–3 d intervals for the first 19 d, alongside the
weaning diet. The water flow was turned off for 1 h and
then turned up to flush out the excess over 1–2 h.

Stomach content analysis of sole one week after the
start of weaning (Table III, Experiment 1) showed that
16 mm sole were feeding at similar rates on particle sizes
within the range 0.15–1.0 mm (χ^2, P > 0.05).

The feeding, growth and survival of 23 mm sole weaned
with and without Artemia supplements for the first 19 d
are summarised in Fig. 2 and 3 (Experiment 2).

Increasing the frequency of live food additions delayed
the onset and slowed down the rate of mortalities, but

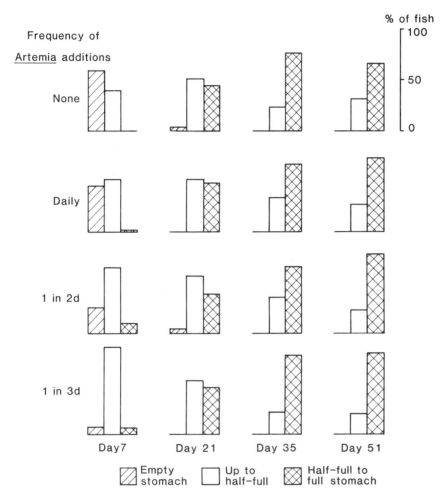

Fig. 2. The stomach contents of sole during weaning on salmon food with Artemia supplements for the first 19 d. (Food D, Experiment 2).

increased the period over which they occurred. Consequently, eventual survival was much the same for all treatments, ranging from 45–52%.

There were some differences in stomach contents and growth rate between treatments during the time that Artemia supplements were being used (Fig. 3). However, from day 21 onwards there were no significant differences in stomach contents (χ^2, $P > 0.05$), or in growth rate ($P > 0.05$) between treatments. The amount of food in the

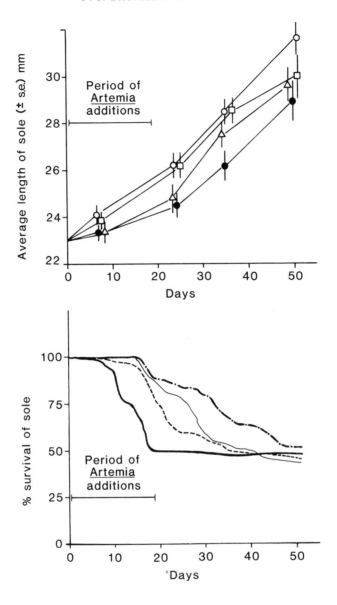

Fig. 3. The growth and survival of sole during weaning on salmon food, with <u>Artemia</u> supplements for the first 19 d. (Food D, Experiment 2). Frequency of <u>Artemia</u> additions: **o** = daily; Δ = 1 in 2 d; □ = 1 in 3 d; ● = none; ▬•▬•▬ = daily; ──────── = 1 in 2 d; ▬▬▬ = 1 in 3 day; ▬▬▬▬ = none.

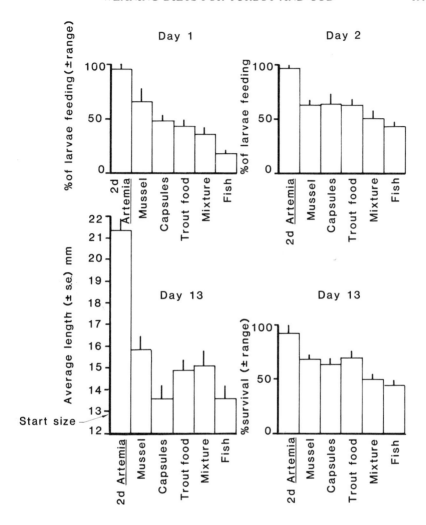

Fig. 4. The feeding, growth and survival of 12.7 mm turbot larvae during weaning on a variety of foods. (Experiment 3).

stomach increased only slowly with time, reaching a maximum on day 35. The amount of food in the stomach one week after the start of weaning was less (χ^2, P = 0.05) than in the previous experiment with 16 mm sole (Table III).

B. Turbot

Experiment 3. The influence of food type on weaning

(Foods A, B, C, F and a mixture of all four).

Three size ranges of larvae were tested. Larvae reared on San Franciscan <u>Artemia</u> to a length of 7.2 and 10.8 mm gave a poor feeding response during weaning and after 5 d only 2-6% of the 7.2 mm larvae and 5-14% of the 10.8 mm larvae were feeding on any of the diets tested.

The feeding response of the 12.7 mm larvae, which had been fed on rotifers for the week prior to weaning, was much improved (Fig. 4) and 19-63% fed within 1 d.

The mussel powder was the most readily accepted of the artificial foods, and the maximum feeding response occurred after 1 d, at which time 63% of larvae were feeding. Similar numbers of larvae fed on the trout food and microcapsules, but the larvae took 2 d to fully establish feeding. The mixture and the fish powder were eaten by somewhat fewer larvae.

Two-way analysis of variance of the number of larvae feeding over the first 4 d on the various artificial foods showed significant differences in feeding response with time ($F = 6.3$, $P = 0.01$, 3 and 12 degrees of freedom) and between diets ($F = 7.4$, $P = 0.01$, 4 and 12 degrees of freedom). This shows that there were significant differences in both the rate of adaptation to the different diets and in the eventual proportion of larvae which commenced feeding. Analysis of the data for days 5-8 showed no further significant change in the numbers feeding with time over this period ($P > 0.05$), but the difference between diets was sustained and was highly significant ($F = 26.6$, $P < 0.001$, 4 and 12 degrees of freedom).

Percentage survival on day 13 (Fig. 4) closely matched the percentage of larvae feeding on day 2, indicating that the success of weaning was determined at an early stage. Most mortalities occurred between days 2-5.

In comparison with the controls fed on 2-day-old <u>Artemia</u>, growth rates were poor during weaning, particularly in larvae feeding on microcapsules and fish powder. The microcapsules appeared to pass through the gut without the coating being ruptured.

Table IV   The influence of Artemia quality on growth and survival during the weaning of turbot larvae (Food E, Experiment 4)

Diet for 24 d prior to weaning	Start			Day 13				
	Number (duplicated)	Length ± s.e. (cm)	Weight ± s.e. (g)	Length ± s.e. (cm)	Weight ± s.e. (g)	% survival	Length increase (mm d^{-1})	Weight gain (% d^{-1})
Weaned controls	11	2.9±0.1	0.41±0.03	4.1±0.1	1.14±0.10	95	0.92	13.7
Brazilian nauplii	31	2.9±0.1	0.31±0.01	3.5±0.1	0.62±0.03	94	0.46	7.7
San Franciscan nauplii	13	2.6±0.1	0.24±0.02	2.9±0.1	0.36±0.06	35	0.23	3.8
San Franciscan nauplii, pre-fed	20	2.5±0.1	0.24±0.02	3.0±0.1	0.34±0.02	57	0.38	3.2
San Franciscan nauplii, pre-fed + algae in tank	21	2.9±0.1	0.36±0.02	3.2±0.1	0.44±0.03	76	0.23	1.7

Experiment 4. The influence of Artemia type and quality
on weaning.

Larvae were fed for 24 d prior to weaning on an excess of
either:

1.   Brazilian Artemia nauplii;
2.   San Franciscan Artemia nauplii;
3.   San Franciscan Artemia nauplii which had been fed
      for 4 h at 28°C on Isochrysis;
4.   As 3, but with an excess of Isochrysis added to
      the tanks as food for the Artemia.

Each day, prior to feeding, twenty food particles were
added to each tank over a 5 min period. The number of
feeding strikes and food particles consumed was recorded.
     When Artemia of differing type and quality were used to
rear turbot larvae the effects on growth and survival
during weaning proved to be considerable (Table IV).
Analysis of variance showed significant differences
(P < 0.05) in percentage survival with time and between
treatments.   Most mortalities occurred between days
5–10.   The feeding response was similarly affected, as
can be judged from the proportion of food particles which
was subjected to feeding strikes and the proportion which
was consumed (Fig. 5) when 20 food particles were added
over a 5-min period.
     Larvae reared on San Franciscan Artemia nauplii fed
poorly during weaning and survival was only 35%.   At the
other extreme, larvae reared on Brazilian Artemia nauplii
readily started feeding on artificial food and survival
was 94%.

     Feeding the San Franciscan Artemia nauplii on
Isochrysis prior to feeding it to the larvae led to
improved weaning survival and growth, and adding
Isochrysis to the tanks led to further improvement in
weaning survival.   However, neither feeding response,
growth rate nor survival during weaning reached the level
achieved by turbot which had been reared on Brazilian
Artemia nauplii.   Prior to weaning, growth had only been
marginally faster on Brazilian Artemia nauplii, which
accounted for the slight size difference at the start of
weaning (Table IV).
     Food capture efficiency, in terms of the proportion of
feeding strikes which resulted in the food being consumed,
was high at the beginning of feeding and by day 7 feeding

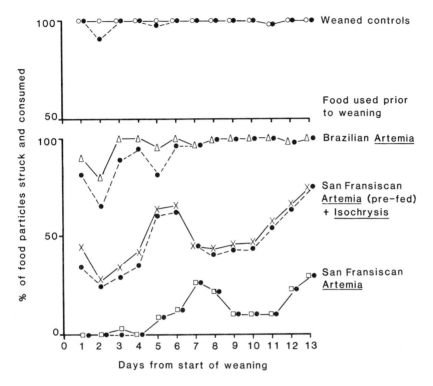

Fig. 5. The percentage of food particles which were subjected to feeding strikes ($\circ,\Delta,\times,\square$) and the percentage consumed ($\bullet$) by turbot larvae which had been fed on Artemia of differing quality prior to weaning. (Food E, Experiment 4).

strikes were almost always successful.

Experiment 5. Rate of development of an adverse weaning response caused by prior feeding on San Franciscan Artemia.

Larvae were fed entirely on rotifers. They were then switched to feed on San Franciscan Artemia and batches were weaned at 3 d intervals over the next 12 d. Larvae reared conventionally on San Franciscan Artemia were used as the controls.

The feeding response and survival of turbot larvae which had been switched from rotifers to San Franciscan Artemia for up to 12 d prior to weaning is shown in Fig. 6 and Table V. Analysis of variance showed significant

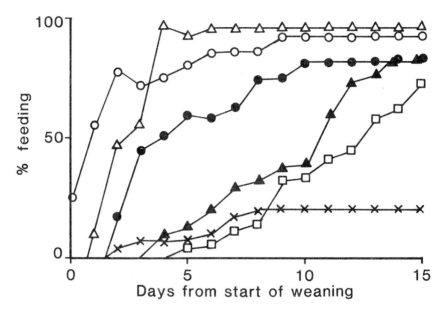

Fig. 6. The feeding response of turbot larvae which had been fed on San Franciscan Artemia for different lengths of time prior to weaning; o = none; Δ = 3 d; ● = 6 d; = 9 d; □ = 12 d; × = controls reared on San Franciscan Artemia. (Food E, Experiment 5).

differences (P < 0.05) in survival and in the numbers of larvae feeding with time and between treatments. There was little difference in the performance of turbot which had been feeding for 3 d on the San Franciscan Artemia, but thereafter the rate of acceptance of weaning food slowed down and mortalities increased.

Weaning survival of the larvae reared in conventional fashion on San Franciscan Artemia, to act as controls, was only 20%, as against 92% survival of larvae reared on rotifers.

During the time spent feeding on Artemia prior to weaning, growth was rapid, as can be judged from the size of the larvae at weaning (Table V).

Experiment 6. Early weaning of turbot larvae from rotifers.

Larvae of 7–8 mm in length, which had been reared for about 15 d on rotifers, readily accepted the standard weaning food (Fig. 7). The average survival for three batches of larvae was 76%, as against 92% for the controls

Table V. The effects of the duration of feeding with San Franciscan _Artemia_ nauplii on weaning survival and feeding response in turbot larvae (Food E, Experiment 5).

Live foods used prior to weaning	Average length of turbot (mm) ± s.e.	Weaning survival (%)	Days taken for 50% of larve to start feeding
San Franciscan _Artemia_ (controls)	15.6 ± 0.3	20	Not reached
Rotifers only	16.1 ± 0.3	92	1
Rotifers + 3 d on San Franciscan nauplii	19.3 ± 0.3	95	2.5
Rotifers + 6 d on San Franciscan nauplii	21.0 ± 0.3	81	4
Rotifers + 9 d on San Franciscan nauplii	23.1 ± 0.4	82	10.5
Rotifers + 12 d on San Franciscan nauplii	26.0 ± 0.4	72	12.5

on rotifers. Growth averaged 0.25 (range ± 0.05) mm d^{-1} on the weaning diet and 0.5 mm d^{-1} on rotifers.

Experiment 7. Feeding responses in 3.6 mm larvae.

Larvae were fed for 2 d on rotifers and then offered either standard weaning food (food A), live or frozen rotifers at a concentration of 10 ml^{-1} for 1 h in 10 l tanks. The stomach contents were dissected out and counted.

In the 1 h food acceptance trials, the standard weaning food (food A) was not eaten (Table VI). A far greater proportion of larvae ate live rotifers compared with those feeding on frozen rotifers ($P < 0.001$). Feeding rates were also considerably higher on live rotifers ($P < 0.001$).

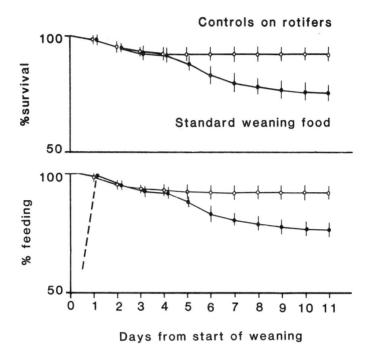

Fig. 7. The survival and growth of 7-8 mm larvae weaned directly from rotifers. The data is pooled for three batches of larvae. (Food A, Experiment 6)

Test diet	Percentage of larvae feeding (± s.e.)	Average number of food particles in the stomachs of feeding larvae (± s.e.)
Live rotifers	80 (7)	4.0 (0.2)
Frozen rotifers	10 (4)	1.3 (0.1)
Standard weaning food (Food A)	0	0

Table VI. The feeding of 3.6 mm turbot larvae on live and dead food for 1 h. The data is pooled for two batches of larvae (Experiment 7).

C. Cod

Experiment 8. Preliminary weaning trial.

Cod of 2.5–3 cm readily accepted salmon food (food D). Survival after 2 weeks ranged from 45–64%. This compares favourably with 52% survival achieved by the controls feeding on Artemia over the same period.
It was clear that many mortalities were due to cannibalism and damage from attacks. Sometimes cod attempted to eat others of a similar size. In this respect cod differs from turbot and sole, where cannibalism was not a significant problem.

IV. DISCUSSION

Turbot, sole and cod could all be weaned by similar methods using dry powdered foods. Frequent feeding to excess, by hand or automatically, reduced the risk of problems caused by the leaching of nutrients (Goldblatt et al., 1979). Simple modifications to the position and strength of the aeration enabled currents to be generated to disperse the food for pelagic larvae. This is particularly suitable for turbot larvae which will swim into a current just below the surface in the path of the food. Food particle sizes of the same order as those of live food proved satisfactory.
A variety of the species have been weaned using a range of approaches and food types, including moist crumbles, pastes and dry powders. The ingredients used, including the levels of vitamins, minerals and taste attractants have also varied (Barahona-Fernandez et al., 1977; Ramos et al., 1979; Bedier, 1981; Alpbaz, 1978; Hussain and Higuchi, 1980; Métailler et al., 1981; Person le Ruyet et al., 1981).
The three main approaches used are: (1) an abrupt change to the weaning food; (2) the addition of live food supplements for a period alongside the weaning food; (3) food organisms are mixed in with the weaning food and then phased out.
The existence of so many variables makes it difficult to generalise on the relative merits of these approaches, but obviously the simplest method which yields good results is the most acceptable. Sole derived no long-term

benefits from Artemia supplements for 19 d.   Those fish
not amenable to weaning were able to survive longer but
did not take advantage of this by learning to eat the
weaning food, so that eventual survival of the whole
population was similar to that of fish weaned abruptly.
However, there is evidence that Artemia supplements every
third day for 45 d improves survival in sole (Bromley,
1979a).   This is a cumbersome procedure and the addition
to the diet of taste attractants, such as glycine betaine
for sole (Cadena Roa et al., 1982; Mackie et al., 1980,
Mackie and Mitchell, this volume) offers a more practical
means of improving survival.   The high survival rates
possible using abrupt weaning methods in turbot also
support the suggestion that complicated weaning procedures
are unnecessary.

Turbot showed a preference for mussel rather than fish
powder.   In this respect, feeding preferences appear to
be similar to those of sole (Bromley, 1979b), whereas
larger turbot, which are piscivorous, respond to inosine
and inosine 5-monophosphate (Mackie and Adron, 1978),
substances more characteristic of fish than invertebrates.
It is perhaps to be expected that turbot larvae would
respond more to feeding attractants which are effective
for other invertebrate feeders than to those to which its
later piscivorous stages respond.

During the course of this work it became clear that in
turbot the overriding factor governing the acceptance of
weaning food was the quality of the live food used to rear
the larvae prior to weaning.   Rotifers, with Isochrysis
in the water, and Brazilian Artemia nauplii were
particularly good in this respect;   San Franciscan nauplii
were poor.   The exclusive use of rotifers before weaning
was undoubtedly one of the important factors contributing
to the 76% survival of 7-8 mm larvae during weaning. This
was much higher than had previously been achieved.
Survival rates of larger larvae which had been reared on
rotifers and Brazilian Artemia reached 90-95%, compared
with 20-35% when San Franciscan Artemia were used.   The
adverse effect of using San Franciscan Artemia on
subsequent weaning success developed quite rapidly,
becoming significant about 6 days after the change from
rotifers and progressing with time.   However, there was
evidence that the adverse effects could be reversed by
transferring the larvae back to rotifers for one week
(Experiment 3).

The effects of Artemia quality do not appear to have
been studied in other species.   However, it may be

significant that the sole reared on Brazilian nauplii (Experiment 1) showed a better initial feeding response than those reared on San Franciscan nauplii (Experiment 2). Early attempts to wean cod which had been reared on San Franciscan Artemia also gave poor results (unpublished data). Adversely affected turbot appear normal and will feed and grow on San Franciscan Artemia.

The cause and mode of action of the adverse weaning response is not known. The problem appears to lie in the area of food recognition. Analysis indicated that San Franciscan Artemia contained no detectable levels of pesticides or PCBs. The levels of 20:4 ω 6 and 20:5 ω 3 fatty acids were lower than in Brazilian Artemia (Howell, personal communication) and the levels in the fish reflected those in the Artemia. However, since feeding the San Franciscan Artemia on Isochrysis improved their food value but did not appreciably alter their fatty acid content, it seems unlikely that fatty acid deficiency was implicated.

Experiments at Lowestoft have shown that in sole, first feeding larvae will eat mussel powder but die after about 10 d, possibly due to digestibility or nutritional problems. Turbot at first feeding have shown little signs of eating artificial food. The best survival rate so far achieved with first feeding turbot larvae using trout food is 0.1%, but there was evidence in this instance that larvae supplemented their diet with the occasional copepod larva which infiltrated the water supply system. The strong preference for live rather than dead rotifers exhibited by 3.6 mm turbot larvae suggests that the swimming movement of the prey may be an important feeding stimulus. The ability to wean later stage larvae successfully may be related to the development of sensory systems other than vision, which is believed to predominate in very early larvae (Iwai, 1980; Govoni, 1981). Other characteristics of the food, such as taste, may therefore become increasingly important in stimulating feeding as the larvae develop. However, this is a field of research which remains relatively unstudied.

REFERENCES

Adron, J.W., Blair, A. and Cowey, C.B. (1974). Fishery Bull. Fish Wildl. Serv. U.S. 72, 353-357.

Alpbaz, A.G. (1978). Zir. Fak. Yayinl., Ege Univ., Turkey (348) 52pp.

Barahona-Fernandes, N.H., Girion, M. and Métailler, R. (1977). Aquaculture 10, 53–63.

Bedier, E. (1981). Rapp. P.-v. Réun. Cons. int. Explor. Mer 178, 530–532.

Bromley, P.J. (1977). Aquaculture 12, 337–347.

Bromley, P.J. (1978). Aquaculture 13, 339–345.

Bromley, P.J. (1979a). In "Finfish Nutrition and Fishfeed Technology" (J.E. Halver and K. Tiews, eds.), 1, 449–455. Heenemann Verlagsgesellschaft, Berlin.

Bromley, P.J. (1979b). Fish Farmer 3, 26–27.

Bromley, P.J. and Howell, B.R. (1983). Aquaculture 31, 31–40.

Cadena Roa, M., Huelvan, C., Le Borgne, Y. and Métailler, R. (1982). J. Wld Maricult. Soc. 13, 246–253.

Castell, J.D. and Tiews, K. (1980). Report of the EIFAC, UINS and ICES Working Group on the Standardisation of Methodology in Fish Nutrition Research. Hamburg, FRG. 21–23 March, 1979. EIFAC Tech. Pap., (36), 24 pp.

Dabrowski, K. and Rusiecki, M. (1983). Aquaculture 30, 31–42.

Fuchs, J. (1982). Aquaculture 26, 339–358.

Girin, M. (1979). In "Finfish Nutrition and Fishfeed Technology", (J.E. Halver and K. Tiews, eds.), 1, 359–366. Heenemann Verlagsgesellschaft, Berlin.

Goldblatt, M.J., Conklin, D.E. and Brown, W.D. (1979). In "Finfish Nutrition and Fishfeed Technology", (J.E. Halver and K. Tiews, eds.), 2, 117–129. Heenemann Verlagsgesellschaft, Berlin.

Govoni, J.J. (1981). Rapp. P.-v. Réun. Cons. int. Explor. Mer 178, 314–315.

Howell, B.R. (1979). Aquaculture 18, 215–225.

Howell, B.R. (1984). In "The Propagation of Cod, Gadus morhua L.", (E. Dahl, D.S. Danielssen, E. Moksness and P. Solemdal, eds.), 657–675. Flodivigen Biological Station, Arendal, Norway.

Hussain, N.A. and Higuchi, M. (1980). Aquaculture 19, 339–450.

Iwai, T. (1980). In "Fish Behaviour and its Use in the Capture and Culture of Fishes", (J.E. Bardach, J.J. Magnuson, R.C. May and J.M. Reinhart, eds), 124–145. ICLARM, Manila, Philippines.

Jones, A. (1972). Lab. Leafl. MAFF Direct. Fish. Res. Lowestoft (24), 16 pp.

Jones A. (1981). Rapp. P.-v. Réun. Cons. int. Explor. Mer 178, 483–484.

Jones, A., Prickett, R.A. and Douglas, M.T. (1981). Rapp. P.-v. Réun. Cons. int. Explor. Mer 178, 522-526.

Lee, C.S., and Hirano, R. (1981). Rapp. P.-v. Réun. Cons. int. Explor. Mer 178, 533-537.

Limborgh, C.L. Van (1979). In "Finfish Nutrition and Fishfeed Technology", (J.E. Halver and K. Tiews, eds.), 2, 3-11. Heenemann Verlagsgesellschaft, Berlin.

Mackie, A.M. and Adron, J.W. (1978). Comp. Biochem. Physiol. 60, 79-83.

Mackie, A.M., Adron, J.W. and Grant, P.T. (1980). J. Fish Biol. 16, 701-708.

Métailler, R., Menn, B. and Morinière, P. (1981). J. Wld Maricult. Soc. 12, 111-116.

Meyers, S.P. (1979). In "Finfish Nutrition and Fishfeed Technology", (J.E. Halver and K. Tiews, eds.), 2, 13-20. Heenemann Verlagsgesellschaft, Berlin.

Person-Le Ruyet, J., Aleandre, J.C. and Le Roux, A. (1981). In "Aquaculture in Heated Effluents and Recirculation Systems", (K. Tiews, ed.), 2, 159-175. Heenemann Verlagsgesellschaft, Berlin.

Purdom, C.E. (1973). Fish Farm. Int. 1, 123-124.

Ramos, J., San Feliu, J.M., Amat, F. and Munoz, F. (1979). Inf. Tecn. Inst. Inv. Pesq. (61), 16 pp.

Watanabe, J., Kitajima, C., Arakawa, T., Fukusho, K. and Fujita, S. (1978). Bull. Jap. Soc. scient. Fish. 44, 1109-1114.

Watanabe, T., Ohta, M., Kitajima, C. and Fujita, S. (1982). Bull. Jap. Soc. scient. Fish. 48, 1775-1782.

EFFECTS OF ARTIFICIAL DIETS ON THE DIGESTIVE PROCESSES OF FISH LARVAE

R. HOFER

Institute of Zoology, University of Innsbruck, Austria

In spite of intensive efforts during recent years little progress has been made in developing artificial diets for fish larvae. During their first stages larvae of many species still have to be reared on expensive live zooplankton. Although artificial diets are accepted by most fish they lead to low growth rates and to high mortality when fed exclusively between hatching and "metamorphosis" of the fish. The reasons for these difficulties are not fully understood:

Flüchter (1982) believes in the existence of an unknown essential substance, present only in native diets, which is necessary for the development of fish larvae. On the other hand, the very short and simple digestive tract of many fish larvae suggests a lower food utilization rate than in adult fish.

Whitefish larvae, for instance, utilize only 70% of cladoceran (Moina sp.) protein (Hofer, unpublished), whereas utilization efficiencies of 80–90% have been reported for animal proteins by adults of several species (Beamish, 1972; Kelso, 1972; Hofer, 1982). Moreover, living prey contain digestive enzymes which support and accelerate the digestive processes of the predator. In whitefish larvae these exogenous proteases represent up to 70% of the total proteolytic activity of the digestive tract (Lauff and Hofer, 1984). However, attempts to improve artificial diets by adding digestive enzymes have had little or no success (Dabrowski and Glogowski, 1977; Ostroumova, 1977; Dabrowska et al., 1979).

NUTRITION AND FEEDING IN FISH
ISBN: 0 12 194055 1

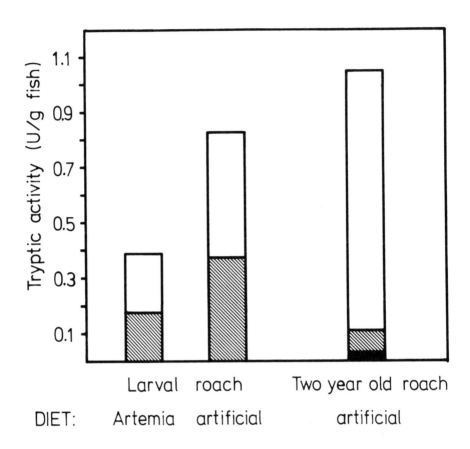

Fig. 1. Tryptic activities (units per g body weight) of the intestinal contents of larval (13 days after hatching) and two year old roach. Data are taken from Hofer and Nasir Uddin (1985) and Hofer (1982).

Total columns: Tryptic activity of total intestinal contents. The activity of Artemia-fed larvae contains also a certain amount of exogenous trypsin.

Hatched columns: Tryptic activity in the contents of the second half of the intestine.

Black columns: Faecal losses of trypsin (measured only in two year old fish).

In larvae the activity of digestive enzymes is generally low but increases with age (Lauff and Hofer, 1984; Dabrowski, 1979). Moreoever, in several species acid proteolysis is developed only at the end of "metamorphosis" (Grizzle and Curd, 1978; Mähr et al., 1983).

As mentioned above, the intestine of fish larvae is very short. In roach larvae the intestine amounts to only 45% of the body length (l_c) compared to about 102% in adults. Since intestinal length and gut passage time are positively correlated in larvae the diet passes the intestine within 2.5 hours at 20°C whereas retention time in adults is extended to about 6 hours. With increasing gut passage time digestion, resorption and recovery of digestive enzymes in the hindgut of the fish are all improved. In adult roach only 3% of all the trypsin produced is lost in the faeces (Hofer, 1982) and in the contents of the second half of the intestine tryptic activity is reduced to only 12% of total activity. In roach larvae, however, tryptic activity in the second half of the intestine amounts to 46% of total activity (Hofer and Nasir Uddin, 1985, see Fig. 1). This compensates for the short intestine by extending the time at which enzymes may act on the food, but, on the other hand, the loss of body proteins is increased. In roach larvae artificial diets induce increased trypsin production which may become twice as high as with native diets and of the same magnitude as in adults (Fig. 1, Hofer and Nasir Uddin, 1985). Whatever the reason for this reaction (impeded digestibility or lack of essential substances), it leads to an increased loss of body proteins. Combined with low utilization of the dehydrated artificial diet, due to the short intestine, the increased loss of enzyme proteins may actually contribute to the difficulties encountered when rearing fish larvae with artificial diets.

REFERENCES

Beamish, F.W.H. (1972). Can. J. Zool. 50, 153-164.
Dabrowska, H., Grudniewski, C. and Dabrowski, K. (1979). Prog. Fish-Cult. 41, 196-200.
Dabrowski, K. (1979). In "Cultivation of fish fry and its live food" (E. Styczynska-Jurewicz, T. Backiel, E. Jaspers and G. Persoone, eds.) pp. 107-126. Europ. Maricult. Soc., Special Publ. 4.

Dabrowski, K. and Glogowski, J. (1977).   Aquaculture 12,
    349-360.
Flüchter, J. (1982).   Aquaculture 27, 83-85.
Grizzle, J.M. and Curd, M.R. (1978).   Copeia 1978,
    448-455.
Hofer, R. (1982).   Comp. Biochem. Physiol. 72A, 55-63.
Hofer, R. and Nasir Uddin, A. (1985).   J. Fish Biol.   In
    press.
Kelso, J.R.M. (1972).   J. Fish. Res. Bd. Canada 29,
    1181-1192.
Lauff, M. and Hofer, R. (1984).   Aquaculture 37, 335-346.
Mähr, K., Grabner, M., Hofer, R. and Moser, H. (1983).
    Arch. Hydrobiol. 98. 344-353.
Ostroumova, I.N. (1977). Physiological-biochemical
    problems in fish nutrition. Fish Nutrition and Diet
    Development, Szarvas; 126-146 (in Russian).

DEVELOPMENT OF PROTEASES AND AN EXAMINATION OF PROCEDURES
FOR ANALYSIS OF ELASTASE ACTIVITY IN DOVER SOLE
(SOLEA SOLEA L)

J. CLARK, N.L. MACDONALD AND J.R. STARK

Department of Brewing and Biological Sciences,
Heriot-Watt University, Edinburgh, U.K.

I.   INTRODUCTION

Interest in digestion and nutrition has been stimulated
by the farming of fish for commercial purposes and the
present work is linked to studies on the development of
microencapsulated diets.   Particular   interest   in this
field is concerned with attempts to rear marine flatfish
on artificial diets (see for example Adron et al., 1974)
and to avoid or minimise the use of Artemia nauplii or
other live feeds.   As part of an assessment of the
nutritional requirements it is therefore of importance to
be able to measure accurately the digestive capabilities
in the gut and to follow the synthesis of specific enzymes
in fish of different ages so that diets can be prepared
specific to the age and the species of the fish.
Following a survey of the proteases in Dover sole
(Clark et al., 1984) we now report the results of
experiments on the development of proteases in fish aged
24 days to adult and also a critical assessment of the
methods for analysis of elastase activity in homogenates.

NUTRITION AND FEEDING IN FISH
ISBN: 0 12 194055 1

II.   METHODS AND MATERIALS

All fish were starved overnight before experimentation and, in addition, the 80 day old, the 200 day old and the adult fish were fed on artificial diets for at least 3 days prior to analysis of the gut and the contents (so there were no contaminating enzymes from live diets in any of the preparations).   For assay of general protease activity, the method of Kunitz (1947) was used and, for elastase measurements, a number of assays were compared as outlined in Table II.

III.   RESULTS AND DISCUSSION

Dover sole intestinal homogenates were examined for endo- and exoproteases. In initial studies using adult fish and casein as substrate, three pH regions of activity were noted. In each of these regions, extracts of the digestive tract homogenates caused a rapid reduction in the viscosity of gelatin indicating the presence of random or endo-acting enzymes. These major activities were at pH 1.7 (pepsin-like), pH 7.8 (trypsin- and chymotrypsin-like) and at pH 9.5 - 10.5 (probably elastase-like).   The strongest activity was present in the alkaline region and the weakest at the acidic pH as measured by both the casein-hydrolysis and the gelatin-viscosity assays. Using the artificial substrates leucine amide, hippuryl phenylalanine and hippuryl arginine, homogenates of adult Dover sole intestine were also shown to contain exoprotease activities corresponding to leucine amino peptidase, carboxypeptidase A and carboxypeptidase B respectively.   Further experiments indicated that these activities were located mainly in the lower regions of the intestine.

The level of these enzymes at different stages of development of the fish have been examined.   The results of these studies using casein as substrate and assaying at different pH values are shown in Table I.   Within the age span examined (24, 49, 80 and 200 day old and adult fish) there was a rise in the 'neutral' proteases (i.e. trypsin and chymotrypsin) and an equally steady rise in the "alkaline" protease.   The pepsin activity measured at pH

1.7 was not detected in the 24, 49 and 80 day old fish but at 200 days a small amount of this activity could be detected. It would therefore appear that with Dover sole, in common with certain other species, pepsin only appears in the gut as the fish matures. It is important to note that the three exoproteases were present in all the samples analysed.

Table I. Protease development in Dover sole intestine

Age of fish (days)	Hydrolysis of casein (µg tyrosine/min/g protein)		
	pH 1.7	pH 7.6	pH 10.1
24	0.00	0.59	0.71
49	0.00	1.46	2.08
88	0.00	1.77	3.82
200	0.80	2.89	4.19
Adult	2.00	4.50	8.90

At all ages the maximum protease activity (as measured by the hydrolysis of casein) was in the alkaline region and since pH–activity studies using BAEE, BTEE and collagen as substrates indicated that trypsin, chymotrypsin and collagenase were all active in the neutral region (pH 7 - 8), elastase was examined as a potential contributor to the alkaline activity. Elastin–orcein, elastin, Congo red elastin, N–succinyl–L–alanyl–L–alanyl–L–alanine p–nitrophenyl ester [N–CBZ–Ala–pNP] were examined as substrates. There are difficulties with all of these substrates. The use of elastin itself is a fairly insensitive method when used in conjunction with absorbance readings at 280 nm or even with the Lowry protein assay and, the use of the ninhydrin method may in fact be measuring the action of exoproteases acting on the elastin. With dyed elastins, problems arise because different batches of the substrates may have different degrees of substitution. Other substrates, Suc(Ala)$_3$-NA and N-CBZ-Ala-pNP have relatively low solubility in water and in addition this latter substrate has the disadvantage of being unstable at alkaline pH values. A further complication arises from the fact that, with crude enzyme preparations, these substrates do not all give the same value for the optimal pH. This is shown in Table II where it can be seen that the values fall into two groups. Those with elastin based substrates: the two dyed elastins and elastin itself with the Lowry assay giving a value in the region 9.4 - 9.8. Whereas the two artificial substrates Suc(Ala)$_3$-NA and N-CBZ-Ala-pNP gave optimal hydrolysis at pH 8.1 - 8.2.

Table II. Assay of elastase with different substrates

Substrate	Optimum pH	Assay Procedure
Casein	10.1	Kunitz (1947)
Elastin-orcein	9.8	Sachar et al. (1955)
Congo-red elastin	9.4	Naughton and Sanger (1961)
Elastin (a)	9.5	Lowry et al. (1951)
Elastin (b)	8.3	Ninhydrin method
Suc(Ala)$_3$-NA	8.2	Beigh et al. (1951)
N-CBZ-Ala-PNP	8.1	Geneste and Bender (1970)

The effect of a range of inhibitors was also examined using casein as substrate. Only phenylmethylsulphonyl fluoride (PMFS) showed any selectivity in inhibiting the hydrolysis of the substrate at different pH values. At a concentration of 0.55 mM PMFS resulted in inhibition of the proteases which act at neutral pH values leaving only 6-8% of the original activity; whereas the protease activity acting at pH 10.0 still showed 65% of its original strength under the same conditions. The elastase and the alkaline protease region are now being further studied using ion-exchange chromatography and chromato-focusing.

IV.   CONCLUSIONS

It is therefore concluded that there is a steady increase in neutral and alkaline protease from 24 days through to maturity. The acid protease, i.e. pepsin activity, is not detectable up to at least 80 days. Elastase activity as measured by elastin-orcein contributed to the alkaline protease activity but there are problems in correlating the results on this activity using different substrates.

REFERENCES

Adron, J.W., Blair, A., and Cowey, C.B. (1974). Fish Bull. Calif. 72, 352-357.

Bieth, J., Spiess, B. and Wermuth, C.G. (1974). Biochem. Med. 11, 350-357.

Clark, J., MacDonald, N.L. and Stark, J.R. (1984). Comp. Biochem. Physiol. (In press).

Geneste, P. and Bender, M.L. (1970). Proc. Natl. Acad. Sci. U.S. 64, 683-685.

Kunitz, M. (1947). J. Gen. Physiol. 30, 291-310.

Lowry, O.H., Rosebrough, N.J., Farr, A.L. and Randall, R.J. (1951). J. Biol. Chem. 193, 265-275.

Naughton, M.A. and Sanger, F. (1961). Biochem. J. 78, 156-163.

Sachar, L.A., Winter, K.K., Sicher, N. and Frankel, S. (1955). Proc. Soc. expt. Biol. Med. 90, 323-326.

FEEDING BEHAVIOUR AND FISH CULTURE

BRIAN KNIGHTS

Applied Ecology Research Group,
Polytechnic of Central London,
115, New Cavendish Street, London W1M 8JS.

I.   INTRODUCTION

Knowledge of feeding behaviour of fish in culture is important so that feeds and feeding techniques can be designed to encourage consumption and hence survival and growth whilst minimising metabolic energy expenditure in feeding.   Furthermore, wastage must be minimised because of high feed costs and the potentially deleterious effects of waste food on water quality.   Commercial culture has tended to rely on the accumulation of empirical data on growth and conversion in relation to feeds and feeding techniques;   this approach is slow in producing data and is prone to interference from uncontrolled variables. This chapter aims to show that there is much to be gained from experimental and observational study of feeding behaviour.   Bioenergetic methodologies can be used to assess growth rates and efficiencies (Knights, 1984). The chapter emphasises intensive culture systems relying on inputs of formulated feed and, especially, work in the author's laboratory on warmwater culture of European eel (Anguilla anguilla L.).   Many useful comparisons can be made, however, with concepts and models developed for fish in the wild feeding on live prey.

NUTRITION AND FEEDING IN FISH
ISBN: 0 12 194055 1

II. APPETITE AND SATIATION

Appetite is the drive state that initiates arousal and appetitive behaviours leading to consummatory behaviour, satiation and negative feedback (drive reduction), as in the scheme:-

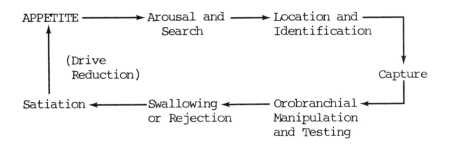

Appetite and satiation are of importance to fish farmers because of the need to ensure that feed regimes (feeding frequencies, ration sizes and time over which they are dispensed) are adjusted to maximise consumption, growth and conversion efficiencies.

Control of appetite in fish involves metabolic, neurophysiological and hormonal mechanisms as reviewed by Peter (1979) and Holmgren et al. (1983). Hypothalamic centres are probably involved and these may be stimulated by gut fullness and/or metabolic factors such as levels of certain metabolites in the blood or temperature changes related to metabolic activities. Fish appear to adjust food consumption to maintain dietary metabolic energy intake and to maintain body weight (Peter, 1979; Jobling, 1980 and 1981; Holmgren et al., 1983; Jobling and Wandsvik, 1983b). Learning and social interactions may also exert psychological effects.

In fish culture, matching of feed regimes to appetite and derivation of feeding tables has largely been achieved by studies of growth and conversion. Most laboratory studies, however, have concentrated on deriving models linking daily ration and food consumption to stomach filling and gastric evacuation (Fänge and Grove, 1979; Jobling, 1981; Holmgren et al., 1983). Many of these studies can be criticised on methodological grounds because they involve pre- or post-feeding starvation, serial autopsy, use of unnatural radiopaque or other labelling materials in the diet or stress due to force-feeding and stomach pumping. Generally, however, it appears that stomach distension inhibits and gastric evacuation excites appetite. Intermittent feeding and short-term deprivation leads to hyperphagia in comparison with the regular feeding used in culture, whilst prolonged deprivation suppresses appetite (e.g. as found in pond-cultured catfish by Randolph and Clemens, 1978).

With regular feeding, growth, assimilation and conversion efficiencies tend to plateau at a certain number of satiation feeds per day (depending on species, body size, temperature and food type). Brett (1971) and other workers suggest that the optimal interval between meals corresponds to gastric evacuation and the first major rise in appetite determined in deprivation experiments, i.e. when the greatest increase in appetite occurs for the shortest deprivation time.

III. EFFECTS OF CULTURE STRESSES ON APPETITE

Culture stresses (e.g. due to water quality, handling, intraspecific interactions, etc.) have been little studied. A 'stressor' can be defined as a stimulus which induces a sequence of 'stress responses'. Initially, neural and hormonal stimulation will occur, leading to secondary changes in behaviour, physiology and morphology (Pickering, 1981; Schreck, 1981). Tertiary responses may follow, e.g. reduced resistance to further stress, increased susceptibility to disease, etc. Stress can also suppress appetite, the extent of the suppression depending on the magnitude and duration of the stress. Chronic exposure may lead to acclimation (Pickering and Stewart, 1984) and habituation may occur with regularly repeated acute exposures (Schreck, 1981). Furthermore, hyperphagia may occur during recovery so that long term energy intake and growth are little affected (Pickering et al., 1982). More research in these areas is required, as is clear from the following discussions of some important stresses.

A. Oxygen and temperature

Feed manufacturers commonly publish empirically-derived feeding tables relating fish size, oxygen, temperature and recommended feed regimes. Critical chronic conditions have largely been determined by growth experiments e.g. by

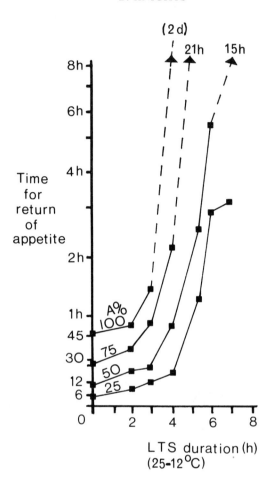

Fig. 1. Effects of duration of low temperature shocks (LTS) on appetite of Anguilla anguilla. Temperature was dropped from 25° to 12° and then returned to 25°C. A%100 represents normal amount of food consumed per test meal, other A figures percentages thereof. See text for further discussion. (Collins and Knights, unpublished results).

Sadler (1979) for temperature in Anguilla anguilla and by Yamagata et al. (1983) for oxygen in A. japonica. Information is lacking, however, on the effects of acute stresses on appetite. One approach is to study feeding behaviour of marked fish in the culture situation, e.g. as carried out by Randolph and Clemens (1976) on pond–cultured channel catfish (Ictalurus punctatus). A more objective approach is to study feeding of fish in the laboratory under controlled stress conditions. This has been done for European eel (Anguilla anguilla) by Collins and Knights (unpublished results). Eel fingerlings were fed dry formulated granules regularly at 25°C, the optimum growth temperature (Sadler, 1979), and the average time to consume 25, 50, 75 and 100% of the average ration was calculated. Fish were then subjected (before the normal feed on the experimental day) to low (LTS) or high temperature shocks (HTS) which can occur in commercial warm–water culture using industrial or power–generation cooling waters. Food was then offered at regular intervals. Figure 1 illustrates the effects of rapidly lowering the temperature to 12°C for various periods of time, then raising it back to 25°C. The results show that return of appetite is progressively delayed, e.g. after a LTS lasting 6 hours, eels take nearly 3 hours to consume 25% and about 5.5 hours to consume 50% of the normal ration. In practical terms, the fish farmer can use such information to decide whether and how much to feed during the working day or whether to cease feeding until fish are fully recovered. Further information of this type is required for acute temperature and oxygen stresses in the culture of eels and other species.

B. Ammonia stress

Ammonia can accumulate in high density culture at low water exchange rates. It is excreted by fish and can also be produced by anaerobic breakdown of waste food and faeces. Growth is generally inhibited at unionised ammonia nitrogen (UIAN) levels of about 0.1 mg dm^{-3} (Alabaster and Lloyd, 1982). This, however, is not necessarily related to feeding inhibition; Knights (1984) claims that energy wasted in ammonia–induced hypermetabolism during post-prandial peaks of ammonia excretion is more important in limiting growth. Appetite could be inhibited, however, at ammonia levels high enough to cause more extensive physiological and morphological stress responses.

C. Stresses due to intraspecific behaviour

It is generally considered that more aggressive (and usually larger) fish in farm populations affect appetite and/or feeding and hence growth of subordinates (e.g. see

Pickering and Stewart, 1984). Dominance and size
hierarchies are therefore interrelated and cause increased
coefficients of variance of body size and positive skews
in size-frequency distributions. These conclusions have,
however, mainly been inferred from changes in population
size-frequency with time. Supportive evidence is
available from laboratory studies of individual growth and
behaviour in fish such as Poecilids (Browne, 1981) but
such evidence is sparse for commercially cultured species.
Deleterious effects of size/aggression on feeding appear
to occur in subordinate hatchery or farmed salmonids
(Kalleberg, 1958; Symons, 1968; Fenderson and Carpenter,
1971; Li and Brocksen, 1977; MacCrimmon and Twongo, 1980;
Jobling and Wandsvik, 1983a), pond-cultured catfish
(Randolph and Clemens, 1976) and carp (Wohlfarth, 1977).
Most studies have, however, been conducted in stream or
tank systems at variable densities which are lower than
those used in intensive culture, thus allowing territories
to be developed. Energetic costs of territorial defence
(Li and Brocksen, 1977) will be reduced in featureless
farm tanks at high densities but subordinates will not be
able to easily disperse and avoid attacks by dominants.
The frequency of agonistic encounters will be highest when
fish first interact and at intermediate densities as
linear dominance hierarchies are established. Aggression
will be reduced at high densities in established
populations (e.g. Fenderson and Carpenter, 1971; Seymour,
1984) as fish adopt an 'average' position in a diffuse
dominance hierarchy. In size-matched fish, initial
dominance may be determined by individual genetic
differences in aggression, sex or prior social
experience. In larvae or wild-caught stock, readiness and
success in first-feeding on formulated diets are important
determinants of later growth and dominance, e.g. as in
eels (Kuhlmann, 1979; Degani and Levanon, 1983; Wickins,
1983) and salmonids (MacCrimmon and Twongo, 1980).

Frequency of agonistic encounters will be high when
fish are most active and aggregate prior to and during
feeding. Randolph and Clemens (1976) have shown that
subordinate catfish learn to approach demand feeders only
after larger dominants have satiated and dispersed.
Relative aggressiveness and position in the hierarchy can
be learnt in fish by associative conditioning and social
learning (McDonald et al., 1968). Increasing feeding
frequencies (or better dispersal of feed) may help
subordinates obtain food, as claimed for Arctic charr
(Salvelinus alpinus L.) and Anguilla anguilla by Jobling

Table I.   Summary of relationships between body size, agonistic behaviour, food consumption and growth of Anguilla anguilla.   See text for further discussion. (Knights, unpublished results).

	Percent of Population		
	Smallest 20%	60% (Mode = 2.1g)	Largest 20%
Weight (g)	0.8 - 1.4	1.4 - 2.8	2.8 - 3.8
Mean agonistic encounters/5 min	1.3	2.1	2.9
Relative dominance (% of encounters)	28.5	45.9	74.3
Avoidance behaviour (% observation time)	43.3	19.4	4.4
Voluntary food consumption (% bw/meal)	0.7	2.1	1.9
Mean specific growth rate (%/day)	-1.20	-0.06	+0.32

(1983) and Wickins (1983) respectively. Periodic size-grading to maintain homogenous populations is also claimed to destroy hierarchies, as well as aiding calculation of food and oxygen requirements and stock assessment (e.g. Gunnes, 1976).

At very high density or when size differentials are very marked, the above techniques may be less effective because appetite is suppressed and subordinates will not feed even if food is available.   This could be due to learning or to stress (Leshner, 1980).   Social stress certainly appears to be important in eels.   Thus subordinates in pairs confined in small tanks show general stress responses but, more specifically, gastric mucosal atrophy (Peters et al., 1980; Peters, 1982).   The latter effect was presumed to be due to hormonally or vagally induced ischemia.   Elvers show similar gastrointestinal degeneration and also enlarged gall bladders (Willemse et al., 1984).   Pickeriong and Stewart (1984) have reviewed evidence for interrenal effects of social stress in salmonids and other fish.

Differential growth rates are particularly marked in warm-water culture of eels (Kuhlmann, 1979). Knights (unpublished results) and Seymour (1984) have shown this is related to effects of agonistic behaviour on appetite and feeding. Eels lack the coloured fins or other means of maintaining relative rank via visual displays as found in other fish species. Such displays are, in any case, ineffective at very high density in culture and biting was the predominant behaviour. Table I summarises the results of studies of individually marked eels of different sizes at moderately high density (Knights, unpublished results). These show that the smallest eels spend much time avoiding other fish (by swimming near the water surface), show low dominance in the few encounters that do occur, consume little food (although it was supplied to excess) and show poor growth. Mortality was also high. Larger fish show the converse picture. The role of learning and/or stress was explored in separate experiments (Knights, unpublished results). Marked elvers and finglerlings were isolated for several days to minimise the effects of prior social experience and then put together in pairs in small observation tanks. Aggression was very high initially, especially in fish well matched in size. Differences in dominance/sub-missiveness and attack/avoidance were particularly marked when the larger fish of the pair was 1.5 times the weight of the smaller. Fish one-third the weight of the larger were always subordinate and spent the majority of the observation time in avoidance swimming. Subsequent learning and/or stress would be expected to correlate with the behaviours, inhibition of appetite, growth and survival discussed above.

The practical implications of these data are two-fold. Firstly they suggest feeding of small fish swimming near the surface could be encouraged by offering paste feeds in suspended baskets or by dropping dry feeds into trays suspended near the surface, leaving larger fish to feed on the bottom. Provision of shelters (e.g. in the form of tubes in which eels can hide) is not practicable in high-density culture so grading is the only other solution. Wickins (1983) recommends fortnightly grading of small eels but the results above suggest other criteria; i.e. that grading should ideally be carried out to ensure no fish is 1.5 times larger than another. They certainly indicate that fish three or more times the size of others should be graded out. In this context, it is interesting that morphometric data (Knights, 1982) show

that at this size differential, the mouth of the larger
fingerlings becomes big enough in relation to trunk
diameter of the smaller ones for the former to grip and
inflict painful bites on the latter.   Cannibalism is also
possible and this can cause significant mortalities in
ungraded elvers. (e.g. Degani and Levanon, 1983).

Direct comparisons between eels and other cultured
species is not strictly valid because of fundamental
differences in basic biology and social behaviour.
Further work on other species might, however, yield
equally useful information on social interactions,
appetite and differential growth.

D. Handling and disturbance stresses

Little work has been carried out on the effects of such
stresses on appetite.   The effects of handling on
salmonids appears variable. Pickering et al. (1982) found
brown trout (Salmo trutta) refused feed for three days
after handling. Wedemeyer (1976) quotes young coho salmon
(Oncorhynchus kisutch) losing appetite for four to seven
days but rainbow trout (Salmo gairdneri), under identical
conditions, resumed feeding the next day.   Differences may
be related to habituation or to genetic differences
between species or races.   More research is required in
this area, especially as to whether subsequent hyperphagia
compensates for lost feeds (Pickering et al., 1982) or not
(Randolph and Clemens, 1978).

IV.   AROUSAL AND SEARCH

Intrinsic increases in appetite lead to arousal and
increased activity and appetitive behaviour.   Demand
feeders can be provided so that, via operant conditioning,
fish learn to feed at will.   The main disadvantage of
demand feeding is that relatively few fish (usually the
more dominant ones) learn to actuate the feeder and some
fish may not be able to obtain enough food.   Increasing
the amount of food released per actuation may help
overcome this problem but it may increase the chances of
wastage or hyperphagia and inefficient conversion in some
fish (Landless, 1976; Webber and Huguenin, 1979).

Fish can learn to anticipate feeding times when on
fixed feeding schedules but arousal and aggregation near

feeders is often due to classical (Pavlovian)
conditioning. Sight or sound of farm workers near feeding
areas can act as conditioned stimuli, for example.
Controlled conditioning has been used in some culture
situations, e.g. Abbott (1972) used a 150–300 Hz pure-tone
audiogenerator to condition rainbow trout to aggregate for
feeding. Fujiya et al. (1980) also used sound (200–700
Hz) to condition red sea bream (Pagrus major) to come to a
feeding spot in an open-sea ranching system.

Social facilitation is also important in high density
in culture, i.e. arousal and excitation of one or a few
fish leads to mass excitation of others. This encourages
learning of feeding cues and demand feeder actuation
(Landless, 1976; Iwai, 1980). It can also help fish to
learn to respond to and take a novel formulated diet. Such
weaning is a particular problem in wild-caught stock or
cultured larval or post-larval stages of species which
require very specific chemical, visual or other innate
releaser stimuli (e.g. as discussed by Mackie in another
chapter). If a species can be bred commercially,
appropriate genetic attributes can be selected for. This
may have occcurred in, for example, rainbow trout and
carp, and strain selection could be important in novel
species, e.g. as shown for largemouth bass (Micropterus
salmoides) by Williamson (1983).

V. LOCATION AND INITIAL IDENTIFICATION

Chemical and physical characteristics of food particles
and feeding techniques need to be matched to the sensory
and motor capabilities and behavioural attributes of any
farmed species. Stage in the life cycle and body size
may also be important. Holling (1959), Atema (1980),
Iwai (1980), Crow (1982) and Simenstad et al. (1982) have
discussed various factors affecting search efficiency and
rates of encounter in the wild.

Rates of encounter can be maximised in the farm
situation by concentrating the food in time and space,
i.e. by regular feeding in a set area and encouraging
aggregation. Location efficiency can be increased by
making food particles more obvious to reduce reactive
distance. This can be done by maximising chemical
attractiveness and/or increasing visibility. The latter
is dependent on size, shape, colour, contrast and movement

of particles and on light intensity and turbidity (Ware, 1971; Wankowski and Thorpe, 1979). The manipulation of such characteristics of lures and baits has long been practised by fishermen and anglers but rarely taken into account in culture. One interesting application, however, has been the staining of Artemia in attempts to improve location and capture success by larval and juvenile Dover Sole, Solea solea (Dendrinos et al., 1984). Manipulation of chemical attractiveness is discussed in detail by Mackie in another chapter.

Visual location is more important in near-surface feeders and in species living in shallow clear waters (Blaxter, 1980). Iwai (1980) concluded that although vision is important in growing teleost larvae, chemoreceptors and mechanoreceptors may also be important. Olfaction can be important in initial detection but location efficiency will be reduced if turbulence prevents the development of distinct odour trails or gradients (Atema, 1980). Gustation, using surface taste buds may also be important in long-range location as well as in contact location and identification. Taste fibres may also possess mechanoreceptor activity (Bardach and Villars, 1974).

Knights (1983) studied location and identification behaviour in eels and found a distinct difference between small (less than 10-15g) and large fish. In small elvers and fingerlings, vision was of minor importance compared with gustation. The great majority of commercially formulated granules were detected on the tank floor by chance encounter with the nose or head (as far back as the pectoral fins). This 'nudge' behaviour led to orientation (i.e. turning of the head towards the food) or to pushing with the nose, a behaviour presumably involving further chemical and perhaps mechanoreceptor assessment. Location efficiency was limited mainly by the likelihood of physical encounter and by size of particles; Fig. 2 shows that particles below a certain diameter were not easily detected, presumably because they didn't offer a sufficiently large chemical stimulus.

Vision became the dominant sense in eels larger than 10-15g. They were able to feed in the dark, presumably using chemical senses, but in the light they did not respond to pellets below 2mm diameter. Increasing visual acuity was shown by their ability to quickly learn to discriminate between larger pellets and to ignore those that were not easily swallowed (Fig. 2 and discussion below).

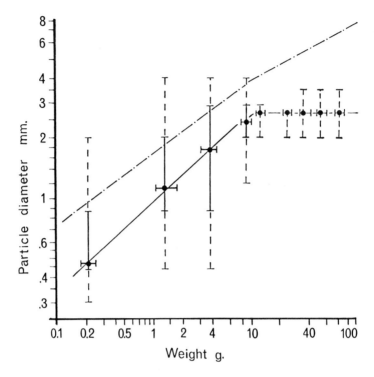

Fig. 2. Relationships between optimum food particle sizes and body weight of <u>Anguilla anguilla.</u> (Dots represent particle sizes with shortest consumption times, solid vertical bars show the range of sizes with longer but not significantly longer consumption time (t-test, P < 0.1). Dashed vertical bars encompass the range of food sizes consumed after a significantly longer location or handling delay and potential wastage. Horizontal bars represent the range of eel weights about a sample mean. Dash-dot lines are regression lines for mouth width (mm) against body weight up to 10g and from 10-100g. From Knights (1984), reproduced by permission from <u>Aquaculture.</u>

Studies of this type are more useful than empirical studies of relationships between feed presentation and growth. They indicate, for example, that eels can feed efficiently in the dark or in turbid water on particles of a certain size (assuming they are chemically attractive; Mackie and Mitchell, 1983; Takeda <u>et al.</u>, 1984). They also suggest that rates of encounter and location efficiency could be improved for small eels by localising food supply, e.g. by using suspended catchment trays below feeders in large tanks with fast self-flushing water currents. Changes in sensory modalities with age are also shown which can be correlated not only with location efficiency but with morphological and neurophysiological changes. For example, Pankhurst (1982), Pankhurst and Lythgoe (1983) and Pankhurst (1984) have shown eye size and retinal morphology change as eels mature whilst the olfactory lamellae atrophy. Such studies also yield information on how fish learn new search images and whether size or factors such as colour and movement are important (Ware, 1971; Wankowski and Thorpe, 1979). This is of great importance in encouraging first-feeding, particularly of larvae of marine fish (Bromley, this volume). Innate or learnt chemical search images may also be important (Mackie, this volume).

VI. CAPTURE

In macrophagous carnivores, capture involves orientation of all or part of the body relative to the food item and then possibly a forward striking movement. Small particles can be taken into the mouth whole and in most teleosts, this is achieved by inertial suction, i.e. a sudden negative pressure is created by rapid expansion of the orobranchial cavity (Hyatt, 1979; Liem, 1980). This causes particles to be sucked into the mouth from a distance.

Capture success in the wild depends on prey size and avoidance behaviour. The latter factor is unimportant in culture using inanimate food particles but passive movement in water currents may cause problems. For example, Thorpe and Wankowski (1979) found the optimal current velocity in this respect for juvenile Atlantic salmon (Salmo salar L.) was five body lengths per second.

Food particle size might be expected to limit capture success in culture. This is not the case, however, if fish are hungry and particles are not excessively large. The eel study quoted above, for example, showed that eels relying on contact location and identification will continue to attack particles much too large to swallow easily. The upper size limit then selected is related to ingestion and not capture problems, as will now be discussed.

VII.   OROBRANCHIAL MANIPULATION AND TESTING

Once in the mouth, food items may have to be
manipulated prior to swallowing and final gustatory
testing occurs. Hardness, abrasiveness and ease of
swallowing will also be tested, leading to:-

VIII.   SWALLOWING OR REJECTION

The importance of taste attractants is discussed in
this volume by Mackie and Mitchell. Optimal particle
sizes for fish of particular size classes (as recommended
in feed tables) have largely been determined from
subjective observations or empirically from growth
experiments (Grassl, 1956; Hastings and Dickie, 1972).
Only a few objective studies of acceptance-rejection
behaviour have been carried out (Fowler and Burrows,
1971; Wankowski and Thorpe, 1979; Knights, 1983). These
show that shape and texture as well as size are of
paramount importance. Ease of location of small particles
sets the lower limit to optimal size but the upper limit
is dictated by morphometrics of the mouth (and possibly
gill rakers if present). The latter are in turn presumably
related to morphometrics of the gastrointestinal tract. A
1:1 relationship between particle size diameter and mouth
width has been found for soft food items (Hartman 1958;
Knights, 1983).   For hard and/or abrasive items,
preferred particle sizes are generally 0.4 - 0.6 of mouth
width (Hyatt, 1979; Thorpe and Wankowski, 1979; Wankowski,
1979; Wankowski and Thorpe, 1979; Knights, 1983). This
relationship for eels is represented in Fig. 2. Large eels
learn to visually ignore large particles (probably because
they are hard and abrasive), although they can easily
swallow larger soft balls of paste feed. Smaller eels
tackled large particles more voraciously, but ingestion
was significantly delayed because granules were repeatedly
taken into the mouth, spat out and pushed with the nose
until they softened and/or disintegrated. Similar delays
in ingestion were observed in Atlantic salmon by Wankowski
and Thorpe (1979). This leads to increased energy
expenditure and potential wastage of food.
A further value of this observational approach is that
it also shows that shape and symmetry of food particles
are important. More rejections and disintegration occur

in pellets that are very much longer than their diameter
(Knights, 1983), emphasising the importance of careful
sizing at the manufacturing stage.

IX. OPTIMAL FORAGING THEORY

Location efficiency, capture success and ease of
ingestion have been proven to be directly related to
growth in Atlantic salmon (Wankowski, 1979; Wankowski and
Thorpe, 1979). This would be predicted from bioenergetic
considerations (Knights, 1984) and from optimal foraging
theory. This theory was propounded to explain feeding
and prey selectivity in wild fish. It proposes that
natural selection favours a predator whose foraging
strategy provides the highest possible rate of energy
intake relative to energy expended in feeding (Pyke et
al., 1977; Krebs, 1978). Interesting parallels are shown
with preceding discussions of fish in culture. The theory
states that energy costs are determined by encounter rate
(time spent locating and identifying food which is
dependent on prey abundance and the predator's perceptual
abilities) and a handling time cost (the energy and
feeding time expended in capture, manipulation and
testing). Energy intake is dependent on the assimilated
energy value of the prey once ingested.

The two extreme optimal strategies are to feed
indiscriminately at low prey abundance or to show
increasing selectivity of larger prey with higher
individual energy content at high prey abundance. The
studies of feeding in eels and salmonids discussed earlier
support the view that changes in sensory abilities and
learning with age are of great importance (Gibson,
1983). Thus feeding appears unselective in first-feeding
and in young fish when appetite is high but before they
posssess the sensory capabilities to distinguish between
potential food items. This leads to high energy
expenditure in locating and capturing very small particles
on one hand and in long handling times for large particles
on the other. With appropriate sensory development,
decreasing appetite and under suitable environmental
conditions of light, etc., sensory discrimination is
possible. Chemical and/or visual search images are then
learnt and fish become more selective.

The practical implications for fish culture are that;
(i) encounter rates need to be maximised by concentrating

food availability in time and space; (ii) food supply
must be matched to appetite; (iii) chemical and physical
characteristics (especially size) of food particles need
to be related to fish species, size and sensory abilities
to aid location, identification and capture; (iv) chemical
and physical characteristics (especially size) should be
designed to minimise handling time and wastage. This
chapter has shown that direct observational studies of
feeding behaviour are essential in clarifying these points.

REFERENCES

Abbott, R.R. (1972). Trans. Amer. Fish. Soc. 101, 35-43.
Alabaster, J.S. and Lloyd, R. (1982). "Water Quality
    Criteria for Fresh Water Fish" (2nd Edtn.). Butterworth
    Scientific Publ., London.
Atema, J. (1980). In "Fish Behaviour and its Use in
    Capture and Culture of Fishes", (J.E. Bardach, J.J.
    Magnuson, R.C. May and J.M. Reinhart, eds.), 57-101.
    ICLARM, Manila, Phillipines.
Bardach, J.E. and Villars, T. (1974). In "Chemoreception
    in Marine Organisms", (P.T. Grant and A.M. Mackie,
    eds.), 49-104. Academic Press, London and New York.
Blaxter, J.H.S. (1980). In "Fish Behaviour and its Use in
    Capture and Culture of Fishes", (J.E. Bardach, J.J.
    Magnuson, R.C. May and J.M. Reinhart, eds.), 32-56.
    ICLARM, Manila, Phillipines.
Brett, J.R. (1971). J. Fish. Res. Bd Can. 28, 409-415.
Browne, K.D. (1981). Ph.D. Thesis, Polytechnic of Central
    London, London.
Crow, M.E. (1982). In "Gutshop '81: Fish Food Habits
    Studies", (C.M. Cailliet and C.A. Simenstad, eds.),
    47-55. Washington Sea Grant Publ. Seattle.
Degani, G. and Levanon, D. (1983). Bamidgeh 35, 53-60.
Dendrinos, P., Dewan, S. and Thorpe, J.P. (1984).
    Aquaculture 38, 137-144.
Fänge, R. and Grove, D.J. (1979). In "Fish Physiology",
    (W.S. Hoar, D.J. Randall and J.R. Brett, eds.), 8,
    161-260. Academic Press, London and New York.
Fenderson, O.C. and Carpenter, M.R. (1971). Anim. Behav.
    19, 439-447.
Fowler, L.G. and Burrows, R.E. (1971). Progr. Fish-Cult.
    33, 67-75.

Fujiya, M., Sakaguchi, S. and Fukuhara, O. (1980). In "Fish Behaviour and its Use in Capture and Culture of Fishes", (J.E. Bardach, J.J. Magnuson, R.C. May and J.M. Reinhart, eds.), 200-209. ICLARM, Manila, Phillipines.

Gibson, R.M. (1983). Trends in Neuro-Sci. 6, 197 and 199.

Grassl, E.F. (1956). Trans. Amer. Fish. Soc. 86, 307-322.

Gunnes, K. (1976). Aquaculture 9, 381-386.

Hartman, G.F. (1958). Copeia 3, 233-234.

Hastings, W.H. and Dickie, L.M. (1972). In "Fish Nutrition", (J.E. Halver, ed.), 327-374. Academic Press, London and New York.

Holling, C.S. (1959). Canad. Entomol. 91, 385-398.

Holmgren, S., Grove, D.J. and Fletcher, D.J. (1983). In "Control Processes in Fish Physiology", (J.C. Rankin, T.J. Pitcher and R. Duggan, eds.), 23-40. Croom Helm, London.

Hyatt, K.D. (1979). In "Fish Physiology", (W.S. Hoar, D.J. Randall and J.R. Brett, eds.), 8, 71-119. Academic Press, London and New York.

Iwai, T. (1980). In "Fish Behaviour and its Use in Capture and Culture of Fishes", (J.E. Bardach, J.J. Magnuson, R.C. May and J.M. Reinhard, eds.), 124-145. ICLARM, Manila, Phillipines.

Jobling, M. (1980). J. Fish Biol. 17, 187-196.

Jobling, M. (1981). J. Fish Biol. 19, 245-257.

Jobling, M. (1983). J. Fish Biol. 23, 177-185.

Jobling, M. and Wandsvik, A. (1983a). J. Fish Biol. 22, 577-584.

Jobling, M. and Wandsvik, A. (1983b). J. Fish Biol. 23, 397-404.

Kalleberg, H. (1958). Inst. F.W. Res. Drottningholm, Rept. No. 39, 55-98.

Knights, B. (1982). Aquacult. Engin. 1, 297-310.

Knights, B. (1983). Aquaculture 30, 173-190.

Knights, B. 91984). In "Fish Energetics: A New Look", (P. Tytler and P. Calow, eds.). Croom Helm, London (In Press).

Krebs, J.R. (1978). In "Behavioural Ecology - An Evolutionary Approach", (J.R. Krebs and N.B. Davies, eds.), 23-63. Blackwell Scientific Publ., Oxford.

Kuhlmann, H. (1979). Rapp. P.-V. Reun. Cons. int. Explor. Mer 174, 59-63.

Landless, P.J. (1976). Aquaculture 7, 11-25.

Leshner, A.I. (1980). Prog. Brain Res. 53, 427-438.

Li, H.W. and Brocksen, R.W. (1977). J. Fish Biol. 11, 324-341.

Liem, K.F. (1980). In "Environmental Physiology of Fishes", (M.A. Ali, ed.), 299–334. Plenum Press, New York.

MacCrimmon, H.R. and Twongo, T.K. (1980). Canad. J. Zool. 58, 20–26.

Mackie, A.M. and Mitchell, A.I. (1983). J. Fish Biol. 22, 425–430.

McDonald, A.L., Heimstra, N.W. and Damkot, D.K. (1968). Anim. Behav. 16, 437–441.

Pankhurst, N.W. (1982). J. Fish Biol. 21, 127–140.

Pankhurst, N.W. (1984). Canad. J. Zool. 62, 335–385.

Pankhurst, N.W. and Lythgoe, J.N. (1983). J. Fish Biol. 23, 229–240.

Peter, R.E. (1979). In "Fish Physiology", (W.S. Hoar, D.J. Randall and J.R. Brett, eds.), 8, 125–159. Academic Press, London and New York.

Peters, G. (1982). J. Fish Biol. 21, 497–512.

Peters, G., Delventhal, H. and Klinger, H. (1980). Arch. Fischwiss. 30, 157–180.

Pickering, A.D. (1981). In "Stress and Fish" (A.D. Pickering, ed.), 1–9, Academic Press, London and New York.

Pickering, A.D., Pottinger, T.G. and Christie, P. (1982). J. Fish Biol. 20, 229–242.

Pickering, A.D. and Stewart, A. (1984). J. Fish Biol. 24, 731–740.

Pyke, G.H., Pulliam, H.R. and Charnov, E.L. (1977). Quart. Rev. Biol. 52, 137–154.

Randolph, K.N. and Clemens, H.P. (1976). Trans. Amer. Fish. Soc. 6, 718–724.

Randolph, K.N. and Clemens, H.P. (1978). Progr. Fish–Cult. 40, 48–50.

Sadler, K. (1979). J. Fish Biol. 15, 499–507.

Schreck, C.B. (1981). In "Stress and Fish", (A.D. Pickering, ed.), 295–321. Academic Press, London and New York.

Seymour, E.A. (1984). Ph.D. thesis, Polytechnic of Central London, London.

Simenstad, C.A., Eggers, D.M., Wissmar, R.C. and Volk, E.C. (1982). In "Gutshop '81: Fish Food Habits Studies", (G.M. Cailliet and C.A. Simenstad, eds.), 33–46. Washington Sea Grant Publ., Seattle.

Symons, P.E.K. (1968). J. Fish. Res. Bd Can. 25, 2387–2401.

Takeda, M., Takii, K. and Matsui, K. (1984). Bull. Jap. Soc. Sci. Fish. 50, 645–652.

Thorpe, J.E. and Wankowski, J.W.J. (1979).   In "Finfish
    Nutrition and Fish Feed Technology", (J.E. Halver and
    K. Tiews, eds.), 1, 501-513. Heenemann Verlag, Berlin.
Wankowski, J.W.J. (1979).   J. Fish Biol. 14, 89-100.
Wankowski, J.W.J. and Thorpe, J.E. (1979).   J. Fish Biol.
    14, 351-370.
Ware, D.M. (1971).   J. Fish. Res. Bd Can. 28, 1847-1852.
Webber, H.H. and Huguenin, H.E. (1979).   In "Finfish
    Nutrition and Fish Feed Technology", (J.E. Halver and
    K. Tiews, eds.), 1, 297-316. Heenemann Verlag, Berlin.
Wedemeyer, G.A. (1976).   J. Fish. Res. Bd Can. 33,
    2699-2702.
Wickins, J. (1983).   Fish Farmer 6, 24-25.
Williamson, J.H. (1983).   Progr. Fish-Cult. 45, 3-7.
Willemse, J.J., Markus-Silvis, L. and Ketting, G.H.
    (1984).   Aquaculture 36, 193-201.
Wohlfarth, G.W. (1977).   Bamidgeh 29, 35-40.
Yamagata, Y., Oonaka, S., Harada, M. and Niwa, M.
    (1983).   Bull. Jap. Soc. Sci. Fish. 49, 1335-1339.

GROWTH AND FEEDING IN JUVENILE ATLANTIC SALMON (SALMO SALAR L.)

P.J. HIGGINS[1] and C. TALBOT[2]

[1]Freshwater Fisheries Laboratory, Pitlochry, PH16 5LB, U.K.; and Department of Zoology, University of Aberdeen, AB9 2TN.
[2]Freshwater Fisheries Laboratory, Pitlochry.

I. INTRODUCTION

Juvenile Atlantic salmon (Salmo salar L.) spend one or more years in freshwater before they smolt and migrate to sea (Jones, 1959). Elson (1957) suggested that a certain size threshold had to be reached by the fish in spring to allow smolting to take place, and it would appear that individual growth rate in fresh water is of major importance in the smolting process. Simpson and Thorpe (1976) and Thorpe (1977) followed the growth of salmon parr reared in a hatchery. They found that sibling populations of parr maintained for their first year in the same tank developed a bimodality both in their length and weight frequency distributions (Fig. 1). The two modes of this distribution were distinguishable some three to four months after first feeding and the separation of the modes became progressively greater over the remaining months of the first season's growth (Thorpe et al., 1980). The fish in the upper growth mode developed into smolts in the spring of their second year while those in the lower mode remained as parr for another year, finally smolting as 2+ fish. This growth and smolting pattern (which is independent of factors within the population such as social hierarchies) was shown to be consistent with the

NUTRITION AND FEEDING IN FISH
ISBN: 0 12 194055 1

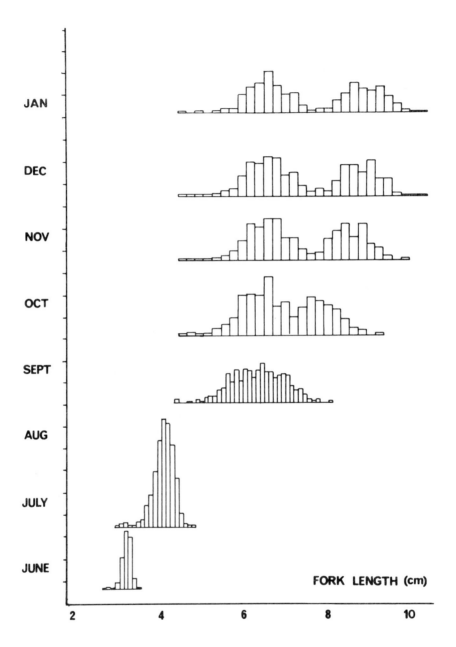

Fig. 1. Development of bimodality of lengths of a typical population of 0+ Atlantic salmon.

migratory age structure of natural populations in four Scottish rivers (Thorpe, 1977). In further hatchery experiments, Thorpe and Morgan (1978) demonstrated that there was a genetic component in the proportion of fish in the two growth modes and in the growth rate and smolting rate within any sibling population. The proportion entering the upper mode is also affected by environmental factors such as crowding and water velocity (Thorpe and Wankowski, 1979) and photoperiod (Villarreal and Thorpe, 1985). Sexual development does not play an important role in the development of bimodality (Villarreal, 1983), though there may be some re-allocation of energy into gonadal development in precocious males which may alter their position within the modes (Saunders et al., 1982). The phenomenon of bimodal length frequency distributions in sibling 0+ Atlantic salmon parr has also been reported in Canadian (Bailey et al., 1980; Saunders et al., 1982) and Norwegian (Knutsson and Grav, 1976) stocks.

The growth rate of fish is ultimately determined by the quantity of food consumed and the way in which nutrients are utilized by the animal. The balanced energy budget of a fish or a population has been given by Windell (1978) as:

$$C = F + U + \Delta B + R$$

Where: C = food consumption; $F+U$ = faecal, urinary and other nitrogenous losses; ΔB = growth in biomass of the soma and gonads; R = energy used in respiration.

The relationship between food consumption and the growth rate which results is affected by a complex interaction of a number of factors which include temperature, light, fish size, appetite, feeding regime and type of food, activity, behaviour and stress. Growth, feeding and the environmental influences on growth in fish have been the subject of major reviews (Fry, 1971; Elliott, 1976, Braaten, 1979; Brett, 1979; Fange and Grove, 1979; and Webb, 1978).

This paper considers some aspects of the energy budget of hatchery reared juvenile Atlantic salmon with particular reference to the phenomenon of bimodality. The results of previous studies carried out at this laboratory are reviewed and new information is presented on growth, proximate components and food consumption; and the influence of season, photoperiod and temperature. For full details of the rearing conditions see Thorpe (1981); and for more detailed description of feeding and growth experiments see Talbot and Higgins (1983) and Higgins (1985a,b).

II. GROWTH STUDIES

A. Specific growth rate

In September 1982, 45 upper (2.1 to 5.0 g) and 45 lower (0.6 to 1.9 g) mode sibling 0+ Atlantic salmon were selected and placed together to form an experimental population, each individual being marked with an X-ray readable microtag inserted into the epaxial musculature, which distinguished it from all others in the tank (Higgins, 1985a). The identification of the microtagged individuals in the experimental population from radiographs at monthly measurements of fork length, allowed the calculation of a monthly specific growth rate for each individual. This was calculated from the formula,

$$S.G.R. = (\log W2 - \log W1)/\text{elapsed time (days)}$$

(after Ricker, 1979)

A mean of all the individual specific growth rates was calculated for each modal group. The microtagged fish demonstrated no adverse growth effects compared to a control (untagged) population (Higgins, 1985a). Ambient water temperatures were recorded continuously, and photoperiod estimated from Whitaker's Almanack. The fish were offered an ad lib. ration, with food dispensed at 15 minute intervals, 24 hours a day by means of automatic feeders.

Throughout the study period all the microtagged individuals stayed within their initial modal group, with none of the upper mode fish dropping back into lower mode or vice versa (Fig. 2b). The upper mode fish maintained a higher growth rate than the lower mode fish throughout the period. This was most notable between 25 October and 25 January when the upper mode maintained growth whilst the lower mode showed almost no growth at all.

For all fish there appeared to be a general association between growth, temperature and photoperiod (Fig. 2), though closer examination revealed conflicting results in

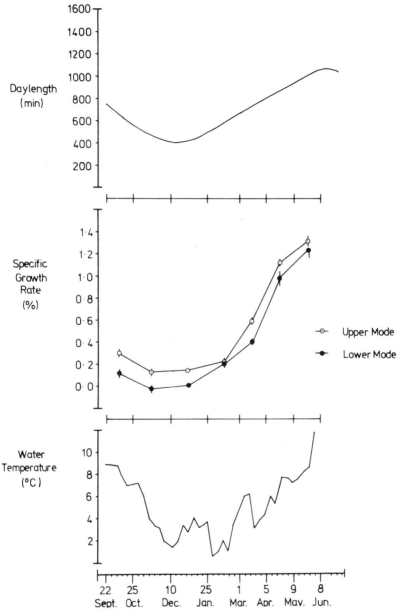

Fig. 2. Mean of individual specific growth rates (+ 1 standard error) of microtagged upper and lower mode salmon in relation to ambient water temperature (°C), and photoperiod (daylength in minutes) from September 1982 to June 1983. Water temperature is displayed as the weekly mean.

the temperature/growth association. Temperatures were
generally higher (2° to 7°C) between 25 October and 10
December than in the two subsequent intervals (10 December
to 25 January, around 3.5°C; and 25 January to 1 March,
around 1°C), yet specific growth rates for both modal
groups were higher during the coldest period (25 January
to 1 March) than in the two preceding intervals.
Furthermore, the average temperature during early spring
(1 March to 5 April) was 5°C whereas during autumn (22
September to 25 October) the average temperature was
8°C. The specific growth rates of both upper and lower
mode fish in spring were approximately twice those found
in autumn. This result is unexpected as the specific
growth rate of fish fed on maximum rations is known to
increase with increasing temperature and to decrease with
increasing fish size (Brett, 1979). Apart from
temperature, the main environmental difference between
autumn and spring is the change in day length, increasing
in spring and decreasing in autumn. The possible role of
photoperiod in regulating growth rate will be discussed
later.

B. Proximate Composition

    A different sibling population of 0+ Atlantic salmon
offered continuous ad lib. feeding as described in the
previous experiment, was monitored for length and weight
at approximately monthly intervals. A representative
subsample of fish from each growth mode was sacrificed at
each monitoring. The water content (following drying to
constant weight at 80°C), lipid content (by the chloro-
form–methanol–water extraction method of Hanson and Olley
(1963)), calorific value (by bomb calorimetry) and ash
content (residue remaining after combustion in the
calorimeter) was determined for whole (i.e. non-
eviscerated) fish. Values obtained (mean + S.E.) are
expressed as percentages of wet fish weight (Figs. 3 a–d).
    A bimodal length frequency distribution was first
discernible in September, some four months after first
feeding. Up to September, there was a marked decrease in
water content and a marked increase in lipid content,
calorific value and ash. At the time when bimodality was
first detectable there were no signficant differences in
water or ash content between fish in the two modes but
there was a significant difference (P<0.01) in calorific
value and lipid content. Thereafter, water and ash

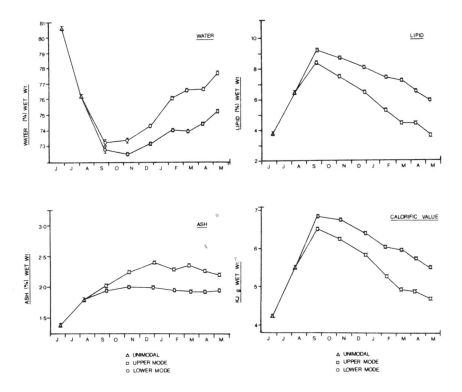

Fig. 3. Changes in water, ash, lipid and calorific value (% wet fish weight, $\pm$ 1 standard error) during the development of bimodality.

content of upper mode fish was significantly (P<0.001) less than in lower mode fish whereas lipid and calorific value was significantly higher (P<0.001). The changes in total calorific content of a typical fish in each mode between samplings (modal fish weight * mean calorific value per unit wet tissue weight) provides an index of calorific growth which is the net product of the energy budget (Fig. 4). The calorific content of lower mode fish reached a maximum of 20.8 kJ/fish in September and then declined slightly throughout the winter and early spring, increasing again in May. Calorific content of upper mode fish continued to increase for longer, reaching 57.5 kJ/fish in November (Fig. 4). There was little change in calorific content of upper mode fish during

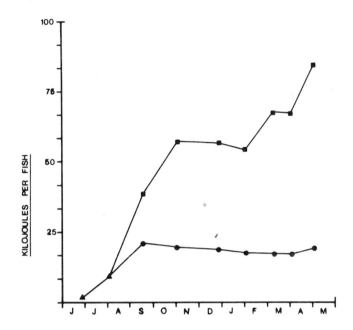

Fig. 4. Changes in calorific content per fish (kJ/g wet weight * fish weight (g)) during the development of bimodality. ▲- unimodal fry, ●- lower mode, ■ - upper mode.

winter but by March a marked increase had resumed which continued until sampling ceased in May. In the periods both before and after winter, upper mode fish showed a more rapid increase in calorific content than lower mode fish and a shorter period during winter when calorific content remained unchanged (Fig. 4). The overall calorific content in May, some 11 months after first feeding, was approximately 5 times higher in upper compared to lower growth mode fish. The difference in calorific growth between the two modes is largely due to differnces in fish weight rather than to calorific value per unit weight of tissue.

III.   FEEDING EXPERIMENTS

Various aspects of the trophic relationships of upper and lower growth mode fish have been investigated using

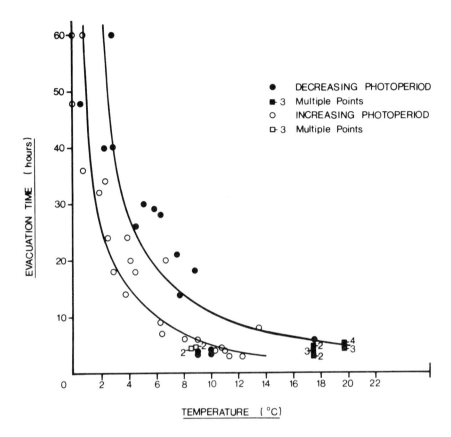

Fig. 5. Changes in whole gut evacuation time with temperature (°C), and seasonal variation in photoperiod.

the method described by Talbot and Higgins (1983), which involves incorporating fine iron powder into the food pellets as a radio-opaque marker. In these experiments, fish were fed ad lib. as described previously.

A. Evacuation rate

For a number of fish species gastric evacuation rate shows a strong temperature dependence (Fange and Grove, 1979), and this appears to be the case for evacuation from the entire gastrointestinal tract of actively feeding juvenile Atlantic salmon (Fig. 5). The relationship between temperature and evacuation time in upper mode fish

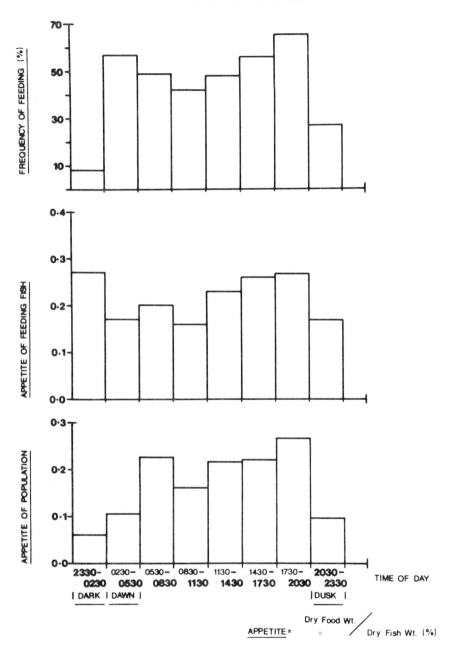

Fig. 6.   Daily feeding pattern of upper mode Atlantic salmon

is plotted separately for spring (increasing photoperiod) and autumn (decreasing photoperiod).   Fish in spring demonstrate a faster rate of evacuation at any given temperature compared with fish on a decreasing photoperiod regime.   The relationship between evacuation time and temperature was calculated by the method of least squares, using a logarithmic model.   The lines of best fit (P<0.001) for the original data are:

Increasing   photoperiod: Evacuation   time   =   106.85* (Temperature)**(-1.04612)
Decreasing   photoperiod: Evacuation   time   =   57.92* (Temperature)**(-1.00349)
A comparison of regression demonstrated significant differences (P<0.001) between intercepts.

B. Daily feeding pattern

The daily feeding pattern (measured as both the % of fish feeding and the food consumption per fish) was determined for a population of 60 1+ salmon (8.8 ± 0.2 cm) in May (water temperature 8° to 11^OC).   The percentage of the population feeding in the hours of darkness is substantially lower than in any other period of the day (Fig. 6a), though relatively few fish also fed at dusk. The quantity of food consumed by those fish which did feed showed little variation throughout the eight 3-hour periods (Fig. 6b).   The food intake of the population as a whole was at a minimum in darkness (Fig. 6c) though low values were recorded for both dawn and dusk.   On each of two occasions when the fish were starved for 30 hours prior to feeding in the dark period, only three fish fed and these fish took relatively small meals (0.1 to 0.2% dry body weight).   These data show that fish in the Almondbank hatchery under ambient light feed primarily between dawn and dusk.

C. Seasonal daily food intake

A bimodal population of Atlantic salmon was used to compare the 24 hour food intake of upper and lower mode fish once a month between October and March.   Irrespective of the ambient photoperiod regime, the daily food intake was calculated from the sum of the intakes during two 12-hour periods (Day: 0900 hours to 2100 hours, and Night: 2100 hours to 0900 hours).

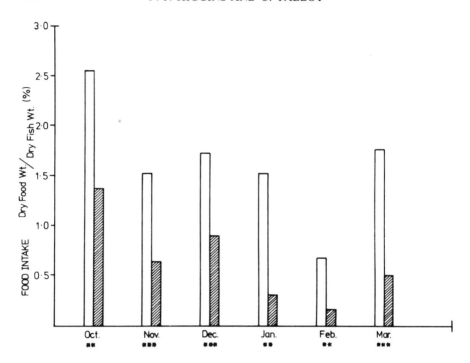

Fig. 7. Daily food intake of upper mode (open bars) and lower mode (hatched bars), between October 1983 and March 1984.

On each of the five (monthly) sampling occasions the upper mode fish took a significantly (P<0.001) larger meal (dry food as a % dry body weight) than the lower mode fish (Fig. 7, Table I). In addition there appeared to be a difference in the feeding of the two modes in the periods of daytime and night-time. On average throughout the period the upper mode fish took 33.4% of their daily food intake during the "night", compared to only 23.0% for the lower mode. This indicates that feeding by upper mode fish is less restricted during the low light levels at twilight and night than the lower mode. The temperature dependence of food intake on these six occasions is also presented (Fig. 8). Lines of best fit were calculated by the method of least squares, assuming the exponential temperature dependence of maintenance ration discussed by Brett (1979). The regression parameters relating temperature and daily food intake of fish in each growth mode are:

Table I. Feeding Experiments. 24-hour Food Intake.

Date	Temp. C	Mode	Length cm	Meal(%) *	S.E.M.	N	P
13 Oct	7.00	upper	7.83	2.95	0.216	15	<0.01
		lower	6.52	1.76	0.342	6	
10 Nov	5.38	upper	8.05	1.51	0.136	13	<0.001
		lower	6.46	0.63	0.125	8	
08 Dec	4.50	upper	8.22	1.72	0.131	12	<0.001
		lower	6.54	0.90	0.116	8	
06 Jan	3.50	upper	8.38	1.52	0.253	13	<0.01
		lower	6.57	0.30	0.111	7	
08 Feb	0.88	upper	8.52	0.67	0.074	15	<0.01
		lower	6.61	0.15	0.030	5	
15 Mar	4.00	upper	8.77	1.76	0.148	14	<0.001
		lower	6.69	0.50	0.162	6	

* - (dry weight food / dry weight fish)*100

Upper mode: Ln (24 hour food intake) = 0.615 + (0.219 * temperature)

Lower mode: Ln (24 hour food intake) = 0.099 + (0.399 * temperature)

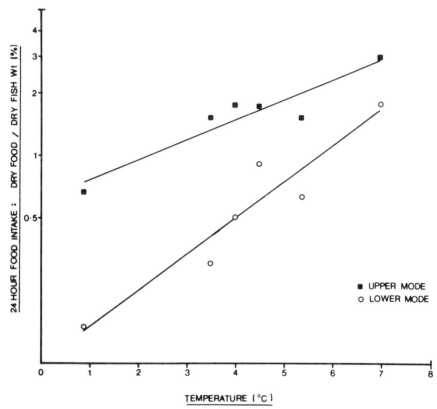

Fig. 8. Temperature dependence of daily food intake btween October 1983 and March 1984.

The upper mode fish demonstrated a significantly (P<0.01) elevated temperature specific food intake compared to the lower mode fish.

D. Conversion efficiency

Between 22 September 1982 and 25 January 1983 the microtagged population used for the specific growth rate experiment was used for the estimation of conversion efficiency. Daily food consumption was estimated for each individual once a week by feeding for 24 hours on the labelled diet. From these results monthly food intake (dry weight) was estimated from the relationship between daily temperatures throughout the month and the estimated daily food intake.

Change in dry fish weight (ΔB) was calculated once a month from the specific growth rate experiment described earlier. Individual gross conversion efficiency was estimated from the relationship:

$$n \text{ (gross)} = \Delta B/C \qquad \text{(after Webb, 1978)}$$

From these individual estimates a mean individual specific growth rate was calculated for each mode.

For each of the three intervals during which conversion efficiency was estimated, the upper mode fish showed a consistently higher efficiency than the lower mode fish. The values for the upper mode remained positive throughout the period whereas two negative values were recorded for the lower mode (Table II). This is a function of weight loss in the lower mode during the winter months.

Table II. Conversion Efficiency.

Dates	Mode	Conversion Efficiency	S.E.M.
22 Sept – 25 Oct	upper	18.6	2.51
	lower	4.8	2.77
25 Oct – 10 Dec	upper	5.5	2.88
	lower	-23.3	5.79
10 Dec – 25 Jan	upper	15.8	3.06
	lower	-15.6	12.98

Conversion Efficiency = Weight Gain / Food Consumed

IV. DISCUSSION

The environmental factors most influential in regulating food intake, growth and smolting of juvenile salmonids appear to be water temperature and photoperiod (e.g. Saunders and Henderson, 1970; Wagner, 1974; Clarke et al., 1978; Villarreal, 1983). Simpson and Thorpe (1976) have speculated that both variables are involved in the development of bimodality. Differences in growth rate which result in growth bimodality must result from differences in biochemical reaction rates under endocrine control, which in turn increase the systemic need for nutrients and hence food consumption. Photoperiod has been suggested as the main factor controlling neuroendocrine activity and hence growth in fish (Saunders and Henderson, 1970; Hoar, 1965; Lundqvist, 1983). Changes in day length and twilight are detected by the fish retina and pineal organ, and conveyed to the various hypothalamic centres where various hypothalamic "factors" are synthesised which stimulate or inhibit the synthesis and release of hormones by the adenohypophysis (for review, see Villarreal, 1983). Amongst these hormone-producing cells the most important for the growth and development of fish are somatotropes, gonadotropes, thyrotropes and lactotropes. For example, in Atlantic salmon kept under long photoperiods during smolting somatotropes increase in size and number (Olivereau, 1954; Komourdjian et al., 1976). Villarreal (1983) has proposed that in Atlantic salmon, photoperiod synchronises a genetic endogenous rhythm, timing the moment of "decision" to follow the upper or lower mode growth pattern, and that cycles of hormonal release by the adenohypophysis could account for these divergent types of development. This proposition supports the original hypothesis of Simpson and Thorpe (1976), who speculated that, as metabolic rates began to decline during late summer in response to falling water temperatures, these biochemical rates may be partially compensated for by a photoperiod induced increase in plasma thyroxine (T4) levels (known for Pleuronectes platessa (Osborn and Simpson, 1973) and Salmo gairdneri (Osborn et al., 1978)). Fish with a low threshold response to T4 would remain responsive to food and continue to feed and grow while those with a high threshold would cease to feed and switch to a catabolic state and become lower mode fish. Though the exact role of somatotropic hormones in the development of bimodality remains to be determined, some support for this original hypothesis has come from recent data. Thorpe et al. (1982), measuring RNA:DNA ratios in epaxial muscle as momentary indices of general protein synthesis, found that ratios for the upper modal group were consistently greater than those for the lower mode from November to May of the first year's growth. Using the same technique for populations held under controlled photoperiods, Villarreal (1983) also showed that modal differentiation and growth rate were under photoperiod control and suggested that the time of initiation of modal division was in a "critical photosensitive period" in June or July.

Brett (1979) has pointed out the important relationship between ration size and growth rate. Above the maintenance ration, growth rate initially increases approxiately linearly with increasing daily ration. However, above the optimum ration size, conversion efficiency begins to decrease, and growth rate increases less rapidly until it reaches a plateau where any excess food is rejected and growth is sustained at a maximum level. Upper growth mode fish have a higher weight specific daily food intake than lower mode fish (independent of temperature and season) and show a higher conversion efficiency (Fig. 6, Table II). They maintain a higher specific growth rate and calorific growth rate during the growing season and a shorter period during winter (about a month either side of the winter solstice) when calorific growth ceases (Figs. 1, 3b). Growth appears to be more closely linked to seasonal changes in photoperiod than water temperature (Fig. 1), a phenomenon noted for the brown trout (Salmo trutta) by Swift (1955) and for the lake whitefish (Coregonus clupeaformis) by Hogman (1968). Swift (1955, 1959) also found a correlation between increasing daylength and growth of brown trout in the spring and increasing endocrine activity (thyroid). Photoperiod induced springtime surges in T3, T4 and cortisol levels and pituitary somatotrophs have also been documented for salmonid smolts (Folmar and Dickhoff, 1980). The effect of photoperiod on growth rate of juvenile salmon appears to be related more to the direction of change rather than absolute daylength.

For any given temperature, whole gut evacuation is more rapid in the spring (increasing photoperiod) than the autumn (decreasing photoperiod) (Fig. 4). Seasonal variations in meal size are unlikely to account for this difference as we have previously reported (Talbot et al.,

1984) that test meals of different sizes are evacuated at similar rates when feeding occurs after the test meal is ingested. Neither should differences in body size affect evacuation rates during the study period (Talbot et al., 1984). These seasonal changes in evacuation rate may therefore be due to neural or hormonal modifications of peristalsis which are mediated by photoperiod effects on growth rate acting through the central nervous system (Fange and Grove, 1979). If growth is stimulated by hormonal changes during periods of increasing photoperiod, an increase in evacuation rate would allow the faster throughput of food necessary to achieve more rapid growth.

The results presented here also support the feeding and growth studies by Gross et al. (1965) on the green sunfish (Lepomis cyanellus). Using a variety of photoperiod regimes, they found that increasing daylength enhanced growth and a decreasing daylength inhibited growth. Furthermore, they found that fish on longer photoperiods fed longer and also had higher conversion efficiencies than fish on shorter photoperiods. Feeding activity is also closely linked to the diurnal rhythm of photoperiod (Fig. 5 a-c) with little feeding occurring during darkness, even after a period of starvation.

The relationships between size, ration, growth, temperature and photoperiod show differences between fish in the upper and lower modal groups, and in many respects these differences are unexpected. For salmonids in general, specific growth rate and maximum ration size decrease with increasing size (weight exponents of approximately 0.6 and 0.7 respectively; Brett, 1979) and one might expect smaller (i.e. lower mode) fish on an unrestricted ration to exhibit a higher weight specific food intake and growth rate. In fact, the results here indicate that for juvenile salmon the converse is the case when comparing between modal groups, and this suggests two distinct physiological populations. Higgins (1985b), found that upper mode fish have higher weight specific resting rates of oxygen consumption than lower mode fish. In the growth experiments described here, food supply was ad lib. and the lower weight specific food intake and specific growth rate shown by lower mode fish must be due to either a depressed appetite compared to upper mode fish, or to differences in feeding opportunity. The upper mode fish appear to achieve their higher weight specific food intake, at least in part, by feeding at a lower light threshold than the lower mode fish and show an elevated temperature response (Fig. 7). These results can be compared with the generalised ration/temperature relationship for sockeye salmon (Oncorhynchus nerka) of an equivalent size range (Brett et al., 1969). The daily meal taken by the upper mode fish is approximately equivalent to the optimum ration size for sustained growth for a young sockeye salmon at the same temperature, though the lower mode food intake is generally in the region of or just above maintenance. As only the food intake in excess of the maintenance ration is available for growth, the lower mode fish have a much reduced scope for growth compared to the upper mode fish.

A number of growth promoting hormones have been shown to increase appetite in fish (Fletcher, 1984), and the higher weight specific food intake, growth rate and metabolic rate shown by upper compared to lower mode fish may be common symptoms of higher titres of these hormones. The physiological evidence presented here seems to support the suggestions of Simpson and Thorpe (1976) and Villarreal (1983), that in the development of bimodality of growth in populations of juvenile Atlantic salmon, the choice of growth strategy by the individual is primarily photoperiod dependent. Seasonal changes in photoperiod may stimulate production of growth hormones through the neuroendocrine system (e.g. pineal-pituitary axis), which increase growth rate and appetite. Differential responses to seasonal and daily changes in photoperiod by individuals may account for the development of bimodality in the population, and also provide the means (through an increased daily and seasonal feeding opportunity) by which higher growth rates are sustained by the upper mode fish.

V.   ACKNOWLEDGEMENTS

The fish populations used in these experiments were maintained by the staff at the Almondbank and Pitlochry hatcheries. Mike Miles provided invaluable technical expertise, and Aileen Shanks gave guidance in statistical analyses. We are also grateful to John Thorpe for assistance in the preparation of the manuscript, and Derek Pretswell who drew the figures. One author (PJH) was supported by an award from the Science and Engineering Research Council.

REFERENCES

Bailey, J.K., Saunders, R.L. and Buzeta, M.I. (1980). Can. J. Fish. Aquat. Sci. 37, 1379-1386.

Braaten, B.R. (1979). In "Finfish Nutrition and Fishfeed Technology", (J.E. Halver and K. Tiews, eds.), 2, 461-504. Heinemann, Berlin.

Brett, J.R. (1979). In "Fish Physiology", (W.S. Hood, D.J. Randall and J.R. Brett, eds.), 8, 599-675. Academic Press, New York.

Brett, J.R., Shelbourn, J.E. and Shoop, C.T. (1969). J. Fish. Res. Bd. Can. 26, 2363-2394.

Clarke, W.C., Shelbourn, J.E., and Brett, J.R. (1978). Can. J. Zool. 56, 2413-2421.

Elliott, J.M. (1976). J. Anim. Ecol. 45, 923-948.

Elson, P.F. (1957). Can. Fish Cult. 21, 1-6.

Fange, R. and Grove, D. (1979). In "Fish Physiology", (W.S. Hood, D.J. Randall and J.R. Brett, eds.), 8, 161-260. Academic Press, New York.

Fletcher, D.J. (1984). Comp. Biochem. Physiol. 78A, 617-628.

Folmar, L.C. and Dickhoff, W.W. (1980). Aquaculture 21, 1-37.

Fry, F.E.J. (1971). In "Fish Physiology", (W.S. Hoar and D.J. Randall, eds.), 6, 1-98. Academic Press, New York.

Gross, W.L., Fromm, P.O. and Roelofs, E.W. (1965). Trans. Am. Fish. Soc. 92, 401-408.

Hanson, S.W.F. and Olley, J. (1963). Biochem. J. 89, 101-102.

Higgins, P.J. (1985a). J. Fish Biol. (in press).

Higgins, P.J. (1985b). Aquaculture (in press).

Hoar, W.S. (1965). Trans. R. Soc. Can. Ser. IV. 3, 175-200.

Hogman, W.J. (1968). J. Fish Res. Bd Can. 25, 2111-2112.

Jones, J.W. (1959). "The Salmon", 192pp. Collins, London.

Knutsson, S. and Grav, T. (1976). Aquaculture 8, 169-187.

Komoudjian, M.P., Saunders, R.L. and Fenwick, J.C. (1976). Can. J. Zool. 54, 544-551.

Lundqvist, H. (1983). Ph.D. thesis, Umea University, Sweden.

Olivereau, M. (1954). Anneé Biol. 30, 63-80.

Osborn, R.H. and Simpson, T.H. (1973). Int. Coun. Explor. Sea, CM 1973/B.23.

Osborn, R.H., Simpson, T.H. and Youngson, A.F. (1978). J. Fish Biol. 12, 531-540.

Ricker, W.E. (1979). In "Fish Physiology", (W.S. Hoar, D.J. Randall and J.R. Brett, eds.), 8, 677–743. Academic Press, New York.

Saunders, R.L. and Henderson, E.B. (1970). J. Fish Res. Bd. Can. 27, 1295–1311.

Saunders, R.L., Henderson, E.B. and Glebe, B.D. (1982). Aquaculture 28, 211–229.

Simpson, T.H. and Thorpe, J.E. (1976). Int. Coun. Explor. Sea. CM 1976/M22, 7 pp.

Swift, D.R. (1955). J. Exp. Biol. 32, 751–764.

Swift, D.R. (1959). J. Exp. Biol. 36, 120–125.

Talbot, C. and Higgins, P.J. (1983). J. Fish Biol. 23, 211–220.

Talbot, C., Higgins, P.J. and Shanks, A.M. (1984). J. Fish Biol. 25, 551–560.

Thorpe, J.E. (1977). J. Fish Biol. 11, 175–184.

Thorpe, J.E. (1981). In "Aquarium Systems", (A.D. Hawkins, ed.), 325–344. Academic Press, London.

Thorpe, J.E. and Morgan, R.I.G. (1978). J. Fish Biol. 13, 549–556.

Thorpe, J.E., Morgan, R.I.G., Ottaway, E.M. and Miles, M.S. (1980). J. Fish Biol. 17, 13–21.

Thorpe, J.E., Talbot, C. and Villarreal, C. (1982). Aquaculture 28, 123–132.

Thorpe, J.E. and Wankowski, J.W.J. (1979). In "Finfish Nutrition and Fishfeed Technology", (J.E. Halver and K. Tiews, eds.), 1, 501–513. Heinemann, Berlin.

Villarreal, C.A. (1983). Ph.D. Thesis, University of Stirling, Scotland.

Villarreal, C.A and Thorpe, J.E. (1985). Aquaculture (in press).

Wagner, H.H. (1974). Can. J. Zool. 52, 219–234.

Webb, P.W. (1978). In "Ecology of Freshwater Fish Production", (S.D. Gerking, ed.), 184–214. Blackwell Scientific Publications, Oxford.

Windell, J.T. (1978). In "Methods for Assessment of Fish Production in Fresh Waters", (T. Bagenal, ed.), 227–254. Blackwell Scientific Publications, Oxford.

CAN AMYLASE INHIBITORS FROM WHEAT REDUCE THE
DIGESTIBILITY OF STARCH AND THE GROWTH RATE IN FISH?

Ch. STURMBAUER AND R. HOFER

Institute of Zoology, University of Innsbruck, Austria.

Native starch is poorly utilized by fish, particularly
by carnivorous species (22-50%), whereas after extrusion
the utilization efficiency of starch increases up to 90%
(Inaba et al., 1963; Smith, 1971; Shimeno et al.; 1977,
Bergot and Braque, 1983). These differences can be
explained mainly by facilitated hydrolysis of gelatinized
starch but partly also by accelerated passage rates when
native starch is fed (Spannhof and Plantikow, 1983) and,
at least with native potato starch, by the absorption of
amylases on starch molecules (Spannhof and Plantikow,
1983). Although the existence of amylase inhibitors in
several grains, like wheat and rye, and their effects upon
amylases of several animals are well known (Silano et al.,
1975; O'Donnell and McGeeney, 1976; O'Connor and McGeeney,
1981) these inhibitors have not been considered as a
factor of importance in the feeding of fish.

Wheat contains several amylase inhibiting albumins
which can be classified into three molecular weight
groups: a 12 500 dalton albumin fraction which affects
insect and other invertebrate amylases, fractions of
24 000 (two subunits) and 60 000 dalton (four subunits)
which inhibit also vertebrate amylases (Silano et al.,
1975).

The inhibitors can be denatured by heating but they are
resistant to acid treatment. All molecular fractions can
be hydrolysed by pepsin but only the high molecular weight
inhibitor is affected by trypsin and chymotrypsin.

In contrast to Silano et al. (1975) who did not find
inhibiting effects of wheat upon amylases in two marine

NUTRITION AND FEEDING IN FISH
ISBN: 0 12 194055 1

species of fish (Scorpaena ustulata and Mugil auratus) we were able to demonstrate drastic inhibition of trout and carp amylases by this type of food (Hofer and Sturmbauer, unpublished observations).

In in vitro experiments simulating natural conditions amylases of both species are inhibited to 10-30% of their initial activity. Because of its higher activity (10-30 fold) the amylase of carp is relatively more affected by the inhibitor than is that of the trout. However, the inhibitor is hydrolysed by proteolytic enzymes of the intestinal fluid. This results in an almost total recovery of amylase activity after four hours in trout whereas in carp recovery is much lower. This despite the fact that proteolytic activity in the intestinal fluid of both species is of equal magnitude. Due to its instability against pepsin temporal storage of the diet in the stomach may result in a further reduction of the inhibitor in trout.

However, in carp fed native or extruded carp diet containing wheat, no significant differences in amylase activity could be found in the intestinal fluids (Hofer and Sturmbauer, unpublished observations). This suggests complete compensation of the effect of the inhibitor, probably by an increase in the production of pancreatic amylase. Since it is doubtful whether the inhibited amylase can be reabsorbed to the same extent as uninhibited enzymes (Hofer, 1982), the increase in amylase production may lead to higher losses of enzyme proteins, and consequently, to a negative influence on the protein balance of the fish.

REFERENCES

Bergot, F. and Breque, J. (1983). Aquaculture 34, 203-212.

Hofer, R. (1982). Comp. Biochem. Physiol. 72A, 55-63.

Inaba, D., Ogino, C., Takamatsu, T., Ueda, T. and Kurokawa, K. (1963). Bull. Jap. Soc. Sci. Fish. 29, 242-244.

O'Connor, C.M. and McGeeney, K.F. (1981). Biochim. Biophys. Acta 658, 387-396.

O'Donnell, M.D. and McGeeney, K.F. (1976). Biochim. Biophys. Acta 422, 159-169.

Shimeno, S., Hosokawa, H., Hirata, H. and Takeda, M.
    (1977). Bull. Jap. Soc. Sci. Fish. 43, 213–217.
Silano, V., Furia, M., Gianfreda, L., Macri, A.,
    Palescandolo, R., Rab, A., Scardi, V., Stella, E. and
    Valfre, F. (1975). Biochim. Biophys. Acta 391, 170–178.
Smith, R.R. (1971).   Prog. Fish-Cult. 33, 132–134.
Spannhof, L. and Plantikow, H. (1983).   Aquaculture 30,
    95–108.

GROSS NUTRITION AND CONVERSION EFFICIENCY OF INTENSIVELY AND EXTENSIVELY REARED CARP (<u>CYPRINUS CARPIO</u> L.).

K.T. O'GRADY AND P.B. SPILLETT

<u>Department of Zoology, Royal Holloway College,</u>
<u>Englefield Green, Surrey TW20 9TY</u>
and <u>Thames Water Authority, Denton House, Iffley Turn,</u>
<u>Oxford OX4 4HT.</u>

I.   INTRODUCTION

Our interest in the gross nutrition of carp arose from the need to produce coarse fish (non-salmonids, initially carp) for the restitution of recreational waters.   Carp for this purpose have been reared in the disused filter beds of the Thames Water Authority, Lea Bridge water works (O'Grady and Spillett, 1981).

In the U.K. carp are at the limit of their climatic range and natural spawning and early survival are unpredictable and unreliable.   This has been particularly true in the Lea Bridge filter beds where early survival has often been less than 7% despite an abundance of zooplankton which are suitable food organisms (Mann, 1961; Matlak and Matlak, 1976). The growing-on of carp of 15-30 g to 200-400 g from May to September in one season has, however, been very successful and economic, with high production levels (O'Grady and Spillett, 1981). Therefore, carp of an appropriate size for stocking the ponds in May have been reared in heated, recirculated water at temperatures suitable for efficient growth and feed conversion, i.e. 25-30°C (Aston and Brown, 1978; Jauncey, 1982).

NUTRITION AND FEEDING IN FISH
ISBN: 0 12 194055 1

There were three main aims of our studies: 1) to assess the contribution of natural foods to the pond rearing of carp; 2) to find a suitable commercially available feed for intensive rearing in these ponds; 3) to find a suitable commercially available feed for the indoor rearing of fry up to about 20 g.   Consideration of the effectiveness of a feed was in relation to: a) growth rate; b) cost; c) conversion ratio and d) logistics, i.e. availability, storage and manpower.   There was also a remit to investigate alternative feeds with a view to reducing costs.   Because of the constraints of (d) this was largely limited to what was available from the suppliers of animal feeds.   This did, however, permit a range of protein, lipid and carbohydrate levels to be used.   In   addition,   activated   sewage   sludge   was incorporated into a conventional fish feed to reduce costs whilst maintaining protein levels.

II.   LABORATORY FEEDING TRIALS

A. Performance of commercially available feeds

Overall, feed I was the most suitable in the laboratory trials (Table 1).   The feed conversion rate (FCR) for 3 and 5% b.w.d.$^{-1}$ (Table II) was about 2.   A superior FCR and specific growth rate (SGR) were obtained with a 5% ration of feed 2 but as this had a higher level of crude protein it gave a poorer protein efficiency ratio (PER) and was more expensive. The feed cost of producing 1 kg of carp was £0.74 for feed 2 and £0.56–£0.62 for feed 1. (At 1984 prices the cost per kg carp was £0.74 for feed 1.)

The efficacy of these feeds was related in part to the protein levels and in part to the relatively high lipid levels. The performance of feed 1 was in keeping with the 38% protein optimum given by Ogino and Saito (1970). Subsequently, Ogino et al. (1976) and Jauncey (1981) have shown   that   35%   crude   protein   is   optimal   if   the metabolisable energy is increased to 3.4 – 3.7 kcal g^{-1}.

Unlike feeds 1 and 2, feeds 3, 4 and 5 were not formulated   for   fish.   Normally   used   for   herbivorous mammals, they are high in carbohydrates and low in protein and lipid.   Feed 5 was an exception to this, having a crude protein to lipid ratio of 2.4:1, approaching that of

Table I.   Composition and costs of commercially available feeds and naturally available foods.

Composition	Feed 1 1980	Feed 1 1982	Feed 2	Feed 3 (a)	Feed 4	Feed 5	ZP (b)	BI (c)
% Crude Protein	38.0	40.0	47.0	9.0	19.0	21.5	48.0	47.7
% Crude Lipid	16.0	15.0	17.5	1.5	3.3	9.0	21.3	13.8
% Crude Carbohydrate	23.5	22.5	15.0	67.4	44.0	46.0	4.4	22.9
% Crude Fibre	3.5	3.5	2.0	4.5	7.7	1.3	7.7	4.0
% Ash	10.0	10.0	9.5	2.6	26.0	22.2	12.4	9.2
% Water	9.0	9.0	9.0	15.0			-	-
Gross Energy $Kj\ g^{-1}$	19.1	19.0	20.4	14.2	13.2	16.4	20.3	20.5
(d) $(kcal\ g^{-1})$	4.57	4.55	4.86	3.4	3.16	3.92	4.86	4.89
Cost $(£)\ kg^{-1}$	0.279	0.312	0.405	0.14	0.20	0.427	-	-
Crude Protein: Crude Lipid	2.4:1	2.7:1	2.7:1	6:1	5.8:1	2.4:1	2.3:1	3.5:1

Notes: Feeds 1 = Ewos T51 trout pellets, 2 = Ewos S30 trout starter pellets,
3 = whole cleaned barley, 4 = Dixon's SG1 rabbit pellet,
5 = Dixon's CDDM mouse pellet, ZP = zooplankton, BI = benthic
invertebrates.

(a) Hickling (1962) (b) Crustacean zooplankton (d.w.) based on a mixture of 40%
Daphnia pulex and 50% Cyclops spp. (d.w.), Yurkowski and Tabachek (1979).
(c) Benthic invertebrates (chironomids) (d.w.), Yurkowski and Tabachek (1979)
(d) calculated on the basis of protein 5.5 kcal g^{-1}, lipid 9.5 kcal g^{-1} and
carbohydrate 4.1 kcal g^{-1}, Winberg (1971).

feeds 1 and 2 and in contrast to about 6:1 for feeds 3 and 4.   The latter feeds, although cheaper to buy, were more expensive because of poor SGR and FCR resulting in costs per kg carp produced of £1.11 (feed 3), and £1.62 (feed 4).   The use of protein for energy at the expense of growth would account for the poor performance of feeds 3 and 4.   Both contained little lipid to spare protein, unlike feed 5, and the large amount of carbohydrate present did not fulfill this role.   Shimeno et al. (1979) reported poor growth of fish on a diet with 10-20% digestible carbohydrate and Spannhof and Plantikow (1983) reported that fish were poor digesters of starch.

According to Bergot and Breque (1983) the available
information on starch digestion in fish indicates
considerable variation in the utilisation of starch. The
exact form of carbohydrate in carp diets will influence
its utilisation. Ufodike and Matty (1983), using rice and
cassava incorporated into experimental diets, showed that
carbohydrate can be well utilised by carp. A high
proportion of cellulose in feeds 3 and 4 may be the reason
for poor utilisation.   In contrast, feed 5 with a high
carbohydrate content was more effective with growth
comparable to feed 1 and resulted in the highest PER
(1.8).   Performance was attributed to the 9% lipid level
enabling protein sparing for growth (Jauncey, 1982).
However, the high cost and poor FCR makes feed 5 expensive
to use, (£1.11 per kg carp produced).

B. Ration size

The optimum ration size for fish growth has been
studied by Brett et al. (1969) for salmonids and Huisman
(1976) for carp and rainbow trout.   Our data indicated
that SGR was asymptotic with ration size. This was
similar to the findings of Brett et al. (1969) and Huisman
(1976) for salmonids but differed from the latter author's
findings for carp which were that the SGR reached an
optimum with a ration size of 7% and above this SGR
declined.   Huisman (1976) found an optimum ration for
growth of 2.2% b.w.d.$^{-1}$. Our observations with smaller
fish, initial weight of 7.3 g, gave an optimum ration of
3.9% b.w.d^{-1}. However, our data with carp of 90 g and
rations of 1, 2 and 3% agree with Huisman's optimum
feeding rate of 2.2%.   Therefore, optimum ration size,
like metabolic rate, declines with increased body size.
This is further supported by the data of Bryant and Matty
(1981) who found that carp post-larvae required 15-17%
b.w.d.$^{-1}$ for optimum growth compared with 10-15%
b.w.d.$^{-1}$ for larger fry (100mg - 3g).

C. Activated sewage sludge

The substitution (0, 5, 10, 20 and 40%) of activated
sewage sludge into a conventional 40% protein fish food
gave SGRs that were not significantly different between
treatments during a seven week study. However, the trends
in growth suggest that it would be imprudent to take the

view that activated sewage sludge does not suppress the growth of carp. The divergence of the 20% and 40% growth curves might lead to significantly different endpoints after a longer period of growth. Moreover, there was a significant reduction in the condition of the carp at higher levels of substitution. Both SGR and FCR were poorer in the 20% and 40% treatments. There was evidence of protein sparing in the 10% and 20% treatments but not at the 40% level.

Incorporation rates of up to 33% of activated sewage sludge were shown by Tacon (1979) to cause no loss of growth or any toxic results in rainbow trout. Similarly, a study by Anwar et al. (1982) showed that up to 70% substitution of activated sewage sludge for cotton seed meal was possible for carp without loss of performance although substitution of 40% gave the best result. Treatments lower than 40%, other than the control, were not used and potentially deleterious components, apart from low energy levels, were not considered. In an earlier study by Tacon and Ferns (1976) a change in the body composition of rainbow trout occurred with increased substitution of activated sewage sludge. It was suggested that this might relate to the presence of anabolic steroids in the sewage sludge. Changes in body composition may also result from heavy metal content. Accumulation of heavy metals from dietary activated sewage sludge by rainbow trout was demonstrated by elevated carcass levels of Pb, Cr, Fe and Ni (Singh and Ferns, 1978). The levels of heavy metals in sewage sludge used in our studies were higher (Moore, 1983) than in the work of Tacon (1979) and Tacon and Ferns (1976). In particular, levels of Pb, Cd, Cu, Ni and Cr were relatively high and increased with increased substitution in the diet. Even at the 5% and 10% level of substitution the concentrations of these metals were appreciably greater than the control. The loss of condition and the reduction of SGR with increased incorporation of sewage sludge may have resulted from the chronic effects of heavy metal accumulation.

III. POND FEEDING TRIALS

A. Extensive rearing

The levels of carp production (300–350 Kgha^{-1}) in our extensive cultivation studies were rather higher than generally reported (Bardach et al., 1972; Huet, 1973) and comparable with the addition of fertilisers, e.g. 300 kg ha^{-1} (Huisman, 1981) and 477 - 518 kg ha^{-1} with heavier fertilisation (Szumiec, 1976). This was in keeping with the eutrophic nature of the site. Low levels of biomass (0.038 - 0.058 g m^{-2}) and production (0.095 - 0.145 g m^{-2} d.w.) by chironomids were apparent. Unless extremely favourable rates of secondary production and/or FCR are assumed, the quantity of chironomids available was unlikely to contribute much to the bulk of the carp diet, although they may play an important qualitative role in the diet of carp. Obtaining reliable estimates of biomass and production of many benthic organisms is problematic because of sampling procedures (Morgan, 1980) and extrapolation from our data is difficult. The standing crop of benthic organisms elsewhere is generally higher than we observed; 3.5 - 13.2 g m^{-2} (Lellak, 1969) and 3.5 - 43.8 g m^{-2} (Hruska, 1961) for conventional carp ponds with rich muddy/sandy substrates. This difference may explain why the contribution of chironomids to the diet of pond carp has been considered of greater importance by other authors. Sarig (1966) discussed the findings from a variety of sources. In some cases a marked preference for chironomids over zooplankton was noted whereas in others the importance of the zooplankton was stressed. In particular, carp of up to 1.5 kg were found to consume large quantities of zooplankton, up to 100 g of Daphnia every five hours.

The zooplankton community in our study had a geometric mean biomass (d.w.) of 2.72 g m^{-2} and a total production (d.w.) of 122 g m^{-2} (1.235 g m^{-2}d^{-1}). This compared favourably with a fertilised but unfed carp pond in the USSR which had a mean seasonal zooplankton biomass of 2.27 g m^{-2} and a production of 34 g m^{-2} for the carp growing period (Kamlyuk et al., 1979). In a similar study of the zooplankton of carp ponds in Poland, Lewkowicz and Lewkowicz (1981) reported a mean monthly biomass of 1-1.9 g m^{-2} (d.w.) and total production of 70.3 g m^{-2} (d.w.) for a pond fed at a moderate level with a relatively low fish density. In these latter two studies the zooplankton communities were dominated by Bosmina longirostris and rotifers. In our study crustacean zooplankton formed the great majority of the biomass, the dominant species being in order of numerical abundance, Daphnia longispina, Cyclops vernalis americanus, Bosmina longirostris, and Cyclops vicinus.

Natural zooplankton food organisms are not fully utilised by carp in ponds (Yashouv, 1954). Consumption of

47% of the zooplankton production by 2 year old carp (of similar size to those in our studies) was observed with a moderate stock density of 50 kg ha^{-1} by Kamlyuk et al. (1979). This food source accounted for 41% of the growth of carp when there was no addition of supplementary feed. Applying a similar utilisation to our extensive pond trial in 1982 but assuming that virtually all of the carp growth derived from this source, as little other food was available, a dry weight FCR of 1.6 resulted (23 for wet weight). In comparison, Kamlyuk et al. (1979) obtained an FCR of 0.65 dry weight (9.3 wet weight). Although approximate, values for FCR of this magnitude are consistent with the protein and lipid content of this food source (Table 1) compared with the FCRs obtained for other diets of approximately similar protein and lipid composition. The FCR for artificial diets may often be based upon the amount of food given and it is assumed that all of this is eaten to produce the observed fish growth. If the FCR is recalculated on the basis of the total zooplankton production, this results in a value of 3.5 (d.w.) (50 w.w.) which may be more strictly comparable with an FCR for artificial foods in intensive pond cultivation.

B. Intensive rearing

The SGRs for intensively reared carp were higher than for extensive rearing because the food resource was not limited despite a higher stock density (Table II). The crude FCRs for the intensive trials were about 2 for feed 1 and 3.3 for the mixture of feeds 1 and 3. Calculated in this way these values assume that the contribution of natural food was slight. The background level of carp production in these ponds, i.e. 300–350 kg ha^{-1} from extensive cultivation, is significant and it might be considered necessary to subtract this value from the intensive production value to obtain a true measure of growth due to the supplementary feed. However, Wirszubsky (1953) believed that production values from unfertilised ponds could not be used as a standard measure to extrapolate to intensive rearing because of the large fluctuations in zooplankton abundance observed. Random variation in the production capacity is a further complicating factor and Wohlfarth and Moav (1968) and Buck et al. (1970) found that random development in organic matter led to dissimilar production capacities in similar

Table II The performance of feeds used

	Laboratory Feeding trials									Pond Feeding trials			
	Feed 1				Feed 2		Feed 3	Feed 4	Feed 5	Feed 1 (1980)	Feed 1 & 3 (1980)	Feed 1 (1982)	Extensive
Ration (a)	3	5	7	10	3	5	3	5	5	2500	1540+3230	4440	–
SGR wt (% day^{-1})	0.9	1.6	1.9	2.0	0.8	1.9	0.6	0.4	1.3	2.0	2.4	1.7	1.4
FCR	2.0	2.0	2.3	3.5	2.4	1.8	7.9	8.1	2.6	1.8	3.5	2.0	1.6
PER	1.2	1.3	1.1	0.9	0.9	1.2	1.4	0.7	1.8	1.5	1.6	1.2	0.6

Note: (a) percentage body weight per day for laboratory trials and Kgha^{-1}y^{-1} for pond trials

ponds. In fact, the zooplankton community structure in
the 1982 intensive trial differed from that in the
extensive trial. The same four species predominated but
Bosmina longirostris was numerically dominant and Daphnia
longispina was much less abundant, only the third most
common species. There was also a reduction in the average
body size of the larger zooplankters with intensification.
The average size of D. longispina was reduced from 0.89 to
0.78 mm and Cyclops vicionus from 0.87 to 0.76 mm.
Consequent upon these changes in community structure was a
reduction in the the geometric mean biomass and total
production to 1.58 g m^{-2} and 40.3 g m^{-2}
(0.41 g m^{-2}d^{-1}) respectively. This overall change
was attributed to the direct effect of carp eating
zooplankton, enrichment caused by increased nutrient
recycling due to the presence of carp, and enrichment
caused by nutrients derived from the supplementary foods.
Intensification generally leads to an increase in
zooplankton biomass and production. Lewkowicz and
Lewkowicz (1981) found an increase from 1 - 1.9 to 1.7 -
5.0 g m^{-2} mean biomass and 70 g m^{-2} to 170 g m^{-2} in
production when a low level of supplementary feeding was
compared with a higher level. Kamlyuk et al. (1979)
reported that at intensive levels with supplementary
feeding the mean biomass rose to 3.31 g m^{-2} (d.w.) and
production to 60.9 g m^{-2} (d.w.). These studies are
broadly comparable with the present one if allowance is
made for differences because of site management and
climate, etc. A similar shift to Bosmina longirostris
was apparent out much of the production in these studies
was due to rotifers especially at the higher level of
supplementary feeding. These and B. longirostris are of
little direct value to larger carp because of their small
size and unlike extensive rearing, utilisation of
zooplankton by carp may be poor under intensive
conditions. The proportions utilised were given as 31%
and 25% by Kamlyuk et al. (1979) and 3-5% of the food
biomass by Okoniewska (1981). The value of zooplankton as
a fish food under intensive conditions may therefore be at
the beginning of the growing season before supplementary
feeding has started or is at a low rate. Assuming the
same FCR to that obtained for extensive cultivation, since
the carp would be eating the same organisms, and a 31%
rate of utilisation (Kamlyuk et al., 1979) of the total
zooplankton production of 40.3 g m^{-2}, only 76 kg ha^{-1}
of the carp production of 2200 kg ha^{-1} was due to
natural foods. The crude FCR for feed 1 in 1982 was 2.0.

This is increased only to 2.09 by allowing for the
contribution of natural food. This is in agreement with
von Lukowicz (1982) who believed that with intensive carp
culture natural foods played little practical role and the
carp fed only on pellets. The FCR obtained in the latter
case ranged from 1.96–2.48 in agreement with our
observations. Rappaport and Sarig (1979) also reported a
similar range of FCR of 2.0–3.4 for carp in Israel but
under very different conditions and with a 25% crude
protein feed. Given that natural foods played little part
in the gross nutrition of intensively reared carp an
estimate may be made of the FCR of feed 3 (barley) in the
1980 trial employing a mixture of feeds 1 and 3. Using
the 1980 FCR value for feed 1, the estimated FCR for
barley was 6.3. This is similar to the value of the 4 –
6 given by Hickling 1962) for cereals and that given by
Huet (1973) for barley. Bardach et al. (1972) reported a
superior FCR of 2.9 for barley but also quoted the crude
protein as 12–27%. The components of barley and other
vegetable materials may therefore be sufficiently variable
to render extrapolation from published FCRs difficult
unless the composition is known to be the same.

IV.   ACKNOWLEDGEMENTS

This work forms part of a project funded by Thames
Water Authority and we are grateful for permission to
publish. We also thank Dr. D.S. Northcott for the
zooplankton data and the NERC for a grant to support that
work.

REFERENCES

Anwar, A., Ishak, M.M., El-Zeiny, M. and Hassanen, G.D.I.
    (1982). Aquaculture 28, 321–325.
Aston, R.J. and Brown, D.J. (1978). Proc. on fish farming
    and wastes. (C.H.R. Pastakia, ed.) Institute of Fish-
    eries Management and Society of Chemical Industry.39–62.
Bardach, J.E., Ryther, J.H. and McLarney, W.D. (1972).
    "Aquaculture", 868pp, Wiley Intersciences.
Bergot, F. and Breque, J. (1983). Aquaculture 34, 203–212.
Brett, J.R., Shelbourn, J.E. and Shoop, C.F. (1969).J.Fish
    Res. Board. Can. 26, 2363–2394.

Bryant, P.L. and Matty, A.J. (1981). Aquaculture 23, 275-286.

Buck, D.H., Thoits, C.F. and Rose, C.R. (1970). Trans. Am. Fish. Soc. 99, 74-79.

Hickling, C.F. (1962). "Fish Culture". Faber and Faber, London. 317pp.

Hruska, V. (1961). Verh. Internat. Verein. Limnol. 14, 732-736.

Huet, M. (1973). "Textbook of fish culture", 436pp, Fishing news (Books) Ltd.

Huisman, E.A. (1976). Aquaculture 9, 259-273.

Huisman, E.A. (1981). In "Bio-engineering for fish culture", (L.J. Allen and E.C. Kinney, eds.), 266-273. FCS Publ. I. American Fisheries Society.

Jauncey, K. (1981). In "Aquaculture in heated effluents and recirculation systems" (K. Tiews, ed.), 249-261. Heeneman GmbH and Co. Berlin.

Jauncey, K. (1982). In "Recent advances in aquaculture" (J.E. Muir and R.J. Roberts, eds.), 4, 217-263. Croom Helm, London.

Kamlyuk, L.V., Lyakhnovich, U.P. and Kopylova, T.V. (1979) J. Ichthyol. 18, 665-669.

Lellak, J. (1969). Verh. Internat. Verein. Limnol. 17, 560-569.

Lewkowicz, M. and Lewkowicz, S. (1981). Acta Hydrobiol. 23, 297-317.

von Lukowicz, M. (1982). Aquaculture Engineering 1, 121-137.

Mann, H. (1961). In "Fish as food" (G. Borgstrom, ed.) 1, 77-102. Academic Press.

Matlak, J. and Matlak, O. (1976). Acta Hydrobiol. 18, 203-228.

Moore, C.M. (1983). Internal Fisheries Report SS/38. Thames Water Authority. 31pp.

Morgan, N.C. (1980). In "The functioning of freshwater eco systems, IBP 22" (E.D. Le Cren and R.H. Lowe-McConnell, eds.), 247-346. Cambridge University Press.

Ogino, C., Chiou, J.Y. and Takeuchi, T. (1976). Bull. Jap. Soc. Sci. Fish. 42, 213-218.

Ogino, C. and Saito, K. (1970). Bull. Jap. Soc. Sci. Fish. 36, 250-254.

O'Grady, K.T. and Spillett, P.B. (1981). Proc. 2nd Brit. Freshw. Fish Conf. P. 17-28. Univ. of Liverpool.

Okoniewska, G. (1981). Foczn. Nauk. Roln. 99, 94-95 (English summary).

Sarig, S. (1966). Synopsis of biological data on common carp Cyprinus carpio (Linnaeus) 1958 (Near East and Europe). F.A.O. Fish Synops. (31.2).

Shimeno, S., Hosokawa, H. and Takeda, M. (1979). In "Finfish nutrition and fishfeed technology" (J.E. Halver and K. Tiews, eds.), 1, 127-143. Heenemann Gmbh and Co. Berlin.

Singh, S.M. and Ferns, P.N. (1978). J. Fish Biol. 13, 277-286.

Spannhof, L. and Plantikow, H. (1983). Aquaculture 30, 95-108.

Szumiec, J. (1976). In "FAO Technical Conference on Aquaculture", Kyoto, Japan FAO-FIR:AQ/CONF/76.E.70. 5p.

Tacon, A.G.J. and Ferns, P.N. (1976). Nutr. Rep. Int. 13, 549-562.

Ufodike, E.B.C. and Matty, A.J. (1983). Aquaculture 31, 31-50.

Winberg, G.G. (ed). (1971). Symbols, units and conversion factors in studies of freshwater productivity. IBP Selection PF. IBP Central Office, London.

Wirszubsky, A. (1953). Bamidgeh 5, 72-87.

Wohlfarth, G.W. and Moav, R. (1968). FAO Fisheries Reports 4, 487-492.

Yashouv, A. (1954). Bamidgeh 6, 103-108.

Yurkowski, M. and Tabachek, J.L. (1979). In "Finfish nutrition and fishfeed technology" (J.E. Halver and K. Tiews, eds.), 1, 435-448, Heenemann GmbH and Co., Berlin.

ESSENTIAL FATTY ACID AND LIPID REQUIREMENT OF FISH

AKIO KANAZAWA

Faculty of Fisheries, University of Kagoshima,
Shimoarata 4, Kagoshima, Japan

I. INTRODUCTION

Much research on the essential fatty acid (EFA)
requirements of fish has been performed during the last
decade.   In contrast to the situation with mammals, the
importance of EFA in fish nutrition has been emphasized
(Kayama, 1964, 1972, 1974, 1977, 1978, 1983; Sinnhuber,
1969; Yone, 1975, 1980; Sargent, 1976; Cowey and Sargent,
1979: Leger, 1980; Watanabe, 1982a; Kanazawa, 1983a).

Recently, we have succeeded in rearing fish larvae on
artificial microparticulate diets.   This work has
contributed to our knowledge of lipid nutrition in the
larval stages of freshwater and marine fish.

This paper concerns the importance of EFA in fish
nutrition and discusses the lipid requirements of fish
larvae.

II. BIOSYNTHESIS OF FATTY ACIDS

Fish produce acetyl–CoA, which is a precursor for fatty
acid biosynthesis, by ß–oxidation of fatty acids and by
catabolism of proteins and carbohydrates.

Mead et al. (1960) have shown by tracer experiments
that Tilapia mossambica is incapable of incorporating the
injected [1-^{14}C] acetate into polyunsaturated fatty
acids.   This suggested a similar pathway of fatty acid

NUTRITION AND FEEDING IN FISH
ISBN: 0 12 194055 1

biosynthesis to that found in mammals.   Also, Klenk and Kremer   (1960)   postulated   that C_{20} and C_{22} highly unsaturated fatty acids (HUFA) occurring in fish could be derived from exogenous sources and their precursors i.e. fatty acids with shorter carbon atom chains.   This idea was based on the fact that the in vitro incubation of liver   slices   of   the   fish   with $[1-^{14}C]$ acetate   gave neither ω3- nor ω6-HUFA.   Recently, Kanazawa et al. (1980a) demonstrated that Tilapia zillii incorporated

Table I. Distribution of radioactivity in the fatty acids of polar and netral lipids isolated from Tilapia Zillii after injection of $(1-^{14}C)$ acetate.

Fatty acid	Distribution % of radioactivity	
	Polar	Neutral
14:0	0.8	4.2
16:0	73.1	11.8
18:0	11.4	12.4
14:1	0.7	4.8
16:1	4.1	31.1
18:1ω9	4.1	28.8
20:1ω9	2.5	1.1
18:2ω6	0.9	1.0
18:3ω3	0.1	0.3
20:3ω6		
18:4ω3	0.4	
20:3ω3		
20:4ω6		1.6
22:4ω6		
22:5ω6		
20:5ω3	1.2	
22:5ω3		
22:6ω3		

Table II.   Fish in which an essential fatty acid requirement has been shown.

Fish	Reference
Freshwater fish:	
Channel catfish, _Ictalurus punctatus_	Stickney and Andrews (1971, 1972)
Carp, _Cyprinus carpio_	Watanabe et al. (1975a,b) Takeuchi and Watanabe (1977a) Farkas et al. (1977)
Rainbow trout, _Salmo gairdneri_	Lee et al. (1967) Castell et al. (1972a,b,c) Sinnhuber et al. (1972) Yu and Sinnhuber (1972, 1976) Watanabe et al. (1974a,b,c) Takeuchi and Watanabe (1976, 1977b,c, 1982) Yu et al. (1979) Castledine and Buckley (1980)
Chinook salmon, _Oncorhynchus tshawytscha_	Nicolaides and Woodall (1962)
Chum salmon, _Oncorhynchus keta_	Takeuchi et al. (1979) Takeuchi and Watanabe (1982)
Coho salmon, _Oncorhynchus kisutch_	Ota et al. (1979) Yu and Sinnhuber (1979) Takeuchi and Watanabe (1982)
Ayu, _Plecoglossus altivelis_	Kanazawa et al. (1982c)
Eel, _Anguilla japonica_	Takeuchi et al. (1980)
Snakehead, _Channa micropeltes_	Cowey et al. (1983b)
Tilapia zillii	Kanazawa et al. (1980b)
Tilapia nilotica	Teshima et al. (1982a) Takeuchi et al. (1983)
Marine fish:	
Red sea bream, _Chrysophrys major_	Yone and Fujii (1975a,b) Fujii and Yone (1976) Fujii et al. (1976)
Black sea bream, _Mylio macrocephalus_	Yone (1978)
Opaleye, _Girella nigricans_	Yone (1978)
Yellowtail, _Seriola quinqueradiata_	Yone (1978) Deshimaru et al. (1982a,b) Deshimaru (1984)
Puffer fish, _Fugu rubripens_	Kanazawa et al. (Unpub.)
Turbot, _Scophthalmus maximus_	Cowey et al. (1976) Gatesoupe et al. (1977b,c)
Plaice, _Pleuronectes platessa_	Owen et al. (1972)
Starry flounder, _Paralichthys olivaceus_	Kanazawa et al. (Unpub.)

[1-^{14}C] acetate into palmitic (16.0), palmitoleic
(16:1ω7), stearic (18:0), and oleic (18:1 ω 9) acids.
However, there was scarcely any incorporation into
linoleic (18:2ω6), linolenic (18:3ω3), eicosa-pentaenoic
(20:5ω3), and docosahexaenoic (22:6ω3) acids, as shown
in Table I.

III. ESSENTIAL FATTY ACIDS

Since fish are incapable of <u>de-novo</u> synthesis of
18:2 ω 6, 18:3 ω 3, 20:5 ω 3, and 22:6 ω 3 acids, dietary
sources of these fatty acids are likely to be essential
for normal growth and survival. In fact, this has been
demonstrated in feeding experiments with a variety of fish
species (see Table II).   With the exception of <u>Tilapia</u>
and snakehead, fish generally required ω3-fatty acids
rather than ω6-fatty acids in contrast to terrestrial

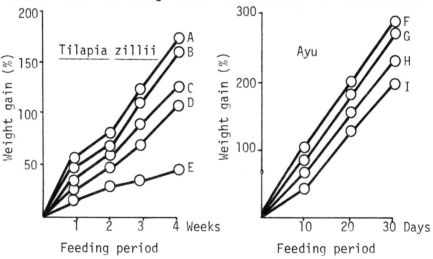

Fig. 1. Effect of essential fatty acids on growth of
freshwater fish

A: 4% 12:0 + 1% 18:2ω6   F: 8% 18:1ω9 + 1% 20:5ω3
B: 4% 12:0 + 1% 20:4ω6   G: 8% 18:1ω9 + 1% 18:3ω3
C: 4% 12:0 + 1% 20:5ω3   H: 8% 18:1ω9 + 1% 18:2ω6
D: 4% 12:0 + 1% 18:3ω3   I: 9% 18:1ω9
E: 5% 12:0

animals which require ω6-fatty acids such as 18:2 ω 6 and
20:4 ω 6. Kayama (1977) suggested that aquatic animals
(poikilothermic animals) may have a requirement for
ω 3-fatty acids because they generally have a lower body
temperature than mammals (homeothermic animals) and
ω 3-fatty acids have a lower melting point than
corresponding ω6-fatty acids of equal carbon chain
length. The efficacy of 18:3ω3 as EFA was similar to
that of either 20:5 ω3 or 22:6 ω3 in freshwater fish such
as the rainbow trout (Yu and Sinnhuber, 1972; Takeuchi and
Watanabe, 1976, 1977c, 1982), chum salmon (Takeuchi et
al., 1979; Takeuchi and Watanabe, 1982), Ayu
(Kanazawa et al., 1982c), and eel (Takeuchi et al.,
1980). In contrast, 18:3ω3 was scarcely effective as an
EFA source for marine fish like the flatfish (Owen et al.,
1972; Cowey et al., 1976; Gatesoupe et al., 1977b, c), red
sea bream (Fujii and Yone, 1976), and puffer fish
(Kanazawa et al., unpub.). For these latter species,
20:5 ω3 was the most effective EFA source. The Tilapia
(Kanazawa et al., 1980b; Teshima et al., 1982a; Takeuchi

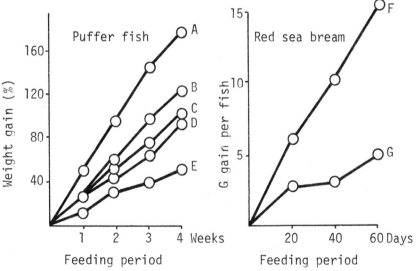

Fig. 2. Effect of essential fatty acids on growth of
marine fish

A: 7% 18:1ω9 + 1% 20:5ω3   F: 6.5% 12:0 + 2.5% HUFA
B: 7% 18:1ω9 + 1% 20:4ω6   G: 5.3% 12:0 + 3.7% 18:3ω3
C: 7% 18:1ω9 + 1% 18:3ω3
D: 7% 18:1ω9 + 1% 18:2ω6
E: 8% 18:1ω9

Table III. Requirements of fish for essential fatty acids

Fish	Requirement		Reference
Rainbow trout	18:3 ω 3	1%	Castell et al. (1972c)
	18:3 ω 3	0.83-1.66%	Watanabe et al. (1974b)
Carp	18:2 ω 6 and 18:3 ω 3	1% 1%)	Takeuchi and Watanabe (1977a)
Eel	18:2 ω 6 and 18:3 ω 3	0.5% 0.5%)	Takeuchi et al. (1980)
Chum salmon	18:2 ω 6 and 18:3 ω 3	1% 1%)	Takeuchi et al. (1979) Takeuchi and Watanabe (1982)
Coho salmon	18:3 ω 3*	1-2.5%	Yu and Sinnhuber (1979)
Ayu	18:3 ω 3 or 20:5 ω 3	1% 1%)	Kanazawa et al. (1982b)
Tilapia zillii	18:2 ω 6 or 20:4 ω 6	1% 1%)	Kanazawa et al. (1980b)
Tilapia nilotica	18:2 ω 6	0.5%	Takeuchi et al. (1983)
Red sea bream	20:5 ω 3 or ω 3 HUFA	0.5% 0.5%)	Yone et al. (1978)
Turbot	ω 3 HUFA	0.8%	Gatesoupe et al. (1977b)

* Trilinolenin

et al., 1983) and snakehead (Cowey et al., 1983) species were exceptional in that they required ω 6-fatty acids rather than the ω 3-fatty acids as found in mammals (Figs. 1 and 2). On the basis of this information, the fatty acid requirements of fish are roughly grouped into the Tilapia-, rainbow trout-, and red sea bream-types. The requirement of fish for EFA is estimated at about 0.5-1.0% of diet, as shown in Table III.

IV. BIOCONVERSION OF LINOLENIC ACID TO ω 3-HUFA

Concerning the metabolism of 18:3 ω 3 acid, Kayama et

Table IV.   Percentage incorporation of (I-^{14}C) linolenic acid into   3 pentaenes and hexaenes of lipids from fish injected with (I-^{14}C) linolenic acid.

Fish	% Incorporation of injected [1-^{14}C]- linolenic acid to ω3-pentaenes and hexaenes (20:5ω3, 22:5ω3 and 22:6ω3)	Relative % incorporation to rainbow trout
Rainbow trout	12.7	100
Ayu	4.5	36
Eel	2.5	20
Red sea bream	1.9	15
Puffer fish	1.6	13
Rockfish	0.9	7

al. (1963) have shown the bioconversion of 18:3 ω3 to 20:5 ω 3 and 22:6 ω 3 in the kelp bass, Paralablax clathratus, by an elaborate technique using radioactive tracers.   Later, Owen et al. (1975) compared the ability for bioconversion of [1-^{14}C]18:3 ω 3 to ω3-HUFA in the turbot, Scophthalmus maximus, and rainbow trout, Salmo gairdneri.   As a result, the rainbow trout was found to convert 18:3 ω3 to 22:6 ω3 more efficiently since about 70% of the label was detected in 22:6 ω 3 acid.   In contrast, there was little incorporation of labelled 18:3ω3 into 20:5ω3 and 22:6ω3 in the turbot.   Kanazawa et al. (1979) have also compared the bioconversion ability from 18:3 ω 3 to ω3-HUFA in some aquatic animals, and demonstrated the relative bioconversion ability (RBCA; rainbow trout = 100).   Some RBCA values are as follows; Ayu (RBCA = 36), eel (RBCA = 20), red sea bream (RBCA = 15), puffer fish (RBCA = 13), and rockfish (RBCA = 7). Marine fish thus appear to have a lower RBCA than freshwater fish (Table IV).   This is further supported by the work of Yamada et al. (1980) from a comparison of the red sea bream, opaleye, stripped mullet, and rainbow trout.   This evidence suggests that 18:3ω3, which is an effective EFA source for rainbow trout, is ineffective for marine fish probably due to their reduced ability for bioconversion of 18:3ω3 to ω3-HUFA.

V.   EFFECTS OF ω3-HUFA ON GROWTH OF LARVAL FISH

Watanabe et al. (1983) have revealed that ω3-HUFA such as 20:5 ω3 and 22:6 ω3 are required for normal growth, not only for adult fish but also for the larvae of Ayu and red sea bream.   In Japan, the seed production of fish has been conducted using the rotifer, Brachionus plicatilis, which was reared on a marine species of Chlorella containing high levels of ω3-HUFA.   In accordance with the development and expansion of seed production, rotifers have more recently been cultured on baker's yeast which is low in ω3-HUFA.   However, a high mortality has been observed among larval fish reared on rotifers cultured in this manner.   In red sea bream, abnormalities such as underdeveloped swim bladder and scoliosis have been observed in larvae reared on rotifer and Artemia, either devoid of ω3-HUFA or possessing only low levels of these lipid fractions containing ω3-HUFA (Watanabe et al., 1980, 1982; Kitajima et al., 1980a, 1980b; Oka et al., 1980, 1982; Watanabe, 1982b).

Kanazawa et al (1982a) have investigated the fate of exogenous radioactive 20:5 ω3 in an attempt to understand the physiological role of 20:5 ω3, the most effective EFA source for fish.   Radioactive measurements of tissues and organs by the combustion method and by autoradiography of the whole bodies, showed high incorporation of label into the gall bladder, swim bladder, liver, and pyloric caecae.   Therefore, 20:5 ω3 is likely to be utilized as a constituent of cellular membranes of these tissues.   This may suggest that relatively large amounts of exogenous 20:5 ω3 acid are necessary for larval fish which are growing at a rapid rate.

VI.   MICROPARTICULATE DIETS AND DIETARY PHOSPHOLIPIDS

The seed production of the red sea bream, knife jaw, flounder, Ayu etc., has been conducted using live foods such as rotifer and Artemia.   However, the culture of these live foods requires considerable man-power and expensive facilities.   Moreover, it is difficult to produce the desired amounts of these live foods constantly because of the variability of yield due to uncontrollable factors such as weather.   The rearing of larval fish with microparticulate diets has been achieved by several workers (Adron et al., 1974; Gatesoupe and Luquet, 1977; Gatesoupe et al., 1977a; Métailler et al., 1979; Teshima et al., 1982b; Kanazawa et al., 1982b; Kanazawa and Teshima, 1983; Dabrowski et al., 1983; Bromley and Howell, 1983). During the course of investigation of microparticulate diets for the rearing of larval fish, we observed that dietary sources of phospholipids are essential for normal growth and survival of fish larvae such as the Ayu. The addition of some phospholipids to microparticulate diets markedly improved both growth and survival of the larval fish.

Table V. Composition (%) of microparticulate diets for the larval red sea bream.

Ingredient	Diet 1	Diet 2	Diet 3
Casein	52	52	52
Gelatin	11	11	11
Dextrin	12	12	12
Amino acid mixture[1]	5	5	5
Mineral mixture[2]	8	8	8
Vitamin mixture[3]	3	3	3
Oleic aicd	6	3	1
Pollack liver oil	3	6	3
Soybean lecithin	0	0	5
Zein	62.5	62.5	62.5

[1] Amino acids (g/100 g dry ingredients except zein): L-phenylalanine, 0.4; L-arginine HCl, 0.9; L-cystine, 0.5; L-tryptophan, 0.2; L-histidine $HCl \cdot H_2O$, 0.2; DL-alanine, 0.9; L-asparaginate Na, 0.7; L-lysine HCl, 0.4; L-valine, 0.5; glycine, 0.3.

[2] USP XII salts and trace metals.

[3] Followed by Halver (1957).

VII.   EFFECTS OF PHOSPHOLIPIDS ON THE LARVAL RED SEA BREAM

Kanazawa et al. (1983a) examined the effects of supplemental phospholipids on the growth of larval red sea bream using the purified microparticulate diets. The composition of the basal diet is shown in Table V. 10-day old larvae reared for 20 days showed improved growth and survival on a diet containing 3% pollack liver oil (PLO) plus 5% soybean lecithin (SBL) than when given diets containing 3% or 6% PLO alone (Fig. 3). The SBL-supplemented diet had a higher nutritive value corresponding to the live food (rotifers) in terms of growth and survival rates. These results indicate that an attempt to substitute the beneficial effects of SBL with ω 3-HUFA was unsuccessful, and lecithin is an essential dietary component for larval fish.

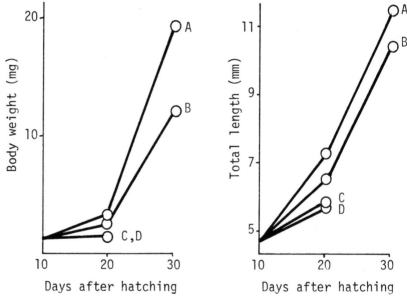

Fig. 3. Effect of soybean lecithin on growth of red sea bream larvae

A: Rotifer
B: Diet 3 (1% 18:1ω9 + 3% Pollack liver oil
    + 5% Soybean lecithin)
C: Diet 2 (1% 18:1ω9 + 6% Pollack liver oil)
D: Diet 1 (6% 18:1ω9 + 3% Pollack liver oil)

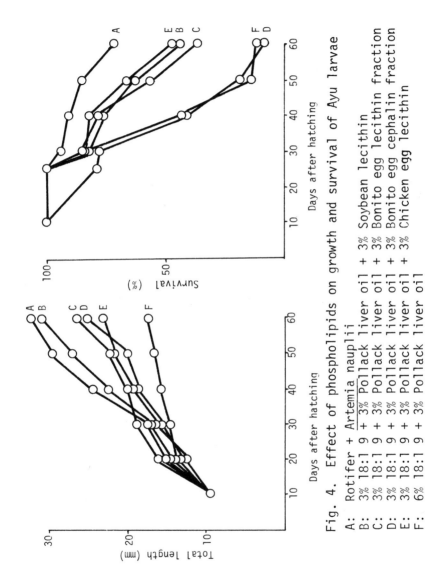

Fig. 4.   Effect of phospholipids on growth and survival of Ayu larvae

A: Rotifer + Artemia nauplii
B: 3% 18:1 9 + 3% Pollack liver oil + 3% Soybean lecithin
C: 3% 18:1 9 + 3% Pollack liver oil + 3% Bonito egg lecithin fraction
D: 3% 18:1 9 + 3% Pollack liver oil + 3% Bonito egg cephalin fraction
E: 3% 18:1 9 + 3% Pollack liver oil + 3% Chicken egg lecithin
F: 6% 18:1 9 + 3% Pollack liver oil

VIII.   EFFECTS OF PHOSPHOLIPIDS ON THE LARVAL AYU

Using a similar type of purified diet to that used for
the red sea bream, Kanazawa et al. (1981, 1983b) have
investigated the phospholipid requirements of 10, 30, and
100 day-old larval Ayu.   Irrespective of age, improved
growth and survival rates were obtained, when the basal
diet was supplemented with either 3% chicken-egg lecithin,
bonito-egg lecithin or soybean lecithin (SBL).   Although
a marked difference in the efficacies was not found among
the types of lecithin, bonito-egg lecithin seemed to have
a slightly higher nutritive value than soybean lecithin
and chicken-egg lecithin (Fig. 4).   The supplemental
effect of cephalin was inferior to that of the
corresponding lecithin.   In feeding trials,
supplementation of the basal diet at the 5% SBL level
enhanced growth and survival rates to a greater extent
than at either the 1 or 3% levels.   Considering the
purity of the SBL used, the true optimum lecithin level in
the diets for larval Ayu appears to be about 1-2% when SBL
is used as the phospholipid source.
In order to clarify which components of bonito-egg
lecithin were most effective for the larval Ayu, Kanazawa
(1983b) has examined the effects of several phospholipid
classes on the growth and survival of Plecoglossus
altivelis.   The fractionation and isolation of each
phospholipid class was achieved by column chromatography
on silica gel.   Good survival rates were obtained with
diets containing phosphatidylinositol plus phosphatidylcholine or phosphatidylcholine alone as the supplemental
phospholipid.   In contrast, phosphatidylethanolamine was
much less effective in improving survival rates.
Regarding weight gain, diets containing
phosphatidylinositol plus phosphatidylcholine again proved
most effective.   Furthermore, Kanazawa (1983b) have
examined the supplemental effects of highly purified
commercial phospholipids on larval Ayu.   Soybean
phosphatidylcholine (purity-98%), chicken-egg phosphatidylcholine (purity-98%, and soybean phosphatidylinositol
(purity-70%) were found to greatly improve survival rates,
where synthetic phosphatidylcholine dipalmitoyl, a phospholipid having a saturated fatty acid moiety, was ineffective.   A similar negative effect was observed with
supplements of cytidine-'5'-diphosphate choline, which is
concerned with the biosynthesis of phosphatidylcholine
from diglycerides, and bile acids having an emulsifying

effect on lipids. Regarding weight gain, soybean phosphatidylinositol showed the greatest activity followed by soybean phosphatidylcholine and chicken-egg lecithin respectively.

In conclusion, larval Ayu were considered to require the molecular form of phospholipids having unsaturated fatty acids at C-2 position and either inositol or choline groups at C-3 position. These compounds, in addition to ω3-HUFA, are believed to be indispensable for normal growth and survival.

IX.   DIETARY PHOSPHOLIPIDS AND THE PREVENTION OF INCIDENCE OF MALFORMATION IN THE LARVAL AYU

The incidence of malformation such as protrusion of the thorax, scoliosis, and twisting of the caudal peduncle is a serious problem in the seed production of Ayu in Japan.   Scoliosis reduces the market value of Ayu remarkably.   During the course of our studies on the microparticulate diets for larval fish, Kanazawa et al. (1981) have found that the incidence of malformation, particularly scoliosis, could be reduced by the addition of phospholipids to the diets.   The incidence (%) of scoliosis in fish reared on the rotifer, Artemia, and commercial formula diets was 63%, whereas it was only 5% with the microparticulate diets containing soybean lecithin or chicken-egg lecithin supplements as shown in Table VI.

X.   PHYSIOLOGICAL ROLES OF DIETARY PHOSPHOLIPIDS IN LARVAL FISH

It is still unclear why larval fish require a dietary source of phospholipids for their growth and survival. We suggest that larval fish require an abundance of phospholipids for the formation of new cell components during the initially short period of rapid growth after hatching.   The biosynthesis of phospholipids may not take place at a sufficiently fast rate to meet this phospholipid requirement.   The difference in the activity among phospholipids examined also implies that dietary

Table VI.   Effect   of   lecithin   on   the   incidence   of
malformation in Agu larvae.

Incidence of malformation	Rotifer + Commercial diet	Rotifer + Microparticulate diet including 3% lecithin
Pughead	1	0
Protrusion of thorax	1	0
Twist of jaw	8	3
Scoliosis	10	0
Twist of caudal peduncle	35	0
Incidence (%)	63	5

phospholipids are likely to be utilized for the formation
of cellular membranes either directly or indirectly.
Furthermore,   Takeuchi   and   Watanabe   (1978)   have
demonstrated   that   the   addition   of   0.01–0.05%
phosphatidylcholine   was   ineffective   in   improving   the
growth rate of juvenile rainbow trout, weighing about
1.5g.   This suggests either insufficient supplementation
of phosphatidylcholine to enhance growth, or that the
requirement for dietary phospholipids may diminish with
increasing age.   This point warrants further examination
in the future.

It has been demonstrated that fish have an essential
requirement for specific dietary lipid fractions.   This
evidence has been applied during the formulation of
synthetic diets.

In Japan, approximately 300 million fish larvae are
produced   annually   for   release   into   the   sea   and
aquaculture.   However, the seed production of fish using
the rotifer-Artemia system is limited.   It is therefore
important that the nutritional requirements of different
fish larvae are identified.   This will permit the
perfection of microparticulate diets which may ultimately
enhance mass fish seed production.

REFERENCES

Adron, J.W., Blair, A. and Cowey, C.B. (1974). Fishery Bull. 72, 353-357.

Bromley, P.J. and Howell, B.R. (1983). Aquaculture 31, 31-40.

Castell, J.D., Lee, D.J. and Sinnhuber, R.O. (1972a). J. Nutr. 102, 93-100.

Castell, J.D., Sinnhuber, R.O., Lee, D.J. and Wales, J.H. (1972b). J. Nutr. 102, 87-92.

Castell, J.D., Sinnhuber, R.O., Wales, J.H. and Lee, D.J. (1972c). J. Nutr. 102, 77-86.

Castledine, A.J. and Buckley, J.T. (1980). J. Nutr. 110, 675-685.

Cowey, C.B. and Sargent, J.R. (1979). In "Fish Physiology" (W.S. Hoar, D.J. Randall and J.R. Brett, eds.) 8, 1-69, Academic Press, New York.

Cowey, C.B., Wee, K.L. and Tacon, A.G.J. (1983). Bull. Japan. Soc. Sci. Fish. 49, 1573-1577.

Cowey, C.B., Owen, J.M., Adron, J.W and Middleton, C. (1976). Br. J. Nutr. 36, 479-486.

Dabrowski, K., Bardega, R. and Przedwojski, R. (1983). Z. Tierphysiol., Tierrernährg. u. Futtermittelkkde. 50, 40-52.

Deshimaru, O. (1984). Feed Oil Abst. No. 20, 1-7.

Deshimaru, O., Kuroki, K. and Yone, Y. (1982a). Bull. Japan. Soc. Sci. Fish. 48, 1155-1157.

Deshimaru, O., Kuroki, K. and Yone, Y. (1982b). Bull. Japan. Soc. Sci. Fish. 48, 1265-1270.

Farkas, T., Csengeri, I., Majoros, F. and Olah, J. (1977). Aquaculture 11, 147-157.

Fujii, M. and Yone, Y. (1976). Bull. Japan. Soc. Sci. Fish. 42, 583-588.

Fujii, M., Nakayama, H. and Yone, Y. (1976). Rep. Fish. Res. Lab., Kyushu Univ., No. 3, 65-86.

Gatesoupe, F.-J. and Luquet, P. (1977). I.C.E.S. Brest, France, 13-20.

Gatesoupe, F.-J., Girin, M. and Luquet, P. (1977a). I.C.E.S. Brest, France, 59-66.

Gatesoupe, F.-J., Leger, C., Metailler, R. and Luquet, P. (1977b). Ann. Hydrobiol. 8, 89-97.

Gatesoupe, F.-J., Leger, C., Metailler, R. and Luquet, P. (1977c). Ann. Hydrobiol. 8, 247-254.

Halver, J.E. (1957). J. Nutr. 62, 225-243.

Kanazawa, A. (1983a). In, "Metabolism in Fish" (F. Nagayama, ed.) 52-67, Koseisha-Koseikaku, Tokyo.

Kanazawa, A. (1983b). Feed Oil Abst. B No. 18, 1-5.

Kanazawa, A. and Teshima, S. (1983). Yoshoku, 20, 97-101.

Kanazawa, A., Teshima, S. and Ono, K. (1979). Comp. Biochem. Physiol. 63B, 295-298.

Kanazawa, A., Teshima, S. and Imai, K. (1980a). Mem. Fac. Fish., Kagoshima Univ. 29, 313-318.

Kanazawa, A., Teshima, S. and Sakamoto, M. (1980b). Bull. Japan. Soc. Sci. Fish. 46, 1353-1356.

Kanazawa, A., Teshima, S. and Sakamoto, M. (1982c). Bull. Japan. Soc. Sci. Fish. 48, 587-590.

Kanazawa, A., Teshima, S., Inamori, S. and Matsubara, H. (1983a). Mem. Fac. Fish., Kagoshima Univ. 32, 109-114.

Kanazawa, A., Teshima, S., Kobayashi, T., Takae, M., Iwashita, T. and Uehara, R. (1983b). Mem. Fac. Fish., Kagoshima Univ. 32, 115-120.

Kanazawa, A., Teshima, S., Imatanaka, N., Imada, O. and Inoue, A. (1982a). Bull. Japan. Soc. Sci. Fish. 48, 1441-1444.

Kanazawa, A., Teshima, S., Inamori, S., Sumida, S. and Iwashita, T. (1982b). Mem. Fac. Fish., Kagoshima Univ. 31, 185-192.

Kanazawa, A., Teshima, S., Inamori, S., Iwashita, T. and NACAO, A. (1981). Mem. Fac. Fish., Kagoshina Univ. 30, 301-309.

Kayama, M. (1964). Yukagaku 13, 511-519.

Kayama, M. (1972). The Aquaculture 20, 247-262.

Kayama, M. 91974). Yushi 27, 110-115.

Kayama, M. (1977). Feed Oil Abst. BNo.6, 6-10.

Kayama, M. (1978). In "Dietary Lipids in Aquaculture" (Japan. Soc. Sci. Fish. eds.) 7-22, Koseisha-Koseikaku, Tokyo.

Kayama, M. (1983). Yakagaku 32, 719-725.

Kayama, M., Tsuchiya, Y., Nevenzel, J.C., Fulco, A. and Mead, J.F. (1963). J. Amer. Oil Chem. Soc. 40, 499-502.

Klitajima, C., Arakawa, T., Oowa, F., Fujita, S., Imada, O., Watanabe, T. and Yone, Y. (1980a). Bull. Japan. Soc. Sci. Fish. 46, 43-46.

Kitajima, C., Yoshida, M. and Watanabe, T. (1980b). Bull. Japan. Soc. Sci. Fish. 46, 47-50.

Klenk, E. and Kremer, G. (1960). Z. Physiol. Chem. 320, 111-125.

Lee, D.J., Roehm, J.N., Yu, T.C. and Sinnhuber, R.O. (1967). J. Nutr. 92, 93-98.

Leger, C. (1980). Ann. Nutr. Alim. 34, 207-216.

Mead, J.F., Kayama, M. and Reiser, R. (1960). J. Amer. Oil Chem. Soc. 37, 438-440.

Metailler, R., Manant, C. and Depierre, C. (1979). In "Finfish Nutrition and Fishfeed Technology" (J.E. Halver and K. Tiews, eds.) Vol II, 181-190. H. Heenemann GmbH and Co., Berlin.

Nicolaides, N. and Woodall, A.N. (1962). J. Nutr. 78, 431-437.

Oka, A., Susuki, N. and Watanabe, T. (1980). Bull. Japan. Soc. Sci. Fish. 46, 1413-1418.

Oka, A., Susuki, N. and Watanabe, T. (1982). Bull. Japan. Soc. Sci. Fish. 48, 1159-1162.

Ota, T., Takaki, T., Odajima, R. and Terao, T. (1979). Bull. Fac. Fish., Hokkaido Univ. 30, 294-300.

Owen, J.M., Adron, J.W., Middleton, C. and Cowey, C.B. (1975). Lipids 10, 528-531.

Owen, J.M., Adron, J.W., Sargent, J.R. and Cowey, C.B. (1972). Mar. Biol. 13, 160-166.

Sargent, J.R. (1976). In "Biochemical and Biophysical Perspectives in Marine Biology" (D.C. Malins and J.R. Sargent, eds.). Vol. 3, 149-212. Academic Press, London.

Sinnhuber, R.O. (1969). In "Fish in Research" (O.W. Neuhaus and J.E. Halver, eds.) 245-261. Academic Press, New York.

Sinnhuber, R.O., Castell, J.D. and Lee, D.J. (1972). Fed. Proc. 31, 1436-1441.

Stickney, R.R. and Andrews, J.W. (1971). J. Nutr. 101, 1703-1710.

Stickney, R.R. and Andrews, J.W. (1972). J. Nutr. 102, 249-258.

Takeuchi, T. and Watanabe, T. (1976). Bull. Japan. Soc. Sci. Fish. 42, 907-919.

Takeuchi, T. and Watanabe, T. (1977a). Bull. Japan. Soc. Sci. Fish. 43, 541-551.

Takeuchi, T. and Watanabe, T. (1977b). Bull. Japan. Soc. Sci. Fish. 43, 893-898.

Takeuchi, T. and Watanabe, T. (1977c). Bull. Japan. Soc. Sci. Fish. 43, 947-953.

Takeuchi, T. and Watanabe, T. (1978). Bull. Japan. Soc. Sci. Fish 44, 733-738.

Takeuchi, T. and Watanabe, T. (1982). Bull. Japan. Soc. Sci. Fish. 48, 1745-1752.

Takeuchi, T., Satoh, S. and Watanabe, T. (1983). Bull. Japan. Soc. Sci. Fish. 49, 1127-1134.

Takeuchi, T., Watanabe, T. and Nose, T. (1979). Bull. Japan. Soc. Sci. Fish. 45, 1319-1323.

Takeuchi, T., Arai, S., Watanabe, T. and Shimma, Y. (1980). Bull. Japan. Soc. Sci. Fish. 46, 345-353.

Teshima, S., Kanazawa, A. and Sakamoto, M. (1982a). Mem. Fac. Fish., Kagoshima Univ. 31, 201–204.

Teshima, S., Kanazawa, A. and Sakamoto, M. (1982b). Min. Rev. Data File Fish. Res. 2, 67–86.

Watanabe, T. (1982a). Comp. Biochem. Physiol. 73B, 3–15.

Watanabe, T. (1982b). Yukagaku 31, 77–90.

Watanabe, T., Kitajima, C. and Fujita, S., (1983). Aquaculture 34, 115–143.

Watanabe, T., Takashima, F. and Ogino, C. (1974c). Bull. Japan. Soc. Sci. Fish. 40, 181–188.

Watanabe, T., Takeuchi, T. and Ogino, C. (1975a). Bull. Japan. Soc. Sci. Fish. 41, 263–269.

Watanabe, T., Kobayashi, I., Utsue, O. and Ogino, C. (1974a). Bull. Japan. Soc. Sci. Fish. 40, 387–392.

Watanabe, T., Ogino, C., Koshiishi, Y. and Matsunaga, T. (1974b). Bull. Japan. Soc. Sci. Fish. 40, 493–499.

Watanabe, T., Ohta, M., Kitajima, C. and Fujita, S. (1982). Bull. Japan. Soc. Sci. Fish. 48, 1775–1782.

Watanabe, T., Oowa, F., Kitajima, C. and Fujita, S. (1980). Bull. Japan. Soc. Sci. Fish. 46, 35–41.

Watanabe, T., Utsue, O., Kobayashi, I anjd Ogino, C. (1975b). Bull. Japan. Soc. Sci. Fish. 41, 257–262.

Yamada, K., Kobayashi, K. and Yone, Y. (1980). Bull. Japan. Soc. Sci. Fish. 46, 1231–1233.

Yone, Y. (1975). Proc. 1st Intern. Conf. Aquaculture Nutr., 39–64.

Yone, Y. (1978). In "Dietary Lipids in Aquaculture", (Japan. Soc. Sci. Fish. eds.) 43–59. Koseisha-Koseikaku, Tokyo.

Yone, Y. (1980). Proc. Pac. Aquaculture Symp., 251–259.

Yone, Y. and Fujii, M. (1975a). Bull. Japan. Soc. Sci. Fish. 41, 73–77.

Yone, Y. and Fujii, M. (1975b). Bull. Japan. Soc. Sci. Fish. 41, 79–86.

Yu, T.C. and Sinnhuber, R.O. (1972). Lipids 7, 450–454.

Yu, T.C. and Sinnhuber, R.O. (1976). Aquaculture 8, 309–317.

Yu, T.C. and Sinnhuber, R.O. (1979). Aquaculture 16, 31–38.

Yu, T.C., Sinnhuber, R.O. and Hendricks, J.D. (1979). Lipids 14, 572–575.

DIGESTION, ABSORPTION AND TRANSPORT OF LIPIDS

C. LEGER

Station de Recherches de Nutrition, C.N.R.Z.,
Institut National de la Recherche Agronomique,
78350 Jouy-En-Josas, France.

I. INTRODUCTION

Digestion, absorption and transport of lipids supplies the animal with fatty acids which are used either as a source of energy, as structural cell wall elements or as precursors of cyclic or non-cyclic derivatives which play an important hormone-like role at the cellular level. These three stages occur in three different sites, i.e. intestinal lumen, enterocyte and lymph or blood. This apparent topographic disparity corresponds to a unity of function as the common goal of the three stages is to provide the cell with the ingested dietary fatty acids.

Hydrolysis of triglycerides – which represent at least 80% of dietary lipids – is catalysed by pancreatic lipase (glycerol-ester hydrolase). Colipase is most likely present in all fish. The presence of non specific bile salt-dependent lipase has also been reported.

In trout, fatty acids are absorbed at the level of the pyloric caeca and in the proximal intestine. The absorption is comparable to that observed in mammals, but it is much slower. The apparent digestibility of dietary lipids depends on their degree of unsaturation and seems to increase with water temperature.

After passage across the intestinal cell wall, dietary lipids are mainly recovered in the lymph, but also in the blood in the form of chylomicrons or very low density lipoprotein (VLDL)-like particles. Lipoprotein-lipase (LPL) present in trout plasma is probably responsible for the catabolism of these two forms of transport. The released fatty acids can then be taken up by the cells. Plasma lipids also circulate as low density lipoproteins (LDL) and high density lipoproteins (HDL). HDL are the major class of lipoproteins, their content in trout is 3-5 fold higher than in man.

These different aspects will be extensively examined in the present chapter.

II. PANCREATIC HYDROLYSIS

The first attempts made to demonstrate a pancreatic lipase activity using the histochemical technique of Gomori (1946) proved to be unsuccessful (Arvy, 1954; Bernard, 1961). By means of a more sensitive histochemical procedure, Arvy and Gabe (1957) showed the existence of a lipase activity in the pancreas, but it could not be considered as a true lipase because of the substrate. Darnton and Barrowman (1969) used an insoluble triglyceride as substrate for the histochemical reaction and were able to detect true lipase activities. Bergot and Leger (unpublished) adapted this technique to the diffuse pancreas of trout. The lipase activity observed in intercaecal tissue sections was located in the cell cluster constituting the exocrine pancreas.

In fish, one of the main difficulties in demonstrating lipase activity in vitro is that the pancreas is a diffuse tissue, except in teleosts such as pike and in all elasmobranchs and Dipneusta. Research was therefore focused on lipase from a compact pancreas like that of skate or shark or from intestinal contents of various teleosts.

A true lipase activity was detected in shark pancreas (Brockerhoff and Hoyle, 1965). The lipase involved was obtained from a pancreatic acetone powder. Like porcine pancreatic lipase, it specifically hydrolysed the 1-and 3-positions of triglyceride molecule in the presence of 4 mM bile salts (Entressangles et al., 1966; Brockerhoff, 1968). The existence of a lipase activity with the same specificity was confirmed in vivo in gut contents of Gadus morhua (Brockerhoff, 1966). Total pyloric caecal extracts (Overnell, 1973) or acetone extracted gut powder

(Brockerhoff, 1966) did not exhibit any lipase activity. In the shark Squalus acanthias, no lipase activity was detected with acetone powder from compact pancreas (Berner and Hammond, 1970).

Some studies have been devoted to the adipo-connective tissue around the pyloric caeca. This tissue was dissected by Leger et al. (1970) in rainbow trout. After homogenisation and centrifugation the lipase activity of the supernatant was 0.4 units/mg protein. Optimum pH was 8.7 and 8.4, respectively in rainbow trout acclimatized to a water temperature of 10° and 20°C. Lipase activity disappared in fresh samples after treatment with organic solvents (Leger, 1972). A simple purification method was suggested, i.e. the intercaecal tissue and pyloric caeca were ground in liquid nitrogen, lyophilised and defatted by solvent mixtures according to the technique of Verger et al. (1969). More than 40% of the initial lipase activity was recovered in the defatted powder. Several purification steps allowed us to preserve 20% of the defatted powder activity in a fraction purified 36 fold.

The properties of pancreatic lipase were studied in rainbow trout (Leger et al., 1979; Leger et al., 1977; Leger and Bauchart, 1972). The enzyme hydrolysed fatty acids in the 1- and 3- positions of the triglyceride molecule. However, contrary to what was observed in pig and skate this lipase also hydrolysed the 2-position if the corresponding acyl chain contained at least one double bond. The medium used to test the specificity of action of the enzyme included no more than 0.8 mM bile salts to prevent any possible interference of a non specific bile salt-dependent lipase (Mattson and Volpenhein, 1966; see also Fig. 1).

Figure 1 (curves A) shows the effect of bile salts (taurocholate + Na glycocholate) on trout pancreatic lipase activity in the presence of tributyrine substrate. It was comparable to that recorded by Leger et al. (1977) in the presence of triolein. At bile salt concentrations between 0.5 and 1 mM, the peak of activity was similar to that observed by other authors in rat (Borgstrom and Erlanson, 1973; Morgan and Hoffman, 1971) pig and dog (Rathelot et al., 1975) in the presence of variable amounts of colipase.

The Ca^{++} ion did not seem to change the initial lipolysis rate, but affected the overall reaction pattern. In the absence of this ion, the reaction velocity rapidly decreased to zero. The same phenomenon was observed in the pig (Benzonana and Desnuelle, 1968).

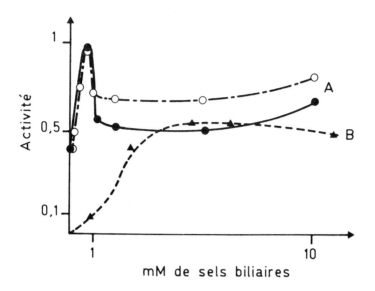

Curves A: -In trout, true (colipase-dependent) lipase
Curve B: -In Triakus semifasciata, bile salt-dependent
          lipase

Fig. 1. Lipase activities in different bile salt concentrations (Patton et al., 1977; Leger, 1980).

The Km was 1.3 x 10^{-6}M expressed in interface concentration. This value was lower than that measured in the pig (Sarda and Desnuelle, 1958) using the same substrate with enzyme preparations of the same degree of purity. The substrate affinity of trout lipase was thus higher than that of porcine lipase. This feature may account for an adaptation of the enzyme to low temperatures.

It was mentioned above that true lipase acted on insoluble triglyceride substrate. In in vivo conditions, the surfactive bile components, i.e. conjugated bile salts and bile phospholipids in most fish, bile alcohols in some of them (Haslewood, 1978), led to formation of a fine and stable emulsion in the gut and "cleaned" the interface of adsorbed fatty acids and proteins. In that way, they increased the available interface surface for enzyme adsorption. However, the oil-water interface coated with these surfactive components became more polar so that the surface pressure increased and lipase was desorbed. In mammals, colipase prevented lipase desorption and thus favoured the catalytic reaction. This colipase is a protein with a molecular weight of 10 000 secreted by the pancreas, but genetically lipase independent (Leger, 1983). Owing to its specific molecular properties, this protein may adsorb to an amphiphilic surface and simultaneously bind lipase.

Sternby et al. (1983) prepared homogenates of intestines and intestinal contents from Myxine glutinosa, pancreatic homogenates from Chimaera monstrosa, skate Raja radiata, shark Somnius microcephalus and pure pancreatic colipase from shark Squalus acanthias. These authors showed the existence of a colipase in these "primitive" fishes similar to that found in mammals. Indeed, this colipase was able to restore the lipase activity inhibited by bile salts, preserved its biological activity after a 10 min treatment at 70°C, had a molecular weight of about 10 000, cross-reacted with rabbit antisera against human and porcine colipase and its biological activity decreased in the presence of increasing amounts of anti-colipase antiserum.

It has also been shown that the reactivation of lipase by colipase is species independent. In fish, shark (S. acanthias) colipase activated porcine lipase (Patton et al., 1978a) and porcine colipase activated trout lipase (Leger et al., 1979). This interspecificity of lipase reactivation in vertebrates indicates the common structure of colipases, on the one hand, and of lipases on the other hand despite the large evolutionary distance between primitive fish and man. This is remarkably confirmed by the work of Sternby et al. (1983) on colipases.

All these results suggest that the lipase–colipase system present in all mammals also exists in fish. However, other types of lipases may be involved in the hydrolysis of triglycerides. Non-specific bile salt-dependent lipases were found in rat (Mattson and Volpenhein, 1968; Morgan et al., 1968) and man (Erlanson and Borgstrom, 1970; Carey, 1980).

Patton et al. (1975) studied the lipolysis of various fatty acid esters in vitro by fish intestinal juice in anchovy, Engraulis mordax and the salmon, Oncorhynchus gorbuscha. Methyl esters of 20:4 and 20:5 fatty acids were hydrolysed while they were resistant to porcine pancreatic lipase (Brockerhoff, 1970). Wax esters which represent a large proportion of the fat supply of marine fish (Benson et al., 1972) were hydrolysed at a lower rate than triglycerides, but at a higher rate than with porcine pancreatic lipase. After a 75% hydrolysis of triglycerides, 50% glycerol was released as against only 25% in the case of porcine pancreatic lipase. Oleic acid in position 2–on glycerol was hydrolysed at the same rate as palmitic and stearic acids in the 1– and 3– positions, whereas stearic acid in the 2–position was poorly hydrolysed. These results are comparable to those obtained in trout with partly purified pancreatic lipase (Leger and Bauchart, 1972). However, they were obtained in the presence of large bile salt concentrations (probably 5mM, but not indicated by the authors). Accordingly, it may be assumed that the enzyme involved is a non-specific, bile salt–dependent lipase. Acetone extracted shark pancreas powder (Triakus semifasciata) contained a non-specific, bile salt–dependent lipase (Fig. 1) whose substrate and positional specificities were comparable to those of E. mordax and O. gorbuscha lipases (Patton et al., 1977; Patton, 1975).

It is noteworthy that in dogfish Squalus sucklei, blue shark, Proniace glauca, and sting ray, Urolophus halleri, pancreatic non-specific lipase levels were very low, less than 5% hydrolysis of the 2–position unsaturated acid (Patton, 1975). Thus, a high level of pancreatic non-specific lipase is not a general feature of all fish and shark digestive systems. A level similar to that of rat can be encountered.

On the other hand, it seems that true lipase exists in leopard shark. Its absence (Patton et al., 1977) could be a consequence of enzyme denaturation during the preparation of the acetone powder (Leger, 1972).

In conclusion, it may be assumed that like rat and man, fish possesses two types of lipases with complementary activities. Morgan et al. (1968) observed that non-specific lipase attacked preferentially micellar lipases, true lipase on emulsified lipids. The activities of the two enzymes were also complementary in the bile salt concentration range of 0.5 to more than 10 mM (Fig. 1) (physiological concentration range of intestinal contents). Bile salt–dependent lipase may strengthen the action of colipase–dependent lipase when the bile salt levels are high, while the latter may replace the bile salt–dependent lipase when the bile salt levels are low. These enzyme activities were also complementary in terms of specificities of position and nature of chain of glyceride fatty acids.

In mammals, the products of intraluminal hydrolysis of triglycerides are diglycerides and especially fatty acids and monoglycerides. In fish, saturated and unsaturated monoglycerides are to a large extent hydrolysed into fatty acids and glycerol because of the probable existence of the 2 lipases. Accordingly, fatty acids and glycerol are the main products of intraluminal hydrolysis of triglycerides.

III. INTESTINAL ABSORPTION OF LIPIDS

By analogy with mammals (Borgström, 1974) it may be assumed that in fish the different lipids present in intestinal contents are partitioned between an oil-phase (mainly triglycerides and diglycerides) and a micellar phase (mixed micelles of bile salts, fatty acids and small amounts of monoglycerides). These mixed micelles represent a form of transport of amphiphates from their site of appearance to their site of uptake in the intestinal lumen.

Fatty acids and glycerol penetrate probably the brush-border of the enterocyte in a monomolecular form (Simmonds, 1974). According to studies made in mammals, fatty acid absorption rate increases with decreasing melting point. Mono- and polyunsaturated fatty acids are better absorbed than saturated fatty acids (palmitic, stearic acids). Saturated fatty acids are more completely absorbed in the form of monoglycerides. Thus, digestibility of fats depends on the nature of their fatty acids and of the position of these fatty acids on glycerol.

Fish oils contain large amounts of mono- and polyunsaturated fatty acids and are particularly well absorbed in fish, the apparent digestibility coefficients being 85 to 96% (Cho and Slinger, 1979; Austreng, 1978). For a given water temperature the digestibility of fats decreases with increasing melting point (Austreng et al., 1980). Conversely, in catfish, Andrews et al. (1978) showed that fat digestibility increased with increasing water temperature. The same result was obtained in trout by Atherton and Aitken (1970). Dietary fat content may also affect the digestibility of lipids, a high level (15 versus 5 and 10%) leading to a low digestibility (Andrews et al., 1978). Finally, it seems that the size of fish may play a part. Thus, Windell et al. (1978) showed that lipid digestibility was lower in trout of 20g than in trout of more than 200 g. However, these authors did not show any influence of the amount of feed ingested per meal.

As in mammals (Johnston, 1970), the absorption of lipids in fish takes place mainly in the proximal intestine or in the pyloric caeca (Greene, 1913; Luzzati, 1936; Sire et al., 1981). These results obtained with histochemical techniques were confirmed by digestibility studies (Austreng, 1978). However, after dietary lipid overloading, the absorption may extend to the distal intestine (Sastry and Garg, 1976).

In mammals, after passage across the brush-border, the fatty acids are diffused until the area of the subapical smooth endoplasmic reticulum (SER), associated with a protein designated as fatty acid binding protein (FABP) is reached (Ocker et al., 1972). Then, the dietary fatty acids which are mainly long-chain, undergo a re-esterification predominantly in the form of triglycerides which, combined with specific phospholipids and proteins (apoproteins), constitute large-sized particles called chylomicrons and VLDL. The diameter of the first ones exceeds 800 A and ranges between 800 and 300 A for the others. They contain 80-50% triglycerides. Their role is to export fatty acids outside the enterocyte and to transport esterified fatty acids. They are found in the chyliferous vessels, then in the lymphatic duct and finally in blood. All these mechanisms, from the passage of fatty acids across the brush-border and of lipoproteins into the lymph, represent the absorption.

In man, absorption begins 10-20 min. after ingestion of milk fat (Bierman et al., 1953). Maximum absorption can be observed 4 to 8 h after meal intake in various mammals (Rampone, 1961; Boucrot and Clement, 1965; Fremont et al., 1970).

Absorption of lipids is much slower in fish (Gohar and Latif, 1963; Bergot and Flechon, 1970a; Noaillac-Depeyre and Gas, 1976; Kayama and Ijima, 1976). Recently Sire et al. (1981) showed that in trout maintained at 12°C a radioactivity could be detected in the plasma 2-4 h after introduction of labelled fatty acids into the stomach and this radioactivity went on increasing between the 4th and the 6th post-prandial hour. It was high after 18 h, while 5-18% of the dose administered were still found in the caecal cell wall. In Hoplias malabaricus kept at a temperature of 29°C, Patton et al. (1978b) observed that labelled oleic acid incorporated into the food appeared in the blood 24 h after the meal and that maximum radioactivity occurred after 31 h. These observations are similar to those of Beamish (1972) in blackbars kept at 25°C.

The slow absorption may depend on the gastric emptying and intestinal transit rates and on the existence of a temporary storage of lipids in the enterocyte (see below). The temperature does not seem to markedly affect the enzymatic mechanisms in the enterocyte since the absorption rate in fish kept in a warm environment does not exceed that of fish in a cold environment.

It is now currently recognized that the enterocyte absorption phase in fish is comparable to that of mammals. According to biochemical studies, fatty acids are esterified in the intestinal mucosa (Sire et al., 1981; Patton et al., 1978b) and it seems that linoleic acid is esterified more rapidly than palmitic acid (Sire et al., 1981). Ijima et al. (1983) confirmed that intestinal enzyme preparations from carp were able to esterify palmitic acid as triglycerides or phospholipids. Synthesis of triglycerides took place through the monoglyceride or phosphatidic acid pathway. Oxidized lipids were able to depress the biosynthesis of triglycerides by affecting the conversion of phosphatidic acid into diglyceride and the acylation of diglyceride.

Since fatty acids and glycerol are the main products of the intraluminal hydrolysis, the glycerol 3-P pathway is most likely the predominant route of biosynthesis of enterocyte triglycerides. Glycerol kinase probably plays a major role in cell lipid metabolism. This was further confirmed by the fact that the USU (1,3-unsaturated fatty acid, 2-saturated fatty acid sn glycerol) triglyceride structure was not preserved during digestion and transport (Leger et al., 1977b).

Microscopic examination of enterocytes in trout (Bergot and Flechon, 1970a; Kimura, 1973; Bauermeister et al., 1979; Sire and Vernier, 1981), carp (Noaillac-Depeyre and Gas, 1974) and tench (Noaillac-Depeyre and Gas, 1976) revealed the presence of particles mainly formed of triglycerides. According to their size, morphology, localisation in the lumen of the endoplasmic reticulum, Golgi vesicles and intercellular spaces, they were assumed to be chylomicron-like particles. However, the variety of sizes (from 600 to 4000 A according to the precited authors), led Sire and Vernier (1981) to examine the effect of the amount of ingested lipids and of the unsaturation of dietary fatty acids on the diameter of these particles. These authors observed that the higher the lipid load and the unsaturation, the larger the size of chylomicrons. The particle size increased from 800 to 2600 A 12-24 h after ingestion of a standard diet

containing 8% lipids of which 14% were 20:5 and 22:6
polyunsaturated fatty acids, up to 6500 A when the diet
contained 10% lipids of which 27% were 20:5 and 22:6
acids.   When the animals received exclusively palmitic
acid, only VLDL-like particles (400-700 A) were visible in
the enterocyte 6-18 h after the meal.   These results are
comparable to those obtained in rat (Ockner and Jones,
1970; Ockner and Isselbacher, 1974; Gangl and Ockner,
1975).   FABP probably exists in fish as in mammals and is
involved in the translocation of fatty acids from the
brush-border to the SER.   The higher affinity of this
protein for unsaturated than for saturated fatty acids
(Ockner et al., 1972) probably leads to a higher
esterification rate of unsaturated fatty acids in the
SER.   It also results in the appearance of large sized
particles as the building of the core of apolar lipids
resulting from the esterification is more rapid than that
of the polar constituents of the particle surface.   Highly
unsaturated but oxidized dietary fats may bring about a
large reduction of the particle size due to an inhibition
of triglyceride synthesis (Ijima et al., 1983).

In fish, a double pathway for the export of lipoprotein
particles was described in trout (Bergot and Flechon,
1979a) and in tench (Noaillac-Depeyre and Gas, 1976): the
blood route as in chicken, the lymph route as in mammals.
Export of lipoproteins via the portal pathways has only
been reported in carp (Noaillac-Depeyre and Gas, 1974).
According to Sire et al. (1981), lipoprotein particles
were almost absent in the lumen of trout blood capillaries
while large amounts of particles appeared in the
intercellular spaces, lamina propria, lymph ducts and
capillary endothelium.

There is now abundant evidence to affirm that lipid
transport outside the enterocyte is similar in fish and
mammals.   However, some authors have reported the export
of free fatty acids (Kayama and Ijima, 1976; Robinson and
Mead, 1973; Patton et al., 1978b) which seemed to appear
during early absorption (1-3 h after the meal) thereafter
they only represented a small proportion of the fatty
acids conveyed into the blood (Sire et al., 1981).   The
chemical form of the ingested fatty acids (free or
esterified) seemed to affect the mode of transport of
fatty acids (Kayama and Ijima, 1976).   The radioactivity
of free plasma fatty acids was low when palmitic acid was
ingested in the form of tripalmitate, whereas it was
higher when the acid was ingested in the free form.   At
the level of the enterocyte the availability of glycerol

determines perhaps to some extent the transport form of fatty acids. This is consistent with the hypothesis that dietary glycerol from the intestinal lumen is probably the only form of glyceride–glycerol precursor in the enterocyte. In this connection it would be interesting to observe the variation in the plasma ratio between free and esterified fatty acids when changing from a triglyceride rich to a wax ester rich diet.

In addition to lipoprotein particles many authors observed a second form of esterified lipids in the enterocyte called fat droplets (Iwai and Tanaka, 1968), "lipides étalés" (Bergot and Flechon, 1970b) or lipid droplets (Noaillac-Depeyre and Gas, 1974; 1976; Stroband and Debets, 1978). They represent extrareticular conglomerates whose diameter may reach several μM. Lipid accumulations have sometimes been observed in mammals in the case of lipid overloading on the intestinal lumen (Sabesin et al., 1975; Snipes, 1977) and abeta-lipoproteinaemia (Dobbions, 1966). These lipid droplets were never found in the extracellular spaces. In fish they probably represent storage pools appearing when the synthesis pathway of the chylomicron-like particles is overloaded. This interpretation is supported by the following observation. Lipid droplets do not seem to appear after ingestion of palmitic acid, but after that of unsaturated fatty acids and their size increases with the degree of unsaturation of the acid (Bergot and Flechon, 1970b; Sire and Vernier, 1981). It was pointed out above that a larger affinity of FABP for unsaturated fatty acids might lead to a faster esterification in the SER. Esterification might then exceed the synthesizing ability of apoproteins which are the surface elements of the chylomicrons. The excess of triglycerides which have not been "packed" by the surface constituents of lipoproteins would then form fine lipid droplets on the cytoplasmic surface of the reticulum which after fusion would form the pre-cited lipid conglomerates.

Large lipid drops also appeared when trout were given a diet containing 85% of the total lipids as wax esters (Bauermeister et al., 1979). They were essentially "conglomerates" of the original small droplets. These conglomerates were seen either free in the cytoplasm or bound by intracellular membranes.

V. TRANSPORT OF PLASMA LIPIDS

Water insoluble lipids (triglycerides, free and esterified cholesterol, phospholipids) and proteins (called apoproteins) are associated in variable proportions in the plasma and form particles or complexes named lipoproteins. They provide an efficient system for transport of lipids into the vascular system from the sites of absorption (enterocytes) and of biosynthesis (mainly hepatocytes and enterocytes) to the sites of conversion, storage or energy utilisation. These structures have been studied especially in man and in some mammals, but they also exist in the plasma of the other vertebrates (Chapman, 1980).

Lipoprotein consists of a hydrophobic nucleus of triglycerides and cholesterol esters and a hydrophilic or amphiphilic envelope of polar constituents (phospholipids, free cholesterol and apoproteins). Plasma lipoproteins are generally classified according to their density, i.e. the relative proportions of low density and high density constituents (lipids and apoproteins, respectively). The classes of lipoproteins are mostly isolated by ultracentrifugation. Table I shows the characteristics of each of these classes for human serum. They were established by Osborne and Brewer (1977) according to data supplied by other authors. Lipoproteins of other species are classified according to these characteristics. The four classes from the lightest to the heaviest are the following: chylomicrons, VLDL, LDL and HDL subdivided into HDL_2 and HDL_3.

There are 5 main families of apoproteins called A, B, C and E. Apo A are predominantly found in HDL, apo B in LDL, apo B, C and E in VLDL and apo A, B and C in chylomicrons. Each apoprotein seems to have a specific function. It has been very well established for apo AI and apo CII (Fielding et al., 1972; La Rosa et al., 1970), which are specific activators of lecithin-cholesterol-acyl-transferase (LCAT) and LPL, respectively, as well as for apo B and apo E which serve as "signals" for lipoprotein catabolism in the tissue by interacting with specific cell membrane receptors (Eisenberg, 1983).

In man, the aggregation of protein and lipid constituents and the secretion of nascent serum lipoproteins, products of this aggregation, take place in the liver and intestine. The liver secretes nascent VLDL and HDL whereas the intestine secretes chylomicrons, VLDL

Table I   Human Serum levels of lipoproteins

Classification based	Origin	Pre-β	β	α	α
- on electrophoresis migration					
- on hydrated density	Chylomicrons	VLDL	LDL	HDL_2	HDL_3
Properties					
- density limits (g/ml)	<1.006	<1.006	1.006–1.063	1.063–1.125	1.125–1.21
- molecular weight	>0.4×10^9	$5–10 \times 10^6$	$2.7–4.8 \times 10^6$	3.9×10^5	1.8×10^5
- diameter (Å)	>750	250–750	200–240	60–140	40–100

From, Osborne and Brewer (1977)

and perhaps small quantities of HDL (see references cited in Chapman, 1982). One of the most striking findings of the last ten years contributing to the understanding of lipoprotein metabolism is that the classes of lipoproteins are not independent, but functionally interrelated (Eisenberg, 1983). Lipoproteins stabilized by non-covalent forces undergo rapid and steady modifications either by non-enzymatic transfer of lipids or apoproteins resulting from excess of hydrophobic or hydrophilic material in the lipoprotein particle, or by enzymatic transfer via three enzymes (LCAT, LPL, and hepatic LPL [HLPL]. Chylomicron and VLDL triglycerides are hydrolysed by LPL and the free fatty acids taken up by the tissues. Excess hydrophilicity resulting from the release of triglycerides leads in turn to the release of excess surface constituents contributing to the formation of mature HDL while chylomicron and VLDL remnants as well as LDL (products of the more advanced VLDL hydrolysis) are taken up by different tissues. The activity of LCAT is required for conversion (maturation) of HDL precursors into HDL_3 and then HDL_2. The HDL precursors might originate either in the excess surface constituents of chylomicrons and VLDL or in a direct hepatic synthesis. During this conversion, HDL which take up free cholesterol from the tissues or other lipoproteins become enriched in cholesterol esters. When passing through the liver, HDL_2 are converted into HDL_3 via the phospholipase activity of HLPL, releasing lysolecithins, cholesterol and perhaps a part of the esterified cholesterol which may then be taken up by the hepatocyte. The remnant cholesterol esters are transferred to other lipoproteins.

Thus, there is a core pathway from the chylomicrons and VLDL to the remnants and LDL which are then included into the tissues and a surface pathway ending with the formation of the pool of HDL (Eisenberg, 1983).

According to the composition and sites of aggregation of lipoproteins as well as to the degradation and conversion pathways it appears that chylomicrons are specialised in the transport of exogenous triglycerides, VLDL in that of both endogenous and exogenous triglycerides, LDL in the transport of esterified cholesterol towards extrahepatic tissues and HDL in the transport to the liver of cholesterol taken up from the extrahepatic tissues.

The three classes of lipoproteins, VLDL, LDL and HDL are present in fish (Mills and Taylaur, 1971; Chapman et al., 1978; Skinner and Rogie, 1978a; Perrier et al., 1979;

Table II   Lipoprotein class distribution in the plasma of fish (mg/100 ml)

Species	VLDL	LDL	HDL
Coelacanth, Latimeria chalumnae (1)	1105	194	127
Hagfish, Myxine glutinosa (1)	1666	710	553
Dogfish, Scyliorhinus canicula (1)	28	154	23
Conger, Conger vulgaris (1)	456	225	nd
Shark, Centrophorus squamosus (2)	415	230	40
Sardine, Sardinops caerula (3)	105	121	560
Salmon, Oncorhynchus gorbuscha (4)	nd	nd	3300
Salmon, Oncorhynchus nerka (5)	167	246	238

nd : not determined

(1) Mills and Taylaur(1973); (2) Mills et al. (1977); (3) Lee and Puppione (1972); (4)

Nelson and Shore (1974); (5) Reichert and Malins (1974).

Fremont et al., 1981; Leger et al., 1981; Fremont and
Marion, 1982; Fremont et al., 1984). Although the
presence of chylomicrons in the serum is not always
reported, their existence is revealed by some authors,
either by electron microscope techniques (Skinner and
Rogie, 1978a; Chapman et al., 1978) or by flotation after
centrifugation at 15000 x g (Fremont et al., 1981; Fremont
and Marion, 1982).

The plasma level of lipids sometimes reaches very high
values, 700 mg/dl in sardines (Lee and Puppione, 1972),
more than 2000 mg/dl in Pacific salmon (Nelson and Shore,
1974), about 1800 mg/dl in mature male trout (Fremont et
al., 1981). It is observed that out of 1850 mg/dl total
plasma lipids, 1726 mg (93%) were recovered in the
lipoproteins, 23 mg in the fraction d > 1.21 g/ml in which
free fatty acids are the main components.

Table III. Lipoprotein class distribution in rainbow
trout plasma (mg/100 ml)

Reference	VLDL	LDL	HDL	Experimental conditions
Skinner and Rogie (1978a)	201 212	392 193	2216 1062	male trout (1.0-1.6 kg) one fish per line
Chapman et al. (1978)	673	466	>1500	female trout (0.7-1.9 kg) pool of 3 fish
Fremont et al. (1981)	586	1156	518	male trout (0.5-1.0 kg) pool of 15 fish
Fremont and Marion (1982)	335[a] 171[b] 47[c]	1189 879 441	331 1371 1013	male trout a: 100 - 120 g immature trout b: 100 - 120 g spermiating trout c: 1.0 - 1.2 kg spermiating trout pool of 50 fish per line
Fremont et al. (1984)	650[a] 100[b]	400+300 250+300	1750 1300	female trout (1.0-1.2 kg) a: in September b: in December (ovulation time) pool of 8-9 fish per line
Sire and Vernier (1979)	248	trace	2344	immature (?) trout (140-200 g) pool of 21 fish

Such plasma lipid levels lead to high levels of
lipoproteins. The values in Tables II and III show that
the lipoprotein levels may exceed 2000 mg/dl in

salmonids.   In trout, HDL are generally predominant and
their plasma level reached between 1500 and 2000 mg/dl.
The distribution of plasma lipoprotein classes varies
widely between species (Table II).   It also varies within
one and the same species (Table III).   These variations
may be due to sexual status (Fig. 2) – sexually mature or
immature fish (Fremont and Marion, 1982) – and to the
sexual cycle (Fig. 3) (Fremont et al., 1984).   Conversely,

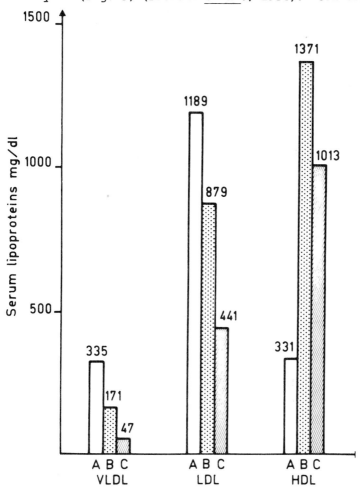

Fig.   2.   Influence   of   the   sexual   status   on   serum
lipoprotein   concentrations.   Samples   of   each   group
represent pooled blood of 50 fish (Fremont and Marion,
1982). A : juvenile male trout; B : spermiating trout (1
st sexual cycle); C : spermiating trout (2nd sexual cycle).

the nutritional conditions seem to slightly affect the distribution of the different classes (Fremont and Marion, 1982).

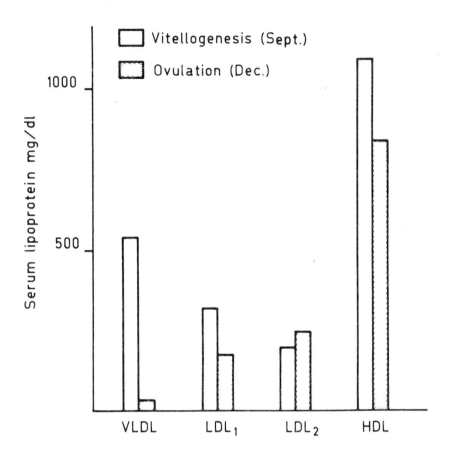

Fig. 3. Total serum lipoprotein contents (mg/dl) in female trout during vitellogenesis (September) and spawning (December). Mean values of analyses (in duplicate or triplicate) of two groups of 8-9 fish whose sera were pooled (Fremont et al., 1984).

One of the difficulties in studying fish lipoproteins resides in the definition of the density intervals of the different classes of lipoproteins. This definition is similar to that adopted in man, but differs from it when the authors take into account the specific fish characteristics. On the basis of polyacrylamide gel electrophoresis, Skinner and Rogie (1978a) defined the following classes in trout: VLDL, d < 1.020; LDL, d 1.020 - 1.085; HDL, d 1.096 - 1.21. Chapman et al. (1978) showed by analysis of flotation rates and immunological techniques that trout LDL could be completely isolated by use of a higher limiting density of approximately 1.080 g/ml instead of 1.063 g/ml. VLDL were isolated at d = 1.015 g/ml which is the non-protein solvent density of trout serum, instead of 1.006 g/ml in human. Fremont and Marion (1982) underlined that lipoproteins in the range of d 1.015 - 1.085 g/ml are not pure LDL in trout. Three populations can be isolated by molecular filtration. These fractions migrated by electrophoresis in polyacrylamide gradient gel (Leger et al., 1979) in positions similar to those of VLDL, LDL and HDL. Two sub-fractions of LDL could be distinguished (Fremont et al., 1984) : LDL_1 (d 1.015 - 1.063) and LDL_2 (d 1.063 - 1.085) corresponding to a VLDL + LDL and a HDL + LDL mixture, respectively. The contamination of sub-fraction LDL_2 by HDL was larger during spermiation (January-March) than during sexual rest (May) in male trout (unpublished results). Therefore the definition of density intervals of lipoprotein classes is not the only difficulty encountered in fish lipoproteins. The second difficulty is that there is an overlapping of lipoprotein classes which seems to vary during the sexual cycle.

Using electrophoretic and chromatographic techniques Nakagawa (1976; 1978) distinguished three classes of lipoproteins in carp whose amino acid compositions resemble human chylomicrons, VLDL and LDL. The fourth class did not show any resemblance to human HDL and albumin. Carp albumin, with a molecular weight of 150,000, contains large amounts of esterified lipids. Because of its high plasma level (about 1 g/dl) it plays a physiological role in the transport of lipids and not only that of free fatty acids as in man. Many authors have studied serum albumin in fish (Perrier et al., 1977). In all cases, the plasma level of albumin was lower than its human counterpart.

The composition of fish lipoproteins is the same as that of human lipoproteins, but the proportions are different and highly variable from one species to another (Table IV). In the most primitive species (coelacanth and hagfish) VLDL, LDL and HDL are very poor in cholesterol. Most constituents are in the free form while the major part is esterified in man and in other fish species. This signifies that the cholesterol esterifying

318 C. LEGER

enzyme activity (LCAT) is low or non-existent and that the
mode of cholesterol transport is particular, probably due
to this lack of activity.

Table IV. Proportions (percent by weight) of lipoprotein
classes in fish.

	Pr	PL	C	CE	TG	ADG	HC
Chylomicrons :							
Trout (7)	4.5	8.3	1.0	2.2	84		
Human (8)	2	8	1	4	84		
VLDL :							
Shark (1)	3.1	15.3	6.7	21.4	23	8.2	18.8
Coelacanth (1)	14.4	11.5	7.0	3.1	64	–	–
Hagfish (1)	12.1	17.3	5.1	2.5	48.2	10.6	4.4
Dogfish (1)	28.4	12.4	7.4	8.3	43.5	–	–
Sardine (2)	nd	1	9*	60	30		
Trout (4)	7.2	16.1	11.5	26.5	38.5		
Trout (5)	9.6	26.5	6.9	15.1	41.9		
Trout (6)	12.8	20.0	5.3	6.1	55.8		
Human (7)	10	18	6	16	50		
LDL :							
Shark (1)	17.6	20.5	8.4	25.9	8.7	10.9	5.9
Coelacanth	27.9	13.6	5.8	3.1	49.7		
Hagfish (1)	21.1	22.4	9.6	3.0	29.5	8.7	5.7
Dogfish (1)	29.8	14.8	12.5	22.8	20.1		
Sardine (2)	nd	35	15*	16	31		
Trout (4)	35.2	14.9	9.5	17.9	12.5		
Trout (4)	24.7	27.1	6.7	15.6	26.9		
Trout (4)	28.3	34.2	3.6	11.3	22.6		
Human (8)	20	22	1.0	40	8		
HDL :							
Shark (1)	47.7	14.5	3.8	13.9	3.4	8.0	6.9
Coelacanth (1)	77.1	7.0	2.2	1.3	12.5		
Hagfish (1)	42.1	29.6	9.6	0.7	10.5	1.5	6.1
Dogfish (1)	53.1	9.8	9.4	15.6	12.2		
Sardine (2)	nd	55	15*	20	10		
Pink Salmon (3)	40	30	3.2	18.3	6.8		
Trout (4)	42.2	27.9	4.1	20.1	5.7		
Trout (5)	46.9	26.5	3.4	7.7	15.5		
Trout (6)	46.0	32.0	2.7	6.8	12.5		
Human (8)	50.0	25	3	15	7		

(1) Mills et al. (1977); (2) Lee and Puppione (1972); (3) Nelson and Shore (1974);
(4) Skinner and Rogie (1978); (5) Chapman et al, (1978); (6) Fremont et al. (1981);
(7) Fremont and Marion (1982); (8) Faegerman (1977).

Abbreviations: Pr = proteins; PL = phospholipids; C: free cholesterol; CE =
cholesterol esters; TG = triglycerides; ADG = alkyldiacylglycerol; * = C + FFA +
diglycerides; HC = hydrocarbons; nd = not determined.

In all fish of Table IV, the level of esterified cholesterol in LDL is definitely lower than in man. Accordingly, LDL are perhaps not the principal form of transport of this constituent in fish. On the other hand, LDL are more triglyceride rich in fish than in man. If we exclude the possibility of contamination of LDL by triglyceride rich VLDL (see above), we may remark that the sum of neutral lipids (cholesterol esters, triglycerides and monoalkyl diacyl glycerol if it exists) known to distribute into the hydrophobic core of lipoproteins, is quite similar in man and in fish (see Table IV and Chapman et al., 1980). Such data seem to indicate that the three–dimensional molecular arrangement in fish LDL is not significantly different from that of man, a predominantly hydrophobic core surrounded by the more polar constituents (protein, phospholipid and free cholesterol). The similar ratio of polar/apolar constituents is consistent with the fact that mean particle size of LDL in hagfish and trout (Mills et al., 1977; Chapman et al., 1978) resemble those of the human fraction (191 A and 238 A, respectively, against 220 A in man).

The relationship between VLDL particle size and the sum of surface constituents established by Sata et al. (1972) in man, seems to be consistent with the results obtained in trout (290 A for 32-40%) and hagfish (310 A for 35%). Thus, VLDL structure in fish and man also seems to be very similar.

The content of polar constituents in fish HDL is similar to that in man. The molecular weight of 170,000 in the salmon (Nelson and Shore, 1974) is closely related to human molecular characteristics of HDL_3. However, the mean diameter of 77 A in trout (Chapman et al., 1978) and the Stokes radius of 80 A in salmon (Nelson and Shore 1974) are substantially lower than that of human HDL_3 (about 130 A) as measured by Aggerbeck et al. (1980) but of the same order as that reported by Osborn and Brewer (1977).

In fish, HDL are probably the most original class of lipoproteins both by their structure and by the amounts present in the plasma. This latter feature provides HDL an important role in the transport of lipids. High HDL levels may be due either to a low degradation rate or to a high hepatic synthesis of nascent particles or to a fast degradation of the very low density particles (chylomicrons and VLDL) by LPL leading to release of apoproteins constituting the HDL. Further investigations would be necessary to explain this high level of HDL.

However, the mean diameter of HDL and the fact that
chylomicrons and VLDL are always very low in the plasma
could be in favour of the last two hypotheses. In this
respect a high HLPL activity would also be necessary for
the rapid conversion of HDL_2 in HDL_3.

Skinner and Youssef (1982) showed that intravenous
injection of heparin into the trout resulted in the
appearance in the plasma of a lipase with LPL properties
(inhibition by 0.6 M NaCl and by protamine sulphate,
activation by trout serum). The enzyme purified by
heparin-Sepharose chromatography displayed properties and
a molecular weight similar to that of mammals. However,
the enzyme was strongly activated by trout VLDL and to a
less extent by trout HDL. This contrasts with the LPL
properties of human LPL, but the difference could be due
to the relative concentration of the activator peptide -
apoprotein C-II in mammals - in the two classes of
lipoproteins.

The LPL also appeared to be present in several tissues:
red and white muscle, heart, brain, liver and adipose
tissue in trout (Black et al., 1983b) and in cod liver
(Black et al., 1983a). It was recently demonstrated
(Fremont et al., unpublished data) that extracts prepared
from acetone-ether powder of trout adipose tissue
exhibited a LPL activity activated by porcine serum. It
can be concluded that lipoprotein degradation by the LPL
pathway exists in fish, leading to the lipid uptake by the
tissues.

The salt-resistant LPL (SR-LPL) appeared to be absent
from trout post-heparin plasma (Skinner and Youssef,
1982), whereas it was present in the liver and several
extrahepatic tissues: brain, red and white muscle, heart
and the adipose tissue of trout and in cod liver (Black et
al., 1983b; Black et al., 1983a). SR-LPL could not be
released by heparin injection from capillary endothelium,
contrasting with the human enzyme counterpart.

A lipase activity appeared in the post-heparin plasma
of Tilapia nilotica (Susuki et al., 1981). No inhibition
took place by addition of 1.0 - 2.0 M NaCl or protamine
sulphate, whereas activation appeared by fish or human
sera. This enzyme seems to be different from both LPL
and SR-LPL as it possesses some properties of both.
Kayama et al. (1979) and Dannevig and Norum (1979)
reported the existence of a cholesterol esterifying enzyme
activity in the carp and the char (Salmo alpinus L.),
counterpart of LCAT activity in mammals.

Resemblances have been noticed between fish and man when comparing the protein moieties, the phospholipid composition and the fatty acid composition of lipid moieties.

The apoproteins of VLDL and LDL on the one hand, and of HDL on the other hand, possess distinct antigenic determinants and amino acid compositions. "This situation clearly resembles that in man, in which the B apolipoprotein is the major component of both VLDL and LDL, while the A apolipoproteins predominate in HDL" (Chapman, 1980).

In contrast, the counterpart of human apo B from hagfish LDL, shark LDL, trout VLDL and LDL-2 closely resemble the apo B from human LDL (table 8 of Chapman, 1980) as shown by amino acid analysis and molecular weight determination. In the same way, two apoproteins exist in trout HDL which possess a molecular weight similar to that of apoprotein A-I and apoprotein A-II of human HDL. Human apoprotein A-I and its apoprotein counterparts in trout and salmon O. gorbuscha (Skinner and Rogie, 1987a; Nelson and Shore, 1974) display similar amino acid compositions. An apoprotein isolated from trout VLDL with the same molecular weight and the same mobility by electro-focusing as human apo C-II was observed by Fremont et al. (unpublished data). This is consistent with the fact that trout VLDL act as a substrate for purified bovine milk LPL (reported by Chapman, 1980) and activate trout LPL (Fremont et al., unpublished data).

Phosphatidylcholine is predominant in fish (54 - 83%) as in human lipoproteins (Chapman, 1980), but sphingomyelin is present in variable and higher proportions (5.6 - 28%) in fish than in man.

Comparison between the fatty acid composition of the different lipoprotein classes (Tables V, VI and VII and table 7 of Chapman, 1980) reveals the existence of common characteristics in fish. The 18:1 acids often represent the major proportion while fatty acids with a greater chain length than 18C are also plentiful. The content of 22:6 (n-3) exceeds that of 18:1 in cholesterol esters CE2 (polyunsaturated fatty acid rich CE fraction, especially 22:6 (n-3)) of shark C. squamosus and trout, in cholesterol esters of sardines as well as in triglycerides and phospholipids of dogfish S. canicula. The main characteristic of fish lipids is the large proportion of highly polyunsaturated fatty acids (HPUFA). These acids are mainly composed of the (n-6) series (of linoleic acid), especially 20:4, and the (n-3) series of (linolenic

acid) (22:5 and especially 22:6).   The (n-3) HPUFA are
absent in Latimeria chalumnae and in cholesterol esters of
Myxine glutinosa.   This is either due to an ancestral
fish trait or to a feed dependent characteristic.

According to the large number of data available in
trout (Tables V, VI and VII), the content of (n-3) series
is much higher than that of (n-6) series in lipoproteins.
This   is   particularly   true   for   phospholipids   and
cholesterol esters in LDL and HDL.   Taking into account
the higher proportion of HDL as compared to LDL in the
plasma, the largest amounts of 22:6 (n-3) were transported
by HDL mainly as phospholipids (Leger et al., 1981;
Fremont et al., 1984).   From a qualitative point of view,
however, both phospholipids and cholesterol esters were
pathways for 22:6 (n-3) transport as shown by the values
of Tables V, VI and VII.   The 22:6 (n-3) belongs to the
essential fatty acids (EFA) in trout and in fish in
general (sec the report on this topic in the present
book).   This fatty acid is probably the physiological
counterpart of 20:4 (n-6) in mammals.   Comparing the high
level of 22:6 (n-3) and 20:4 (n-6) in lipo-protein
phospholipids and cholesterol esters of fish and rat,
respectively, it can be suggested that there may be a
relationship between EFA activity and distribution of EFA
into the lipid fractions of lipo-protein whatever the
series to which EFA belongs.

Vitellogenin is a form of lipid transport specifically
encountered in mature oviparous female and oestrogen-
injected male species of Amphibia, birds and fish (Hara
and Hirai, 1978; Wallace, 1970; Deeley et al., 1975;
Bergink and Wallace, 1974; Plack et al., 1971; Emmersen
and Petersen, 1976).   It is a very high density
lipoprotein (d 1.21 - 1.28 g/ml) containing about 80%
proteins and 20% lipids mainly containing phospholipids,
synthesized by the liver and rich in EFA (Leger et al.,
1981; Fremont et al., 1984).   It is a precursor form of
two egg components, lipovitellin and phosvitin.   No
antigenic community has been observed between protein
moieties of egg and plasma lipoproteins (Skinner and
Rogie, 1978b).   High levels (>5 g/dl) can be reached at
the spawning period.   As shown by Fremont et al. (1984),
fish fed an (n-3) deficient diet for six months are able
to elevate the EFA content of lipoprotein and especially
vitellogenin as compared to fish fed the deficient diet
for three r.onths.   A compensatory mechanism in which
hepatic acyltransferase could be involved is most likely
responsible for the maintenance of sufficiently high

Table V   Simplified fatty acid composition of the lipid esters of trout very low density lipoproteins

LP-lipids	References	16:0	16:1	18:0	18:1 (n-9)	18:2 (n-6)	20:4 (n-6)	18:3 (n-3)	20:5 (n-3)	22:6 (n-3)	Σ(n-6)	Σ(n-3)
VLDL-TG	(1)	16.6	9.0	3.5	41.9	10.1	1.9	5.8	–	6.9	nd	nd
	(2)	15.3	10.6	5.3	40.7	4.3	0.3	0.3	0.6	1.9	5.9	6.2
	(3)	15.5	7.2	4.3	28.6	6.5	0.7	0.9	3.7	12.3	9.1	19.4
		13.3	5.3	3.7	21.8	10.0	0.9	1.4	4.8	17.4	13.4	26.6
		15.4	8.4	4.8	24.2	9.3	0.9	1.5	4.4	14.8	12.7	23.4
VLDL-CE	(1)[a]	7.0	2.4	3.1	3.3	0.8	5.5	–	6.7	65.5	nd	nd
	(2)	25.8	5.6	4.4	17.1	3.6	0.8	0.2	2.2	12.0	6.7	20.0
	(3)	18.8	5.1	4.2	19.5	3.8	0.9	0.3	3.6	20.9	7.3	26.0
		18.2	3.1	2.5	13.3	4.4	1.5	0.4	5.2	36.2	9.5	43.1
VLDL-PL	(1)	25.0	3.5	11.5	14.1	8.3	1.6	2.3	–	23.7	nd	nd
	(2)	32.8	5.3	12.8	18.2	2.0	0.6	–	–	4.2	2.9	4.2
	(3)	32.7	4.6	6.9	19.5	2.2	2.4	0.2	3.7	25.5	6.6	30.4
		24.0	4.5	7.0	11.0	3.4	3.6	0.3	4.2	33.9	9.2	39.3

(1) Chapman et al. (1978);   (2) Fremont et al. (1981);   (3) Fremont and Marion (1982)

[a] The fatty acid percentages of the fraction CE-2 are reported here

nd = not determined; TG = triglycerides; CE = cholesterol esters; PL = phospholipids

Table VI   Simplified fatty acid composition of the lipid esters of trout low density lipoproteins

LP-lipids	References	16:0	16:1	18:0	18:1 (n-9)	18:2 (n-6)	20:4 (n-6)	18:3 (n-3)	20:5 (n-3)	22:6 (n-3)	Σ(n-6)	Σ(n-3)
LDL-TG	(1)	17.2	8.9	3.6	42.8	10.4	0.7	5.2	–	8.2	nd	nd
	(2)	14.7	8.1	5.1	38.6	6.6	0.7	0.5	1.5	6.5	10.5	10.1
	(3)	13.8	6.0	3.7	29.5	6.2	0.9	1.0	4.6	15.2	9.2	23.5
		9.8	4.4	3.3	23.5	9.1	1.2	1.2	5.4	24.2	13.5	33.8
		11.4	5.1	3.1	28.8	9.7	1.5	1.6	4.3	19.6	14.3	28.5
LDL-CE	(1)[a]	4.8	2.3	2.5	2.5	1.3	5.9	0.8	6.9	64.5	nd	nd
	(2)	20.7	3.8	0.4	16.0	5.5	1.7	0.4	4.4	25.7	10.9	31.6
	(3)	12.8	4.7	2.5	17.3	4.1	1.4	0.4	5.5	29.9	8.7	37.8
		13.3	3.3	1.6	11.2	5.0	1.7	0.4	5.8	42.1	10.4	50.2
		20.7	2.1	2.5	12.0	6.9	3.7	0.6	6.5	35.0	13.5	43.5
LDL-PL	(1)	25.7	3.3	11.6	14.6	8.7	–	2.5	–	25.6	nd	nd
	(2)	44.0	6.1	10.0	20.5	2.1	–	–	0.2	–	2.8	2.6
	(3)	21.9	3.2	5.7	12.6	2.2	3.7	0.2	4.6	35.0	7.8	41.2
		24.1	3.0	4.3	9.6	2.8	3.5	0.2	3.9	40.6	8.5	45.8
		25.4	2.7	5.6	12.1	5.1	6.4	0.4	4.4	29.3	14.0	35.9

(1) Chapman et al. (1978) ;   (2) Fremont et al. (1981) ;   (3) Fremont and Marion (1982)

[a] The fatty acid percentages of the fraction CE-2 are reported here

nd = not determined;   TG = triglycerides;   CE = cholesterol esters;   PL = phospholipids

Table VII   Simplified fatty acid composition of the lipid esters of trout high density lipoproteins

LP-lipids	References	16:0	16:1	18:0	18:1 (n-9)	18:2 (n-6)	20:4 (n-6)	18:3 (n-3)	20:5 (n-3)	22:6 (n-3)	Σ(n-6)	Σ(n-3)
HDL-TG	(1)	17.2	8.9	3.5	40.7	10.3	1.4	4.8	–	9.7	nd	nd
	(2)	15.3	8.3	5.2	39.2	6.4	0.7	–	1.5	6.1	9.4	8.5
	(3)	14.4	5.9	4.1	28.5	6.1	0.7	0.8	4.0	14.1	8.6	21.5
		12.7	5.2	3.5	24.9	9.6	1.1	1.2	5.1	19.1	13.6	28.7
		12.2	5.2	3.2	30.4	10.1	1.4	1.7	1.6	16.8	14.6	25.5
HDL-CE	(1)[a]	4.2	2.1	1.8	2.8	3.2	6.0	0.5	6.5	66.9	nd	nd
	(2)	22.5	3.8	4.3	14.8	5.0	1.7	–	5.3	29.0	9.4	36.0
	(3)	16.4	5.2	3.2	15.2	3.4	1.1	0.3	4.7	27.4	7.0	34.3
		15.2	3.3	2.0	12.8	4.8	1.9	0.5	6.0	38.1	10.4	46.5
		20.5	2.2	2.6	13.4	7.4	3.8	0.6	6.4	32.8	13.6	41.2
HDL-PL	(1)	24.8	2.9	10.5	13.3	8.7	2.4	3.0	–	28.6	nd	nd
	(2)	31.0	5.9	6.4	14.7	3.8	2.9	–	2.5	18.2	8.4	21.3
	(3)	23.7	3.5	6.3	12.2	2.3	3.2	0.2	4.6	34.3	7.4	40.4
		24.3	2.8	1.4	10.8	3.5	4.1	0.3	4.0	37.8	9.3	43.6
		24.8	2.5	5.2	12.3	5.4	5.7	0.4	5.0	30.3	13.6	37.6

(1) Chapman et al. (1978);   (2) Fremont et al. (1981);   (3) Fremont and Marion (1982)

[a] The fatty acid percentages of the fraction CE-2 are reported here

nd = not determined;   TG = triglycerides;   CE = cholesterol esters;   PL = phospholipids

tissue and egg contents of essential fatty acids.

Apart from the specific carrier involved in the deposition of egg reserves (encountered in oviparous animals), the observations concerning both the protein moieties of the carrier and the carried lipid moieties, made sometimes in phylogenetically very different species, strongly suggest the great role of lipoproteins in lipid transport. Furthermore, the three main enzymes involved in the degradation and interconversion of lipoproteins in mammals also exist in fish (except LCAT probably absent in primitive fish). Thus, the mechanisms of lipid transport are most likely the same in all vertebrates. The very different plasma levels of lipoproteins from one species to another may be explained by differences in the adjustment of the processes leading to the synthesis of the constituents and to lipoprotein formation and degradation.

VI. ACKNOWLEDGEMENTS

The author wishes to acknowledge that Mme K. Ferat prepared this translation of the French paper into English.

REFERENCES

Aggerbecq, L.P., Yates, M. and Gulik-Krywicki, I. (1980). Ann. N.Y. Acad. Sci. 348, 352-364.
Andrews, J.W., Murray, M.W. and David, J.M. (1978). J. Nutr. 108, 749-752.
Arvy, L. (1954). C.R. Assoc. Anat. 41, 836-843.
Arvy, L. and Gabe, M. (1957). Ann. Histochem. 2, 141-148.
Atherton, W.D. and Aitken, S. (1970). Comp. Biochem. Physiol. 36B, 719-745.
Austreng, E. (1978). Aquaculture 13, 265-272.
Austreng, E., Skrede, A. and Eldegard, A. (1980). Aquaculture 19, 93-95.
Bauermeister, A.E.M., Pirie, B.J.S. and Sargent, J.R. (1979). Cell Tissue Res. 200, 475-486.
Beamish, F.W.H. (1972). Can. J. Zool. 50, 153-164.
Benson, A.A., Lee, R.E. and Nevenzel, J.C. (1972). Biochem. Soc. Symp. 35, 175-187.

Benzonana, G. and Desnuelle, P. (1968). Biochim. Biophys. Acta. 164, 47–58.

Bergink, E.W. and Wallace, R.A. (1974). Ann. Zool. 14, 1177–1193.

Bergot, P. and Flechon, J.E. (1970a). Ann. Biol. anim. Biochim. Biophys. 10, 459–472.

Bernard, F. (1961). Travaux du laboratoire d'Hydrobiologie et de Pisciculture de Grenoble, 141–145.

Berner, D.L. and Hammond, E.G. (1970). Lipids 5, 558–562.

Bierman, H.R., Byron, R.L., Kelly, K.H., Gilfillan, R.S., White, L.P., Freeman, N.E. and Petrakis, N.L. (1953). J. Clin. Invest. 32, 637–649.

Black, D., Kirkpatrick, S.A. and Skinner, E.R. (1983a). Biochem. Soc. Trans. 11, 708.

Black, D., Youssef, A.M. and Skinner, E.R. (1983b). Biochem. Soc. Trans. 11, 93–94.

Borgstrom, B. (1974). In "Biomembranes", (D.H. Smyth, ed.) Vol 4B, 555–620. Plenum Press, London, New York.

Borgstrom, B. and Erlanson, C. (1973). Eur. J. Biochem. 37, 60–68.

Boucrot, P. and Clement, J. (1965). C.R. Acad. Sci. Paris. 260, 4083–4086.

Brockerhoff, H. (1966). J. Fish. Res. Board Canada 23, 1835–1839.

Brockerhoff, H. (1968). Biochim. Biophys. Acta 159, 296–303.

Brockerhoff, H. (1970).Biochim. Biophys. Acta 212, 92–101.

Brockerhoff, H. and Hoyle, R.J. (1965). Biochim. Biophys. Acta 98, 435–436.

Carey, M.C. (1980). Ital. J. Gastroenterol. 12, 140–145.

Chapman, M.J. (1980). J. Lipid. Res. 21, 789–853.

Chapman, M.J. (1982).Gastroentérol. clin. biol. 6, 482–499.

Chapman, M.J., Goldstein, S., Mills, G.L. and Leger, C. (1978). Biochemistry 17, 4455–4464.

Cho, C.Y. and Slinger, S.J. (1979). In "Finfish Nutrition and Fishfeed Technology", (J.E. Halver and K. Tiews, eds.) II, 239–247. H. Heeneman GmbH and Co., Berlin.

Dannevig, B.H. and Norum, K.R. (1979). Comp. Biochem. Physiol. 63B, 537–541.

Darnton, S.J. and Barrowman, J.A. (1969). Histochem. J. 1, 551–557.

Deeley, R.G., Mullinix, K.P., Wetekam, W., Kronenberg, H.M., Meyers, M., Eldridge, J.D. and Goldberger, R.F. (1975). J. biol. Chem. 250, 9060–9066.

Dobbins, W.O. (1966). Gastroenterology 50, 195–210.

Eisenberg, S. (1983). Klin. Wochenschr. 61, 119–132.

Emmersen, B.K. and Petersen, I.M. (1976). Comp. Biochem. Physiol. 54B, 443-446.

Entressangles, B., Sari, H. and Desnuelle, P. (1966). Biochim. Biophys. Acta 125, 597-600.

Erlanson, C. and Borgström, B. (1970). Scand. J. Gastroenterol. 5, 395-400.

Faegerman, O. (1977). Acta Med. Scand. Suppl. 614, 3-29.

Fielding, C.J., Shore, V.G. and Fielding, P.E. (1972). Biochem. Biophys. Res. Commun. 46, 1493-1498.

Fremont, L., Flanzy, J. and Francois, A.C. (1970). Ann. Biol. anim. Biochim. Biophys. 10, 271-289.

Fremont, L., Leger, C. and Boudon, M. (1981). Comp. Biochem. Physiol. 69B, 107-113.

Fremont, L., Leger, C., Petridou, B. and Gozzelino, M.T. (1984). Lipids, in press.

Fremont, L. and Marion, D. (1982). Comp. Biochem. Physiol. 73B, 849-855.

Gangl, A. and Ockner, R.K. (1975). Gastroenterology 68, 167-186.

Gohar, H.A.F. and Latif, A.F.A. (1963). Publ. mar. Biol. Stat. Al Ghardaga (Red Sea) 12, 43-64.

Gomori, G. (1946). Am. J. clin. Pathol. 16, 347-352.

Greene, C.W. (1913). Bull. U.S. Bur. Fish. 33, 149-175.

Hara, A. and Hirai, H. (1978). Comp. Biochem. Physiol. 59B, 339-343.

Haslewood, G.A.D. (1978). In "The biological importance of bile salts", (A. Neuberger and E.L. Tatum, eds.) North-Holland Publishing Company, Amnsterdam, New York, Oxford.

Ijima, N., Zama, K. and Kayama, M. (1983). Bull. Jap. Soc. Sci. Fish. 49, 1465-1470.

Iwai, T. and Tanaka, M. (1968). Bull. Jap. Soc. Sci. Fish. 34, 871-875.

Johnston, J.M. (1970). In, "Comprehensive Biochemistry", (M. Florkin and E.H. Stotz, eds.) 18, 1-18, Elsevier Publishing Company, Amsterdam, London, New York.

Kayama, M. and Ijima, N. (1976). Bull. Jap. Soc. Sci. Fish. 42, 987-996.

Kayama, M., Mankura, M. and Dalimunthe, D. (1979). Bull. Jap. Soc. Sci. Fish. 45, 523-525.

Kimura, N. (1873). Jap. J. Ichthyol. 20, 13-24.

La Rosa, J.C., Levy, R.I., Herbert, P., Lux, S.E. and Frederickson, D.S. (1970). Biochem. Biophys. Res. Commun. 41, 57-62.

Lee, R.E. and Puppione, D.L. (1972). Biochim. Biophys. Acta 270, 272-278.

Leger, C. (1972).   Ann. Biol. anim. Biochim. Biophys. 12, 341–345.

Leger, C. (1980).   In "Nutrition des Poissons", (M. Fontaine, ed.) 69–77. C.N.R.S., Paris.

Leger, C. (1983).   Diabète Métab. 10, 52–62.

Leger, C. and Bauchart, D. (1972).   C.R. Acad. Sci., Paris, Série D 275, 2419–2422.

Leger, C., Bauchart, D. and Flanzy, J. (1977a).   Comp. Biochem. Physiol. 57B, 359–363.

Leger, C., Bergot, P., Flanzy, J. and Francois, A.C. (1970).   C.R. Acad. Sci., Paris, Série D 270, 2813–2816.

Leger, C., Bergot, P., Luquet, P., Flanzy, J. and Meurot, J. (1977b).   Lipids 12, 538–543.

Leger, C., Ducruet, V. and Flanzy, J. (1979).   Ann. Biol. Anim. Biochim. Biophys. 19, 825–832.

Leger, C., Fremont, L., Marion, D., Nassour, I. and Desfarges, M.F. (1981).   Lipids 16, 593–600.

Luzzati, E. (1936).   Bol. Zool. Torino 7, 167–171.

Mattson, F.H. and Volpenhein, R.A. (1966).   J. Lipid. Res. 6, 536–543.

Mattson. F.H. and Volpenhein, R.A. (1968).   J. Lipid. Res. 9, 79–84.

Mills, G.L. and Taylaur, C.E. (1971).   Comp. Biochem. Physiol. 40B, 489–501.

Mills, G.L. and Taylaur, C.E. (1973).   Comp. Biochem, Physiol. 44B, 1235–1241.

Mills, G.L., Taylaur, C.E., Chapman, M.J. and Forster, G.R. (1977).   Biochem. J. 163, 455–465.

Morgan, R.G.H., Barrowoman, J., Filipek-Wender, H. and Borgström, B. (1968).   Biochim. Biophys. Acta 167, 355–366.

Morgan, R.G.H. and Hoffman, N.E. (1971).   Biochim. Biophys. Acta 248, 143–148.

Nakagawa, H. (1978).   Bull. Jap. Sco. Sci. Fish. 45, 219–224.

Nakagawa, H., Kayama, M. and Asakawa, S. (1976).   Bull. Jap. Soc. Sci. Fish. 42, 677–685.

Nelson, G.J. and Shore, V.G. (1974).   J. biol. Chem. 249, 536–542.

Noaillac-Depeyre, J. and Gas, N. (1974).   Cell Tissue Res. 155, 353–365.

Noaillac-Depeyre, J. and Gas, N. (1976).   Tissue Cell. 8, 511–530.

Ockner, R.K. and Isselbacher, K.J. (1974).   Rev. Physiol. Biochem. Pharmacol. 71, 107–146.

Ockner, R.K. and Jones, A.L. (1970).   J. Lipid. Res. 11, 284–292.

Ockner, R.K., Pittman, J.P. and Yager, J.L. (1972). Gastroenterology 62, 981-992.

Osborne, J.C. and Brewer, H.B., Jr. (1977). Adv. Protein. Chem. 31, 253-337.

Overnell, J. (1973). Comp. Biochem. Physiol. 46B, 519-531.

Patton, J.S. (1975). Lipids 10, 562-564.

Patton, J.S., Albertsson, P.A., Erlanson, C. and Borgström, B. (1978a) J. biol. Chem. 253, 4195-4202.

Patton, J.S., Haswell, M.S. and Moon, T.W. (1978b). Can. J. Zool. 56, 787-792.

Patton, J.S., Warner, T.G. and Benson, A.A. (1977). Biochim. Biophys. Acta 486, 322-330.

Perrier, H. and Perrier, C. (1977). Ichtyophysiol. Acta. 1, 22-29.

Perrier, H., Perrier, C., Peres, G. and Gras. J. (1979). Comp. Biochem. Physiol. 62B, 245-248.

Plack, P.A., Pritchard, D.J. and Fraser, N.W. (1971). Biochem. J. 121, 847-856.

Rampone, A.J. (1961). Proc. Soc. Exp. Biol. Med., 108, 278-282.

Rathelot, J., Julien, R., Canioni, P., Coeroli, C. and Sarda, L. (1975). Biochimie 57, 1117-1120.

Reichert, W.L. and Malins, D.C. (1974). Nature 247, 569-570.

Robinson, J.S. and Mead, J.F. (1973). Can. J. Biochem. 51, 1050-1058.

Sabesin, S., Holt, P. and Clark, S. (1975). Lipids 10, 840-846.

Sarda, L. and Desnuelle, P. (1958). Biochim. Biophys. Acta 30, 513-521.

Sastry, R.V. and Garg, V.K. (1976). Z. Mikrosk. anat. Forsch. 90, 1032-1040.

Sata, T., Havel, R.J. and Jones, A.L. (1972). J. Lipid Res. 13, 757-768.

Simmonds, W.J. (1974). In "Physiology Series One, Gastrointestinal Physiology", (E.D. Jacobson and L.L. Sanbour, eds.) 4, 343-376, Butterworths, London and University Park Press, Baltimore.

Sire, M.F., Lutton, G. and Vernier, J.M. (1981). J. Lipid Res. 22, 81-94.

Sire, M.F. and Vernier, J.M. (1979). Bull. Soc. Zool. France 104, 161-166.

Sire, M.F. and Vernier, J.M. (1981). Biol. Cell. 40, 47-62.

Skinner, E.R. and Rogie, A. (1978a). Biochem. J. 173, 507-520.

Skinner, E.R. and Rogie, A. (1978b). "Protides of the biological fluids, 25th. Colloquium". (H. Peeters), 491–494, Pergamon Press, Oxford.

Skinner, E.R. and Youssef, A.M. (1982). Biochem. J. 203, 727–734.

Snipes, R.L. (1977). Acta Anat. 99, 435–439.

Sternby, B., Larsson, A. and Borgström, B. (1983). Biochim. Biophys. Acta 750, 340–345.

Stroband, H.W.J. and Debets, F.M.H. (1978). Cell Tissue Res. 187, 181–200.

Suzuki, M., Tsujita, T. and Okuda, H. (1981). Bull. Jap. Soc. Sci. Fish. 47, 1515–1520.

Verger, R., De Haas, G.H., Sarda, L. and Desnuelle, P. (1969). Biochim. Biophys. Acta 188, 272–282.

Wallace, R.A. (1970). Biochim. Biophys. Acta 215, 176–183.

Windell, J.T., Foltz, J.W. and Sarokon, J.A. (1978). Trans. Am. Fish. Soc. 167, 613–616.

ROLES OF VITAMIN E AND SELENIUM IN THE PREVENTION

OF PATHOLOGIES RELATED TO FATTY ACID OXIDATION IN

SALMONIDS

J.G. BELL and C.B. COWEY

N.E.R.C. Institute of Marine Biochemistry,

St. Fittick's Road, Aberdeen AB1 3RA

I.   INTRODUCTION

The reactions involved in fatty acid autoxidation have been established for some time; the oxidation is referred to as autoxidation because the rate increases as the reaction proceeds. A simplified outline of the steps involved is shown in Fig. 1.

The free radical chain reaction mechanism involves three stages (i) Initiation, in which an unsaturated molecule loses a proton to form a free radical. The divinyl methane structure present in all polyunsaturated fatty acids (PUFA) is particularly susceptible to hydrogen abstraction. (ii) Propagation, oxygen adds at the double-bond leading to an autoxidation reaction with the formation of peroxy radicals, hydroperoxides and new hydrocarbon radicals. New radicals formed may contribute to the chain by reacting with other oxygen molecules. (iii) Termination, the formation of non-radical products, occurs when two radicals interact.

One of the first stable products of the initiation and propagation reactions are hydroperoxides. As their concentration in a system increases, these begin to decompose to a variety of products. Thus a possible

NUTRITION AND FEEDING IN FISH
ISBN: 0 12 194055 1

(i) Initiation

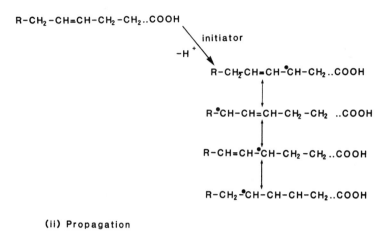

(ii) Propagation

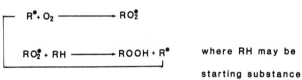

where RH may be

starting substance

(iii) Termination

$$2R^\bullet \longrightarrow RR$$

$$2RO_2^\bullet \longrightarrow O_2 + ROOR$$

$$RO_2^\bullet + R^\bullet \longrightarrow ROOR$$

Fig. 1. Diagrammatic outline of stages involved in fatty acid autoxidation.

reaction is the monomolecular decomposition to an alkoxy and a hydroxy radical, the former can then readily give rise to aldehydes, ketones and alcohols (Fig. 2).

After lipid peroxidation has been initiated the rate-limiting step is the reaction of a peroxy free radical ($RO_2^\bullet$) with another fatty acid. This rate is dependent on fatty acid structure

$$(CH_3(CH_2)_x \ (CH = CH_2)_n(CH_2)_y \ COOH$$

and increases according to the ratios 0.025:1:2:4:6:8 as the number of double bonds 'n' increases from 1 to 6

(Witting and Horwitt, 1964; Witting, 1965). Thus tissue lipid PUFA content and composition are critical factors in lipid peroxidation. As fish tissues and fish diets typically contain large quantities of highly unsaturated (n-3) series fatty acids they may be more at risk from peroxidative attack than are mammals.

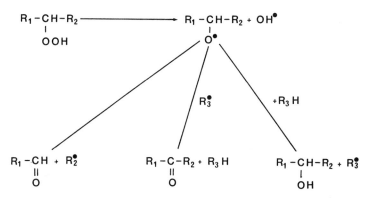

Fig. 2. Monomolecular decomposition of a hydroperoxide and further possible reactions of the radical products.

These highly unsaturated fatty acids are essential components of all biomembranes. They exist here in an arrangement that may permit maximum interaction between the individual molecules and so also contribute to maximum damage to the cell.

There is also a further potential risk to fish in that virtually all practical diets contain greater or lesser amounts of fishmeal which, in turn, contains appreciable amounts of unsaturated lipid. Autoxidation of unsaturated fat in fish oils or fishmeals may result from the effects of energy in the form of heat, light or ionizing radiation. It may also be a consequence of catalysis by pro-oxidant metals. The latter effect is a real possibility in complete diets for fish where fish oils and mineral supplements are intimately mixed.

II. FATTY ACID OXIDATION IN VIVO

Free radicals also arise in vivo as intermediates in the normal course of metabolism. They are mainly toxic, or potentially toxic, highly reactive metabolites of oxygen. In the four electron transfers of oxidative phosphorylation between O_2 and H_2O three important states occur: $HO_2^{\bullet}$; H_2O_2 and $^{\bullet}OH$. In the cytosol, purine metabolism (xanthine oxidase) may generate the superoxide anion radical, $O_2^{\bullet}$ and other oxidases such as D-amino acid oxidase may generate H_2O_2. The extremely damaging and reactive hydroxyl radical $^{\bullet}OH$ is thought to arise in tissues by an iron or other transition metal-catalyzed Haber-Weiss reaction:

$$H_2O_2 \; + \; Fe^{2+} \longrightarrow \; ^{\bullet}OH \; + \; OH^{-} \; + \; Fe^{3+}$$

$$O_2^{\bullet -} \; + \; Fe^{3+} \longrightarrow \; O_2 \; + \; Fe^{2+}$$

The seriousness of the problems that may arise from free radical-initiated chain reactions and the probability of their actual occurrence is suggested by the complex multi-level defence system, that exists to eliminate radicals in tissues. This includes (i) Free radical dismutation catalysed by the enzyme superoxide dismutase (SOD) which converts the hydroperoxyl radical to O_2 and H_2O_2.

$$2HO_2^{\bullet} \longrightarrow O_2 \; + \; H_2O_2$$

Eukaryotic cells have a copper/zinc SOD in the cytosol and a manganese SOD in mitochondria. (ii) Catabolism of potentially damaging hydroperoxides which are a potential source of new free radicals (cf. formation of hydroxyl radical by Haber-Weiss reaction above) by peroxidases. Catalase, a peroxisomal enzyme, has a high Km value for H_2O_2 and is not an efficient scavenger of it (Misra, 1974). The selenium metallo-enzyme glutathione (GSH) peroxidase is able to convert fatty acid hydroperoxides to innocuous hydroxy fatty acids, and since it has a low Km value for H_2O_2 it is an efficient scavenger at low peroxide levels. A non-selenium glutathione peroxidase activity has been found in the soluble fraction of some animal tissues and is thought to be due to their GSH S-transferase enzymes (Prohaska and Ganther, 1977). It will destroy lipid hydroperoxides but not H_2O_2. Differing activities of this enzyme in some animal tissues are seen as a possible cause of differing responses between species deficient in Se and vitamin E (Lawrence and Burk, 1978). (iii) Interception of secondary free radicals; termination of free radical chain reactions. Vitamin E (AH) competes with polyunsaturated fatty acids for lipid peroxy free radicals.

$$RO_2^{\bullet} \quad + \quad RH \quad \longrightarrow \quad ROOH \quad + \quad R^{\bullet}$$

$$RO_2^{\bullet} \quad + \quad AH \quad \longrightarrow \quad ROOH \quad + \quad [A]$$

Free radicals are thus withdrawn from the system via quinone formation or dimerization of vitamin E.

A general summary of the inter-relationships between reactive oxygen species, cellular components and anti-oxidant systems are shown in Fig. 3. Normal enzymic reactions generate free radicals and H_2O_2 which may interact to produce the hydroxyl radical and then singlet oxygen. Adventitious initiation of lipid peroxidation may produce lipid hydroperoxides which unless removed may cause tissue damage. Nutritional factors involved in defence of the cell against oxidative damage are, (i) copper, zinc and manganese as functional components of the superoxide dismutases; (ii) selenium as a component of GSH peroxidase; (iii) vitamin E as a scavenger of free radicals. Studies in rainbow trout have concentrated on the latter two components.

III.   DIETARY REQUIREMENT FOR VITAMIN E

The vitamin E requirement of rainbow trout, of mean initial weight 10g, was measured at a constant water temperature of 15° using diets with graded levels of vitamin E (0-10 mg/100g diet). The diets contained low levels of PUFA (1% linolenic acid) and there were no complicating factors such as selenium deficiency or autoxidation products.

Trout increased their weight by nearly 10-fold over a 16 week period and there were no differences between treatments irrespective of vitamin E intake. No pathologies occurred nor were there any mortalities. At low vitamin E intake haematocrit values were significantly reduced and erythrocyte fragility values significantly elevated (Table I). Lipid peroxidation in liver

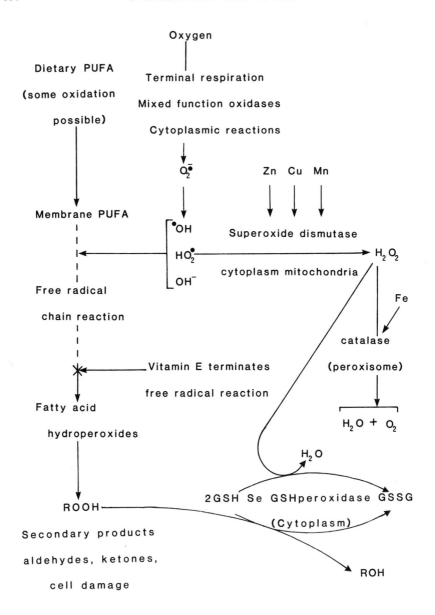

Fig. 3. Possible inter-relationships between reactive metabolites of oxygen, cellular components and anti-oxidant systems.

microsomes, incubated under defined oxidizing conditions
in vitro and assessed by the amount of malondialdehyde
formed gave reproducible dose/response curves (dietary
vitamin E versus malondialdehyde formed - Cowey et al.,
1981). Microsomal susceptibility to lipid peroxidation in
this sytem is mainly determined by the ratio, vitamin E:
peroxidizable PUFA in the membrane.

Table I. Weight gain, erythrocyte fragility and other
measures of dietary vitamin E sufficiency in rainbow trout
given diets containing different concentrations of vitamin
E for 16 weeks

Vitamin E Concentration in diet	Mean initial weight	Mean final weight	Erythrocyte fragility	Haemat	Microsomal lipid peroxidation
mg/kg	g	g	% haemolysis	%	nmoles malondialdehyde formed/mg protein
0	10.3	51.9	46.9	21.0	36.7
100	10.6	54.3	5.5	41.0	2.4

Data from Cowey et al,(1981).

From the data on haematocrit, erythrocyte fragility and
lipid peroxidation in microsomes in vitro (signs of
subclinical vitamin E deficiency) a vitamin E requirement
of 2 mg/100g diet was obtained.

When the experiments were repeated but using a higher
level of PUFA (10%) in the diet similar results were
obtained (Cowey et al., 1983).   Vitamin E requirement was
elevated to 5 mg/100g diet but there were no differences
in growth rate between trout depleted of vitamin E and
those given diets supplemented with vitamin E.   No
mortalities occurred nor were there any pathologies.

These results are in general agreement with those of
other workers carried out under similar conditions. Smith

(1979) using rainbow trout of mean initial weight 13g at a water temperature of 15° did not find any reduction in growth rate nor any pathologies when the fish were given diets lacking vitamins E and C; pathologies developed only when the diets contained rancid fat and lacked both vitamins. Hung et al. (1981) similarly found that the absence of supplementary vitamin E from practical type diets did not affect growth rate or feed conversion nor result in pathologies in trout of mean initial weight 2g grown at 15° for 24 weeks.

The results demonstrate that even after tissues have been severely depleted of vitamin E by giving diets deficient in vitamin E remaining defence mechanisms in rainbow trout are sufficient to prevent any tissue damage that might arise should free radicals arising in the normal course of metabolism multiply.

The effectiveness of vitamin E in preventing peroxidative damage as, for example, in the experiments of Smith (1979) and Hung et al. (1981) appears to be largely

Table II. Concentrations of vitamin E in subcellular fractions of liver from rainbow trout given diets lacking or supplemented with vitamin E for 16 weeks

	Diet lacking vitamin E		Diet supplemented with 100 mg vitamin E/kg	
	µg/fraction/g liver	% of total vitamin E in liver	µg/fraction/g liver	% of total vitamin E in liver
Cytosol	0.56	7.9	2.57	3.6
Nuclear fraction	1.50	21.3	16.03	22.5
Mitochondria	3.76	53.4	32.21	45.2
Microsomes	1.22	17.3	20.39	28.6

Data from Cowey et al. (1981)

a result of its inclusion within the membrane, a position in which it appears to exert maximum anti-oxidant effect in actual membrane preparations. The subcellular distribution of vitamin E in liver of normal and vitamin E deficient rainbow trout is shown in Table II.

By contrast with these findings on rainbow trout Poston et al. (1976) using Atlantic salmon of mean initial weight 0.9g at a water temperature of 15° found a number of pathologies developing in vitamin E deficient fish after 16 weeks. These included anaemia, exudative diathesis, dermal depigmentation and muscular dystrophy. Vitamin E activity was reported as 5.0 I.U./100g liver and 0.5 I.U./100g carcass in these salmon. These values are appreciably greater than those in the vitamin E deficient rainbow trout which did not develop pathologies (Cowey et al., 1981). Reasons for the different results obtained in these closely related species will be considered later.

IV. VITAMIN E DEPLETION AT VARYING WATER TEMPERATURE

The experiments mentioned above were all carried out at water temperatures of 15°. As trout in many areas normally inhabit water at considerably lower temperatures for much of the year the effects of vitamin E deficiency and of the presence in the diet of moderately oxidized oil (peroxide value 94 mEq/kg) were examined in a 2 x 2 factorial experiment carried out at water temperatures (of 12-6°) such as occur in Scotland in late summer and autumn (Cowey et al., 1984).

In contrast with earlier results trout given diets supplemented with vitamin E gained significantly more weight (irrespective of the quality of the oil) than those given diets without supplementary vitamin E. The moderately oxidized oil was as effective in sustaining growth as was the fresh oil, when the diets contained added vitamin E (Table III). Haematocrit values and erythrocyte fragility values were in line with the growth results. As in earlier experiments there was a marked reduction in vitamin E levels in liver and muscle of deficient fish. Likewise malondialdehyde formation in hepatic mitochondria incubated under oxidizing conditions in vitro was much greater in vitamin E deficient fish. Fatty acids from the polar lipids of the liver of vitamin E deficient fish had reduced amounts of 22:6 (n-3) and this was compensated by increased amounts of 18:1(n-9).

Severe muscle damage was evident in those fish given diets without added vitamin E. The damage consisted in an

Table III. Weight gain, haematocrit and erythrocyte fragility of rainbow trout given diets containing either normal (non-oxidized) oil or moderately oxidized oil with or without supplementary vitamin E for 14 weeks in outdoor tanks at natural varying water temperatures.

Vitamin E in diet	(mg/kg)	395.2	18.4	388.4	7.4
Peroxide value of oil in diet at start	(mEq/kg)	4.0	4.0	94.0	94.0
Peroxide value of oil in diet at end	(mEq/kg)	15.6	234.0	420.2	666.6
Mean initial weight	(g)	9.36	7.30	7.59	7.82
Mean final weight	(g)	51.14	37.55	48.29	35.33
Feed/gain		1.05	1.20	1.05	1.38
Mortalities		0	3	0	6
Haematocrit (%)		45.5	13.2	39.9	20.3
Erythrocyte (% haemolysis)		50.8	94.9	57.7	73.9

Data from Cowey et al. (1984)

alteration of fibre size with the fibres being more rounded, partly swollen and partly shrunken. The degeneration of fibres was more marked in trout given the diet containing moderately oxidized oil (and lacking added vitamin E).

Thus the substitution of a moderately oxidized oil for fresh oil in diets containing supplementary vitamin E did not affect the performance of the trout. The absence of supplementary vitamin E did, on the other hand, have marked effects on the trout including effects on growth rate and the appearance of muscle pathology. These results contrast with those obtained previously.

In these earlier experiments basal (adventitious) levels of vitamin E in the deficient diets were from zero to 2 mg/100g diet. The latter value is similar to the levels present in the vitamin E deficient diets in this factorial experiment carried out at varying (natural) temperatures. In line with this, tissue concentrations of vitamin E deficient and control fish in analogous treatments of the various experiments were very similar, for vitamin E deficient fish these were 5-8 ug/g liver and 2-3 ug/g muscle.

Consequently other factors, in addition to a low vitamin E intake, were responsible for the major differences in growth rate and histopathology between the two experiments, the main factor probably being the low and variable temperatures used in the second experiment. The maintenance of fluidity in biomembranes is more demanding in terms of polyunsaturated fatty acids at low than at high temperatures (Hazel, 1980) and the evidence is that trout may be more susceptible to vitamin E deficiency at low water temperatures. It has been observed that there can be no single vitamin E requirement for rainbow trout under all practical situations (Hung et al., 1980). It now appears that water temperature should be taken into account when the vitamin E level in diets is being assessed.

V.   VITAMIN E AND SELENIUM DEPRIVATION

A synergism between dietary selenium and vitamin E was first inferred in mammals when it was shown that, in the rat, a single deficiency of either of these dietary components seldom led to liver damage.

However a combined deficiency of both nutrients resulted in liver necrosis (Schwarz and Folz, 1957). This synergism has generally been explained on the basis of the role of Se in the metalloenzyme GSH peroxidase.

Little information on this inter-relationship in fish is yet available. Poston et al. (1976) in the experiments on Atlantic salmon already referred to demonstrated that dietary supplements of both vitamin E and Se were necessary to significantly reduce mortality in small fish (mean weight 0.1g) during the first six weeks after yolk sac absorption. In larger fish (0.9g live weight) both vitamin E and Se were necessary to prevent muscular dystrophy. On the other hand Hilton et al. (1980) using rainbow trout of 1.3 g mean initial weight could find no deficiency symptoms at dietary Se levels of 0.07 ug/g with 0.4 ug Se/l of rearing water and at a dietary vitamin E level of 0.4 I.U./g diet (water temperature 14-15°).

This apparent lack of effect of Se depletion in rainbow

trout may have been due to the presence in the fish of a
Se-independent GSH peroxidase or of a compensatory
increase in its activity. The presence of such an enzyme
has been claimed in bullheads said to be deficient in Se
(Heisinger and Dawson, 1983). In some mammals GSH
S-transferase activity has been identified as the
Se-independent GSH peroxidase activity (Lawrence et al.,
1978).

This possibility was examined by purifying GSH
S-transferase from trout liver and testing it for
peroxidase activity. In addition the inter-relationship
between Se and vitamin E in trout was examined in a 2 x 2
factorial experiment with diets either adequate or low in
Se or vitamin E or both. Fish had a mean initial weight
of 11g, the experiment lasted 40 weeks at a water
temperature of 15°.

Glutathione S-transferase was purified many fold from
trout liver cytosol by ion exchange and affinity
chromatography (Bell et al., 1984a). No GSH-peroxidase
activity was present in it nor was Se independent GSH
peroxidase activity detected in any fraction of liver
homogenate.

Growth of trout given a diet depleted of both Se and
vitamin E was significantly lower than that of trout given
a complete diet deficient only in selenium or in vitamin
E. There were no mortalities and the only pathology seen
was exudative diathesis in the dually deficient trout
(Bell et al., 1984b).

Synergism between the two nutrients was evident from a
significant interaction between them with respect to
haematocrit value (significantly reduced only in the
dually deficient fish) and to malondialdehyde formation in
the in vitro NADPH-dependent microsomal lipid peroxidation
system (low value only when both nutrients were present).
Also for plasma there was a significant effect of dietary
vitamin E on Se concentration (Bell et al., 1984b).

Levels of GSH peroxidase activity in liver and plasma
are shown in Table IV. Ratios of hepatic GSH peroxidase
activity measured with cumene hydroperoxide and H_2O_2
were the same for all treatments. As the Se-independent
GSH peroxidase functions only with organic peroxides while
the Se-dependent GSH peroxidase functions with both
organic and hydrogen peroxide the constancy of this ratio
confirms the absence of a Se-independent GSH peroxidase
activity in trout liver.

Glutathione S-transferase activity was essentially the
same in all treatments (Table IV) there being no

Table IV. Activities (nmoles substrate converted or of thioester bond formed/min/mg protein) of certain enzymes in plasma and livers of rainbow trout given diets* of different vitamin E and selenium content

	Diet 1		Diet 2		Diet 3		Diet 4	
	Mean	SEM	Mean	SEM	Mean	SEM	Mean	SEM
Liver GSH** peroxidase	27.67^a	1.73	8.18^b	0.70	26.41^a	1.28	5.23^b	0.77
Liver GSH*** peroxidase	22.94^a	2.21	6.84^b	0.65	19.44^a	1.89	4.11^b	0.42
Plasma GSH** peroxidase	6.32^a	0.31	2.44^b	0.4	5.98^a	0.47	2.09^b	0.11
Liver GSH S-transferase	96.10	10.47	96.23	7.73	107.16	9.36	95.13	11.20

*   Concentrations of vitamin E in diets 1, 2, 3 and 4 were respectively (mg/kg): 40.6,

       40.6, 2.14 and 1.96; concentrations of selenium in diets 1, 2, 3 and 4 were respectively

       (mg/kg): 0.869, 0.060, 0.877 and 0.060

**   Cumene hydroperoxide as substrate

***   Hydrogen peroxide as substrate

       Values in the same row with different superscripts are significantly different; for

       GSH peroxidase (P<0.01).

       Mean of measurements on six fish per treatment

compensatory increase in Se deficiency.

Although these experiments demonstrate a synergism with respect to certain parameters, between Se and vitamin E they do not provide an explanation of why both nutrients are necessary to prevent muscular dystrophy in very small salmon (Poston et al., 1976) but that no pathologies develop in rainbow trout depleted of one or other nutrient. The induction or increase in activity of a Se-independent GSH peroxidase is eliminated as an explanation for their non-appearance in Se depletion.

It may be that the diets used by Poston et al. (1976)

had lower Se concentrations than those used by Hilton et
al. (1980) or by ourselves. This question cannot be
resolved as Poston et al. (1976) did not measure Se levels
in either diets or fish tissues.

Another possibility is that the low level of dietary
polyunsaturated fatty acid (10g linolenic acid/kg)
together with synthetic anti-oxidant used by us compared
to the 100g stripped corn oil/kg diet used by Poston et
al. (1976) may explain the lack of pathology in our
fish. But this is not consistent with the fact that
Hilton et al. (1980) used larger quantities of more highly
unsaturated fatty acids (150g salmon oil/kg diet) without
synthetic antioxidants.

Another factor that may be important is the size of the
fish used. Vos et al. (1981) showed that in ducklings
myopathy does not occur if vitamin E depletion is delayed
until the birds are 2 weeks of age and provided dietary Se
content is not too low (0.074 mg/kg). Under these
conditions mortality is very low and growth normal over a
14 week period despite low levels of vitamin E in serum,
liver and muscle. The observation is explained by the
extremely high rate of growth during the first 2 weeks of
age when it reached a peak.

Similar effects may extend to fish and may explain the
lack of any pathology in our Se-depleted trout and the
absence of muscular dystrophy in our dually deficient
fish. Thus the salmon used by Poston et al. (1976) were
0.9g, much smaller than those used in our experiments.
However the fish used by Hilton et al. (1980) were similar
in size to those of Poston et al. (1976) - initially 1.3g
and it would seem that in the presence of adequate vitamin
E, moderate Se depletion does not lead to muscular
dystrophy or other pathologies in trout.

REFERENCES

Bell, J.G., Cowey, C.B. and Youngson, A. (1984a).
    Biochim. Biophys. Acta. 795, 91-99.
Bell, J.G., Cowey, C.B., Adron, J.W. and Shanks, A.M.
    (1984b). Br. J. Nutr. In press.
Cowey, C.B., Adron, J.W., Walton, M.J., Murray, J.,
    Youngson, A. and Knox, D. (1981). J. Nutr. 111,
    1556-1567.
Cowey, C.B., Adron, J.W. and Youngson, A. (1983).
    Aquaculture 30, 85-93.

Cowey, C.B., Degener, E., Tacon, A.G.J., Youngson, A. and
Bell, J.G. (1984). Br. J. Nutr. 51, 443–451.

Hazel, J.R. (1979). Am. J. Physiol. 236, R91–R101.

Heisinger, J.F. and Dawson, S.M. (1983). J. Exp. Zool.
225, 325–327.

Hilton, J.W., Hodson, P.V. and Slinger, S.J. (1980). J.
Nutr. 110, 2527–2535.

Hung, S.S.O., Cho, C.Y. and Slinger, S.J. (1980). Can. J.
Fish. Aquat. Sci. 37, 1248–1253.

Hung, S.S.O., Cho, C.Y. and Slinger, S.J. (1981). J.
Nutr. 111, 648–657.

Lawrence, R.A. and Burk, R.F. (1978). J. Nutr. 108,
211–215.

Lawrence, R.A., Parkhill, L.K. and Burk, R.F. (1978).
J. Nutr 108, 981–987.

Misra, H. (1974). J. biol. Chem. 249, 2151–2155.

Poston, H.A., Combs, G.F. and Leibovitz, L. (1976).
J. Nutr. 106, 892–904.

Prohaska, J.R. and Ganther, H.E. (1977). Biochem.
Biophys. Res. Commun. 76, 437–445.

Schwarz, K. and Folz, C.M. (1957). J. Am. Chem. Soc. 79,
3293–3298.

Smith, C.E. (1979). J. Fish Diseases, 2, 429–437.

Witting, L.A. (1965). J. Am. Oil Chem. Soc. 42, 908–913.

Witting, L.A. and Horwitt, M.K. (1964). J. Nutr. 82,
19–33.

Vos, J., Hulstaert, C.E. and Molenaar, I. (1981). Ann.
Nutr. Metab. 25, 299–306.

FATTY ACID METABOLISM IN FISH

R.J. HENDERSON and J.R. SARGENT

NERC Institute of Marine Biochemistry,
St. Fittick's Road, Aberdeen AB1 3RA.

I. FATTY ACID SYNTHESIS

A. Tissue Sites and Carbon Source

The pathway of fatty acid biosynthesis in fish is assumed to be basically similar to that operating in mammals (Fig. 1). The two-carbon acetyl-CoA unit is carboxylated by acetyl-CoA carboxylase to malonyl-CoA which is converted to fatty acid by the fatty acid synthetase complex via a series of condensation and reduction reactions involving the utilisation of NADPH (Volpe and Vagelos, 1976; Gurr and James, 1980). For storage, the fatty acid synthesized in this way is activated to its fatty acyl-CoA derivative and esterified to glycerol 3-phosphate along with another acyl-CoA to form phosphatidic acid. After removal of the phosphate group by phosphatidate phosphohydrolase, a third acyl-CoA is added to produce triacylglycerol, the major neutral lipid in fish.

In mammals, which store triacylglycerols in a distinct adipose tissue, both liver and adipose tissue are capable of fatty acid and triacylglycerol synthesis to an extent which varies with species (Pearce, 1983). Whilst some teleost fish such as the rainbow trout possess definite perivisceral adipose tissue, other pelagic species including herring, capelin and mackerel have more obvious sub-cutaneous lipid depots sometimes penetrating quite far into muscle and often assumed to be muscle adipose stores

NUTRITION AND FEEDING IN FISH
ISBN: 0 12 194055 1

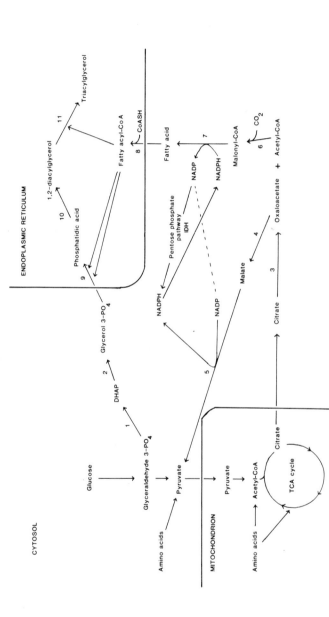

Figure 1   Schematic Pathways of Lipid Synthesis

TCA, tricarboxylic acid; DHAP, dihydroxyacetone phosphate; IDH, isocitrate dehydrogenase. 1. triose-phosphate isomerase; 2. glycerol phosphate dehydrogenase; 3. citrate cleavage enzyme; 4. malate dehydrogenase; 5. malic enzyme; 6. acetyl-CoA carboxylase; 7. fatty acid synthetase; 8. acyl-CoA synthetase; 9. glycerol phosphate acyltransferase; 10. phosphatidate phosphohydrolase; 11. diacylglycerol acyltransferase

(Ackman, 1980); demersal species like the cod generally store lipid in their livers. Henderson and Sargent (1981) compared the lipogenic capabilities of liver and adipose tissue in rainbow trout and reported that, in terms of DNA, the two tissues had similar rates of fatty acid synthesis as measured by the rate of incorporation of tritium from tritiated water, a measure independent of carbon source. Since DNA is an index of cell number, this implies that the functional unit of adipose tissue has the same capacity as that of liver to synthesize fatty acids de novo. However, liver contains considerably more DNA i.e. more cells, per unit weight than adipose tissue and on a whole body basis the liver is the main site of fatty acid biosynthesis in trout. In comparison with liver, adipose tissue is more effective in the incoporation of glucose-carbon into triacylglycerol-glycerol in vitro, and the rate of esterification of palmitic acid by adipose tissue increases with the level of lipid in the diet (Henderson and Sargent, 1981). Lin et al. (1977a) found that the specific activities of several NADPH-producing enzymes and citrate cleavage enzyme, the enzyme which generates acetyl-CoA for fatty acid synthesis in the cytosol, were all higher in the liver than adipose tissue of coho salmon. Thus, on the basis of studies of substrate incorporation and enzyme activities, liver is the principal site of fatty acid synthesis in salmonids whilst adipose tissue is adapted for the uptake and storage of fatty acids originating from the diet or hepatic synthesis. The rate of fatty acid synthesis from alanine was approximately six times greater than that from glucose in trout liver slices when the two substrates were supplied at the same concentration (Henderson and Sargent, 1981). This suggests that amino acids may be a better carbon source for fatty acid synthesis tnan glucose and might reflect the low carbohydrate and high protein contents of natural fish diets.

The visceral adipose tissue of trout is composed of distinct fat-cells or adipocytes which can be liberated by digestion of the tissue with collagenase. These free adipocytes are more fragile than rat adipocytes but are still capable of incorporating glucose, alanine and palmitic acid into triacylglycerols (Henderson and Sargent, unpublished data).

B. Products of Fatty Acid Synthesis

In comparison with the fatty acid synthetase of microbes and mammals, the nature of this enzyme complex and its products in fish has been less well studied. Mammalian and avian fatty acid synthetases produce palmatic acid (16:0) together with lesser amounts of stearic (18:0) and myristic (14:0) acids, and have a molecular weight of 400,000 to 500,000 (Gurr and James, 1980). Wilson and Williamson (1970) purified fatty acid synthetase from the liver of plaice and demonstrated that it produced, from ^{3}H–acetyl–CoA, 16:0 and 18:0 in the ratio 3:2 but no unsaturated fatty acids. The fatty acid synthetase present in the cytosol of catfish liver synthesized 16:0 and 18:0 in the ratio 2:3 from ^{14}C–acetate with 21% of the incorporated radioactivity being recovered in the fraction containing 18:2(n–3) and 21– to 27–carbon saturates (Warman and Bottino, 1978). Evidence that fish fatty acid synthetase is similar to that of mammals and birds comes from the work of Hansen and Knudsen (1981) who purified the enzyme to homogeneity from flounder liver, estimated its molecular weight to be 457,000 and showed that its main product was 16:0 with lesser amounts of 18:0, 14:0 and butyric acid (4:0).

C. Effect of Dietary Lipid Levels on Fatty Acid Synthesis

Whilst endogenous fatty acid synthesis in mammals is markedly depressed and augmented by increasing the levels of dietary lipid and carbohydrate respectively (Volpe and Vagelos, 1976), the situation in fish is not so definite. Lin et al. (1977b) increased the amount of lipid in the diet of coho salmon from 5% to 20% at the expense of the carbohydrate dextrin and showed that the activities of several NADPH–producing enzymes were depressed in the liver. Several weeks were required before the enzyme activities changed in response to such dietary changes. In contrast, Henderson and Sargent (1981) found no relationship between levels of dietary lipid in the range 2 to 10% and the rate of fatty acid synthesis in trout liver. However, the high carbohydrate level (27–35%) employed in their study may have had an augmenting effect on fatty acid synthesis which could over–ride changes in relation to dietary lipid levels. The activities of acetyl–CoA carboxylase and fatty acid synthetase in catfish liver have proved to be insensitive to changes in

the carbohydrate and lipid contents of the diet (Warman
and Bottino, 1978). Similarly, de la Higuera et al.
(1977) reported that the activities of several other
enzymes of intermediary metabolism in trout liver were not
influenced by high levels of dietary lipid.

Polyunsaturated fatty acids are more potent inhibitors
of fatty acid synthesis in mammalian liver than saturated
or monoenoic fatty acids, exerting their effect by
decreasing the quantity of the lipogenic enzymes (Volpe
and Vagelos, 1976; Toussant et al., 1981). Considering
that fish diets are generally rich in polyunsaturated
lipid it is perhaps surprising that fish livers have
substantial rates of fatty acid synthesis.

D. Desaturation and Elongation of Fatty Acids

Whereas the products of endogenous fatty acids are
predominantly saturated, the fatty acids of fish lipids
are characteristically rich in unsaturated fatty acids
(Ackman, 1980; Sargent, 1976). The fatty acid
composition of dietary lipids undoubtedly influences the
pattern of tissue fatty acids observed in both marine and
freshwater fish (Watanabe, 1982) and the fatty acid
composition of body lipids can be regarded as a final
blend of endogenous and exogenous fatty acids after any
modification by processes of desaturation-elongation.

The sequence of desaturation-elongation of fatty acids
arising from endogenous synthesis or the diet is outlined
in Fig. 2. The three families of unsaturated fatty
acids, (n-9), (n-6) and (n-3), are acted upon by a common
enzyme system of alternating desaturation and elongation
to give a series of fatty acids of increasing length and
unsaturation. The requirements of fish for the (n-6) and
(n-3) series of polyunsaturates are described elsewhere in
this volume. Cowey and Sargent (1979) have discussed the
essential fatty acid (EFA) requirements of carnivorous
fish in relation to desaturase and elongase activities and
their dietary supply of fatty acids.

The tissue lipids of fish, particularly marine species
consuming a natural diet, are generally rich in
polyunsaturated fatty acids of which the (n-3) series
greatly exceeds the (n-6) series. This predominance of
the (n-3) polyunsaturates in fish lipid reflects the
abundance of this series in the marine food chain and in
particular the retention of these fatty acids at the
trophic levels phytoplankton-zooplankton and zooplankton-
fish (Sargent and Whittle, 1981). The storage

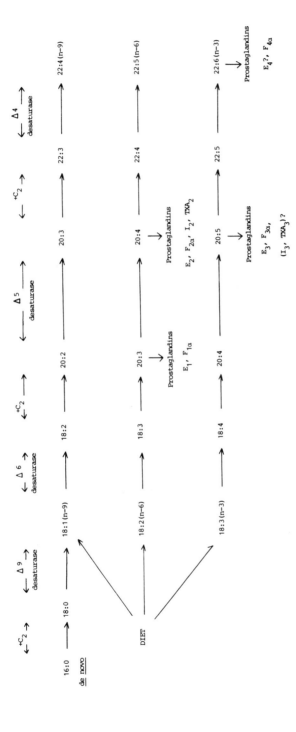

Figure 2 Desaturation and Elongation of the (n-9), (n-6) and (n-3) series of unsaturated fatty acids, and their conversion to prostaglandins. Δ refers to the number of carbons from the carboxyl carbon of the fatty acid e.g. Δ9 desaturase inserts a double bond at the 9, 10-position. (n-x) indicates the nearest double bond to the terminal methyl group is x number of carbons distant from it.

triacylglycerols of fish have a lower polyunsaturate content than the phospholipids which play an important role as structural components of biomembranes.

The degree of unsaturation of the fatty acids in membrane phospholipids of poikilotherms such as fish is inversely related to the acclimation temperatures (Hazel and Prosser, 1974). The high proportion of polyunsaturates has been studied in relation to the activities of the desaturation and elongation enzymes. Nino et al. (1974) demonstrated the presence of microsomal $\Delta 9$, $\Delta 6$ and $\Delta 5$ desaturases in the liver of the freshwater fish Pimelodus maculatus and proposed that lowering the environmental temperature enhanced the desaturation activity. De Torrengo and Brenner (1976) later showed that the activities of the desaturation and elongation enzymes in Pimelodus were higher in liver microsomes from fish maintained at 14-15° than from those kept at 29-30°C. More recently, Sellner and Hazel (1982) demonstrated that hepatocytes from trout acclimated at 5° or 20°C had a substrate preference linolenic acid, 18:3 (n-3) > linoleic acid, 18:2 (n-6) > oleic acid, 18:1 (n-9) for desaturation and elongation, especially when assayed at 5°C. The authors suggested that this specificity could explain the decrease in the (n-9), little change in the (n-6) and significant increase in the (n-3) series of unsaturated fatty acids which they observed in hepatocyte lipids from 5°C-acclimated trout in comparison with trout acclimated at 20°C. The enrichment of phospholipids with (n-3) polyunsaturates in fish reared at low temperatures may be ensured by the selective uptake of the (n-3) fatty acids into phospholipids whilst the (n-6) series is incorporated preferentially into triacylglycerols (Hazel, 1979).

The effect of environmental temperature on the rate of fatty acid synthesis de novo in fish is still uncertain. Hazel and Sellner (1979) found that the rate of incorporation of tritium from tritiated water into fatty acids was higher in hepatocytes from cold (5°C)-than warm (20°)-acclimated trout regardless of assay temperature. However, rates of fatty acid synthesis from ^{14}C-acetate do not appear to differ significantly between hepatocytes from cold- and warm- acclimated trout with the highest amount of incorporated radioactivity always being recovered in 18:1(n-9) (Hazel, 1979).

The relative rates of conversion of (n-6) and (n-3) polyunsaturated fatty acids to prostaglandins (Fig. 2) in fish tissues is currently of interest but will not be discussed here.

II.   FATTY ACID CATABOLISM

A. Catabolism of Lipids and Ketone Body Formation

The capelin (<u>Mallotus villosus</u>) is an example of an Arctic fish where the metabolism of lipid is linked strongly to the life cycle of the fish.   During the summer the capelin feeds heavily on the abundant lipid-rich zooplankton and deposits large reserves of neutral lipid in its flesh (Jangaard, 1974).   The population of capelin in Balsfjorden, northern Norway, feed very little during over-wintering and rely very largely on their own body reserves for the production of gonads which occurs during this period.   Both the males and females lose 76% of the lipid originally present in their flesh during the four months prior to spawning, but whereas the males catabolise all of the mobilised lipid, the females deposit 38% of it in the roe (Henderson <u>et al</u>., 1984a).   During this period of sexual maturation when lipids are being heavily catabolised for gonad formation the capelin is also effectively starving and the situation can be compared with starvation in mammals when lipids are also mobilised from reserve depots.

Fatty acids mobilised by mammals, e.g. during prolonged starvation, are transported to the liver where they are oxidised <u>in lieu</u> of carbohydrate for the provision of energy.   However, the rates of supply and ß-oxidation of fatty acids can overwhelm the capacity of the TCA cycle to oxidise the acetyl-CoA produced (Fig. 3), in which case the resultant acetyl-CoA is utilised in the formation of the ketone bodies, acetoacetate and 3-hydroxybutyrate. These ketone bodies can be transported from the liver to extrahepatic tissues where they are converted back to acetyl-CoA which can be oxidised or used as a lipogenic substrate (Williamson, 1981).

In the livers of overwintering capelin no detectable 3-hydroxybutyrate dehydrogenase activity was found but 3-oxoacid-CoA transferase was very active.   This situation is in contrast to that in mammalian livers (McGarry and Foster, 1980) but identical to the observation made by Zammit <u>et al</u>. (1979) in the livers of several species of teleosts, both marine and freshwater. A substrate cycle between acetoacetyl-CoA and acetoacetate in teleost livers was proposed by Zammit <u>et al</u>. (1979) who suggested that a high activity of 3-oxoacid-CoA transferase reduces the rate of ketone body formation by

effectively removing acetoacetate by its conversion back
to acetoacetyl-CoA. The latter is both a product
inhibitor of acetoacetyl-CoA thiolase and a substrate
inhibitor of HMG-CoA synthetase. Thus any
acetoacetyl-CoA formed is converted back to acetyl-CoA for
oxidation, and ketone bodies are maintained at very low
levels.

Zammit and Newsholme (1979) compared ketone body
production from lipids in marine elasmobranchs and
teleosts and reported that whilst ketone bodies were not
produced by the bass, the concentrations of both
3-hydroxybutyrate and acetoacetate increased several-fold
in the blood of dogfish during starvation. Whilst the
low and high activities of 3-hydroxybutyrate dehydrogenase
and 3-oxoacid-CoA transferase respectively prevent the
formation of ketone bodies in teleosts as described above,
3-hydroxybutyrate dehydrogenase is always present in
elasmobranch liver and along with acetoacetyl-CoA thiolase
activity, increases significantly during starvation.
These increased enzyme activities together with a low
3-oxoacid-CoA transferase activity, which is not
influenced by starvation, lead, in the livers of
elasmobranchs, to the production of ketone bodies which
can be utilised as fuel by the fishes' muscles.
Elasmobranchs store most of their reserve lipid in the
liver and Zammit and Newsholme (1979) suggest that these
lipid stores are mobilised as ketone bodies rather than
free fatty acids for oxidation in other tissues. In
contrast, capelin and other teleosts store their reserve
lipid in extrahepatic tissues such as muscle and adipose
tissue and transport the mobilised lipid as fatty acids.

B. Mitochondrial and Peroxisomal Fatty Acid Oxidation

Free fatty acids are an important metabolic fuel in
fish tissues especially the dark muscle of actively
swimming fish (Bilinski, 1974). Similarly, mammalian
cardiac muscle also utilises free fatty acids as its main
fuel for constant rhythmic contractions. The
mitochondrial pathway for the oxidation of fatty acids in
fish tissue is essentially the same as that of mammals
whereby fatty acids enter the mitochondrion as their
acylcarnitine derivatives and are subsequently oxidised
via ß-oxidation and the TCA cycle to produce ATP (Fig. 3).

Several species of pelagic fish including herring and
mackerel consume large quantities of wax ester-rich

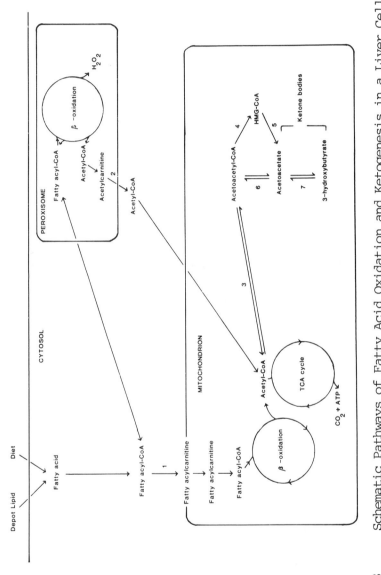

Figure 3 Schematic Pathways of Fatty Acid Oxidation and Ketogenesis in a Liver Cell TCA, tricarboxylic acid; HMG-CoA, hydroxy methylglutaryl-CoA. 1. carnitine acyltransferase; 2. carnitine acetyltransferase; 3. acetoacetyl-CoA thiolase; 4. HMG-CoA synthetase; 5. HMG-CoA lyase; 6. 3-oxoacid-CoA transferase; 7. 3-hydroxybutyrate dehydrogenase.

calanoid copepods in their natural diets. The major
fatty alcohols in these wax esters, 22:1(n-11) and
20:1(n-9), are dehydrogenated to their corresponding fatty
acids, cetoleic acid, 22:1(n-11) and gadoleic acid,
20:1(n-9) which are incorporated into triacylglycerols in
fish intestinal mucosa. A microsomal dehydrogenase is
responsible for this conversion of fatty alcohols to fatty
acids with the concomitant formation of NADH (Bauermeister
and Sargent, 1979). When trout were maintained on a diet
of lipid-rich copepods in which 22:1(n-11) comprised 25%
of the total alkyl/acyl units, it was notable that
22:1(n-11) accounted for only 8% of the fatty acids in the
total lipid of the fish (Henderson et al., 1982).
Similarly, relative to the amounts ingested, 22:1(n-11)
was the least deposited of all the principal dietary fatty
acids when trout were fed herring oil (Yu et al., 1977).
22:1(n-11) is not found to any great extent in structural
phospholipids of fish biomembranes and it may be utilised
specifically as an energy source.

    Feeding large amounts of oils rich in 22:1, either as
erucic acid, 22:1(n-9), in rape seed oil or as 22:1(n-11)
and other isomers in partially hydrogenated marine oils,
can cause a transient cardiac lipidosis in rats
(Beare-Rogers, 1977). Therefore, interest has been
centred on the catabolism of 22:1 fatty acids by mammals.
In response to high-fat diets rich in 22:1 an additional
pathway of fatty acid oxidation located in peroxisomes is
induced in the livers of mammals (Osmundsen, 1982; Bremer
and Norum, 1982). Peroxisomal ß-oxidation of fatty acids
has been well studied in mammals and is known to be
cyanide-insensitive since it is not directly linked to the
mitochondrial electron transfer chain or coupled to a
phosphorylating system. It has been suggested that
peroxisomes specifically chain-shorten fatty acid by
oxidising the very long chain monoenes to shorter chain
acyl-CoA's which are better substrates for mitochondrial
ß-oxidation (Osmundsen, 1982). Thus peroxisomal
ß-oxidation is induced in rats to make excesses of dietary
22:1 compatable with mitochondrial ß-oxidation. By
virtue of its high lipid and 22:1 (n-11) contents, a diet
of calanoid copepods might be expected to induce high
peroxisomal ß-oxidation in livers of fish consuming such a
diet. Peroxisomes have been detected by electron
microscopy in the livers of trout fed zooplankton,
although their population density was much less than that
of mitochondria (Henderson et al., 1982). The
activities of peroxisomal palmitoyl-CoA oxidation in

livers of trout fed either a synthetic control diet, krill or calanoid copepods were similar and not influenced by the contents of lipid or 22:1(n-11) in the three diets (Henderson et al., 1982). The plasticiser, di-(2-ethylhexyl)-phthalate (DEHP) is a potent inducer of peroxisomal ß-oxidation in rat livers and occurs as a micro-pollutant in the marine environment (Osumi and Hashimoto, 1978; Musial et al., 1981). However, inclusion of DEHP in a diet of freeze-dried calanoid copepods had no effect on the activity of peroxisomal palmitoyl-CoA oxidation in the livers of trout fed this diet (Henderson and Sargent, 1983).

The activity of carnitine palmitoyltransferase, a possible rate-limiting enzyme for the mitochondrial oxidation of palmitoyl-CoA (McGarry and Foster, 1980), was much greater than that of peroxisomal palmitoyl-CoA oxidation in livers of trout and capelin (Henderson and Sargent, 1984; Henderson et al., 1984b). This demonstrates that, in relation to mitochondrial ß-oxidation, peroxisomal ß-oxidation is quantitatively minor in fish as in normal mammals (Osmundsen, 1982).

When trout were maintained on a diet containing 11.5% partially hydrogenated fish oil plus 3.5% capelin oil, the cyanide-insensitive palmitoyl-CoA oxidation activity was double that observed in livers of fish consuming 15% capelin oil (Henderson and Sargent, 1984). The ratio of (20:1 + 22:1) to polyunsaturates in the former diet was 6:1 but only 1:1 in the latter. In copepod lipid the ratio is approximately 1.5:1. This suggests that peroxisomal ß-oxidation in trout is only induced by feeding diets containing an excess of very long chain monoenes in relation to polyunsaturates, a situation which never arises in natural fish diets.

Although 22:1 has been postulated as a substrate for oxidation in mammalian peroxisomes, only low rates of 22:1-CoA oxidation were observed with peroxisomes isolated from rat liver, the optimum substrates being 14:0 and 16:0-CoA's (Osmundsen, 1982; Bremer and Norum, 1982). Similarly, the rates of acyl-CoA oxidation by isolated trout liver peroxisomes were low with long chain monoenoic and polyunsaturated substrates in comparison with shorter-chained substrates (Fig. 4) (Henderson and Sargent, unpublished data).

Given that peroxisomal ß-oxidation activity is low in fish and is not specific for very long chain monoenes, then the oxidation of dietary 22:1(n-11) must proceed via mitochondrial ß-oxidation. Murata and Higashi (1979)

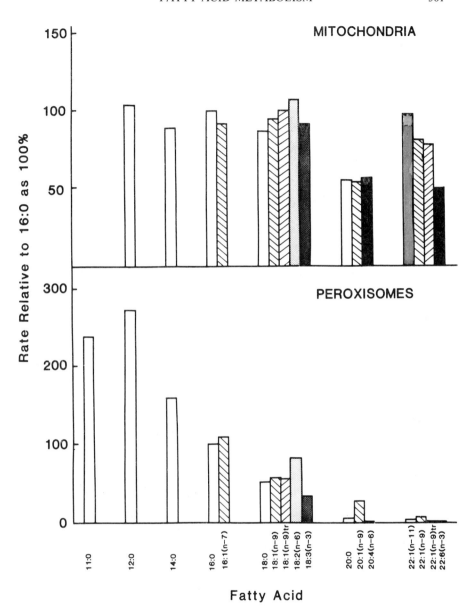

Fig. 4. Chain-length specificities of mitochondial and peroxisomal ß-oxidation in trout liver in vitro. Fatty acids were supplied as fatty acylcarnitines to isolated peroxisomes. Mitochondrial ß-oxidation rates were measured by manometry and peroxisomal oxidation as described in Henderson and Sargent (1984).

showed that 18:1 and 16:1 were oxidised at higher rates
than other fatty acids present in the lipids supplied as
substrates by mitochondria isolated from carp. Similarly,
22:6 was shown to be inferior to 18:1 as a substrate for
ß-oxidation in liver mitochondria from eel, tilapia, trout
and bream (Murata, 1979). However, when the substrate
specificity of ß-oxidation in mitochondria isolated from
trout liver was studied using acylcarnitine derivatives,
all fatty acids were oxidised at similar rates with the
exception of 20-carbon fatty acids and 22:6 (Fig. 4)
(Henderson and Sargent, unpublished data). Most notably,
22:1(n-11) and 16:0 served equally well as substrates, in
contrast to mammalian mitochondria in which 20 and
22-carbon fatty acylcarnitines are poorly oxidised in
vitro (Osmundsen and Bremer, 1978).

The ability of trout mitochondria to oxidise both very
long chain monoenoic and polyunsaturated fatty acids
indicates that fish mitochondria are well adapted to
utilise the spectrum of fatty acids present in natural
fish diets, but not usually encountered in the diet of
terrestrial animals.

REFERENCES

Ackman, R.G. (1980). In "Advances in Fish Science and
    Technology", (J.J. Connell, ed.), pp. 86-103. Fishing
    News Books Ltd., Farnham, Surrey.
Bauermeister, A. and Sargent, J.R. (1979). Trends in
    Biochem. Sci. 4, 209-211.
Beare-Rogers, J.L. (1977). Prog. Chem. Fats other Lipids
    15, 29-56.
Bilinski, E. (1974). In "Biochemical and Biophysical
    Perspectives in Marine Biology" (D.C. Malins and J.R.
    Sargent, eds.), 1, 239-299. Academic Press, London.
Bremer, J. and Norum, K.R. (1982). J. Lip. Res. 23,
    243-256.
Cowey, C.B. and Sargent, J.R. (1979). In "Fish
    Physiology", (W.S. Hoar, D.J. Randall and J.R. Brett,
    eds.), 8, 1-69. Academic Press, London.
De Torrengo, M.A.P. and Brenner, R.R. (1976). Biochim.
    Biophys. Acta. 424, 36-44.
Gurr, M.I. and James, A.T. (1980). "Lipid Biochemistry",
    pp. 25-88. Chapman and Hall, London.

Hansen, H.O. and Knudsen, J. (1981). Comp. Biochem. Physiol. 70B, 515-520.

Hazel, J.R. (1979). J. Exp. Zool. 207, 33-42.

Hazel, J.R. and Prosser, C.L. (1974). Physiol. Rev. 54, 620-677.

Hazel, J.R. and Sellner, P.A. (1979). J. Exp. Zool. 209, 105-114.

Henderson, R.J. and Sargent, J.R. (1981). Comp. Biochem. Physiol. 69C, 31-37.

Henderson, R.J. and Sargent, J.R. (1983). Comp. Biochem. Physiol. 74C, 325-330.

Henderson, R.J. and Sargent, J.R. (1984). Comp. Biochem. Physiol. 78B, 557-564.

Henderson, R.J., Sargent, J.R. and Hopkins, C.C.E. (1984a). Mar. Biol. 78, 255-263.

Henderson, R.J., Sargent, J.R. and Pirie, B.J.S. (1982). Comp. Biochem. Physiol. 73B, 565-570.

Henderson, R.J., Sargent, J.R. and Pirie, B.J.S. (1984b). Mar. Biol. Letts. 5, 115-126.

de la Higuera, M., Murillo, A., Varela, G. and Zamora, S. (1977). Comp. Biochem. Physiol. 56A, 37-41.

Jangaard, P.M. (1974). Bull. Fish. Res. Bd Can. 186, 1-70.

Lin, H., Romsos, D.R., Tack, P.I. and Leveille, G.A. (1977a). J. Nutr. 107, 846-854.

Lin, H., Romsos, D.R., Tack, P.I. and Leveille, G.A. (1977b). J. Nutr. 107, 1477-1483.

McGarry, J.D. and Foster, D.W. (1980). Ann. Rev. Biochem. 49, 395-420.

Murata, H. (1979). Bull. Jap. Soc. Scient. Fish. 45, 379-383.

Murata, H. and Higashi, T. (1979). Bull. Jap. Soc. Scient. Fish. 45, 211-217.

Musial, C.J., Uthe, J.F., Sirota, G.R., Burns, B.G., Gilgan, M.W., Zitko, V. and Matheson, R.A. (1981). Can. J. Fish. Aquat. Sci. 38, 856-859.

Ninno, R.E., De Torrengo, M.A.P., Castuma, J.C. and Brenner, R.R. (1974). Biochim. Biophys. Acta. 360, 124-133.

Osmundsen, H. (1982). Annals N.Y. Acad. Sci. 386, 13-29.

Osmundsen, H. and Bremer, J. (1978). Biochem. J. 174, 379-386.

Osumi, T. and Hashimoto, T. (1978). J. Biochem. 83, 1361-1365.

Pearce, J. (1983). Proc. Nutr. Soc. 42, 263-271.

Sargent, J.R. (1976). In "Biochemical and Biophysical Perspectives in Marine Biology", (D.C. Malins and J.R. Sargent, eds.), 3, 149–212. Academic Press, London.

Sargent, J.R. and Whittle, K.J. (1981). In "Analysis of. Marine Ecosystems", (A.R. Longhurst, ed.),pp. 491–533. Academic Press, London.

Sellner, P.A. and Hazel, J.R. (1982). Arch. Biochem. Biophys. 213, 58–66.

Toussant, M.J., Wilson, M.D. and Clarke, S.D. (1981). J. Nutr. 111, 146–153.

Volpe, J.J. and Vagelos, P.R. (1976). Physiol. Rev. 56, 339–417.

Warman, A.W. and Bottino, N.R. (1978). Comp. Biochem. Physiol. 59B, 153–161.

Watanabe, T. (1982). Comp. Biochem. Physiol. 73B, 3–15.

Williamson, D.H. (1981). Biochem. Soc. Trans. 9, 346–347.

Wilson, A.C. and Williamson, I.P. (1970). Biochem. J. 117, 26–27.

Yu, T.C., Sinnhuber, R.O. and Purnam, G.B. (1977). Lipids 12, 495–499.

Zammit, V.A., Beis, A. and Newsholme, E.A. (1979). FEBS Lett. 103, 212–215.

Zammit, V.A. and Newsholme, E.A. (1979). Biochem. J. 184, 313–322.

GROWTH, GILL STRUCTURE AND FATTY ACID COMPOSITION
OF PHOSPHOLIPIDS IN THE TURBOT (SCOPHTHALMUS MAXIMUS)
IN RELATION TO DIETARY POLYUNSATURATED FATTY ACID
DEFICIENCIES

M.V. BELL, R.J. HENDERSON, B.J.S. PIRIE AND J.R. SARGENT

N.E.R.C., Institute of Marine Biochemistry,
St. Fittick's Road, Aberdeen AB1 3RA.

In freshwater fish both the (n-3) and (n-6) series of
polyunsaturated fatty acids (PUFA) are nutritionally
important. The fatty acid requirements of marine fish
are less well defined and though the (n-3) series of PUFA
is generally considered essential for marine species the
requirement for the (n-6) series is less certain (reviewed
by Watanabe, 1982). The (n-3) PUFA requirement of turbot
has been variously reported as 0.8% dry weight of the diet
of long chain PUFA (Gatesoupe et al., 1977) or 0.55%
(Leger et al., 1979) while a higher requirement of 1.3%
was found for larval turbot (LeMillinaire et al., 1983).
In this study young turbot (1-20g live weight) from
Cardigan Bay, Wales, were kept in fibre glass tanks
containing 120 litres of circulating seawater at
10-13°C, with 102 fish per tank at the start of the
experiment. The three groups of turbot were maintained
on standard diets, fed at 2g per 100g fish per day,
containing different types of lipid: 1) 10% of the dry
weight of the diet as natural fish oil, equivalent to 2.5%
(n-3) PUFA and 0.23% (n-6) PUFA; 2) 10% of the dry weight
of the diet as palmitic acid, i.e. no PUFA; 3) 8.7%
palmitic acid and 1.3% of the dry weight as (n-3) PUFA
with negligible (n-6) PUFA. The composition of the lipid
component of the diets is shown in Table 1. The exact
composition of the diets and the preparation of the (n-3)
concentrates has been described (Bell et al., 1985). All

NUTRITION AND FEEDING IN FISH
ISBN: 0 12 194055 1

Table I. Fatty acid composition of the fish oil used for the preparation of diet 1 and the lipids added to diets 2 and 3. The isomers of the 16:2 and 16:3 fatty acids were not determined. Data are expressed as weight %.

	Diet 1	Diet 2	Diet 3A	Diet 3B
14:0	8.4	0	0	0
16:0	20.6	100.0	87.0	87.0
16:1(n-7)	10.5	0	0	0
16:2	1.1	0	0	0
16:3	1.2	0	0	0
16:4(n-3)	1.8	0	2.6	3.8
18:0	3.5	0	0	0
18:1(n-9)	10.1	0	0	0
18:1(n-7)	3.8	0	0	0
18:2(n-6)	1.4	0	0	0
18:3(n-3)	0.8	0	0	0
18:4(n-3)	2.1	0	0	0
20:1(n-9)	1.8	0	0	0
20:4(n-6)	0.9	0	0	0
20:5(n-3)	13.0	0	8.3	6.3
22:5(n-3)	1.5	0	0.4	0.1
22:6(n-3)	7.2	0	0.6	2.8
20:5/22:6	1.9	0	13.8	2.2

the constituents of the diet were extracted with chloroform/methanol 2:1 (v/v) to remove contaminating fatty acids before incorporation into the diet.

Over the 15 week experimental period only the fish

given diet 1 (the control diet) showed significant growth
from a total biomass of 500g to 837g.   The fish given
diets 2 and 3 showed high mortality and those fish which
remained were very thin with little flesh at the end of
the experiment.   The smallest fish fed diets 2 and 3
showed the highest mortality (Table II).   The rapid rate
of mortality of the fish given diet 3 occurred with a
20:5(n-3) to 22.6(n-3) ratio of 13.8 (diet 3A).   When this
ratio was decreased after 10 weeks to 2.2 (diet 3B), close
to that of the natural fish oil used in diet 1, the
mortality rate rapidly dropped to that of the control fish.

Table II.   Mortality of fish on the different diets

	% mortality of no. in original weight class		
Wt. class	diet 1	diet 2	diet 3
0 - 2.49 g	29	91	100
2.5 - 4.9 g	7	55	65
5.0 - 9.9 g	6	52	44
10.0 + g	0	18	11

During the course of the experiment a gross change in
gill structure occurred in fish fed diets 2 and 3.   Light
microscopy showed an initial disappearance of the chloride
cells along the primary filaments.   The basement
epithelium then pulled off the primary filament and was
replaced by a new epithelium.   This in turn "sloughed"
off and there was a progressive infilling of the
interlamellar spaces with tissue.   During this process
some haemorrhaging occurred as blood cells appeared in the
mass of tissue.   Eventually the entire epithelium
sloughed away from the gill filaments leaving a skeleton
of cartilage and connective tissue.   This change in gill
structure is similar to that noted in fish exposed to a
variety of toxic substances (Schweiger, 1957; Christie and
Battle, 1963; Kamaraguru et al., 1982).   It is interesting
to note that essential fatty acid deficiency in mammals
leads to blood in the urine and serious kidney damage
(Burr and Burr, 1929).

After an average of 14 weeks on the diets, the liver, gut, gills and muscle of fish on the three diets were taken for fatty acid analysis of the phospholipids. The total amounts of PUFA in the different phospholipids, phosphatidylcholine, phosphatidylethanolamine, phosphatidylserine, phosphatidylinositol and sphingomyelin, of fish fed on the three diets showed little change. However, the proportion of the 3 main PUFA's arachidonic acid 20:4(n-6), eicosapentaenoic acid 20:5(n-3) and docosahexaenoic acid 22:6(n-3) altered. Fish maintained on diet 2, totally deficient in PUFA, retained 20:4(n-6) and 22:6(n-3) at the expense of 20:5(n-3), so that during the weight loss which occurred there was selective retention of 20:4(n-6) and 22:6(n-3) and selective catabolism of 20:5(n-3). Fish maintained on diet 3 deficient in (n-6) PUFA contained decreased amounts of 20:4(n-6) and 22:6(n-3) while retaining 20:5(n-3). It should be remembered that for the first 10 weeks of treatment 3 (diet 3A) this diet was probably also deficient in 22:6(n-3). The data support the finding of Cowey et al. (1976) that turbot cannot elongate 20:5 to 22.6.

CONCLUSIONS

1. Fish fed on the two PUFA deficient diets showed a serious gill pathology, ultimately leading to the disintegration of the epithelium. The gill epithelium appears to be a sensitive indicator of essential fatty acid deficiency in this species.

2. Both the mortality data from treatment 3 and the fatty acid analyses lead to the conclusion that 22:6(n-3) is an essential fatty acid in turbot.

3. Within the experimental period it was not possible to conclude whether or not 20:4(n-6) is essential. However, the importance of this fatty acid in phosphatidylinositol metabolism suggests that it is essential, but at what dietary level remains to be determined.

4. PUFA are avidly retained in phospholipids in the face of dietary deficiency.

REFERENCES

Bell, M.V., Henderson, R.J., Pirie, B.J.S. and Sargent, J.R. (1985). J. Fish Biol. 26, 181-191.

Bell, M.V., Simpson, C.M.F. and Sargent, J.R. (1983). Lipids 18, 720-726.

Burr, G.O. and Burr, M.M. (1929). J. Biol. Chem. 82, 345-367.

Christie, R.M. and Battle, H.I. (1963). Can. J. Zool. 41, 51-61.

Cowey, C.B., Adron, J.W., Owen, J.M. and Roberts, R.J. (1976). Comp. Biochem. Physiol. 53B, 399-403.

Gatesoupe, F.J., Leger, C., Metailler, R. and Luquet, P. (1977). Ann. hydrobiol. 8, 89-97.

Kumaraguru, A.K., Beamish, F.W.H. and Ferguson, H.W. (1982). J. Fish Biol. 20, 87-91.

Leger, C., Gatesoupe, F.J., Metailler, R., Luquet, P. and Fremont, L. (1979). Comp. Biochem. Physiol. 64B, 345-350.

LeMillinaire, C., Gatesoupe, F.J. and Stephen, G. (1983). C.R. Acad. Sci. Paris. 296, 917-920.

Schweiger, G. (1957). Arch. Fischereiwiss 8, 54-78.

Tocher, D.R. and Sargent, J.R. (1984). Lipids 19, 492-499.

Watanabe, T. (1982). Lipid Nutrition in Fish. Comp. Biochem. Physiol. 73B, 3-15.

THE EFFECTS OF DIFFERENT RATION ON FECUNDITY AND EGG
QUALITY IN THE RAINBOW TROUT (<u>SALMO GAIRDNERI</u>)

J.R.C. SPRINGATE, N.R. BROMAGE and P.R.T. CUMARANATUNGA

Fish Culture Unit, University of Aston,
Birmingham B4 7ET, U.K.

I. INTRODUCTION

In the wide literature relating to egg production and the population dynamics of fish it is often implied that the supplies of food are of prime importance in determining the reproductive potential of different fish stocks (Woodhead, 1960; Nicolskii, 1969; Bagenal, 1973). However, much of the evidence is circumstantial mainly because it is derived from records of wild stocks of fish, where dietary influences are difficult to quantify and to separate from other environmental variables. Thus, McFadden <u>et al</u>. (1965) reported that brown trout from oligotrophic streams had lower fecundities and reached sexual maturity later than similar sized fish from more fertile waters. Fry (1949) similarly suggested that the variation in fecundity of lake trout from year to year occurred as a result of differences in diet. Martin (1970) in an exhaustive study of the same salmonid species proposed that the increases in fecundity and egg size shown in the later years of a 21 year series were due to improved food supplies. Better feeding conditions were also said to advance the age of first spawning and increase fecundity in brook trout (Vladykov, 1956), although this finding was not substantiated in a similar study of the same species and area by Gibson <u>et al</u> (1976).

NUTRITION AND FEEDING IN FISH
ISBN: 0 12 194055 1

Working on non-salmonid species Hodder (1965), Bagenal
(1966) and Raitt (1968) related variations in the
fecundities of different stocks of haddock, plaice and
Norway pout, respectively, to alterations in population
density and/or food supplies. Various studies of the
roach have indicted that diminished food supplies reduced
fecundity (MacKay and Mann, 1969; Kuznetzov and Khalitov,
1978), delayed maturation (Mackay and Mann, 1969) but did
not affect egg size (Kuznetzov and Khalitov, 1978).

Primarily, because of the inherrent difficulties of
associating cause and effect in the determination of
fecundity and egg composition amongst wild stocks of fish,
the above data, at best, offers only supportive evidence
for a direct relationship between nutrition and
reproduction. Laboratory investigations of the effects of
modified ration on egg size, number and quality (i.e.
survival) would improve our understanding of this
relationship but surprisingly, few such studies have been
conducted. Scott (1962), in a three year investigation
of the effects of varying ration on the rainbow trout,
showed that the proportion of fish which became mature was
lower in fish fed on approximately half ration; these
fish also produced fewer eggs although the eggs were
unchanged in size. Some questions, however, remain
regarding these findings as less than 5% of all the fish
matured by the end of the experiment. Working with the
brown trout, Bagenal (1969a,b) showed that diet
restriction reduced total fecundity and delayed
maturation; there were also alterations in the mean wet
and dry weights of the eggs, although these changes were
probably due to the measurements being made on eggs from
prespawned fish, and these would have included oocytes at
different stages of growth and final maturation. Baiz
(1978) in a study of the fecundity of the rainbow trout
also reported that a period of starvation reduced egg
numbers, but like Scott (1962), could find no effect on
egg size. Hislop et al. (1978) showed that egg production
and feed levels were positively correlated in laboratory
maintained haddock. There was also a suggestion that a
lower proportion of the fish under the lowest ration
matured, and that their eggs were lighter on a dry weight
basis. In contrast, Kato (1975) and Ridelman et al.
(1984) reported that diet restriction for either 4 months
or 40 days before spawning, respectively, produced no
changes in either fecundity or egg size in the rainbow
trout. In an extensive séries of papers on the
stickleback, Wootton and co-workers (see review Wootton,

1982) have shown that high food levels increase both the percentage of fish maturing and their spawning frequency and, that by improving the growth of fish, fecundity was increased.   Food level however had no effect on egg size.   More recently Townshend and Wootton (1984) showed for the convict cichlid that both fecundity and egg size were posively correlated with ration and that fish size per se had negligible effects on these parameters. Clearly, the weight of evidence points to direct effects of nutrition on varying aspects of reproduction, but the details of such changes remain obscure.

It is also not clear how the possible alterations in fecundity and egg size are achieved.   It has been suggested that food deprivation reduces oocyte numbers by inducing atresia (Vladykov, 1956) and/or by modifying the recruitment of oocytes into vitellogenesis (Robb, 1982). However, Henderson (1963) reported that the levels of atresia in the brook trout were too low to account for these changes, and Townshend and Wootton (1984), although finding a reduction in ooocyte recruitment in convict cichlids on reduced ration, concluded that the relative importance of this process and atresia in determining fecundity could not be ascertained.

In view of the wide range of reported influences of diet on fish reproduction and the unresolved questions relating to atresia and recruitment, the present study investigates the effects of altered ration on the timing of reproduction, and the number, size and quality of the eggs produced in the rainbow trout under carefully controlled experimental conditions; and also by histological examination the ovarian changes which could mediate these changes.

II.   MATERIALS AND METHODS

Groups of 40 female rainbow trout (Salmo gairdneri) were maintained in 2m circular tanks and fed in replicate at either 0.35% (half-ration) or 0.7% (full-ration) body weight day^{-1} on a dry commercial trout pellet (Ewos-Baker: Pellets 7 and 8.   Proximate analysis: total protein 47%, carbohydrate 22%, ash 13%, moisture 9%, fat 7%, fibre 2%).   Water inflow to each tank was 40L. min^{-1} at a constant temperature of 10°C.   The fish, which were of North American origin, but with an

October/November spawning time under local conditions, were 2 years old at the beginning of the experiment on 13th October and weighed 0.581 $\pm$ 0.005 kg. Only fish which had spawned for the first time during the week before the experiment was begun were used.

The fish were individually marked with numbered tags attached by plastic ties through the dorsal fin. At approximately monthly intervals fish were individually weighed under phenoxyethanol anaesthesia (1 in 15,000), and also examined for signs of sexual maturation and the presence of ripe eggs. At the same time, blood samples were taken from the Cuverian Sinus and, after separation, the serum was deep frozen at $-20^{\circ}C$ for later analyses of calcium (as an index of vitellogenin) and testosterone using methods already described (Elliott et al., 1984).

As maturity approached the fish were examined each week for the presence of ripe or ovulated eggs. The eggs were removed from each mature fish by gentle pressure on the abdominal wall (i.e. stripping) and separately dry-fertilized in a plastic bowl with an aliquot of sperm from a pool of milt derived from several ripe male fish. Post-stripped fish weights and length were also recorded. 1 minute after fertilization the eggs were washed in running water and after water-hardening for one hour in the same bowls, the volume of eggs derived from each female was determined and the mean diameter of the eggs calculated by counting the number of eggs which could be aligned along a 30cm long groove in a measuring board. The number of eggs from each fish (i.e. the fecundity) was then calculated from the volume of eggs and their mean diameter using the method of von Bayer (1950). This method provides a consistent measure of fecundity which is not significantly different from fecundity determinations based on total egg counts (Springate and Bromage, unpublished observations).

After measurement, the eggs were transferred to hatchery trays and the fertilization rates and subsequent mortalities at eying and as feeding fry recorded using methods already described (Springate et al., 1984). Parallel groups of water-hardened, fertilized eggs from each female were taken for estimation of wet and dry weights (by weighing to constant weight after drying in a hot air oven for 24 hours at $70^{\circ}C$) and for analyses of their proximate composition. Total protein was measured by microkjeldahl analysis, total fats using a Soxhlet apparatus and extracting for 4 hours with petroleum ether ($BP.40^{\circ}-60^{\circ}C$), free amino acids using a Locarte

Analyser, mineral ions with a Perkin-Elmer 373 atomic absorption spectrophotometer and free fatty acids using a Pye-Unicam 304 gas liquid chromatograph. Ash content was determined by weighing to constant weight after heating samples in a muffle furnace for 24hr at 500°C.

After swim-up the fry were fed ad libitum on commercial fry diets (Ewos-Baker Ltd) and when they had reached a mean weight of approximately 1g (in March) they were transferred to 1.5m diameter fry tanks. Throughout this period, mortalities were recorded and, at approximately 3-week intervals from the time of first feed, individual fry weights were taken.

Ovarian samples were taken from the fish from each group approximately 14 days pre- and post-ovulation for histological examination after fixation in Bouin's fixative, alcohol dehydration and JB4 plastic (Polysciences) embedding. Sections were cut at approximately 1µm thickness. Parallel ovarian samples were also fixed and separated in Gilson's fluid for determination of the total numbers of each of the seven oocyte stages (van den Hurk and Peute, 1979). The levels of atresia in prespawning fish were expressed as percentages of the total number of vitellogenic and atretic oocytes whereas in the spawned fish the numbers of ovulated follicles were also included in the total count.

Differences between means were compared with a student's 't' test and in the case of percentages after 'arc sine' transformation. Regression analysis was carried out using a 'Minitab' statistical package on a Harris main frame computer. The estimated statistical parameters are given $\pm$ 1 standard error (SE) of the mean.

III.   RESULTS

By the time of the first sampling in February, the differences in dietary input were clearly shown by the significant difference in growth between the groups (Fig. 1, P < 0.05). The growth divergence became more pronounced as the trial progressed and from May onwards the differences between means was highly significant (P < 0.001). At all times there was an overlap in the range of fish sizes in the two groups and at spawning the half-ration fish were 0.835 $\pm$ 0.020 kg in weight (range 0.580-1.225), whereas the full-ration fish were 1.330 $\pm$ 0.040 kg (range 0.500-2.000).

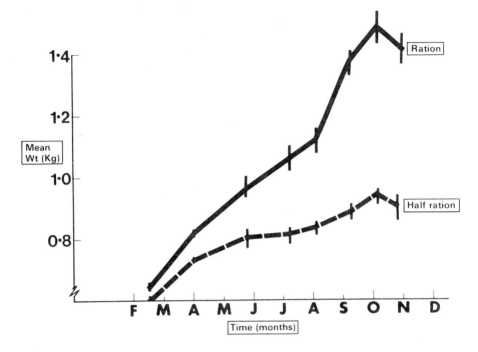

Fig. 1. Growth of rainbow trout fed on 0.35% (half-ration) and 0.7% (full-ration) body weight day^{-1} (Mean $\pm$ SE).

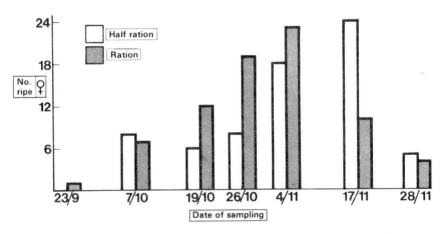

Fig. 2. Spawning profile of the fish on half- and full-ration.

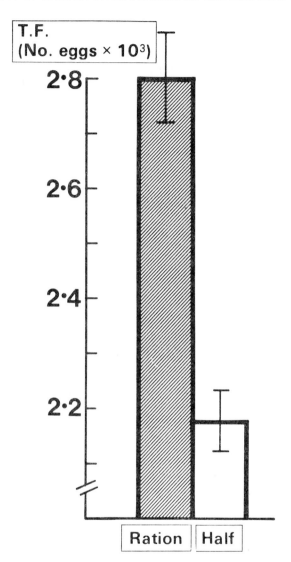

Fig. 3. Total fecundity (No. of eggs fish^{-1}) of the fish on half- and full-ration (Mean $\pm$ SE).

The first fish to be stripped were those under full-ration, 2–3 weeks earlier than those on half-ration (Fig. 2). No relationship could be seen between fish size and their spawning times. However, all the fish which had been fed full rations spawned, whereas 11% of the half-ration group failed to mature.

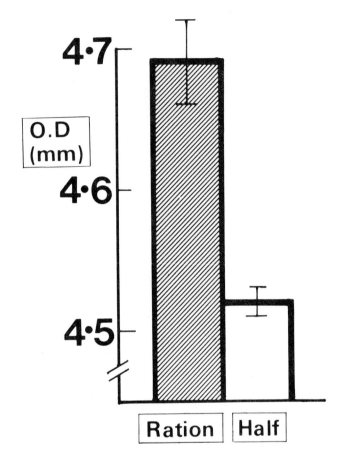

Fig. 4. Diameter (mm) of the eggs from the half- and full-ration fish (Mean + SE).

Determinations of fecundity showed that the full-ration fish produced significantly more eggs per fish than those on half-ration (Fig. 3, P < 0.001). However, the eggs from the full-ration group were significantly larger (Fig. 4, P < 0.001). The concomitant changes in fecundity and egg size in the two groups were reflected in a significant increase in relative fecundity in the fish fed with half-rations (Fig. 5, P < 0.001) when compared with the full-ration group.

Measurements of serum calcium (as an index of vitellogenin) and testosterone revealed similar profiles to those reported elsewhere (Elliott et al., 1984) with peak values occurring around the time of ovulation. The

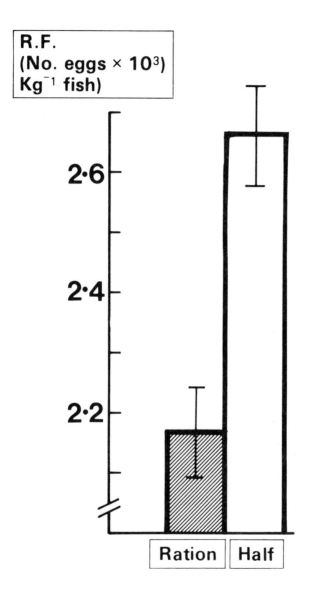

Fig. 5. Relative fecundity (No. of eggs kg^{-1} post-spawned fish weight) of the fish on half and full-ration (Mean $\pm$ SE).

peak heights for both calcium and testosterone were
reduced in the half-ration fish (Fig. 6).

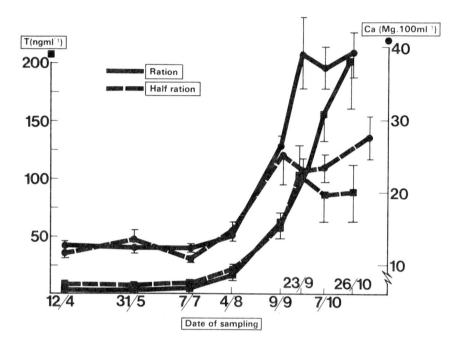

Fig. 6. Serum levels of calcium (Ca) (as an index of
vitellogenin) and testosterone (T) in the half-and
full-ration fish.

The eggs of the full-ration fish were significantly
heavier on a dry weight basis than those from fish on
reduced ration (Fig. 7, $P < 0.001$) although the proportion
of water to dry matter was the same in the two groups
(Table I).

The proximate composition of the water-hardened eggs
from the two treatment groups are shown in Table I.
Proximate analyses showed no changes in either total fat
or protein levels. The amino acid profiles of the eggs
from the full- and half-ration fish were similar, as were
the concentrations of mineral ions, both expressed per
unit weight of egg (Table II and III). There were few
changes in free fatty acid composition although a moiety
approximately described as 20:0 was consistently present
in small amounts in the eggs from fish on half-ration but
absent from the eggs of fish on full-ration (Table IV).

Similar survivals of the eggs were seen at fertilization, and eying (Table I), and in the fry and fingerlings up to six months of age there were overall mortalities of 55% in both groups.

Initially, there were highly significant differences in the size of the fry (Fig. 8, P < 0.001) and for the next 4 months this difference was maintained. Subsequently, the variances in growth within each group increased and there were no significant differences between the means.

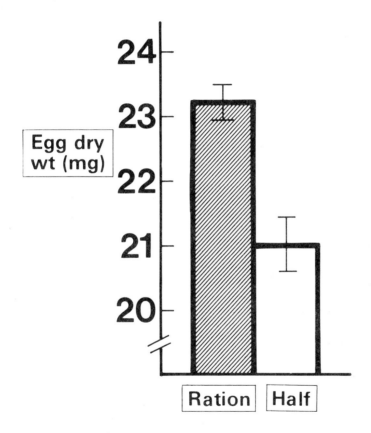

Fig. 7. Dry weight (mg) of the eggs from the half- and full-ration fish (Mean $\pm$ SE).

Histological examination of the preovulatory samples revealed that atresia was present in vitellogenic oocytes, stages V–VII (van den Hurk and Peute, 1979), of the ovaries of both full- and half-ration fish. However, the

Table I.   Proximate analyses of the eggs.

	Half Ration			Full Ration			
	mean	± SE	n	mean	± SE	n	Significance of difference: P value
Wet Wt. (mg)	47.4	0.7	50	51.0	0.8	50	< 0.01
Dry Wt. (mg)	21.0	0.4	44	23.2	0.4	49	< 0.001
% water	55.7	0.4	44	54.5	0.3	49	NS*
Ova Diam (mm)	4.54	0.02	70	4.69	0.03	76	< 0.001
Dry weight							
% Protein	69.8	2.0	10	69.1	3.3	10	NS*
% Fat	7.5	0.2	10	7.3	0.1	10	NS*
% Ash	3.6	0.1	10	3.7	0.2	10	NS*
Survival Rates							
% Fert.	92.0	1.9	9	86.3	5.9	9	NS*
% Eying	82.5	5.8	9	74.8	9.0	9	NS*
Parent Size (at spawning)							
Wt (kg)	0.835	0.020	70	1.330	0.040	76	< 0.001
Lth (cm)	41.6	0.3	70	46.0	0.5	76	< 0.001

*
  With arcsine transformation

overall atresia levels of 6.9 + 2.1% of the total numbers of vitellogenic oocytes in the full-ration fish were significantly different from the 21.9 + 1.2% found in half-ration fish (P < 0.05).   True atresia was not seen in stages I-IV oocytes in either treatment group although some stage IV oocytes particularly from the full-ration group were showing early signs of this process.

Total counts of the oocytes in the preovulatory ovaries of both half- and full-ration fish revealed similar numbers of vitellogenic oocytes to the numbers of fully-ripe eggs which would have been stripped at full maturity.   The total numbers of oocytes of all stages were higher in the fish on full-ration as might have been predicted from the mean total fecundity of this group at spawning.   There was also a delay in the development of vitellogenesis in the ovaries of the half-ration fish. At the time of sampling of the preovulatory fish, most of the vitellogenic oocytes (i.e. stage V–VII) had reached late stage VI or early stage VII, whereas in the half-ration fish the majority of the vitellogenic oocytes

Table II.   Levels of free amino acids (nmol g^{-1} dry wt egg x 10^3).

	Half-Ration			Full-Ration		
	mean	$\pm$	SE	mean	$\pm$	SE
Asp	17.3		0.2	15.6		1.1
Thr	12.4		0.4	12.8		0.4
Ser	15.8		1.1	15.7		0.8
Glu	21.2		0.4	21.3		0.5
Pro	17.3		0.5	1/.2		0.7
Gly	10.4		0.5	11.1		0.3
Ala	20.1		0.2	20.0		0.3
Val	15.9		0.4	15.4		0.1
Met	6.5		0.1	6.5		0.1
Ile	11.8		0.2	11.5		0.2
Leu	14.9		0.2	16.2		0.4
Tyr	7.2		0.1	7.2		0.1
Phe	8.9		0.1	9.1		0.1
His	5.5		0.1	5.6		0.1
Lys	13.8		0.2	13.8		0.1
NH_3	16.1		0.2	14.9		0.5
Arg	11.7		0.3	8.9		0.2

were only in the early portion of stage VI.   No stage V oocytes were present in either ration group.   Examination

of the post-ovulatory ovaries showed that in the
full-ration fish only a small number of vitellogenic eggs
remained unovulated. In contrast, up to 7% of the same
stages remained in the ovaries of half-ration fish,
although the significance of this change just failed to
reach the $P < 0.05$ probability level. Atresia levels
were 11.9% and 17.5% respectively in the full and
half-ration groups, although this difference was not
significant.

IV. DISCUSSION

The most significant effect of feeding a low ration to
female rainbow trout was a 22% reduction in total
fecundity, expressed as the number of ripe eggs produced
per fish at stripping. Similar reductions in fecundity
following experimental deprivation of food have also been
reported for salmonids by other workers (Scott, 1962;

Table III. Mineral concentration (mg/g g^{-1} egg dry
weight; n = 6).

Element	Half ration mean ± SE	Full ration mean ± SE
Na $(mg.g^{-1})$	1.7 ± 0.7	2.1 ± 0.7
K $(mg.g^{-1})$	4.7 ± 0.5	4.5 ± 0.2
Ca $(mg.g^{-1})$	2.0 ± 0.1	2.5 ± 0.2
Mg $(mg.g^{-1})$	1.9 ± 0.2	2.0 ± 0.1
Zn $(g.g^{-1})$	86.7 ± 7.1	108.0 ± 7.1
Fe $(g.g^{-1})$	60.4 ± 2.7	66.0 ± 4.4
Cu $(g.g^{-1})$	8.8 ± 3.6	11.3 ± 0.9

Bagenal, 1969a; Baiz, 1978). However, only Scott (1962)
and Baiz (1978) determined fecundity from measurements of
ripe fish. Furthermore, in Scott's study overall

maturity levels in the experimental fish were very low probably because the fish on the highest ration only reached 150g in weight at three years of age. Non-salmonid species also experience reductions in fecundity following decreases in ration size (Wootton, 1973; Townshend and Wootton, 1984). Full interpretation of the results of the majority of these studies is,

Table IV. Percentage composition of fatty acid in the total lipid extract (n = 6).

Free Fatty Acid	Half ration mean ± SE	Full ration mean ± SE
14 : 0	3.3 ± 0.2	3.5 ± 0.1
16 : 0	18.6 ± 0.9	17.4 ± 0.4
16 : 1	7.4 ± 0.4	7.7 ± 0.2
18 : 0	3.1 ± 0.2	2.5 ± 0.2
18 : 1	16.9 ± 2.5	16.4 ± 1.4
18 : 2	6.5 ± 0.4	4.9 ± 0.2
18 : 3	0.9 ± 0.04	0.9 ± 0.04
20 : 1	4.0 ± 0.2	4.2 ± 0.4
20 : 2	0.7 ± 0.04	0.7 ± 0.08
20 : 3	1.4 ± 0.1	1.5 ± 0.1
20 : 4	2.2 ± 0.3	2.6 ± 0.6
20 : 5	7.2 ± 1.0	7.2 ± 0.4
22 : 5	2.5 ± 0.1	2.5 ± 0.1
22 : 6	22.1 ± 1.8	27.5 ± 0.7

however, complicated by the effects of diet on somatic growth because fecundity is primarily determined by fish size (Bagenal, 1973; Wootton, 1982). Consequently, if one is aiming to determine the direct influence of ration on fecundity then the primary effects of diet on fish size must be first removed by appropriate experimental

techniques (Wootton, 1982). Few studies are able to offer
such differentiation and, even where such analyses have
been possible, they have shown that there is considerable
interspecific variation.   Thus, in the stickleback, egg
production is primarily a function of fish size, whereas
in the convict cichlid the reductions in fecundity
produced by lower rations were greater than would be
expected from the reductions in fish weight (Wootton,
1982; Townshend and Wootton, 1984).   A direct correlation
of fecundity with the amount of food received, even after
the size differences were taken into account, was also
shown for the brown trout (Bagenal, 1969a).   However,
there is little evidence for a direct effect of ration on
fecundity in the rainbow trout.   The present work shows a
significant correlation of size with fecundity in the
full-ration fish ($r = 0.51$, $P < 0.001$), but not for those
on reduced ration, suggesting that diet may have had a
direct influence in this group.   However, fish of
equivalent sizes in the two ration groups had similar
fecundities.   Further partitioning of the multiple effects
of diet in the rainbow trout must await factorial
experimentation with a variety of ration levels.

In parallel with the change in fecundity, both the
diameter of the eggs and their mean dry weight were
significantly reduced in the fish on half-ration. Hislop
et al. (1978) have also reported similar changes in
laboratory-maintained haddock.   In contrast, Bagenal
(1969a) reported that diet restriction in brown trout led
to the production of larger eggs by dry weight. However
Bagenal's measurements were conducted on preovulatory fish
and, as the feeding regime also delayed maturity, the
sampling procedure would have included eggs of varying
stages of final ripeness and hydration.   Generally, other
investigations on salmonids have shown that egg size is
not affected by reduced ration (Scott, 1962; Ridelman et
al., 1984) or, as in the study of Baiz (1978), by a period
of starvation enforced by disease problems in the
experimental fish.   Reductions in ration also failed to
change egg size expressed as either wet or dry weight in
the stickleback (Wootton, 1973) and the convict cichlid
(Townshend and Wootton, 1984).   However, both these
species are multiple spawners and the length of the
interspawning interval, which is extended by decreased
ration, may also have effects on egg size.   Increases in
egg size have also been reported to occur in the rainbow
trout after a delay in spawning time (Bromage et al.,
1984).

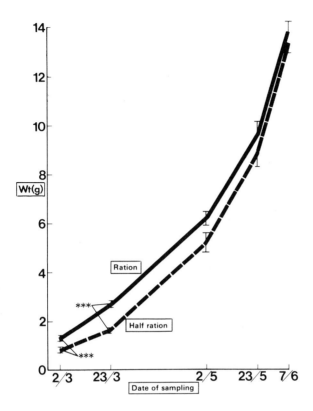

Fig. 8.   Weight of fry (Mean ± SE) derived from the eggs of half- and full-ration fish.

Although there were no differences in percentage wet and dry weights of the eggs, the absolute dry weights of the eggs was reduced in the fish on half-ration and closely paralleled the reduction of egg diameter in this group.   Possibly, some of the varied effects of diet on egg size described above relate more to the changes in water relations experienced by the eggs during their final maturation rather than to ration per se.   Such difficulties would be minimised by only comparing the sizes of water-hardened, ovulated eggs.

Proximate analyses of the gross protein, fat and ash constituents of the eggs revealed no differences between the ration groups nor were there any alterations in mineral or amino acid composition, if expressed in terms of concentration.   Apart from relatively low levels of fat, which probably reflect the levels of lipid in the feed, the proximate composition of the eggs was similar to that reported by other workers (Takeuchi et al., 1981; Ridelman et al., 1984). The absence of any measurable difference between the eggs as far as proportional composition is concerned does not preclude a role for the absolute amounts of these materials in each egg, because ultimately each hatched fry will be solely dependent on this nutrient supply for its development. Experimental reductions of either mineral or fat levels in broodstock feeds for rainbow trout have been shown to decrease the quality of the eggs produced (Takeuchi et al., 1981). Bearing in mind that the modest difference in egg diameter between the treatment groups represent a 10% difference in volume, then it is possible that the additional amounts of material possessed by the larger eggs may be of selective advantage.

Certainly, like other workers (Bagenal, 1969b) we have shown that larger eggs produce larger fry and it is possible that, under adverse conditions as for example those experienced in the wild, these larger progeny might show better survivals. However, despite clear differences in size of the eggs and hatched fry of the two ration groups, there were no reductions in viability expressed on the basis of fertilization and eying rates of the eggs and mortality levels of the fry and fingerlings. The overall survival levels were also similar to those reported for other rainbow trout stocks (Ridelman et al., 1984). The absence of any reduction in viability of the developing eggs and hatched fry derived from small eggs supports the conclusion reached by Phillips and Dumas (1959) in their study of the brown trout that ample materials for viable embryo production exist even in the smallest egg.

In addition to the differences in egg number and size there was also a two week delay in spawning time in fish on half-ration. However, the failure of 11% of the low ration group to achieve maturity is probably of more significance. Delays of spawning and extensions of the interspawning interval after diet restriction have been reported for some multiple spawners (Wootton, 1982; Townshend and Wootton, 1984), whereas salmonids stocks appear to respond to lowered ration by reducing the overall percentage of maturing fish (Scott, 1962; Bagenal, 1969a). In the present work the fish on low ration which failed to spawn had a lower mean weight (0.68+0.05Kg) than the spawning members of this group. Low fish size may have also been the reason for the very low levels of maturity described by Scott (1962) for fish on both high and low rations.   Although, it is possible that a fish has to reach a certain weight before it can mature, from the present results, it would appear that size is not of importance in determining the timing of ovulation within the spawning spread of a stock.   This is in contrast to the results of Kato (1975) who suggested that it was the larger fish amongst stocks of rainbow trout which spawned first.

Turning now to the possible mechanisms by which the alterations in fecundity and/or egg size are achieved, it is apparent even from the most cursory examination of the ovary of fish throughout the year that enormous reductions in oocyte number occur during development.   In the present study up to 50,000 oocytes were present in the ovary a few weeks after ovulation but only 5-6000 of these would have been expected to reach full maturity at the following spawning.   Three mechanisms might account for these changes: the first involves atresia or the resorption of oocytes particularly those undergoing yolk incorporation; the second the recruitment of stage I-IV oocytes into vitellogenesis; and lastly the extent of oogonial multiplications.

Although the relative importance of these processes in determining fecundity and egg size may vary with different fish, in the rainbow trout the most significant change following a reduction in food was an increase in the level of atresia up to 22% of the total numbers of vitellogenic oocytes present in pre-spawning fish.   Much lower levels were found in the fish on full-ration.   Levels up to 27% were also reported by Scott (1962) even for the group of fish which were fed on the highest rations of food.   However, closer examination of the final weights of these fish would suggest that all the experimental and control groups were being subjected to restricted rations.   Vladykov (1956) described 80% and 45% reductions in oocyte numbers up to 1mm and 3.5mm in diameter respectively in the brook trout and again suggested that this reduction was due to atresia.   Levels of 27% atresia were also recorded for natural populations of the chubsucker although figures for individual fish ranged from 4-72% (Wagner and Cooper, 1963).   In contrast Henderson (1963) found far fewer atretic oocytes in the brook trout although the levels, averaging 4.0%, were of the same order as those found in the fish on full-ration in the present experiment, probably because both groups were maintained under equivalent hatchery conditions and fed to full-ration according to feed manufacturers' tables. It is clear that the levels of atresia reported here commonly occur in the rainbow trout in the months leading up to spawning. Furthermore, their alteration in response to reductions in ration suggests a physiological role for atresia in the determination of fecundity in the rainbow trout.

An effect of diet on the recruitment of oocytes is more difficult to assess from the present results primarily because the numbers of fish under experiment would not allow histological samples to be taken at more frequent intervals throughout the year and more specifically at the time of onset of vitellogenesis. Reductions in recruitment as a result of feeding low rations have been reported for the winter flounder (Tyler and Dunn, 1976), a cichlid (Townshend and Wootton, 1984) and Poecilia, an ovoviviparous fish (Hester, 1964). In contrast de Vlaming (1971) showed that starvation induced atresia in the yolky oocytes of the goby but did not affect recruitment. There was evidence from the present work that vitellogenesis was more advanced in the fish in full-ration. However, this apparent difference was probably due to an increase in the rate of maturation of these fish and the sampling of both groups on the same day. Vitellogenin and testosterone levels were significantly lower at spawning in the half-ration fish and although the reductions in size and number of eggs in these fish could be attributed to these serum changes, the relationship remains unclear. There were no changes in the proportion of eggs undergoing vitellogenesis in the full-ration fish despite the higher fecundities of this group and the presence in the pre-spawning ovaries of much higher numbers of yolky oocytes. One must conclude that effects on recruitment or the oogonial divisions, if present, must have occurred much earlier in the year-long cycle of ovarian development.

As a consequence of the parallel changes in total fecundity and egg size, there was an increase in relative fecundity i.e. the number of eggs per kilogram of body weight, in the fish on half-ration. The decrease in relative fecundity of the larger full-ration fish is partly explained by the increased size of their eggs. Other workers have also reported that larger fish often produce fewer eggs than would be expected from the regression of fecundity and fish size (Rounsefell, 1957; Nicholls, 1958). A probable explanation is that the rainbow trout and possibly other salmonids, produce a volume of eggs at stripping which bears a constant relationship to body weight and that reductions in either fecundity or egg size, possibly caused by alterations in diet, will involve corresponding increases in the other parameter. A similar conclusion regarding a 'trade off' between egg size and number was also reached by Rounsefell (1957) in his extensive review of the fecundity of North American Salmonidae. Although the production by the trout of a weight-related volume of eggs would not preclude direct effects of ration or nutrient on fecundity and egg size it might provide a finite range of egg size and number on which subsequent alterations in atresia or recruitment induced by nutritional and other environmental changes might be superimposed.

The presence of a reciprocal relationship involving egg size and number which can be modified by dietary change, together with the decrease in relative fecundity and increase in egg size with increased body weight are potentially of considerable commercial importance. Currently, salmonid eggs are sold by number and not by size and the potential production of a hatchery is determined by the total weight of broodstock which can be maintained on the farm. Under such constraints, an increase in the total numbers of eggs from the same weight of broodstock might be achieved by varying the feeding regime or by using more broodfish but of smaller size. Providing the consequent decreases in size of the eggs do not affect their viability or their acceptance for general sale, such approaches may confer considerable economic advantage.

In summary, the present results provide evidence for multiple effects on the fecundity, egg size and rate of maturation of rainbow trout. Further work is necessary to investigate the effects of varying nutrient composition in the diet and of different feeding rates at different times of the year.

V.   ACKNOWLEDGEMENTS

This work was supported by a NERC grant to N.B. and during the tenure of a Commonwealth Staff Scholarship to P.C.

REFERENCES

Bagenal, T.B. (1966). J. Mar. biol. Ass. U.K, 46, 161-186.
Bagenal, T.B. (1969a). J. Fish Biol. 1, 167-182.
Bagenal, T.B. (1969b). J. Fish Biol. 1, 349-353.
Bagenal, T.B. (1973). Rapp. P.-v. Reun. Cons. int.
  Explor. Mer 164, 186-198.
Baiz, M. (1978). Ecologia 3, 57-64.
Bayer, H. von (1950). Prog. Fish-Cult., 2, 105-107.
Bromage, N.R., Elliott, J.A.K., Springate, J.R.C. and
  Whitehead, C. (1984). Aquaculture (in press).
Elliott, J., Bromage, N. and Springate, J. (1984).
  Aquaculture (in press)
Fry, F.E.J. (1949). Biometrics 5, 27-67.
Gibson, R.J., Kerkhoven, P.C. and Haedrich, R.L. (1976).
  Naturaliste Can. 103, 417-423.
Henderson, N.E. (1963). J. Fish. Res. Bd Can. 20,
  899-908.
Hester, F.J. (1964). J. Fish. Res. Bd Can. 21, 757-764.
Hislop, J.R.G., Robb, A.P. and Gauld, J.A. (1978). J.
  Fish Biol. 13, 85-98.
Hodder, V.M. (1965). ICNAF Spec. Publ., 6, 515-522.
Hurk, R. van den and Peute, J. (1979). Cell Tissue Res.
  199, 289-306.
Kato, T. (1975). Bull. Fresh. Fish. Res. Lab. 25, 83-115.
Kuznetsov, V.A. and Khalitov, N. Kh. (1978). J.
  Ichthyol. 18,
  63-70.
Mackay, I. & Mann, K.H. (1969). J. Fish. Res. Bd Can.
  26, 2795-2805.
Martin, N.V. (1970). J. Fish. Res. Bd Can. 27, 125-146.
McFadden, J.T., Cooper, E.L. & Andersen, J.K. (1965).
  Limnol. Oceanog. 10, 88-95.
Nicholls, A.G. (1958). Aust. J. Mar. Freshwat. Res. 9,
  526-536.
Nikolskii, G.V. (1969). "Theory of Fish Population
  Dynamics as the Biological Background for Rational
  Exploitation and Management of Fishery Resources"
  (Translated by J.E.S. Bradley). Oliver & Boyd
  Edinburgh.
Phillips, A.M. and Dumas, R.F. (1959). Prog. Fish-Cult.
  21, 161-164.
Raitt, D.F.S. (1968). Mar. Res. 5, 1-24.
Ridelman, J.M., Hardy, R.W. and Brannon, E.L. (1984).
  Aquaculture 37, 133-140.

Robb, A.P. (1982).   J. Fish Biol. 20, 397–408.

Rounsefell, G.A. (1957).   Fish Bull. Fish. Wildl. Serv. U.S. 57, 451–468.

Scott, D.P. (1962).   J. Fish. Res. Bd Can. 19, 715–731.

Springate, J.R.C., Bromage, N.R., Elliott, J.A.K. and Hudson, D.L. (1984).   Aquaculture (in press).

Takeuchi, T., Watanabe, F.T., Ogino, C. Saito, M. Nishimura, K. and Nose, T. (1981).   Bull. Jap. Soc. Scient. Fish 47, (5) 645–654.

Townshend, T.J. and Wootton, R.J. (1984).   J. Fish Biol. 24: 91–104.

Tyler, A.V. and Dunn, R.S. (1976).   J. Fish. Res. Bd Can. 33, 63–75.

de Vlaming, V.L. (1971).   Biol. Bull. Mar. Biol. Lab. Woods Hole 141, 458–471.

Vladykov, V.D. (1956).   J. Fish. Res. Bd. Can. 13, 799–841.

Wagner, C.C. & Cooper, E.L. (1963).   Copeia 1963, 350–357.

Woodhead, A.D. (1960).   Proc. Nutr. Soc. 19, 23–28.

Wootton, R.J. (1973).   J. Fish Biol. 5, 89–96.

Wootton, R.J. (1982).   In "Reproductive Physiology of Fish", (C.J.J. Richter and L.M.J. Th Coos, eds.), 201–219. Pudoc. Wageningen.

IMPORTANCE OF THE STUDY OF BROODSTOCK NUTRITION FOR FURTHER DEVELOPMENT OF AQUACULTURE

TAKESHI WATANABE

Laboratory of Fish Nutrition, Tokyo University of
Fisheries, Tokyo 108, Japan.

I. INTRODUCTION

Up to the present more than 300 different species of finfish have been cultivated throughout the world, and the number of species produced is still increasing every year with the advance of rearing techniques and methods for mass production of live foods. Most fish seed comes from natural sources; these are clearly inadequate to supply the present and future needs of farmers in the world. In other words economically productive aquaculture is heavily dependent upon an adequate supply of seed, of fertile eggs and juvenile fish, with which to stock ponds, enclosures, and other cultivation systems. Thus one of the most important and fundamental approaches to aquaculture is to ensure a year-round, rather than a seasonal, supply of fertile eggs of high quality which produce high survival and growth rates.

For this purpose broodstock which produce such eggs must be cultivated. Nutrition is known to have a profound effect upon gonadal growth and fecundity. Although precise information on the nutritional requirements for gonadal maturation in broodstock is lacking, it has been generally agreed that quality and quantity of feed, as well as the feeding regime, are important for spawning and egg quality. However, research on broodstock has long laid emphasis mainly on other factors which affect gonad maturation and spawning behaviour such as induced spawning

NUTRITION AND FEEDING IN FISH
ISBN: 0 12 194055 1

by hormone injection, selective breeding and
hybridization, and environmental factors such as
temperature, hours of daylight (photoperiod), stocking
density, and rainfall. Nutritional requirements of
broodstock during gonad development may possibly differ
from those of young fish. Little information is
available on broodstock nutrition, although brief accounts
of recent work are provided by Takeuchi et al. (1981b),
Watanabe et al. (1984a,b,c,d,e) and Yu et al. (1979).

The purpose of this review is, therefore, to summarize
and discuss recent advances in knowledge of broodstock
nutrition and to indicate the necessity for further
research on detailed nutritional requirements of
broodstock. For the initiation of studies on the
nutrition of broodstock it is necessary to determine
whether or not spawning and egg quality are influenced by
nutritional quality of broodstock diets. Recent studies
have indeed demonstrated that the reproduction of rainbow
trout and red sea bream is greatly affected by the
nutritional quality of broodstock diets. The present
review is mainly based on the results obtained in these
species.

II.   AYU FISH Plecoglossus altivelis

The nutritional requirement of broodstock Ayu for
vitamin E was investigated by Takeuchi et al. (1981a).
Vitamin E plays an important role in reproductive
physiology in fish as it does in birds and mammals.
Takeuchi et al. examined the effects of dietary vitamin E
on its distribution in fish body, on spawning,
hatchability of eggs and mortality of the hatched fry.
This was done by feeding Ayu fish with diets containing
different levels of vitamin E, ranging from 1 to 239 mg of
vitamin E per 100 g diet for about 3 months before
spawning. It was found that the duration of spawning
behaviour was different from group to group, although
there were little difference in growth, feed efficiency
and mortality of the fish due to dietary levels of vitamin
E. In the group fed on the lowest vitamin E diet, one
third of total female broodstock did not spawn, while the
broodstock in the other groups completed their spawning.
The survival rate to eyed stage of the fertilized eggs
from the former broodstock was the lowest (46.6%) as was

hatchability. In addition, the mortality of hatched larvae from these eggs was highest among the experimental groups. The authors concluded that dietary vitamin E transported to the eggs greatly helped survival of the young; the requirement of Ayu broodstock for vitamin E was estimated to be 3.4 mg per 100g diet.

The importance of vitamin E for reproduction of fish was also confirmed in other species such as carp (Watanabe and Takashima, 1977), rainbow trout (Kinumaki et al., 1972) and red sea bream (Watanabe et al., 1984f,g). The concentration of vitamin E is, in general, high in eggs and low in tissues of broodstock after spawning, suggesting some physiological function of this vitamin in spawning, fertilization and hatching. This is also supported by the high concentration of egg vitamin E being rapidly consumed during egg development in chicks (Higashi et al., 1970) and salmonid fish (Kinumaki et al., 1972; Watanabe et al., unpublished data). In the study by Takeuchi et al. (1981a) the vitamin E level in the fish fed on the diet containing 3.4 mg of vitamin E was lower than that in wild fish, and a dietary vitamin E level of more than 10 mg/100g was recommended if the levels in wild fish are to be reached.

As with vitamin E, fatty acid distribution in eggs is readily affected by dietary lipids. Shimma et al. (1977) compared fatty acid distribution in the eggs of Ayu broodstock fed diets containing single cell protein (SCP) with those from wild Ayu. The proportion of 18:3ω3 and 20:5ω3 was higher in the latter eggs, suggesting that, if eggs from wild fish are superior to those from cultured fish, then lipids rich in these fatty acids should be supplied in broodstock diets. The same difference in fatty acids between wild and cultured Ayu has been observed by many workers (Ohshima et al., 1982; Hirano and Suyama, 1983; Hirano, 1984). The percentage of 18:3ω3 and 20:5ω3 in wild Ayu, was derived mainly from the attached diatom they ate, and these fatty acids were carried over to their eggs.

Recently, Watanabe et al. (unpublished data) examined the effect of broodstock diets on spawning and on the chemical components in the eggs of Ayu. Feeding a diet without supplemental phosphorus resulted in the lowest growth of fish together with the lowest egg production. It did not however result in any marked difference in the proximate composition nor in proportions of different lipid classes in the eggs produced by each group of experimental broodstock fed diets of different nutritional quality. Even the concentration of phosphorus in the eggs together withu Ca and ash was not markedly different as a consequance of the phosphorus–deficient diet; this contrasts with results obtained on red sea bream (Watanabe et al., 1984b). Fatty acids in the Ayu eggs were, however, reflected by dietary fatty acids, although precise information on relationship between fatty acid distribution in eggs and their quality is lacking.

Nutritional studies on fish like Ayu which grow to fully matured broodstock in a year should be conducted intensively, for studies on other species of fish are time consuming, as they require at least two years to reach gonadal maturation and spawning.

III. CARP Cyprinus carpio

The weight of the gonad and gonad–somatic index of carp which had been fed on α-tocopherol deficient diet for 17 months were significantly lower than those of control fish (Watanabe and Takashima, 1977), gonad–somatic index ranged from 0.7 to 2.0% compared with 10 to 20% in control fish. This suggests that reproductive disorders were induced by a lack of α-tocopherol and is in agreement with the results of histological studies. In the deficient ovaries none of the oocytes accumulated yolk–granules or yolk-vesicles. In the study of vitamin E requirements in fish, experiments have mainly been done on young fish or fingerlings, however, these results on broodstock carp demonstrate that α-tocopherol deficiency retarded oocyte development - essentially the same effect as that observed in mammals; they showed also that α-tocopherol is indispensable for successive development of oocytes in carp. The tocopherol deficiency revealed basically the same histological changes as those recognized in carp fingerlings, for example apparent muscular dystrophy characterized by a marked loss of flesh from the back.

Tocopherol greatly affected gonadal growth of carp. The average weight of ovaries and gonad–somatic index were respectively 68.1 and 14.1 in the control fish, but 6.3 and 3.3 in deficient fish. The chemical components in ovary were also greatly affected by tocopherol deficiency. In the ovaries from the deficient fish moisture levels ranged from 76–82%, compared to 63–66% in the control fish. These considerably higher levels of moisture were reflected in significantly lower levels of

both protein and lipid.   The average percentage of polar
lipids in the ovary was 5.6% in the control group and 1.8%
in the deficient group.   This reduced level of polar
lipid in the deficient ovaries may be closely related to
the retardation of oocyte development.   The most marked
change in fatty acid composition was the absence of $18:2\omega6$
level   and   increase   in $18:1\omega9$ and $20:3\omega9$ in   both
triglyceride and polar lipid fractions in the deficient
ovaries.   These changes in fatty acid pattern are very
similar to those seen in essential fatty acid (EFA)
deficiency in both fish and mammals.   Thus the depletion
of tocopherol from the diet was found to exert significant
effects on the pituitary–ovarian system and this clearly
indicates that α–tocopherol plays an important role in
reproductive physiology in fish.   The significance of
α–tocopherol in the reproduction of fish must be analysed
more precisely to establish actual dietary requirements of
broodstock, although the requirement of fingerlings or
young fish for this vitamin is relatively low (Watanabe et
al., 1970; Cowey et al., 1983; Watanabe et al., 1981).

   Shimma et al. (1977) examined the effect of diets on
the reproduction of common carp by feeding them diets
containing, respectively, fish meal, methanol–grown single
cell   protein   (SCP)   and   ethanol–grown   SCP   as   protein
sources   for   2   years.   The   hatching   rate   in   the   eggs
produced by individual experimental broodstock fluctuated
largely from fish to fish ranging from 50 to 24%, thus the
effect of the feeds was not clear other than for some
cases where a relationship between the rate of hatching
and   fatty   acid   distribution   in   eggs   was   observed.
Hatchability was low in the eggs containing less than 10%
by   weight   of $22:6\omega3$,   and   the   authors   suggested   a
relationship between   the   rate   of   hatching   and   the
proportion of $22:6\omega3$ in eggs of carp.   The requirement for
$22:6\omega3$ for normal hatching was estimated to be about 20%
by weight, although an optimum amount of $22:6\omega3$ in eggs
for maximum hatching was not determined.

   Fatty acid distribution in egg lipids, especially 3
highly unsaturated fatty acids (HUFA) such as $20:5\omega3$ and
$22:6\omega3$, may possibly be used as one criterion of egg
quality as with an EFA index.   But attention must also be
paid to the fact that, in the case of rainbow trout and
red sea bream, even eggs high in HUFA content were of low
quality as described later.

IV. RAINBOW TROUT Salmo gairdneri

Fat-soluble vitamin needs of rainbow trout broodstock were investigated by Kinumaki et al. (1972) by examining the distribution of the vitamins in broodstock tissues, eggs and hatched fry, after feeding them with diets containing different levels of the vitamins for 7 or 8 months. A diet containing 800 IU of supplementary vitamin A per 100g diet did not result in any deposition of the vitamin, but a marked accumulation in liver and other tissues of the broodstock did occur when the diet contained more than 10,000 IU per 100g diet. The vitamin was transferred to the eggs and the level in fry just after hatching was 0.6-1.2 IU per fry, decreasing during the hatching process. Vitamin D level in mature eggs was 0.15-0.71 IU per egg and was not much affected by dietary levels of the vitamin. Dietary vitamin E was also observed to be efficiently transferred to eggs and fry: its level in mature eggs was 4.4-5.1 g per egg in broodstock given a vitamin E deficient diet, compared with 21.5-35.4 g per egg in other groups. There was little change in concentration of the vitamin in the egg during hatching and floating. From these results suitable levels of these vitamins in diets for broodstock were estimated as 1,000-2,000 IU of vitamin A and more than 10mg of vitamin E per 100g diet; the requirement of broodstock rainbow trout for vitamin D appeared lower than for either of these vitamins, although quality of eggs produced by each experimental broodstock was not evaluated in this experiment.

No difference in growth, prespawning mortality, egg development, or egg hatchability were observed when two diets, one containing 90 mg DL-α-tocopheryl acetate/kg diet and the other lacking α-tocopherol were given to rainbow trout broodstock. The concentration of α-tocopherol in the eggs differed significantly between the treatments only during December (King et al., 1983). The analytical results indicate that the fish had sufficient tissue stores of α-tocopherol at the start of the study to supply the needs of developing ovaries without further dietary supplementation.

The influence of diet composition on the chemical composition of hens eggs was also extensively investigated (Neber, 1979). As a group, the fat-soluble vitamins are transferred from the diet of the laying hen to the egg with some facility. The liver plays an important role in the uptake of dietary trace nutrients and their subsequent release to other body tissues and to the ovary for egg yolk deposition.   Intermediate storage of a nutrient in the liver may alter the pattern of egg deposition by moderating the increase in egg content of the nutrient in response to increased dietary concentration of the nutrient. High liver storage levels of a nutrient will also tend to stabilize egg content of that nutrient by nutrient release from the liver during periods of restricted nutrient intake.   Thus the pattern of nutrient distribution in broodstock liver may prove to be useful as a criterion of quality of eggs to be hatched.

Recently the effect of variation in dietary level of protein, vitamins, lipids and minerals on reproduction of broodstock has been extensively studied in salmonid fish. Takeuchi et al. (1981b) have carried out nutritional experiments on rainbow trout in which fingerlings (3.5g live weight) were grown at natural water temperatures (5-20°C) for 3 years and given either a commercial diet (43-47% crude protein) or one of three experimental diets (two of these were low protein/high energy diets, 33-35% crude protein, 390 kcal/100g and the other contained no trace element supplement).   Average gain over the period was 1.5 kg except for the trout given the diet lacking a trace metal supplement (these gained 1 kg on average). During this time the fish spawned twice but quality of eggs was examined only at the second spawning as eggs produced at the first spawning are usually of low quality.   At this second spawning there were no differences between treatments in egg production per female (approximately 3,000), egg diameter (average 5.2 mm), the proportion of eggs reaching the eyed stage (90%) and the proportion hatching (87%) other than for trout given the diet lacking supplementary trace minerals. The respective values for that group were 2,000 eggs/female, 5.1 mm egg diameter, 3.7% of eggs reaching the eyed stage and 0.4% hatching (Table I).   These results demonstrate that a diet containing a lower protein content than that normally employed but with a high energy level is as effective for both fingerlings and broodstock of rainbow trout as the more conventional diets of high protein content.

These results also indicated that the requirement of rainbow trout for EFA had not changed throughout their life cycle, because the dietary EFA were present only in amounts which satisfy the EFA requirement of fingerling rainbow trout (Castell et al., 1972; Watanabe et al.,

Table I. Effects of low-protein diets of high-calorie content and of deletion of trace elements from the fish meal diet on the spawning and the quality of eggs of rainbow trout (the results from 2nd. spawning in January, 1980).

	Total number of egg production	Average egg diameter (mm)	Eyed rate (%)	Total Hatch (%)
Commercial diet	3,631±836*	5.3±0.25	89.0±4.3	87.2±3.7
Low protein-high calorie (beef tallow 5%)	3,954±1,006	5.2±0.29	90.5±4.9	87.4±1.0
Low protein-high calorie (beef tallow 7%)	3,050±1,156	5.1±0.12	86.2±6.3	86.3±6.3
No trace metal supplement	1,975±342	5.1±0.00	3.7±5.0	0.4±0.9

* Mean ± SD (n=3-12).

1974; Watanabe and Takeuchi, 1976; Takeuchi and Watanabe, 1977) but they were adequate throughout this long-term feeding experiment. By contrast a trace metal supplement in the diet is shown to be indispensable for reproduction of rainbow trout. Of the mineral analyses the most striking change was in manganese concentration, this fell from 4.1 g/g eggs in females given a commercial diet to 1.6 g/g eggs in females given the experimental diet lacking a trace metal supplement. The significance of this metal for reproduction is not known.

In a second experiment with rainbow trout by Watanabe et al. (1984e), broodstock were given experimental diets for only 3 months prior to spawning. Four of the treatments were used to examine further the effects of protein and energy balance on egg quality. It was confirmed that broodstock given a diet containing 36% crude protein and 18% lipid performed as well as those given a diet with 46% crude protein and 15% lipid. It was also shown that beef tallow used at a level of 7% as an energy source had no adverse effect on the reproduction of rainbow trout. A similar result was also obtained by Roley (1983). The dietary protein requirement for maximum growth was between 37 and 47% in a diet containing

2.8 kcal metabolizable energy/g.   Dietary protein level did not affect prespawning mortality, spawning success or the duration of spawning, and also did not have a significant effect on the absolute or relative number of eggs spawned, relative egg size or embryo survival.

Table II. Quality of eggs produced at the first spawning

	Total number of egg production[*1]	Average egg diameter (mm)[*2]	Eyed rate[*3] (%)	Total hatch[*3] (%)
Control (18:2ω6)	1,937	5.04	88.4	82.4
EFA-deficient	1,429	4.92	53.9	46.4

*1 Average value of 6 fish.
*2 20 eggs were used for determination.
*3 Two broodstock were pooled for analysis in each determination.

Watanabe et al. (1984e) also examined the effect of EFA deficiency on the reproduction of rainbow trout broodstock. As anticipated the use of partially defined diets deficient in EFA led to much the lowest values for total egg production, percentage of eyed eggs produced and total hatch (Table II). It is of particular interest that addition of linoleic acid, 18:2ω6 to the EFA deficient broodstock diet led to marked improvement in percentage of fertilization, percentage of eyed eggs and total hatch compared with broodstock given diets lacking EFA. Linoleic acid is known to be inferior to linolenic acid, 18:3ω3 as an EFA for rainbow trout fingerlings but the situation seems different with broodstock.   Feeding the EFA-deficient diet did not lead to any increase in the abnormal polyenoic acid "20:3ω9" in either liver of broodstock or eggs produced. This fatty acid is usually seen in fingerling rainbow trout fed a diet deficient in EFA.   However, the fatty acid distribution in sperm was found to be affected by the EFA-deficiency, quite differently from the eggs.   The EFA-deficient diet resulted in an increased level of 20:3ω9 in the lipid of sperm and the level was effectively reduced by feeding

Table III. Fatty acid distribution in eggs and sperm produced by rainbow trout broodstock fed on a diet deficient in EFA or a diet containing ethyl linoleate (18:2ω6) as EFA (the results of the first spawning).

Fatty acid	Egg				Sperm	
	EFA-deficient		18:2ω6		EFA-deficient	18:2ω6
	Polar	TG	Polar	TG	Total	Total
12:0	1.0	12.1	1.0	7.5	-	-
14:0	3.2	7.9	2.8	6.2	3.2	3.2
16:0	16.3	12.4	15.8	13.1	21.9	22.2
16:1	4.7	10.7	3.4	9.2	4.7	2.1
18:0	10.2	2.6	11.7	3.1	5.2	5.0
18:1	18.9	32.9	15.4	29.1	25.3	13.0
18:2ω6	5.2	5.0	6.5	12.0	3.4	10.1
18:3ω3	0.3	0.3	-	0.3	-	-
20:1	3.1	2.4	2.6	2.6	1.6	0.5
20:2ω6	2.7	0.9	3.8	2.4	0.7	1.7
20:3ω9	-	-	-	-	2.0	0.9
20:3ω6	4.0	1.2	4.8	2.4	2.0	2.9
20:4ω6	3.1	0.7	7.1	2.2	3.6	12.2
20:4ω3	0.2	0.2	-	tr	-	-
20:5ω3	2.7	0.9	1.8	-	5.5*	4.8*
22:1	-	0.3	-	1.0	-	-
22:5ω6	tr	tr	tr	tr	1.4	6.9
22:5ω3	1.5	0.6	1.1	0.5	1.5	1.1
22:6ω3	20.7	6.3	15.9	4.4	18.1	12.2
Σω6	16.8	8.3	27.7	21.6	11.1	33.8
Σω3	24.5	8.4	18.9	6.3	25.1	18.1

* The concentration of 20:5ω3 in sperm of other groups ranged from 11.1 - 17.9% in contrast with 4.0 - 7.1% in eggs.

18:2 ω6 (Table III). In addition the percentage of 20:5ω3 was characteristically high in the sperm lipid. A further experiment is necessary to clarify whether the difference in fatty acid distribution in sperm lipids is responsible for activity of spermatozoa and affects rate of fertilization or proportion of eyed eggs.

Thus EFA play important roles in reproduction of fish. The eggs with a low content of 22:6ω3 from the EFA-deficient broodstock gave low rates of fertilization

and hatchability as had been observed previously in the
eggs of carp (Shimma et al., 1977). However, the eggs
from the broodstock receiving ethyl linoleate were also
low in percentage of 22:6ω3 but their egg quality was not
different from those of the control group. This suggests
that the role of 22:6ω3 in egg quality is not unique but
may possibly be replaced by 20:4ω6, although it depends
upon fish species. In this context it is of considerable
interest that rainbow trout have been grown through a
generation using a semipurified diet containing 1%
linolenic acid as the sole dietary EFA (Yu et al., 1979).
However, the eggs produced contained a small amount of
arachidonic acid 20:4ω6. This demonstrates that the
trout broodstock had tenaciously retained the small
amounts of ω6 fatty acids present in the incompletely
extracted diet ingredients such as casein, dextrin and
gelatin. It remains possible that there is a small but
absolute requirement for ω6 fatty acids in rainbow trout.

Rainbow trout eggs produced by broodstock receiving
normal diets have, in general, high rates of both eyed egg
production and hatchability, thus it is difficult to
evaluate whether or not quality of eggs is improved by
changes in composition of diets. Recently, two batches
of eggs from the same broodstock have been obtained in one
year. This has been achieved in rainbow trout by
adjustment of the endocrine balance through variation in
photoperiod regime. However, eggs released in spring or
summer are low in quality, their hatchability being about
60%. Elevation of this value to that obtained in winter
eggs is a problem requiring urgent solution. It is not
yet known whether nutritional status of broodstock is a
factor.

V.   RED SEA BREAM Pagrus major

Among the marine species mass-produced in Japan red sea
bream is the most important and popular, and the total
production has markedly increased following establishment
of techniques for natural spawning and mass production of
live foods. Reproduction and egg quality have also been
found to be deeply affected by the nutritional value of
the diets.

In the first experiment red sea bream broodstock were
given experimental diets for approximately 5 months in
floating net cages in the sea, and then were transferred

to spawning tanks in the aquarium for the investigation of
spawning and quality of eggs (Watanabe et al., 1984a).
Five of the treatments were used to examine the effect of
diets low in protein, low in available phosphorus and of
EFA–deficient diets; in addition the relative values of
white fish meal and of cuttlefish meal as sources of
protein were compared. The results of natural spawning
by red sea bream broodstock fed respectively diets of
different nutritional quality are shown in Table IV. In
the case of red sea bream the percentage of buoyant eggs,
floating on the water surface, is very important for
evaluation of egg quality (Yamaguchi 1975). Buoyant eggs
have, in general, high rates of hatching and normal
development. On the other hand, deposited eggs, sinking
to the bottom of tanks, consist mainly of unfertilized or
dead eggs. As shown in Table IV, in the broodstock fed
on the control diet (diet 1, white fish meal diet with 45%
of crude protein) the average number of eggs produced
during the experimental period was 100.5×10^4 per fish,
80.9% of these eggs were buoyant. These values in the
control group are almost equivalent to those obtained by
two–year–old red sea bream broodstock at usual fish
farms. In the group fed the low–protein diet (diet 2) or
the diet without supplemental phosphorus (diet 3) values
were lower than those in the control. The proportion of
buoyant eggs produced by the EFA–deficient broodstock
given the corn oil diet rich in 18:2 6 was the lowest
recorded among the experimental groups, more than 75% of
eggs produced were deposited, in marked contrast to
rainbow trout broodstock mentioned above. Values for
both parameters were highest in the group receiving the
diet containing cuttlefish meal as a protein source
(173.5×10^4 eggs per fish, 88.5% being buoyant).
Abnormal eggs with more than 2 oil globules (normal red
sea bream eggs possess, in general, one oil globule)
amounted to as much as 70.7, 67.9 in the groups fed the
low–protein, the phosphorus–deficient and the
EFA–deficient diets, respectively, in comparison with
30.7% in the control group. The rate of hatching was
also significantly lower in these eggs (Table IV). The
eggs produced by the females given diet containing
cuttlefish meal, mainly consisted of normal buoyant eggs
with a high rate of hatching, leading to high productivity
of viable larvae as fish seed.

These results have demonstrated a close relationship
between nutritional quality of broodstock diet and
reproduction of red sea bream, although the effect of the

Table IV. Effect on the spawning and egg quality of red
sea bream <u>Pagrus major</u> of broodstock diets of different
composition.

	1 Control	2 Low protein	3 Low phosphorus	4 EFA deficient	5 Cuttle- fish meal
Egg					
Eggs produced (x10^4/fish)[*1]	100.5	72.7	84.1	116.5	173.5
Buoyant egg[*1] (%)	80.9	54.4	62.1	23.9	88.5
Abnormal egg[*2] (%)	30.7	70.7	67.9	93.7	2.7
Av number of oil globules	1.7	3.5	3.1	6.2	1.0
Hatched larvae					
Rate of hatching (%)	69.4	23.6	26.3	0.9	93.9
Deformity (%)	23.3	84.1	75.5	-	1.9
Normal larvae (%)	62.4	3.8	6.2	-	97.6
Final productivity of fish seed from total eggs produced (%)	24.3	0.1	0.3	-	78.9

[*1] Normal eggs floating on the water surface.
[*2] Eggs with more than 2 oil globules.

duration of the period over which diets are fed, which may
greatly affect gonadal maturation and spawning, were not
clear in this experiment. In red sea bream it is well
known that acceptable diets are actively eaten by the
broodstock   even   during   spawning   and   that   feeding
broodstock with krill, Mysis, shrimp, crab wastes and so
on results in pigmentation of eggs produced within a
matter of hours. This suggests that the nutritional
value of the diet given to broodstock shortly before
spawning may affect the results of spawning. It also
indicates that pigments and other fat-soluble materials in
diets are easily incorporated into eggs and quality of
eggs may possibly be improved by feeding broodstock with
some fat-soluble nutrients such as EFA and vitamins.
Trials   were   conducted   with   salmonids   to   enhance
pigmentation in both skin and eggs by feeding them

crustacean pigments, but no clear evidence was obtained as
to whether or not egg quality is improved by pigmentation
(Kitamura, 1978).

The position has been studied by Watanabe and his
colleagues (Watanabe et al., 1984d). They used
broodstock that had been reared on diets containing either
55% protein (from fishmeal) and 10% lipid (3% cuttlefish
oil and the remainder from fishmeal) or 45% crude protein
(a mixture of fishmeal and cuttlefish meal) and 10% lipid
(3% cuttlefish oil and remainder from both the meals)
until shortly before spawning. At this point some of the
broodstock were transferred to diets containing one or
other of carotenoid pigments (ß-carotene 0.1%,
canthaxanthin 0.3%), krill oil extract (9%; containing
astaxanthin mono- and di-esters) or corn oil (at a level
of 10% and replacing cuttlefish oil), some of the
broodstock were given raw krill and others maintained on
the original diet (Table V). Supplementation of diets
with ß-carotene and canthaxanthin or with krill oil
extract led to a slight decrease in total number of eggs
produced but the percentage of buoyant eggs increased from
49.1% to 56.4% and 69.6% respectively in the fish given
diets supplemented with pigments. Feeding frozen raw
krill led to marked improvements in both total eggs
produced and percentage of buoyant eggs. However, the use
of large amounts (10%) of corn oil in the diet resulted in
a marked reduction in the proportion of buoyant eggs
produced (Table V). Abnormalties in the number of oil
globules in the eggs (% of eggs with more than 2 oil
globules) were effectively reduced by the use of pigments,
krill oil extract or frozen raw krill. The effect was
most marked in the latter treatment where the percentage
of abnormalities was 8.1% compared with the original value
of 77.5% in the high protein group. In eggs from
broodstock fed the diet containing corn oil, abnormalities
in number of oil globules increased to 94%. Rate of
hatching (83.1%) was not improved by addition of
ß-carotene and canthaxanthin (77.4%) or krill oil extract
(67.5%) but abnormality in the number and position of oil
globules in the hatched larvae was reduced to very low
levels. Consequently, the proportion of normal larvae
obtained was increased from 51.6% in the original high
protein diet to 74.3% (ß-carotene and canthaxanthin
supplemented diet) and 88.2% (krill oil extract) in these
treatments. The value obtained for those broodstock
given frozen raw krill -91.2%- was even more striking. By
contrast in the broodstock fed on the diet containing 10%

Table V. Effect of broodstock diets of different composition on the spawning and egg quality of red sea bream.

	High protein	Fish meal +Cuttlefish meal	β-Carotene + canthaxanthin	Krill oil extract	Frozen raw krill	Corn oil
Egg						
Eggs produced (x10^4/fish)	149.5	121.6	120.4	90.1	202.1	58.7
Buoyant egg [1] (%)	49.1	68.6	56.4	69.6	82.7	18.2
Abnormal egg [2] (%)	77.5	22.1	37.0	20.9	8.1	94.0
Av number of oil globules	2.4	1.5	1.8	1.2	1.1	3.4
Hatched larvae						
Rate of hatching (%)	83.1	93.7	77.4	67.5	90.3	27.3
Deformity (%)	14.8	4.7	15.0	8.4	2.0	43.2
Normal larvae (%)	51.6	82.2	74.3	88.2	91.2	24.0
Final productivity of fish seed from total eggs produced (%)	21.1	52.8	39.1	41.4	68.1	1.2

[1] See Table 4.
[2] Eggs with more than 2 oil globules.

corn oil only 24% of normal larvae were produced.

Thus nutritional quality of diets given to broodstock of species like red sea bream which can accept diets actively even during spawning is seen to be important and may affect reproduction and egg quality greatly. Frozen raw krill was especially suitable as a food for red sea bream at this time. The superior results (over krill oil extract, and pigments) obtained by its use suggest that other factors, in addition to pigments, contribute to its value - perhaps quality and ease of digestion of protein. The deleterious effect of diets containing corn oil at a level of 10% may partly reflect the accumulation of linoleic acid in the eggs and the inability of this species to convert it to $20:4\omega6$. It cannot be inferred that small quantities of the latter fatty acid are not useful or even desirable in the diet of broodstock red sea bream. The results do indicate a need for careful balance of EFA in broodstock diets.

The metabolism of dietary carotenoids in eggs in this experiment was also investigated (Miki et al., 1984). Levels of carotenoids incorporated in the eggs were approximately 60 g/100g irrespective of the amount and kind of carotenoid supplemented in the diet, and only keto and non-esterified carotenoids were detected in the eggs. Dietary canthaxanthin was transferred into eggs but not ß-carotene, and astaxanthin esters were converted largely to non-esterified astaxanthin and partly to doradexanthin. Idoxanthin present in the eggs was presumed to be derived from non-esterified astaxanthin in the diets. In contrast to the integumentary carotenoids of red sea bream the composition of which has been shown to be fairly complex (Fujita et al., 1983), the composition of the egg carotenoids was rather simple.

The egg quality was improved by enhancing incorporation of carotenoids into the eggs, but no carotenoids were detected in the high quality eggs of broodstock fed on the cuttlefish meal diet. This suggests that carotenoids fulfill some physiological function such as antioxidant rather than their being an absolute need for the pigment itself.

The effect of carotenoids on survival of eggs and alevins of salmonids has also been studied by many workers. The relationship between the carotenoid content and quality is not so far resolved. Deufel (1965) reported that dietary canthaxanthin improved egg production and rate of fertilization in rainbow trout. Salmonids mobilise their carotenoid pigments, astaxanthin and canthaxanthin, in the flesh and deposit them in eggs and skin during sexual maturation. This active metabolism of carotenoids suggests a specific function either during reproduction, early life, or both. From this viewpoint Torrissen (1983) conducted an experiment with Atlantic salmon. Differently pigmented eggs and alevins were incubated in darkness and exposed to light of different wavelength. Highly pigmented eggs were found to be sensitive to light. In darkness there was no significant effect of the carotenoid level on survival of eggs and alevins. Diets supplemented with synthetic astaxanthin and canthaxanthin promoted growth during the early feeding period. The function of carotenoids in reproductive physiology clearly requires further analysis.

Watanabe et al. (1983) conducted a further experiment to clarify the effect of the duration of the period over which diets are fed and to reconfirm the dietary value of cuttlefish meal and raw krill for red sea bream broodstock. The percentage of buoyant eggs was again effectively improved by replacement of cuttlefish liver oil with krill oil extract. Addition of 200 mg of DL-α-tocopheryl acetate (VE) to the control diet also resulted in an elevation of the value from 42.7 to 77.9%. These results suggest that incorporation of fat-soluble materials such as VE and astaxanthin or phospholipids into eggs by broodstock is effective in improving spawning. On the other hand, substitution of cuttlefish liver oil by corn oil again resulted in deterioration of egg quality. A harmful effect of 18:2ω6 on the spawning of red sea bream is confirmed in this experiment. While in the eggs produced by the broodstock fed on the diet containing cuttlefish meal as a protein source, the percentage of buoyant eggs was as high as 98.4%, highest among the experimental groups, almost all the eggs produced being available as seed for mass propagation of juvenile fish. Feeding broodstock with frozen raw krill resulted in elevation of the percentage. The value was also found to be improved from the original value of 30.6% to 91.7% by feeding frozen raw krill shortly before the initiation of spawning after separation from the broodstock which had been given the corn oil diet. In the previous experiment quality of eggs from the broodstock, which had been given a nutritionally high quality diet, decreased markedly when they were fed the corn oil diet even for a short period before spawning; this experiment in which raw krill was fed after the corn oil diet provided a converse response. The total quantity of fish seed produced by each experimental broodstock calculated from numbers of buoyant eggs, the rate of hatching and the percentage of normal larvae was lowest in the corn oil group, and was effectively improved by feeding raw krill just before spawning. The proportion of normal larvae, obtained from total egg production, was about 26% in the control group, and was improved to 58.4 and 65.0% by addition of 200 mg of VE or replacement of cuttlefish liver oil with krill oil extract. The value was as high as 92% in the cuttlefish meal group.

Thus the indications that nutritional quality of diets given to broodstock shortly before spawning affect reproduction greatly was verified and, in fish such as red sea bream, which can accept diets actively even during spawning, the quality of diets fed to broodstock during spawning becomes very important for their reproduction and egg quality. Frozen raw krill was again shown to be suitable as a food for red sea bream broodstock from this viewpoint.

Finally Watanabe et al. (1984f) fractionated both cuttlefish meal and krillmeal into fat-soluble and nonfat-soluble fractions to identify the effective components in both meals for reproduction of red sea bream. The effective components for the reproduction of red sea bream were found mainly in the non-lipid fraction in cuttlefish meal and in the lipid fraction of krill meal, although the principal factors involved were not identified. The effectiveness of VE and krill oil including polar and nonpolar fractions on the reproduction of red sea bream suggest common factors between them such as antioxidants. Further experiments will be necessary to identify the effective components e.g. by comparing the chemical composition of the non-lipid fractions of cuttlefish meal with that of white fishmeal or the two fractions, polar and nonpolar, of krill oil. In addition feeding experiments with diets containing different levels of polar and nonpolar lipid fractions will be needed.

Until comparatively recently, little research has been directed toward broodstock nutrition. More research effort is now required on broodstock nutrition together with physiological, genetic and environmental areas for further advancement of fish production.

VI.   ACKNOWLEDGEMENT

The author expresses here his sincere thanks to Dr. C.B. Cowey, N.E.R.C. Institute of Marine Biochemistry, Aberdeen, Scotland, who kindly read the manuscript and gave valuable suggestions.

REFERENCES

Castell, J.D., Sinnhuber, R.O., Wales, J.H. and Lee, J.D. (1972).   J. Nutr. 102, 77–86.

Cowey, C.,B., Adron, J.W., Walton, M.J., Youngson, A. and Knox, D. (1981).   J. Nutr. 111, 1556–1567.

Deufel, J. (1965).   Archiv. für Fish. 16, 125–132.

Fujita, T., Satake, M., Watanabe, T., Kitajima, C., Miki, W., Yamaguchi, K., and Konosu, S. (1983).   Bull. Japan. Soc. scient. Fish. 49, 1855–1861.

Higashi, H., Nakamizo, S., Ozaki, N., Terada, K., Kagaya, K. and Nakahira, T. (1970).   Vitamins 42, 1–17.

Hirano, T. and Suyama, M. (1983).   Bull. Japan. Soc. Scient. Fish. 49, 1459–1464.

Hirano, T. (1984).   Food-chemical studies on the quality of cultured Ayu.   Doctoral Thesis), Kyoto University.

King, I., Hardy, R.W. and Halver, J.E. (1983).   Abstracts of the International Symposium on Salmonid Reproduction. Seattle, Washington, p. 24–25.

Kinumaki, T., Sugii, K., Iida, H. and Takahashi, T. (1972).   Bull. Tokai Reg. Fish. Res. Lab. 71, 133–160.

Kitamura, S. (1978).   In "Carotenoids of Aquatic Animals" (Japan. Soc. scient. Fish. eds.), 132–141.   Suisangaku series NO. 25, Koseisha-Koseikaku, Tokyo.

Miki, W., Yamaguchi, K., Konosu, S. and Watanabe, T. (1984).   Comp. Biochem. Physiol. 77B, 665–668.

Neber, E.C. (1979).   Poultry Science 58, 518–528.

Ohshima, T., Widjaja, H.D., Wada, S. and Koizumi, C. (1982).   Bull. Japan. Soc. Scient. Fish. 48, 1795–1801.

Roley, D.D. (1983).   Abstracts of the international Symposium on Salmonid Reproduction, Seattle, Washington, p. 25.

Shimma, Y., Suzuki, R., Yamaguchi, M. and Akioyama, T. (1977).   Bull. Freshwater Fish. Res. Lab. 27, 35–48.

Shimma, Y., Ikeda, K. and Murayama, T. (1980).   Bull. Natl. Res. Inst. Aquaculture 1, 61–69.

Takeuchi, T. and Watanabe, T. (1977). Bull. Japan. Soc. scient. Fish. 43, 947-953.

Takeuchi, M., Ishii, S. and Ogiso, T. (1981). Bull. Tokai Reg. Fish. Lab. 104, 111-122.

Takeuchi, T., Watanabe, T., Ogino, C., Saito, M., Nishimura, K. and Nose, T. (1981). Bull. Japan Soc. scient. Fish. 47, 645-654.

Torrissen, O. (1983). Pigmentation of salmonids: Effect of carotenoids in eggs and start feeding diet on survival and growth rate. Abstracts of the International Symposium on Salmonid Reproduction, October 30-November 2, Seattle, Washingston, p. 21.

Watanabe, T., Takashima, F., Ogino, C. and Hibiya, T. (1970). Bull. Japan. Soc. scient. Fish. 36, 972-976.

Watanabe, T., Takashima, F. and Ogino, C. (1974). Bull. Japan. Soc. scient. Fish. 40, 181-188.

Watanabe, T. and Takeuchi, T. (1976). Bull. Japan. Soc. scient. Fish. 42, 893-906.

Watanabe, T., Takeuchi, T., Wada, M. and Uehara, R. (1981). Bull. Japan. Soc. scient. Fish. 47, 1463-1471.

Watanabe, T. & Takashim, F. (1977). Bull. Japan. Soc. scient. Fish. 43, 819-830.

Watanabe, T., Koizumi, T., Suzuki, H., Satoh, S., Takeuchi, T., Yoshida, N., Kitada, T. and Tsukashima, Y. (1983). Annual Meeting of Japan. Soc. Sci. Fish. October 1983, Abstract p. 91.

Watanabe, T., Arakawa, T., Kitajima, C. and Fujita, S. (1984a). Bull. Japan. Soc. scient. Fish. 50, 495-501.

Watanabe, T., Ohhashi, S., Itoh, A., Kitajima, C. and Fujita, S. (1984b). Bull. Japan. Soc. scient. Fish. 50, 503-515.

Watanabe, T., Itoh, A., Kitajima, C. and Fujita, S. (1984c). Bull. Japan. Soc. scient. Fish. 50, 1015-1022.

Watanabe, T., Itoh, A., Murakami, A., Tsukashima, Y., Kitajima, C. and Fujita, S. (1984d). Bull. Japan. Soc. scient. Fish. 50, 1023-1028.

Watanabe, T., Takeuchi, T., Saito, M. and Nishimura, K. (1984e). Bull. Japan. Soc. scient. Fish. 50, 1207-1215.

Watanabe, T., Satoh, S., Takeuchi, T., Yoshida, N., Kitada, T. and Arakawa, T. (1984f). Annual Meeting of Japan. Soc. Sci. Fish. October 1984, Abstract p.20.

Yamaguchi, M. (1975). Tai-Yoshoku no Kiso to Jissai, Ist ed. Koseisha-Koseikaku, Tokyo, pp. 133-150.

Yu, T.C., Sinnhuber, R.D. and Hendricks, J.D. (1979). Lipids, 14, 572-575.

RECENT ADVANCES IN VITAMIN NUTRITION AND METABOLISM
IN FISH

JOHN E. HALVER

School of Fisheries, University of Washington,
Seattle, Washington 98195, U.S.A.

I. INTRODUCTION

New knowledge has accumulated in the past five years on
the specific quantitative water-soluble and fat-soluble
vitamin requirements of fish with respect to different
fish species, fish size, and environment in which they are
reared. Much of this information has been summarized in
two recent U.S. National Academy of Sciences, National
Research Council bulletins on Nutrient Requirements of
Coldwater Fishes (NAS/NRC 1981), and Nutrient Requirements
of Warmwater Fishes and Shellfishes (NAS/NRC 1983). A
summary of vitamins required for cultivated salmonids was
printed in 1982 (Halver, 1982) which contained a table on
vitamin requirements of coldwater fishes, test diets for
vitamin studies, and a table on signs of vitamin
deficiences in salmonids. The FAO manual on Fish Feed
Technology contained more extensive descriptions of
general physiological and biochemical functions of the
water-soluble vitamins and included discussions of
techniques to minimize loss of these during fish feed
manufacturing techniques (FAO, 1980). A more complete
description of vitamin chemistry can be found in the
treatise Fish Nutrition (Halver, 1972).
Exciting new data have appeared in the role of
water-soluble vitamin intake and fish health with respect
to disease vectors or other stressors which fish encounter
in freshwater or saltwater fish husbandry. Macro-

NUTRITION AND FEEDING IN FISH
ISBN: 0 12 194055 1

components of fish diet formulations influence the need for several water-soluble vitamins and more information has been developed on carbohydrate intake level and thiamin and niacin requirements, on inter-relationship between tocopherols and polyunsaturated fatty acids in the diet, on the nature and type of ascorbate in the diet and environmental pollutants of fish pathogens, and on amelioration of aflatoxicosis by increased intake of either vitamers C or vitamers K.

II. WATER SOLUBLE VITAMINS

A. Thiamin requirement and metabolism

Thiamin pyrophosphate is required for the decarboxylation of pyruvic acid and of alpha-ketoglutaric acid in the metabolism of carbohydrates and lipids. It is also involved in tissue transketolase activity which is essential for direct oxidative cellular metabolism of glucose. Morito and Hilton (1984) have suggested that the rainbow trout requirement for thiamin was not over 2 milligrams thiamin per kilogram feed. This is within the NAS/NRC recommendations and is higher than that reported for channel catfish fingerlings by Murai and Andrews (1978) and by Aoe et al. (1967) for carp, and is similar to the thiamin requirement of turbot reported by Cowey et al. (1975). Carp and catfish utilize dietary carbohydrate as an active energy source, whereas many carnivorous fish such as salmonids, turbot, tuna and sea bream metabolize carbohydrates less efficiently (Hilton and Atkinson, 1982; Lin et al., 1978). The original work of Brin (1962) to use erythrocyte transketolase activity as a measure of thiamin nutritional status (Brin, 1966) has been adequately demonstrated as applicable to thiamin status in several species of fish (Cowey et al., 1975; Halver, 1982; Morito and Hilton, 1984). Thiamin is one of the more labile vitamins and the pyrimidine and thiazole moieties can be severed by the thiaminase present in tissues of certain fresh fish and molluscs, or the vitamin rendered inactive by excessive heat during feed mixing, compaction, or extrusion (FAO, 1980). Therefore, it is prudent to ensure a thiamin content of 10 to 15 milligrams per kilogram diet in most fish feed preparations. Lower levels may be used with impunity in catfish or carp diet preparations, but carnivorous coldwater species need high levels for nutrient safety in fish production. Table I indicates levels of water-soluble vitamins which should be present in some fish diets. Table II lists vitamin deficiency signs observed in fish hatcheries or on fish farms.

Table I. Recommended levels of water soluble vitamins for coldwater carnivores (mg/kg dry diet)

Vitamin	Recommended level
Thiamin	5-10
Riboflavin	5-15
Pyridoxine	5-10
Pantothenic acid	10-20
Nicotinic acid	100-150
Biotin	0.5-1
Folic acid	2-5
Vitamin B_{12}	0.01-0.02
Choline	2000-3000
Myo-inositol	200-400
Ascorbic Acid	100-800

B. Riboflavin requirement and metabolism

Riboflavin functions in flavoprotein enzymes and is present in prosthetic groups of many enzymes involved in oxidation-reduction reactions. Stimulation of erythrocyte glutathione reductase activity has been used as a sensitive biochemical measurement of riboflavin status in animals (Tillotson and Sauberlich, 1971) and has been found applicable to measure riboflavin status in fish (Hughes, 1980; Hughes et al., 1981). Woodward has suggested that D–amino acid oxidase, a flavin dependent enzyme, is a more sensitive indicator of riboflavin status (Woodward, 1982). The role of this vitamin in inter-mediary metabolism of salmonid fish has been summarized by Walton and Cowey (1982) and Woodward (1984). Trout requirements for riboflavin appear to be between 5 and 10 milligrams per kilogram dry diet, but maximum liver storage levels in salmonids are not achieved until at least 10 milligrams riboflavin per kilogram dry diet are fed.

Hughes and Rumsey (1984) have reviewed the many causes for lenticular cataracts induced by several nutrient deficiences, including riboflavin, as one major vector for the disease. Comparative descriptions of other eye diseases induced by deficiences or imbalance of thiamin, methionine–cystine, zinc, tryptophan, or vitamers A were also described.

C. Pyridoxine requirement and metabolism

Pyridoxal phosphate is the coenzyme of many amino-transferases. Since pyridoxine requirement is related to protein intake, adequate pyridoxine in the diet is essential for good fish health and rapid fish growth. Young trout and salmon require between 5 and 10 milligrams of pyridoxine per kilogram diet, and marine fish appear to have a higher requirement when high protein diets are fed (Halver, 1982; Jurss, 1978). Alanine aminotransferase activity in erythrocytes is a good assay technique to measure pyridoxine status (Jurss, 1978).

D. Pantothenic acid, niacin, biotin, folic acid, and vitamin B_{12}

Pantothenic acid requirements and metabolism have been reviewed recently (Halver, 1982). Similar discussions were included for niacin, biotin, folic acid, and vitamin B_{12}. The NAS/NRC bulletins have good discussions on deficiency signs for both subclinical or gross clinical manifestations of the water–soluble vitamin deficiencies. The recommendations for requirements for these water-soluble vitamins have not been modified and diets manufactured to contain the levels recommended have produced salmonids in both freshwater and marine environments without the appearance of gross or subclinically detectable vitamin deficiencies. These recommendations for dietary content of the water-soluble vitamins are listed in Table I.

Table II. Signs of vitamin deficiences

Nutrient	Clinical	Subclinical
Water-soluble vitamins		
Thiamin	Poor growth, anorexia, hyperirritability, convulsions, edema	Low transketolase activity in erythrocytes and kidney, loss of equilibrium, increased pyruvate in muscles
Riboflavin	Impaired growth, anorexia blindness	Lens cataract, adhesion of lens and cornea, impaired activity or erythrocyte glutathione reductase and D-amino acid oxidase
Pyridoxine	Poor growth, anorexia, epileptiform convulsions, hyperirritability, lowered resistance to handling, erratic spiral swimming, rapid breathing and gasping, flexing of opercles, rapid onset of rigor mortis	Reduced muscle and erythrocyte amino transferase
Pantothenic Acid	Poor growth and survival, anorexia, clubbed, exudate-covered gills	Artophied pancreatic acinar cells, vacuoles and hyaline bodies in kidney tubules
Niacin	Poor growth and feed conversion, anorexia, skin lesions, anemia, muscle spasms	Colon lesions, NAD or NADP enzyme systems impaired
Biotin	Reduced growth and feed conversion, increased mortality, degeneration of gill lamellae, skin lesions ("blue slime")	Reduced liver acetyl CoA carboxylase and pyruvate carboxylase, altered fatty acid synthesis, lipid infiltration of liver, degeneration of pancreatic acinar cells; glycogen storage in kidney tubules
Folic Acid	Slow growth, anorexia, poor feed conversion, anemia, pale gills	Large, immature, segmented erythrocytes, limited proerythrocytes in anterior kidney
B_{12}	Anemia, fragmented erythrocytes	Small erythrocytes, low hemoglobin
Choline	Impaired growth, poor feed conversion	Fatty livers, reduced cholinesterase
Inositol	Anorexia, reduced growth, anemia	
Ascorbic Acid	Lordosis, scoliosis, lethargy, hemorrhagic exophthalmia, ascites, anemia, intramuscular hemorrhage, petechial hemorrhage, other scurvy symptoms	Reduced concentrations of ascorbic acid in liver and anterior kidney, abnormal histology of support cartilage in eye, gill, and fin, reduced serum thyroid hormone (T3), elevated plasma cholesterol and triglycerides

Continued

Table II. Signs of vitamin deficiencies – continued

Nutrient	Clinical	Subclinical
Fat-soluble vitamins		
A	Impaired growth, exophthalmos, eye lens displacement, edema ascites, depigmentation	Corneal thinning and expansion, degeneration of retina
D	Poor growth, tetany of white skeletal muscle	Impaired calcium homeostasis
E	Reduced survival and growth, anemia, ascites	Immature erythrocytes, poikilocytosis, variable-size erythrocytes, anisocytosis, erythrocyte fragility and fragmentation, nutritional muscular dystrophy, exudative diathesis, lipid peroxidation
K	Prolonged blood clotting, anemia	Reduced hematocrit, visceral and fin hemorrhage

E. Vitamers C, requirements and metabolism

Ascorbic acid is required for numerous hydroxylation reactions in fish metabolism. A review of ascorbate metabolism in fish has recently been published (Tucker and Halver, 1984a). Impaired hydroxylation of lysyl and prolyl groups in procollagen, as it is secreted by fibroblasts, results in classical symptoms of scurvy. Subclinical, impaired collagen formation can occur before the onset of clinical signs of scurvy. The hydroxyproline to proline ratio is a useful indicator of vitamin C deficiency in fish at an early stage of development. The mechanical strength of connective tissue is dependent upon cross linking of collagen and elastin, this is dependent upon the activity of lysyloxidase which is also regulated by ascorbate.

The dietary requirement of salmonids for ascorbic acid depends upon several factors, including fish size, the growth rate, other dietary components and stressors for the fish under production. An apparent requirement of 100 milligrams of L–ascorbic acid per kilogram diet may be increased to 500 to 1000 milligrams when the fish are wounded or are under severe stress. A description of the apparent requirement of L–ascorbic acid necessary to promote maximum wound repair was reviewed by Halver (1982) and by Tucker and Halver (1984a, 1984b).

Mixed function oxidases are involved in the catabolism of xenobiotics, toxicants, steroids, and drugs. Induction of mixed function oxidase activity is directly related to ascorbate concentrations in the media (Zannoni et al., 1982). An increased tolerance by fish to environmental pollutants has been observed when tissue stores of ascorbate are high. Effects of pesticides, PCB, DDT, heavy metal, and toxaphene poisoning are diminished when ascorbate intake is high. Dietary ascorbic acid facilitates absorption of iron in the gut, and spleen iron levels are affected by ascorbate tissue levels.

Ascorbic acid is rapidly oxidized to dehydroascorbic acid, and can be reduced back to L-ascorbic acid to conserve total ascorbate in fish tissues. An active dehydroascorbate reductase has been reported in trout liver and kidney. The ratio of reduced L-ascorbic acid to dehydroascorbic acid may reflect or control cell biosynthetic processes. In salmonids, dietary L-ascorbic acid is readily converted to ascorbate-2-sulfate, a chemically stable form of ascorbate, which is stored in connective tissue throughout the body (Halver, 1982; Tucker and Halver, 1984a, 1984b). Benitez and Halver (1982) have shown that over 90% of dietary ascorbate can be converted into the ascorbate-2-sulfate and that an enzyme system, ascorbate-2-sulfohydrolase, exists in fish tissues which can readily convert ascorbate-2-sulfate back to L-ascorbic acid for oxidation-reduction reactions in the tissues. This ascorbate-2-sulfatase is inhibited by L-ascorbic acid, and therefore serves as a modulator to control the levels of circulating ascorbic acid in the tissues and with the complementary ascorbate-2-sulfate sulfosynthetase serves to conserve excess L-ascorbic acid by converting it into tissue stored ascorbate-2-sulfate. Ascorbate-2-sulfate is then available to maintain essential levels of ascorbic acid in the circulatory and intracellular tissue systems.

Further recent work (Tucker and Halver, 1984b) has shown that the total ascorbate pool in young growing fish is present in three compartments similar to the ascorbate pools in man. One pool is a rapidly exchanging pool between dietary intake and liver levels of ascorbic acid. A second is a slowly exchanging pool reflected by ascorbate-2-sulfate levels in the tissues, and the third pool is a slowly exchanging pool reflected by the ascorbate concentrations of the brain. The total body pool estimates reflect the dietary ascorbic acid intake. Isotope dilution analysis has shown that the total ascorbate is directly related to the ascorbic acid intake. Since ascorbate sulfatase is a glycoprotein, it will be

associated with cell membranes where ascorbic-2-sulfate
hydrolysis may occur.   The half life of ascorbic acid in
rainbow trout fed a low ascorbic acid diet for 3 months
and then transferred to a repletion diet was shown from
excretion analysis to be approximately 40 days (Tucker and
Halver, 1984b).   However the half life of ascorbate in
trout tissues varies with nutritional status as shown by
results in Table III, the half life in each organ except
brain being inversely proportional to dietary intake of
ascorbate (Tucker and Halver, 1984b).

Table III. Effect of dietary ascorbic acid intake on half
life (days) of radioactivity from [1^{14}C) ascorbic acid
given orally.

No. of feeds* per week	Tissue			
	Liver	Head kidney	Skin	Brain
12	30	20	20	—
3	70	80	100	140

*   Feed contained 100 mg vitamin C/kg dry diet

Previous   feeding   studies   have   shown   that
ascorbate-2-sulfate and L-ascorbic acid are effective in
equimolar   concentrations   for   meeting   the   vitamin   C
requirements of young trout and salmon (Halver et al.,
1975).   Ascorbate-2-sulfate is chemically stable and is
not lost during processing of fish diets during the air
exposure,   during   mixing,   or   the   heat   treatments
encountered during compaction or extrusion.   The large
losses   of   L-ascorbic   acid   which   occur   during   these
processes suggest that it would be advantageous to use
ascorbate-2-sulfate   for   fish   feed   formulations   whenever
stable content of vitamin C is necessary.   The vitamers C
include   L-ascorbic   acid,   dehydro-ascorbic   acid,   and
ascorbate-2-sulfate,   and   can   be   called   vitamin C_1,
dehydro C, and vitamin C_2 for trivial nomenclature.
     Vitamin C requirements for fish cannot be easily
defined. A requirement for rapid growth of 100 milligrams
per   kilogram   dry   diet   under   pristine   environmental
conditions may be increased to 5 to 10 fold when the fish

are exposed to environmental contaminants, physical or environmental stress or exposure to fish pathogens. Li and Lovell (1984) have shown that mortality rates of fish experimentally infected with a pathogen can be decreased when increased levels of dietary L-ascorbic acid are fed. Mortality rates ranged from all fish succumbing when fish were fed an ascorbic acid deficient diet to no mortality when fish were fed up to 10 to 20 times the apparent requirement for L-ascorbic acid. Antibody response also reflected dietary ascorbic acid intake at high levels of L-ascorbic acid in the diet. Significantly higher antibody production and complement activity was observed. These studies were conducted with channel catfish, but the principles may be extended to other fish husbandry systems. Therefore, vitamin C requirements should be increased to potentiate maximum resistance of fish to environmental stressors, to fish pathogens, and to pollutants which may inadvertently contaminate the water supply. Requirements of L-ascorbic acid should therefore be increased to a minimum of 300 milligrams per kilogram dry diet, and further increased to 1000 milligrams per kilogram dry diet, when fish are exposed to known pathogens or environmental stressors. Since ascorbic acid is rapidly lost upon processing and more slowly lost upon storage, equivalent amounts of vitamin C_2 or ascorbate-2-sulfate should be considered in the diet formulation to assure maintenance of adequate and projected amounts of this vitamin in the diet.

F. Choline and inositol requirements and metabolism

Choline is a desirable methyl donor in methylation reactions in intermediatory metabolism. Since it is involved in acetyl-coenzyme A activity to form the neurotransmitter, acetylcholine, and is also involved in phospholipid formation, large amounts of this nutrient are required for growth of all fish reared in fish farming. Clinical deficiency signs are listed in Table II. Recommendations for dietary levels can be found in Table I. The requirements will vary with growth rate, methionine and cystine intake, and type of lipid ingested by the fish. A summary of choline requirements and metabolism is included in recent reviews Halver, 1982; NAS/NRC 1981, 1983).

Inositol is a structural component of living tissues and is normally present in adequate amounts in most fish diet preparations. Some agricultural commodities contain water-insoluble phytin which is a complex calcium-magnesium salt of inositol hexaphosphate, the inositol can not be released from this complex by gut enzymes and so is not available for growth or metabolic requirements. Inositol requirements have been reviewed by Halver (1979).

G. Para-aminobenzoic acid

P-aminobenzoic acid is a constituent of pantothenic acid and thus is not specifically required by any finfish studied. Synthesis of pantothenic acid by gut bacteria in fishes has not been reported for any species in amounts necessary for normal growth and metabolism. Therefore, supplementation of fish diets with p-aminobenzoic acid is not warranted and will only serve to promote gut flora division and growth.

III.   FAT SOLUBLE VITAMINS

A. Vitamers A

The efficacy of beta-carotene to satisfy the vitamin A requirement of salmonids is dependent on water temperature. Salmonids can utilize precursors of vitamin A at 12-15°C, but only small amounts of the ß-carotene are hydrolyzed at temperatures below 10°C (Poston et al., 1977). The enzyme which oxidizes ß-carotene to retinol in the intestinal mucosa is apparently restricted at temperatures below 10°C. Therefore the potency of ß-carotene as a source for vitamin A is dependent on water temperature. Hypervitaminosis vitamin A can be encountered when intake exceeds 1 million international units of vitamin A per kilogram of diet (Poston et al., 1966). Poston and Livingston (1971) have reviewed the levels of vitamin A which cause necrosis of the caudal fin, reduced growth, low hematocrit, and reduced body fat and liver size in trout. Therefore requirements for vitamin A should be monitored and kept between 2000 and 4000 international units of vitamin A per kilgram diet. Recommended levels for coldwater carnivore diets are listed in Table IV.

Table IV.   Recommended levels of fat soluble vitamins for coldwater carnivores (I.U./kg dry diet)

Vitamin	Recommended level
Vitamers A	2000 to 3000
Vitamers D	2000 to 3000
Vitamers E	20 to 40
Vitamers K	5 to 10

B. Vitamers D

Vitamin D_3 is the precursor of the hormone, 1,25-dihydroxy D_3 which is the biologically active form of the vitamin; it facilitates absorption of calcium ions from the gastrointestinal tract. A deficiency of vitamin D in salmonids is difficult to induce because of the absorption of calcium through the gill membranes into the bloodstream.   Thus, salmonids can sequester adequate amounts of calcium from the environment to satisfy most of the calcium requirements.   In low ionic strength water however, a requirement for vitamin D becomes apparent, and impairment of calcium homeostasis is manifested by subclinical or clinical signs of tetany in the white muscle fibres.   In addition, an increase in plasma triiodothyronine has been reported (Leatherland et al., 1980).   An estimate of the vitamin D requirement can be placed at about 200 international units of vitamin D_3 per kilogram diet.   Five hundred to 1000 times this intake will result in hypercalcium calcemia and some liver necrosis;   therefore, it is prudent to add about 2000 international units of vitamin D per kilogram dry diet for fish feed preparation, but it is necessary to restrict excessive intake of fish liver oils, which contain large amounts of vitamin D, in order to prevent subclinical or clinical hyper-vitaminosis D.

C. Vitamers E

Many tocopherols with vitamin E activity occur in fats and oils. Each tocopherol has different biological activity with D-α-tocopherol the most biologically active. These tocopherols act as lipid-soluble intracellular antioxidants to limit oxidation of polyunsaturated fatty acids present in the biological membranes. Oxidative degradation of these membranes impairs cell membrane permeability and consequently, efficiency of cell function. Therefore, the dietary requirement for the vitamers E depends upon the type and amount of polyunsaturated fatty acids in the diet, and in addition, upon the level of other antioxidants present in the fish tissues. The enzyme glutathione peroxidase protects against peroxidative degradation and contains one atom of selenium per molecule of enzyme protein. Ascorbic acid also acts synergistically with vitamin E and glutathione peroxidase activity in preventing damaging, uncontrolled peroxidations. The deficiency signs of vitamin E hypovitaminosis have been reviewed (Halver, 1982) and include many signs of cell membrane functional loss. Fragility and fragmentation of erythrocytes lead to anemia, susceptibility to loss on handling, oedema, and dystrophy of the skeletal muscle bundles. Hypervitaminosis E can also occur when one or more grams of tocopherol per kilogram diet is fed. The tocopherol requirement lies between 10 and 30 international units per kilogram diet, and is correlated with the amount and type of polyunsaturated fat fed to the fish. Some natural tocopherols occur in fish fats, and larger amounts are present in vegetable oils such as corn oil or soybean oil. Vitamin E supplements should, therefore, be at about 30 milligrams of added tocopherol per kilogram diet for most salmonid diets which contain 6 to 15 percent fat in the ration.

King (1984) has recently shown that vitamers E measured as D-α-tocopherol are rapidly mobilized into developing oocytes in maturating rainbow trout females. She reported all necessary tocopherol was present in developing ova at least 3 months prior to spawning. No deficiences in egg maturation, hatchability, or in yolk-sac absorption and fry development were observed, and tocopherol levels were adequate until feeding of fry was initiated. Therefore, vitamin E supplementation must be focused upon early maturation of the female fish, and is less critical during final maturation and spawning activity (King, 1984).

D. Vitamers K

The vitamin K compounds are naphthoquinones, and are involved in electron transport and oxidative phosphorylation reactions. Salmonids require vitamin K for the synthesis of prothrombin and thromboplastin, which are involved in blood coagulation. Vitamin K is readily synthesized by microflora in terrestrial animals, but these naphthoquinones have not been detected in appreciable amounts in the intestines of coldwater carnivores. Menadione is a chemically synthesized compound with biological vitamin K activity. Vitamin K is also required as a cofactor for microsomal enzyme systems that carboxylate glutamyl residues to γ-carboxyl-glutamic acid in other proteins of the blood coagulation cascade. Requirements for menadione or menadione sodium bisulfate have been reported at 0.5 to 1 milligram per kilogram of diet, but even 2 grams per kilogram diet of the menadione did not adversely affect growth or induce hypervitaminosis K (Poston, 1971); therefore, fish diets generally are designed to contain about 5 to 10 milligrams of vitamin K per kilogram diet to assure normal blood clotting mechanism. A recent observation on aflatoxicosis in channel catfish has indicted higher amounts of vitamin K may reduce the hemorrhages commonly encountered with aflatoxin intake (Griffith, 1984). Channel catfish ingesting 100 to 300 parts per billion of crude aflatoxin had hemorrhagic fins, pale livers, and acute anemia. These same fish fed 50 to 100 milligrams of menadione bisulfate per kilogram diet showed a rapid improvement in hemopoiesis and a return to normal hematocrit and red blood cell count within one week after the vitamin K supplementation. Fish fed the diet with 10 milligrams vitamin K per kilogram diet and the aflatoxin contamination continued to die from anemia and blood loss through the hemorrhagic fins. One symptom of acute afla-toxicosis is the massive hemorrhagic effect encountered in trout, salmon, and other fish susceptible to the fungal toxin. At intermediate levels of aflatoxicosis, increased blood clotting time and petechial hemorrhages occur throughout the intraperitoneal cavity and into the musculature. Additional intake of vitamin K can ameliorate this hemorrhagic effect of aflatoxins in other fish besides the channel catfish. Table IV lists the fat-soluble vitamin requirements of coldwater carnivores.

IV. CONCLUSIONS

Water-soluble and fat-soluble vitamin requirements vary with fish size, species, environment, age, and state of maturation. Requirements for maximum growth under optimum conditions can be increased 3-10 fold under other conditions of stress or disease. Techniques have been developed, however, which can be used to assay biological activity and to determine the true nutritional status and metabolic health of these animals reared in fish husbandry.

REFERENCES

Aoe, H., Masuda, I., Saito, T. and Komo, A. (1967). Bull. Jap. Soc. Sci. Fish. 33, 355-360.

Benitez, L.V. and Halver, J.E. (1982). Proc. Natl. Acad. Sci. USA 79, 5445-5449.

Brin, M. (1962). Ann. N.Y. Acad. Sci. 98, 528-535.

Brin, M. (1966). In "Methods in Enzymology, IX Carbohydrate Metabolism", (W.A. Wood, ed.) 506-514. Academic Press, N.Y.

Cowey, C.B., Adron, J.W. and Knox, D. (1975). Br. J. Nutr. 34, 383-390.

FAO/UNDP ADCP/REP (1980). Fish Feed Technology, FAO Press, Rome, 395pp.

Griffith, W. (1984). Personal communication.

Halver, J.E. (1972). "Fish Nutrition". Academic Press, N.Y. 490 pp.

Halver, J.E. (1979). In "Finfish Nutrition and Fishfeed Technology", (J.E. Halver and K. Tiews, eds.) 1, 45-58. H. Heenemann GmbH and Co., Berlin.

Halver, J.E. (1982). Comp. Biochem. Physiol. 73B, 43-50.

Halver, J.E., Smith, R.R., Tolbert, B.H. and Baker, E.M. (1975). Ann. N.Y. Acad. Science 258, 81-102.

Hilton, J.W. and Atkinson, J.L. (1982). Br. J. Nutr. 47, 597-607.

Hughes, S. (1980). M.S. Thesis. Cornell University.

Hughes, S.G., Rumsey, G.L. and Nickum, J.G. (1981). Prog. Fish-Cult. 43, 167-172.

Hughes, S.G. and Rumsey, G.L. (1984). Prog. Fish-Cult. In press.

Jurss, K. (1978). Comp. Biochem. Physiol. 61B, 385-389.

King, Irena (1984). Personal communication.
Leatherland, J.F., Barnett, B.J., Cho, C.Y. and Slinger,
    S.J. (1980a). Env. Biol. Fish. 5, 167–173.
Li, Y. and Lovell, R.T. (1984). J. Nutr. In press.
Lin, H., Romsos, D.R., Tack, P.I. and Leveille, G.A.
    (1978). Comp. Biochem. Physiol. 59A, 189–191.
Morito, C.L. and Hilton, J.W. (1984). J. Nutr. In press.
Murai, T. and Andrews, J.W. (1978). J. Nutr. 108, 176–180.
National Academy of Sciences/National Research Council
    (1981). Nutrient requirements of coldwater fishes.
    Academy Press, Washington, D.C. 63 pp.
National Academy of Sciences/National Research Council
    (1983). Nutrient requirements of warmwater fishes and
    shellfish. Academy Press, Washington, D.C. 102 pp.
Poston, H.A. (1971). Fish. Res. Bull. No. 34, 41–42. St.
    of N.Y. Conser. Dept., Albany, N.Y.
Poston, H.A. and Livingston, D.L. (1971). The influence
    of dietary levels of protein and vitamin A on the liver
    vitamin A level, lipid metabolism and growth of brook
    trout. Fish. Res. Bull. No. 34, 27–34. St. of N.Y.
    Conserv. Dept., Albany, N.Y.
Poston, H.A., Livingston, D.L., Pyle, E.A. and Phillips,
    A.M. (1966). Fish Res. Bull. No. 29, 20–24. St. of
    N.Y. Conserv. Dept., Albany, N.Y.
Tillotson, J.A. and Sauberlich, H.E. (1971). J. Nutr.
    101, 1459–1466.
Tucker, B.W. and Halver, J.E. (1984a). Nutr. Rev. 42,
    173–179.
Tucker, B.W. and Halver, J.E. (1984b). J. Nutr. 114,
    991–1000.
Walton, M.J. and Cowey, C.B. (1982). Comp. Biochem.
    Physiol. 73B, 59–79.
Woodward, B. (1982). J. Nutr. 112, 908–913.
Woodward, B. (1984). J. Nutr. In press.
Zannoni, V.G., Holsztynska, E.J. and Lau, S.S. (1982). In
    "Ascorbic acid: Chemistry, metabolism and uses", (P.
    Seib and B. Tolbert, eds.) 349–368. Am. Chem. Soc.,
    Washington, D.C.

STANDARDIZATION OF THE NUTRITION OF FISH
IN AQUATIC TOXICOLOGICAL TESTING[1]

DAVID A. BENGTSON[2], ALLAN D. BECK[3] and
KENNETH L. SIMPSON[2]

[2]Department of Food Science and Technology,
Nutrition and Dietetics, University of Rhode Island,
Kingston, Rhode Island 02881, USA.

[3]U.S. Environmental Protection Agency.
Environmental Research Laboratory,
Narragansett, Rhode Island 02882, USA.

I. TOXICITY TESTS: A BRIEF OVERVIEW

In the past few decades, increased public concern with
environmental pollution has led to legislation and the
formation of government agencies to regulate the addition
of contaminants to the environment.   Research is required
to provide the scientific data that support the agencies'
regulatory activities. One very important aspect of this
research is toxicity testing of both individual chemicals
and complex effluents using living organisms.   The
testing is done not only by government laboratories, but
also by industrial and contract laboratories.   In a
toxicity test, groups of organisms are exposed to
different toxicant concentrations and their responses
(mortality, growth, reproduction, behaviour, etc.) are

[1]   Contribution Number 2233 from the University of
Rhode Island Agricultural Experiment Station and
Contribution Number 639 from the Environmental
Research Laboratory, Narragansett.

observed, quantified and compared with responses of organisms in a control treatment, not exposed to the toxicant. Toxicity tests can be generally subdivided into two categories, short-term, or acute, tests and long-term, or chronic, tests.

Historically, most toxicity tests conducted with aquatic organisms have been acute 48-h or 96-h exposures to a single chemical. The toxicant concentration necessary to kill 50% of the organisms (LC50) was calculated and provided a relative measure of the toxic properties of the chemical. Many of the tests were conducted with juvenile or adult organisms under static conditions. Feeding of the test organisms was prohibited not only during the test, but also for two days prior to it, in order to ensure the physiological similarity of the test organisms and to prevent fouling of the water. The philosophy and protocol of not feeding organisms during acute tests is still maintained (ASTM, 1980), even though the emphasis has switched to flow-through tests. Thus, consideration of the nutrition of the test organisms has been limited to ensuring that test organisms are not manifestly diseased or abnormal at the start of the test.

More recently, researchers have observed that larval organisms are often more sensitive to toxicants than their juvenile or adult stages and have also realized the importance of long-term sublethal toxicant effects. Toxicity testing has evolved to the point that longer term tests and tests utilizing larval organisms require that the organisms be fed during the test. One example of this evolution is the fish early life-stage (ELS) test (see, e.g., Woltering, 1984). ELS tests usually begin with 24-h old embryos that are placed in several toxicant concentrations plus a control. The test includes embryonic development, hatching, larval development and metamorphosis to the juvenile stage and can last from 28 to 120 days depending on species. Both survival and growth of the fish (i.e. both lethal and sublethal effects) are recorded. (In life-cycle tests with fishes and invertebrates, reproduction is measured in addition to survival and growth).

In order to ensure the interlaboratory comparability and legal defensibility of toxicity test data, standard methods for their conduct are being developed under the auspices of the American Society for Testing and Materials (ASTM) and the Organization for Economic Cooperation and Development (OECD). In the draft documents presently under consideration, it is recommended that fish in an ELS test be fed brine shrimp nauplii (Artemia), rotifers, or commercially available prepared diets, depending on the fish species used. Available evidence, some of which is presented below, shows that diet can significantly affect the results of toxicity tests and that such broad recommendations may be insufficent to ensure standardization of toxicity tests.

II. EFFECTS OF NUTRITION IN TOXICOLOGICAL TESTING

The Committee on Laboratory Animal Diets, in a report to the U.S. National Academy of Sciences (NRC, 1978), stated that: "The role of animal nutrition as an experimental variable has been overlooked for too long. Adequate, controlled nutrition for laboratory animals is essential to the reproducibility of data, and in the long run it results in a net saving of time and money. The Committee believes that few if any other factors can influence the results of a study as profoundly as diet." Although written with regard to mammalian species, their conclusions apply to fish species as well.

Mehrle et al. (1974) fed six prepared diets to separate groups of juvenile rainbow trout (Salmo gairdneri) for six weeks prior to their use in a 96-h acute toxicity test with chlordane. The LC50 values for the groups of fish varied more than five-fold, from 8.2 μg/l to 47 μg/l. In particular, the fish fed a synthetic low-protein diet were significantly more sensitive than fish fed a high protein diet. Mehrle et al. (1977) later found that a) when juvenile rainbow trout and bluegills (Lepomis macrochirus) were fed two different diets during a 30-day chronic toxicity test, one diet caused both species to be more sensitive to the PCB Arochlor 1254 than did the other diet; b) dietary methionine concentration caused significant differences in the toxicity of DDT and dieldrin to adult rainbow trout in a chronic test; c) increased vitamin C in the diet of juvenile channel catfish (Ictalurus punctatus) increased their tolerance in a chronic test with toxaphene.

Several other studies, both short- and long-term, have been conducted on dietary effects in toxicological tests with rainbow trout. Phillips and Buhler (1979) fed fingerlings on tubificid worms or a commercial pelleted diet during chronic exposure to a sublethal concentration

of dieldrin.   The fish fed tubificids had reduced fat
elaboration and reduced body concentrations of dieldrin
than the fish fed pellets.   Yamamoto et al.   (1981) showed
that increased dietary L-ascorbic acid resulted in
decreased copper uptake in an 18-week chronic exposure to
that metal.   Increased carbohydrate content in the diet
resulted in nearly a 2-fold increase in copper toxicity in
a short-term test (Dixon and Hilton, 1981).   Two commercial
diets led to significantly different hepatic enzyme
responses of trout exposed to carbon tetrachloride for
24 h (Pfeifer et al., 1980).

Even when fish are fed live Artemia nauplii from
different geographical sources, toxicity test results can
be significantly altered.   Bengtson et al. (in press)
found that acute toxicity of cadmium to 25-day old
Atlantic silversides (Menidia menidia) differed by
2 1/2 times, depending on which of two geographical
strains of Artemia the fish had been fed prior to
testing.   Schimmel (1981) has pointed out that
intralaboratory variability for repeated determinations of
LC 50 for a single species is generally less than a factor
of two;   interlaboratory variability should be less than a
factor of four.

The effects of nutrition on aquatic toxicity testing
are not limited to fish, but have also been demonstrated
for several crustaceans, among them cladocerans (Winner et
al., 1977; Taylor, in press), copepods (Sosnowski et al.,
1979; Cooney et al., 1983) and mysids (Bengtson et al., in
press).

In some of the studies just cited, diets were of known
composition and were purposely caused to vary.   In others,
diet composition was unknown.   In either case, however,
two aspects of the diet are important with regard to
toxicity testing: nutrient levels and contaminant levels.

Specific nutrient requirements are known for relatively
few species of fish (e.g., some trout and salmon species,
channel catfish, carp) and are unknown for many species
commonly used in toxicity tests, e.g. fathead minnows
(Pimephales promelas), sheepshead minnows (Cyprinodon
variegatus), silversides (Menidia spp.).   For commercially
available formulated diets, the proximate composition is
very likely the only available nutritional information on
the package.   For commercially available Artemia cysts,
it is unlikely that any nutritional information is
available.   Thus, the toxicologist knows almost nothing
about his test organisms' nutrition unless he analyzes
batches of diets himself.

III. THE NUTRITIONAL VARIABILITY OF DIETS

Literature reports of analyses of variability in nutrient levels in commercially available products are not encouraging. Crawford and Law (1972) and Tacon and DeSylva (1983) found that mineral composition was highly variable in the diets they tested. Fatty acid composition of Artemia has been shown to vary significantly with geographical source (Watanabe et al., 1978b; Fujita et al., 1980; Schauer et al., 1980; Seidel et al., 1982) and that of rotifers (Brachionus plicatilis) has been shown to vary with culture conditions (Watanabe et al., 1978a).

Contaminant levels in commercial fish feeds have been analyzed and the results again indicate great variability. Brauhn and Schoettger (1975) found DDT levels ranging from nondetectable to 390 ppb and PCB levels from nondetectable to 320 ppb in the diets they analyzed. Fish oils used in those diets had the highest concentration of organic contaminants of all the components used. Crockett et al. (1975) detected DDTs of 20 to 840 ppb and lesser levels of five other organic contaminants in catfish feed. Gruger et al. (1976) measured 110 ppb total chlorobiphenyls in the diet used for a study of sublethal effects of chlorobiphenyls in salmon. They pointed out the need that researchers have for contaminant-free fish food, but acknowledged that the development of a clean diet without nutritional deficiencies would take years. Parejko and Wu (1977) analyzed two commercial diets fed to hatchery trout and found heptachlor levels of 21 and 15 ppb, DDE levels of 260 and 200 ppb, and total Arochlor levels of 118 and 639 ppb. Mac et al. (1979) found PCB concentrations from 100 to 300 ppb and DDE concentrations from undetectable to 470 ppb in different lots of one commercial fish feed. They also found 26 ppb DDE and 140 ppb PCB in brine shrimp nauplii and suggested that the nauplii should not be considered as an alternative feed to avoid contamination. They concluded that "the presence of organic contaminants in fish feed demonstrated in this and other studies is evidence that all feed used in contaminant-exposure studies should be analyzed."

The contamination of Artemia nauplii by chlorinated hydrocarbons and heavy metals has also been shown to vary tremendously with geographical source of the Artemia. The results of Olney et al. (1980) and Seidel et al. (1982) indicated that total DDTs ranged from 2 to 422 ppb and total PCBs ranged from 1 to 66 ppb depending on source.

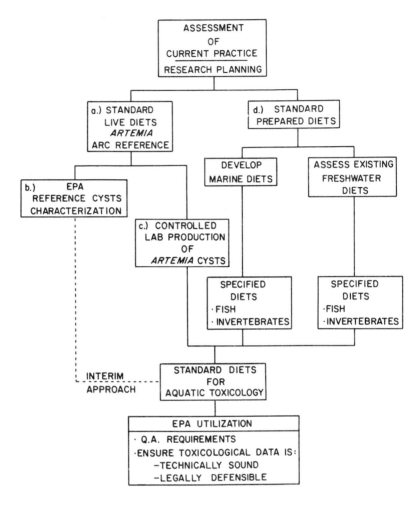

Fig. 1. Research strategy for nutrition in aquatic toxicology.

Considerable information exists, therefore, to show the large amount of variability of both nutrients and contaminants in both living and prepared diets for fish. Two major questions that remain, however, are: at what concentrations do dietary contaminants affect the biology of the fish?; and at what concentrations do dietary contaminants interact with toxicant effects in toxicity tests? Present ASTM (1980) recommendations for maximum contaminant levels in food for toxicity test organisms are < 150 ppb organic chlorine or < 300 ppb total organochlorine pesticides plus PCBs.

Mammalian toxicologists have long understood the importance of nutrition of animals prior to and during testing (NRC 1976, 1978). Certified diets are now available (Shelton, 1980), in which certain contaminants are certified not to exceed specific minimum levels. Greenman et al. (1980) and Bercz (1981) have reported on unacceptable contaminant levels in uncertified mammalian diets and have given examples of toxicity test data that had to be discarded for that reason.

The use of standard certified diets should be adopted by aquatic toxicologists as well, in order to reduce a potentially serious source of experimental variability. Our research strategy toward the accomplishment of that goal for the U.S. Environmental Protection Agency is outlined in Fig. 1. Standardization of both live and prepared diets is necessary. We have so far completed the interim approach (standardization of Artemia) and are just beginning work on the development of prepared diets for marine larval fish and the certification of existing diets for freshwater fish.

IV. STANDARIZATION OF BRINE SHRIMP NAUPLII

The concept of a standard, or reference, lot of brine shrimp cysts for use in scientific research was originally proposed (Simpson et al., 1980) in response to the variability in nutritional quality of different geographical strains of Artemia cysts (see literature reviewed in Beck and Bengtson (1982) or Seidel et al. (1982)). The availability of a standard lot, referred to as Reference Artemia Cysts (RAC), was announced to the scientific community (Sorgeloos, 1980) and samples have been sent to scores of scientists around the world.

Because of the importance of Artemia nauplii as a food for fish in ELS tests (as well as for several invertebrate species), the U.S. EPA has acquired and tested a large homogeneous lot of brine shrimp cysts, designated RAC II, as a standard diet for marine organisms used by EPA in toxicity testing. Testing of RAC II included several biochemical analyses and evaluation as a diet for two fish and two crustacean species, following methods of Beck et al. (1980), Johns et al. (1980, 1981), Klein-MacPhee et al. (1980), Olney et al. (1980), Schauer et al. (1980), and Seidel et al. (1980). Analysis for chlorinated hydrocarbons (Table I) indicated that RAC II was

Table I. Chlorinated hydrocarbons in Reference Artemia
Cysts II (RAC II) nauplii.   Results are given as ng/g or
ppb.

Chlorinated Hydrocarbon	Concentration
HCB	< 0.1
α -BHC	< 0.4
γ -BHC	< 0.6
cis-chlordane	< 0.5
trans-chlordane	< 0.6
nonachlor	< 0.3
dieldrin	< 1.4
Σ DDTs (ppDDE, ppDDD, opDDT, ppDDT)	< 10
Σ PCBs (1016 + 1254)	< 20

relatively free of contamination, with < 10 ppb total DDTs
and < 20 ppb total PCBs.   Fatty acid data (Table II) show
that the level of the essential fatty acid 20:5ω3, while
less than that for RAC and Brazilian samples, is certainly
adequate for marine organisms (Schauer et al., 1980).
Essential amino acid requirements (for chinook salmon) are
also met by RAC II (Table III).   Proximate and mineral
analyses (Table IV) also suggest that RAC II may be a good
larval fish diet.
     Laboratory evaluation of the RAC II diet included its
acceptability as measured by survival, growth and
reproduction of species commonly used in toxicity tests.
Fish larvae were fed RAC II, RAC (known good-quality
diet), or San Pablo Bay (known poor-quality diet) and
survival and growth were measured.   The fish survived and
grew as well on RAC II as on RAC (Table V).   Evaluation
as a diet for two crustacean species (Table VI) showed
that RAC II allowed good survival to the megalops stage
for mud crab larvae, which show a clear response to

Table II. Weight percent fatty acid composition of RAC II
Artemia nauplii.   Data from other high-quality Artemia
nauplii are included for comparison (RAC data from Seidel
et al. (1982), Brazil data from Schauer et al. (1980)).
(nd = not detected).

FAME	RAC II	RAC	Brazil
14:0	1.93	1.79	1.57
15:0	0.50	nd	0.67
15:1	0.42	nd	0.24
16:0	14.81	12.70	15.42
16:1	16.82	16.78	10.79
16:2 ω 4	4.12	4.33	3.88
18:0	4.30	4.07	2.79
18:1 ω 9	34.82	30.37	35.86
18:2 ω 6	11.80	9.62	9.59
20:0	0.23	nd	0.52
20:3 ω 3/20:4 ω 6	5.16	5.82	nd
20:5 ω 3	5.14	8.45	8.98

inadequate diets by complete mortality at metamorphosis to
megalops (Johns et al., 1980), and provided good
reproduction by mysids, also a good indicator of diet
adequacy (Johns et al., 1981).

We recommend that RAC II be used as a certified diet
because it has been extensively characterized for its
chemical constitutents and it has met biological
requirements for species used in marine toxicity tests.
The availability of this standard diet reduces the
variable of nutrition of test organisms, which may reduce
variations seen in interlaboratory comparison of data, and
should improve the quality of the toxicity test data
produced.

Table III. Amino acid profiles for RAC II <u>Artemia</u>
nauplii. Data from Seidel et al. (1980) for <u>another</u>
high-quality <u>Artemia</u> strain (Brazil) and the dietary
essential amino acid requirements for chinook salmon
(Mertz, 1969) are also listed for purposes of comparison.
Values are expressed as g amino acid/ 100 g protein.

Amino Acid	RAC II	Brazil	Chinook Salmon
Aspartic acid	10.3	11.0	-
Threonine	5.5	5.2	2.5
Serine	5.1	4.5	-
Glutamic acid	14.1	13.1	-
Proline	6.9	5.7	-
Glycine	7.4	6.0	-
Alanine	7.8	4.6	-
Valine	6.8	5.3	3.25
Methionine	3.3	2.2	1.5
Isoleucine	5.9	5.6	2.5
Leucine	9.3	8.9	4.0
Tyrosine	4.7	10.5	-
Phenylalanine	4.6	5.1	5.25
Histidine	4.3	4.9	1.75
Lysine	10.3	11.7	5.0
Arginine	9.8	11.5	5.75

Table IV.   Proximate analysis and mineral analysis of RAC II nauplii.

a) Proximate analysis (%)

Moisture		Protein	Fat	Fiber	Ash
		Dry			
82.4		47.0	20.8	5.2	6.1

b) Mineral analysis

Na %	1.86
K %	1.27
Mg %	0.15
P %	0.11
Ca ppm	303
Mn ppm	13.9
Zn ppm	118
Fe ppm	269
Cu ppm	15.5

This standard diet, however, is effective only as long as the supply lasts, estimated to be 3 years. After that, a new standard will have to be established. Reliance on Artemia cysts from natural populations presents several problems. Unpredictable climatic conditions, unreliable biological management of salinas (salt pans), and availability or cost of cysts in fluctuating world market conditions all mitigate against the likelihood that cysts can even be purchased from the same geographical source, let alone that they might be similar in quality.

The production of Artemia cysts under controlled laboratory conditions (Versichele and Sorgeloos, 1980; Lavens and Sorgeloos, in press) may provide a long-term solution to the problem of variability of Artemia from natural populations. The U.S. EPA is presently funding a portion of the research being done on lab cyst production

Table V.   Survival and growth of two fish species, Atlantic silversides (Menidia menidia) and winter flounder (Pseudopleuronectes americanus) raised on nauplii of Reference Artemia II (RAC II), Reference Artemia (RAC) or San Pablo Bay Artemia (SPB). Silversides were reared for 21 days, flounder for 26 days, on different diets. Data are mean ± standard deviation.

| Food | *M*. menidia | | *P*. americanus | |
	Survival (%)	Final wet wt. (mg)	Survival	Final wet wt. (mg)
RAC II	89.4 ± 5.9	16.8 ± 4.6	83.7 ± 6.3	2.60 ± 3.33
RAC	79.3 ± 6.8	19.3 ± 5.4	76.2 ± 9.5	1.55 ± 2.36
SPB	21.8 ± 5.2	19.3 ± 6.3	17.8 ± 14.2	0.60 ± 0.58

at the Artemia Reference Center in Ghent, Belgium. If cysts can be produced in sufficient quantity and quality under controlled conditions of feeding, temperature, water quality, etc., then reliance by toxicologists on natural Artemia populations could be curtailed.

V.   RESEARCH NEEDS

Beyond the controlled laboratory production of Artemia cysts, standard nutrition of fish in toxicology requires research in three general areas. The first is the development of certified diets for species whose nutrient requirements are (at least partially) known and which are used for toxicity testing, e.g., rainbow trout and channel catfish. Progress has been made in this direction with the development of reference research diets at the U.S. Fish and Wildlife Service Laboratory at Columbia, Missouri (Brauhn and Schoettger, 1975). The second is the investigation of nutrient requirements of those species used in toxicology whose requirements are not known and the development of formulated diets for them. This aspect is especially applicable to marine fish larvae. Finally, we need to better determine the maximum levels of contaminants allowable in fish diets that are used in toxicology.

The studies of Murai et al. (1981) and Hodson and Hilton (1983) are helpful in this regard. We especially need to detemine at what concentrations certain dietary contaminants have interaction effects with the toxicants being studied.

Table VI. a) Survival and growth of two crustacean species, mud crab (Rhithropanopeus harrisii) and mysid (Mysidopsis bahia) raised on nauplii of Reference Artemia II (RAC II), Reference Artemia (RAC), or San Pablo Bay Artemia (SPB). Mud crabs were raised to the megalops stage, mysids were raised for 10 days after hatching. b) Survival, growth and reproduction of mysids raised for 25 days (full life cycle). Survival is percentage of the original 35 mysids per replicate that survived to the end of the experiment, dry weight is the average of dry weights of those survivors and juvenile production is the number of juveniles produced per adult female at the end of the experiment. Data are means + standard deviation.

a)

	R. harrisii		M. bahia	
Food	Survival(%)	Final dry wt. (ug)	Survival(%)	Final dry wt. (ug)
RAC II	78.6 + 12.5	104 + 26	73.6 + 9.4	138 + 30
RAC	78.3 + 10.2	122 + 34	70.0 + 0.0	180 + 57
SPB	0.0	--	48.0 + 16.5	181 + 47

b)

Food	Survival(%)	Dry weight (ug)	Juvenile production
RAC II	76.7 + 0.0	518 + 154	6.85 + 1.06
RAC	56.7 + 0.0	523 + 145	5.00 + 1.21
SPB	50.0 + 9.4	459 + 124	0.19 + 0.04

ACKNOWLEDGEMENTS

We thank C. Seidel and H. Leibovitz for biochemical analyses and G. Klein-MacPhee for work with larval flounder. Helpful comments on the manuscript were provided by W.J. Berry, G.R. Gardner, D.J. Hansen and D.M. Johns. This work was supported by EPA Cooperative Agreements CR-806735-03 and CR-811042-01-0 with the University of Rhode Island.

REFERENCES

American Society for Testing and Materials (1980). "ASTM Annual Book of Standards, Designation E729-80". Amer. Soc. for Testing and Materials, Philadelphia.

Beck, A.D. and Bengtson, D.A. (1982). In "Aquatic Toxicology and Hazard Assessment: Fifth Conference, ASTM STP 766" (J.G. Pearson, R.B. Foster and W.E. Bishop, eds.), 161-169. Amer. Soc. for Testing and Materials, Philadelphia.

Beck, A.D., Bengtson, D.A. and Howell, W.H. (1980). In "The Brine Shrimp Artemia" (G. Persoone, P. Sorgeloos, O. Roels and E. Jaspers, eds.), 3, 249-259. Universa Press, Wetteren, Belgium.

Bengtson, D.A., Beck, A.D., Lussier, S.M., Migneault, D. and Olney, C.E. (in press). In "Ecotoxicological Testing for the Marine Environment" (G. Persoone, C. Claus and E. Jaspers, eds.). European Mariculture Society.

Bercz, J.P. (1981). "Temporal Variability of Toxic Contaminants in Animal Diets. EPA-600/S1-81-040". U.S. Environmental Protection Agency, Health Effects Research Laboratory, Cincinnati, Ohio.

Brauhn, J.L. and Schoettger, R.A. (1975). "Acquisition and Culture of Research Fish: Rainbow Trout, Fathead Minnows, Channel Catfish, and Blue-gills. EPA-660/3-75-011". U.S. Environmental Protection Agency, Ohio.

Cooney, J.D., Beauchamp, J.J. and Gehrs, C.W. (1983). Environ. Toxicol. Chem. 2, 431-439.

Crawford, D.L. and Law, D.K. (1972). Prog. Fish-Cult. 34, 126-130.

Crockett, A.B., Wiersma, G.B., Tai, H. and Mitchell, W.
    (1975). Pestic. Monit. J. 8, 235-240.
Dixon, D.G. and Hilton, J.W. (1981).   J. Fish Biol. 19,
    509-517.
Fujita, S., Watanabe, T. and Kitajima, C. (1980). In "The
    Brine Shrimp Artemia", (G. Persoone, P. Sorgeloos, O.
    Roels and E. Jaspers, eds.), 3, 277-290. Universa
    Press, Wetteren, Belgium.
Greenman, D.L., Oller, W.L., Littlefield, N.A. and Nelson,
    C.J. (1980). J. Toxicol. Environ. Health 6, 235-246.
Gruger, E.H., Jr., Hruby, T. and Karrick, N.L. (1976).
    Environ. Sci. Technol. 10, 1033-1937.
Hodson, P.V. and Hilton, J.W. (1983). In "Environmental
    Biogeochemistry",   (R.   Hallberg,   ed.),   335-340.
    Publishing House of Swedish Research, Stockholm.
Johns, D.M., Berry, W.J. and Walton, W. (1981). J. exp.
    mar. Biol. Ecol. 53, 209-219.
Johns, D.M., Peters, M.E. and Beck, A.D. (1980). In "The
    Brine Shrimp Artemia", (G. Persoone, P. Sorgeloos, O.
    Roels and E. Jaspers, eds.), 3, 291-304. Universa
    Press, Wetteren, Belgium.
Klein-MacPhee, G., Howell, W.H. and Beck, A.D. (1980). In
    "The Brine Shrimp Artemia" (G. Persoone, P. Sorgeloos,
    O. Roels and E. Jaspers, eds.). 3, 305-312. Universa
    Press, Wetteren, Belgium.
Lavens, P. and Sorgeloos, P. (in press). Aquacultural
    Engineering.
Mac, M.J., Nicholson, L.W. and McCauley, C.A. (1979).
    Prog. Fish-Cult. 41, 210-211.
Mehrle, P.M., Johnson, W.W. and Mayer, F.L. (1974). Bull.
    Environ. Contam. Toxicol. 12, 513-517.
Mehrle, P.M., Mayer, F.L. and Johnson, W.W. (1977). In
    "Aquatic Toxicology and Hazard Evaluation, ASTM STP
    634", (F.L. Mayer and J.L. Hamelink, eds.), 269-280.
    Amer. Soc. for Testing and Materials, Philadelphia.
Mertz, E.T. (1969). In "Fish in Research", (O.W. Neuhaus
    and J.E. Halver, eds.), 233-244.   Academic Press, New
    York and London.
Murai, T., Andrews, J.W. and Smith, R.G., Jr. (1981).
    Aquaculture 22, 353-357.
National Research Council (1976). ILAR News 19, L1-L25.
National Research Council (1978). ILAR News 21, A1-A11.
Olney, C.E., Schauer, P.S., McLean, S., Lu, Y. and
    Simpson, K.L. (1980). In "The Brine Shrimp Artemia"
    (G. Persoone, P. Sorgeloos, O. Roels and E. Jaspers,
    eds.), 3, 343-352. Universa Press, Wetteren, Belgium.
Parejko, R. and Wu, C.J. (1977). Bull. Environ. Contam.
    Toxicol. 17, 90-97.

Pfeifer, K.F., Weber, L.J. and Larson, R.E. (1980). Comp. Biochem. Physiol. 67C, 91–96.

Phillips, G.R. and Buhler, D.R. (1979). J. Fish. Res. Bd. Can. 36, 77–80.

Schauer, P.S., Johns, D.M., Olney, C.E. and Simpson, K.L. (1980). In "The Brine Shrimp Artemia", (G. Persoone, P. Sorgeloos, O. Roels and E. Jaspers, eds.), 3, 365–373. Universa Press, Wetteren, Belgium.

Schimmel, S.C. (1981). "Interlaboratory Comparison – Acute Toxicity Tests Using Estuarine Animals. EPA-600/4-81-003." U.S. Environmental Protection Agency, Environmental Research Laboratory, Gulf Breeze, Florida.

Seidel, C.R., Johns, D.M., Schauer, P.S. and Olney, C.E. (1982). Mar. Ecol. Prog. Ser. 8, 309–312.

Seidel, C.R., Kryznowek, J. and Simpson, K.L. (1980). In "The Brine Shrimp Artemia", (G. Persoone, P. Sorgeloos, O. Roels and E. Jaspers, eds.), 3, 375–382. Universa Press, Wetteren, Belgium.

Shelton, D.C. (1980). Lab. Animal 9, 42–45.

Simpson, K.L., Beck, A.D. and Sorgeloos, P. (1980). In "The Brine Shrimp Artemia" (G. Persoone, P. Sorgeloos, O. Roels and E. Jaspers, eds.), 3, 409–411. Universa Press, Wetteren, Belgium.

Sorgeloos, P. (1980). Mar. Ecol. Prog. Ser. 3, 363–364.

Sosnowski, S.L., Germond, D.J. and Gentile, J.H. (1979). Water Res. 13, 449–452.

Tacon, A.G.J. and DeSylva, S.S. (1983). Aquaculture 31, 11–20.

Taylor, M.J. (in press). In "Aquatic Toxicology and Hazard Assessment: Seventh Conference, ASTM STP", (R.D. Cardwell and R. Commotto, eds.). Amer. Soc. for Testing and Materials, Philadelphia.

Versichele, D. and Sorgeloos, P. (1980). In "The Brine Shrimp Artemia", (G. Persoone, P. Sorgeloos, O. Roels and E. Jaspers, eds.), 3, 231–246. Universa Press, Wetteren, Belgium.

Watanabe, T., Kitajima, C., Arakawa, T., Fukusho, K. and Fujita, S. (1978a). Bull. Jap. Soc. scient. Fish. 44, 1109–1114.

Watanabe, T., Oowa, F., Kitajima, C. and Fujita, S. (1978b). Bull. Jap. Soc. scient. Fish. 44, 1115–1121.

Winner, R.W., Keeling, T., Yeager, R. and Farrell, M.P. (1977). Freshwater Biol. 7, 343–349.

Woltering, D.M. (1984). Aquatic Toxicology 5, 1–21.

Yamamoto, Y., Hayama, K. and Ikeda, S. (1981). Bull. Jap. Soc. scient. Fish. 47, 1085–1089.

THE APPLICATION OF NUTRITIONAL FINDINGS TO THE FORMULATION OF PRACTICAL DIETS

V.O. CRAMPTON

Ewos-Baker Ltd., Westfield, Bathgate, West Lothian, EH48 3BP, U.K.

I. INTRODUCTION

This paper is intended to show the approach taken by one fish feed manufacturing company in deciding upon the formulation of practical rations. The subject is examined with regard to the formulation of salmonid diets in the U.K. but the principles outlined will apply equally to other species in all countries. The first consideration has to be the market value of the fish when finally ready for sale and the fixed or non-feed costs involved in producing the fish. Having examined economic considerations, research findings can then be applied as appropriate.

II. ECONOMIC CONSIDERATIONS

A. Effect of Product Value

A fish farmer makes a living by converting fish feed into fish flesh and in this sense is no different to any manufacturing company. The fact that the product is a living animal is an extra problem but should not change the essential nature of the process. Consequently the fish farmer is interested in converting the raw material

NUTRITION AND FEEDING IN FISH
ISBN: 0 12 194055 1

(fish feed) into the finished product (live fish) as quickly and as efficiently as possible.   But the relative importance of growth rate and conversion efficiency will vary depending upon the cost of feed in relation to the value of the fish.   In fact the value of fish grown in the U.K. varies considerably with fish size and species. Fig. 1 illustrates the market value of four different groupings of fish.

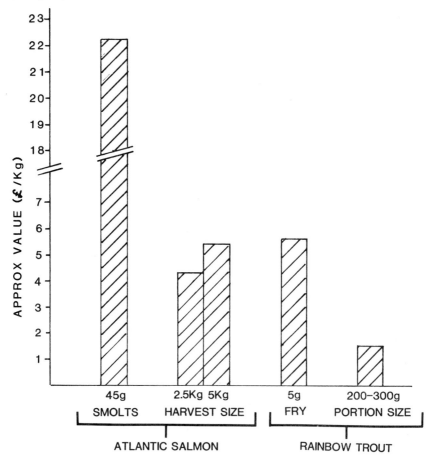

Fig. 1.   Comparative value of fish of different species and sizes.

Atlantic salmon smolts weighing 45g each and selling at £1 each are worth £22.2/kg.   This compares to £1.50/kg for portion sized rainbow trout (200–300g) and £5.60/kg for rainbow trout fry (5g).   Harvest size Atlantic salmon

prices vary with size; a 2.5kg fish will sell at around
£4.30/kg, whilst a 5kg fish will fetch approximately
£5.40/kg. (Data from Fish Farmer Vol. 7 Nos. 1-3, 1984).

These differences in price have a definite bearing upon
what the fish farmer wants from his feed. The Atlantic
salmon smolt producer buys feed for around £0.65/kg and so
the value of his fish is approximately 34 times higher
than the cost of his feed. He needs to convert a
relatively low value item into a much higher value one and
so is primarily interested in maintaining high growth
rates in order that turnover may be increased thus
reducing the contribution of fixed or overhead costs.
Reduced feed costs or increased feed efficiency would not
have much effect upon increasing profitability of smolt
farming.   In fact most smolt farmers spend only
approximately 4% of turnover on feed. However, increased
growth rate or survival levels would have a very marked
effect on profitability and it is by these two criteria
that most smolt farmers will judge competing feeds.
Producers of this size and species would be quite prepared
to pay increased prices for a feed that was able to give
only small improvements in growth or survival.

This situation should be compared to the farmer
producing portion-sized rainbow trout. Feed costs are
around £0.40/kg and so the value of the feed is
approximately 27% of the value of the fish. These farmers
will typically spend about 40% of their turnover on feed
(Lewis, 1979). Because the value of the feed is not very
far removed from the value of the fish, such a farmer is
very concerned with obtaining maximum feed efficiency.
Growth rate is still important in helping to reduce the
contribution of fixed costs but does not have the same
over-riding importance that is present with salmon smolt
production. Many rainbow trout farmers do not feed to
satiation, preferring instead to maximise conversion
efficiency rather than growth rate and so formulation
changes that increase growth rate without affecting
conversion efficiency will not always be viewed as
improvements.

The producers of rainbow trout fry and of harvest size
Atlantic salmon obtain prices between the two extremes
already discussed. The fry producer pays around £0.60/kg
for feed which represents only 10% of the value of his
fish when sold at 5g. Since fixed costs of production
are high then the primary criteria of feed are that it
returns high growth and provides high survival levels.
Cost of feed and conversion efficiency are of a much
lesser importance.

The price obtained per unit weight for harvest sized Atlantic salmon is dependent largely upon the weight of the fish.   Since there is a limited time in which to grow these fish, the farmer is concerned with maximising growth rate so that a larger fish and a higher market price can be obtained.   Also by increasing the market size, production costs may be reduced by spending less (per unit weight of fish produced) on fixed costs and the purchase of smolts.

For these reasons then the criteria by which farmers judge a feed depends upon the species which they are growing.   For producers of Atlantic salmon smolts, harvest sized Atlantic salmon and rainbow trout fry, the growth rate obtained is much more important than conversion efficiency or absolute feed costs.   For the producer of portion sized rainbow trout, conversion efficiency and absolute feed costs are at least as relevant as growth rate and for most farmers, more easily measured.

B. Effect of Economic Requirements upon Formulation

From a nutritional viewpoint, the economic considerations should not affect formulation.   Since salmonids eat to a set energy level, any improvement in diet will lead to an improvement in conversion efficiency when the fish are fed to satiation.   If the fish are being fed at a restricted rate, any improvement in diet will lead to an improvement in growth rate and conversion efficiency.   Given this, it might be argued, the approach to formulating salmon diets should be the same as when formulating trout diets.   The economic considerations, it may be argued, should not conflict with the nutritional considerations.

However, such an approach neglects one important factor - that of palatability.   The work of Adron et al. (1973) and Adron and Mackie (1978) showed that fishmeal in general and certain amino acids in particular are effective at stimulating increased feeding levels.   Tacon (1983) also found that increased feed intake and growth could be attained through the use of attractants which did not contribute significant nutritional value.   A number of years of experience has also convinced feed manufacturers that energy intake can be increased through the increased use of high quality raw materials.   Such materials only marginally affect the nutritional composition of the diet but do seem to be effective at increasing the palatability of the feed.   Unless such changes are made, palatability can limit the feed intake of certain fish species.   This seems true of salmon and trout fry and particularly of larger salmon (greater than 1kg) at low water temperatures (less than 10°C).   But there are no unequivocal results to support this and of course palatability is a difficult parameter to measure.   However, if palatability is a limiting factor in fish growth and accepting that it cannot be measured precisely then the effect of formulation changes on growth rate become unpredictable though profound.   Because of this uncertainty, formulation changes are rarely made for salmon diets or for diets for rainbow trout fry.   Furthermore, findings regarding the optimal dietary composition (e.g. amino acid content) cannot be fully used until it is certain that growth is not limited by non-nutritional considerations or until the full effect of such changes on feed intake is known.

For salmonids, at least, the fishmeal content seems to be the determining factor in palatability.   In particular, fish meals that release feeding stimulants into the water quickly, or in greater quantity, because either components of the fishmeal are water soluble, or because less severe heat treatment during processing leaves most of these components intact and undamaged, are the most effective stimulants of feed intake.   Palatability does not seem to have a very limiting effect upon feed intake of rainbow trout above approximately 10g.   Current prices and availability of fish meals mean that more often it is nutritional considerations that determine formulations.   For this reason and because of the need to maintain efficient protein conversion, nutritional findings are readily applied usually with the aid of computerised, least cost, linear programming systems to feeds for rainbow trout larger than approximately 10g.   These are discussed in the following section.

III.   NUTRITIONAL CONSIDERATIONS

Computerised linear programming systems allow data on nutritional requirements of fish to be used easily but, as will become clear, such data must be reported in a comparable form, and must be related to available information on the raw materials offered for inclusion. The requirements and outputs of the system will be illustrated by an example.

A. Raw Material Specification

The starting point is a description of each of the raw
materials the user has available and wishes to offer for
inclusion.   Information is needed on the price of the
material and on the level of each of the nutrients of
interest.   Note   that   there   are   no   pre-programmed

Table I.   Illustration of a raw material specification for
use in computerised linear programming

MATERIAL: Fish Meal, Scottish

Price: £358 per tonne

Nutrient	LEVEL
Volume (%)	100
Metabolizable energy (Mcal.kg)	3.41
Protein (%)	69
Lipid (%)	9
Carbohydrate (%)	0
Fibre (%)	0
Ash (%)	14
Methionine (%)	2.1
Met. + Cys. (%)	2.85
Lysine (%)	5.8
Available lysine (%)	5.4
Fishmeal content (%)	100
etc.	

---

nutrients; it is entirely up to the user to choose what
nutrient parameters be used, to describe each of the
available raw materials and to decide what levels be
assigned to each of these parameters. Typically about
30-40 different nutrient parameters can be stored by the
computer. Information on nutrient levels of various raw
materials is available from industrial and government data

Table II. Constraints imposed on the selection of raw
materials by computerised linear programming (example
illustration).

MATERIAL	MINIMUM	MAXIMUM
	%	%
Fish meal, Scottish	15	100
Fish meal, Danish	15	100
Fish meal, spray-dried	0	15
Blood meal, spray dried	0	5
Soyabean meal, ext.	0	15
Meat and Bone meal	0	10
Fish oil	2	13
Wheat	0	20
Poultry by-products meal	0	5
Distillers by-products meal ..	0	5
Vitamin pack	1	1
Mineral pack	1	1
Pellet binder	0.1	0.1

sheets, (e.g. Bolton and Blair, 1974). Table I shows part
of an example raw material specification for fish meal.

B. Diet Specification

Having detailed the price and composition of each of
the raw materials available, the user must then specify
which raw materials may be included along with any
constraints on their inclusion (i.e. their minimum and
maximum levels for inclusion). An example is given in
Table II.

Finally, minimum and maximum levels must be applied to
each of the nutrients used in the raw material
specification. An example is shown in Table III.

Table III. Constraints imposed on the nutrient
composition of a diet in computerised linear programming
(example illustration).

ANALYSIS	MINIMUM	MAXIMUM
Volume (%)	100	100
Metabolizable energy (Mcal/kg)	3	100
Protein (%)	45	100
Lipid (%)	15	100
Carbohydrate (%)	5	20
Fibre (%)	0	100
Ash (%)	5	18
Methionine (%)	0.75	100
Met. + Cys. (%)	1.75	100
Lysine (%)	2.3	100
Available lysine (%)	2	100
Fishmeal content (%)	45	100
etc.		

C. Optimum Diet

Once the user has posed the problem the computer will, in a matter of seconds, produce the lowest cost diet which satisfies all the constraints imposed. Such an output is shown in Table IV. At this or at any other point, the user may go back to re-define the constraints involved.

Alternatively the computer will not find the problem feasible, that is no diet will satisfy all the constraints imposed. If this latter output occurs, the user will need to redefine the problem or accept that such a diet is not possible under the given constraints.

Table IV. Composition of an optimal diet produced by computerised linear programming (example illustration).

	INCLUSION
	%
Fish meal, Scottish	15.0
Fish meal, Danish	30.0
Soybean meal ext.	15.0
Meat and bone meal	0.1
Fish oil	9.9
Wheat	20.0
Poultry by-product meal	4.8
Distillers by-product meal	3.1
Vitamin pack	1.0
Mineral pack	1.0
Pellet binder..........................	0.1
TOTAL	100.0

Before describing the other outputs, the assumptions involved with any linear programming (LP) system (manual or computerised) will be reviewed.

D. Assumptions of LP Systems

Such a quick and easy aid does have its drawbacks. One is that an LP system assumes a linear relationship between each of the ingredients used and each of the nutrient levels. This will not be true in a number of instances, for example the contribution to metabolizable energy of the first 10% of wheat in a diet may not be the same as the second 10%. The marginal utility (in terms of metabolizable energy) of wheat inclusion is not constant though a linear programming model will assume that it is. Formulating practical rations then becomes a problem of deciding just how non-linear such relationships are and when the point is reached where the difference between what is assumed to be true and what is actually true becomes too large to be tolerated. Reducing the range of inclusion levels from which to select the optimum ration will help to minimise the errors involved in this assumption but may also exclude the optimum ration. Industry requires unequivocal information on the exact relationship between utilization of an ingredient and its level in the diet for the most common ingredients.

A second assumption is that the parameters of interest can be stated in numeric terms. This can be difficult for parameters such as digestibility, since data are not present for all raw materials currently available. With other factors such as palatability, expression in numeric terms is almost impossible. This assumption then does not so much invalidate the use of an LP model as make it rather difficult to use.

The two other assumptions involved in linear programming need not bother us. The first of these is that the LP problem must be soluble given the raw materials available and the restrictions, if any, on their inclusion. The second is that there must be restrictions on one or more of the nutrient parameters specified. Neither of these is likely to cause any difficulty.

However, the value of LP as an aid in formulating practical diets is also dependent upon the quality and quantity of information about nutrient requirements and what is provided, in the way of these nutrients, by the raw materials available. This of course is true of any method for formulating diets, it is not peculiar to LP formulations. However, a computerised LP system creates much greater demands upon the information provided by nutritional findings since it is much easier to use and much more versatile than manual formulations. A large data base on nutritional requirements can be used but it does mean that the work has to be expressed in a standard fashion. Consequently standardised terminology is required not just for the advancement of nutritional studies but also for their application to practical diets.

Other outputs from LP system are described below.

E. Analysis of Optimal Diet

An example of an analysis of the optimal diet is shown in Table V. The parameters shown are exactly those used to define the raw materials offered for inclusion.

Table V. Analysis of an optimal diet produced by computerised linear programming (example illustration)

NUTRIENT PARAMETER	ANALYSIS
Volume (%)	100
Metabolizable energy (Mcal/kg)	3.4
Protein (%)	45.1
Lipid (%)	15.0
Carbohydrate (%)	20.0
Fibre (%)	1.6
Ash (%)	10.6
Methionine (%)	1.2
Met. + cys. (%)	1.75
Lysine (%)	3.2
Available lysine (%)	2.0
Fishmeal content (%)	45.0

F. Cost Ranging

The effect of price changes of raw materials included in the optimal diet upon the cost and composition of it is also given. An example showing the effect of cost changes in two materials is given in Table VI.

Table VI. Cost ranging of two of the materials included in an optimum diet (example illustration).

MATERIAL: MEAT AND BONE MEAL	£/Tonne		%
Current Price	187.00	Inclusion	0.1
Lower Range	181.40	Inclusion	7.0
Upper Range	211.80	Inclusion	0.0

MATERIAL: POULTRY BY-PRODUCTS	£/Tonne		%
Current Price	275.00	Inclusion	4.8
Lower Range	262.70	Inclusion	5.0
Upper Range	340.30	Inclusion	4.7

It shows for example that meat and bone meal would be included in the optimum ration at 7% if the price fell to £181.40 per tonne. Similarly even if the price of poultry offal increased to £340 per tonne (a £65 per tonne rise), the optimum inclusion would fall by only 0.1% (to 4.7%). Such information is useful in seeing what price changes of raw materials have upon inclusion levels and the ration type. Raw materials vary in their sensitivity to price changes; an output such as shown in Table VI can help the user to persuade raw material suppliers to reduce their offered price for a return in increased usage of that raw material (meat and bone meal in this example). Equally such an output will highlight those raw materials where an increase in cost could not be mitigated by substitution with an alternative (poultry offal in this example). Also it is very useful in deciding upon the cost of including a raw material at a different level other than that featured in the optimum solution. Thus if the user decided to include meat and bone meal at 7% (perhaps to spread reliance of raw materials) he would know the approximate extra cost involved (£187 - £181.40 x 0.07 = £0.4). Raw materials offered but not included in the optimum solution are shown in Table VII along with the price at which they would have to be offered to merit inclusion. Here, two high quality, spray dried materials are not included in the ration and the price offered would have to fall substantially before they would be included. Again, this type of output can be used as an aid in negotiating prices (when they are negotiable) with raw material suppliers.

Table VII. Inclusion costs of materials not included in the optimum diet (example illustration).

	INCLUSION PRICE (£/Tonne)	INCLUSION LEVEL (%)
Blood Meal	333.10	0.5
Fish Meal (spray dried)	383.60	0.8

In this example the nutrient parameters used measure the level of only three amino acids and with the exception of lysine, take no account of their digestibility. This will favour inclusion of lower priced ingredients which are high in these amino acids but which may not be very digestible. That is, the exclusive use of such measures means that expensive raw materials equally high in digestibility will not usually be featured in an optimum diet.

F. Sensitivity of Constraining Factors

Table VIII shows the raw materials and nutrient parameters which are effective in limiting the optimal solution. Thus soybean meal and wheat are both being used at their maximum allowed inclusion level (15% and 20% respectively) whilst Scottish herring meal is at its

Table VIII. Sensitivity of the constraining materials used in the optimum diet (example illustration).

MATERIAL: SOYBEAN MEAL

Current Restriction	15.0%	Unit Cost (£/%):	0.03
Looser Restriction	17.12%	Saving (£):	0.06
Tighter Restriction	13.95%	Cost (£):	0.03

MATERIAL: WHEAT

Current Restriction	20%	Unit Cost (£/%):	0.11
Looser Restriction	21.41%	Saving (£):	0.16
Tighter Restriction	19.78%	Cost (£):	0.02

MATERIAL: FISH MEAL SCOTTISH

Current Restriction	15%	Unit Cost (£/%):	0.03
Looser Restriction	0%	Saving (£):	4.78
Tighter Restriction	15.68%	Cost (£):	0.02

---

minimum (15%).   The marginal cost of each percentage inclusion is given in the first column followed by the savings or cost of the next step change with the new constraint level.   In this example, each percentage change in soya inclusion would cost approximately 3p, as would each percentage change in the cost of Scottish herring meal.   Whilst the figure for wheat inclusion is approximately 11p for each percentage unit, none of these are very significant.   Each of these marginal unit costs will apply only to the current step, but the marginal cost at the next step will usually be similar to the cost at the current step and so it is possible to predict the effect of changes on constraints for quite a wide range of changes.

The marginal unit costs of two of the constraining nutrient parameters are shown in Table IX.   It is immediately apparent that in this example small changes in the specified level of methionine plus cystine can have a relatively large effect upon the cost of the optimal ration.

Table IX.   Sensitivity of two of the constraining nutrient parameters which detail the optimum diet (example illustration).

PARAMETER: METHIONINE AND CYSTINE CONTENT

Current Restriction:	1.75% Unit Cost (£/%)	33.29
Looser Restriction	1.746% Saving (£)	0.15
Tighter Restriction	1.753% Cost (£)	0.08

PARAMETER: FISH MEAL CONTENT

Current Restriction	45.00% Unit Cost (£/%)	0.88
Looser Restriction	44.71% Saving (£)	0.25
Tighter Restriction	45.81% Cost (£)	0.71

The absence of crude protein level as a limiting factor indicates that the optimum solution is heavily dependent upon the specified level of these amino acids.   The carbohydrate and lipid levels also constrain the optimum solution in this example.

G. Choice of Constraints

No matter how sophisticated an LP system is, the optimum diet it produces will only be as close to or as far from the true optimum as the constraints chosen allow.

The choice of constraints are largely determined by research findings, and it is vital that the findings on requirements are readily interpreted in terms of the nutrient levels in the raw materials.   Thus the results should be expressed in a comparable form and ideally as a proportion of a single index (such as net or metabolizable energy).

IV. PRACTICAL CONSIDERATIONS

Diet formulation must take account of practical considerations and it is useful to review these since they influence the extent to which nutritional findings can be applied to formulation.

A. Materials Handling

A feed mill is essentially concerned with material handling. Even a small feed mill produces 10,000 tonnes of feed per year which means it not only has to send 10,000 tonnes of material to its customers but also buy the same amount of raw materials from suppliers as well as process one into the other.   Some of the larger feed mills will produce around 250,000 tonnes per year. Consequently there is always pressure to accept any changes that make materials handling and processing easier and to reject anything which makes them more difficult.

A diagrammatic representation of a typical feed mill is shown in Fig. 2.   Raw materials come in the form of bagged or bulk, dry or liquid ingredients.   It is more expensive to use bagged ingredients since the price of bags adds about £10 per tonne to the cost of the material whilst labour costs are much more expensive too.   Most of the more specialist raw materials are only available in bags and an excessive use of such materials means that the extra cost of manufacture can outweigh the nutritional advantages to be gained.   It is essential to maintain a quick turnover of raw materials, thus the use of a large number of different vitamin mixes, for instance, becomes impractical though it may be advantageous for a nutritionally efficient diet.

The use of bulk materials (either dry or liquid) is limited by the number of storage bins available.   The amount of oil or other liquid ingredients is limited by the fact that it is not possible to achieve more than around 18% oil in a pelleted ration without experiencing problems with pellet durability.   The moisture content of the diet needs to be less than 12% to ensure a shelf-stable product.

Raw materials must also be available continuously and be of consistent quality.   For instance, only two feed grade amino acids are available (methionine and lysine) whilst many distillery by-products are not available throughout the year.   The feed must also be able to be

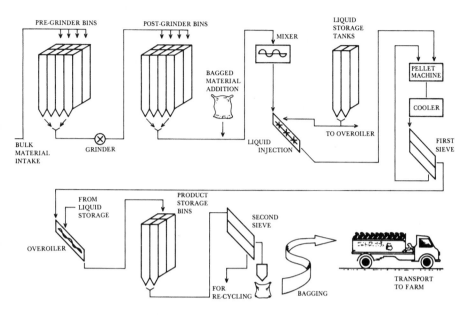

Fig 2. Simplified, schematic, flow diagram of fish feed manufacturing plant.

pelletted and remain so until used. Some raw materials particularly those high in ash, fibre or oil produce non-durable pellets and their use must be limited, or if unlimited, must be combined with increased usage of pellet-binding agents.

B. Buoyancy

A diet that floats does have some distinct advantages over one that sinks, the most important is that it allows the farmer to see how much feed remains uneaten and so regulate feeding much more closely. Such diets need high levels (around 20-30%) of carbohydrate inclusion to ensure that they are expanded during processing and this obviously affects the composition of the rest of the diet.

C. Marketing Considerations

The feed is made to be sold and if it cannot be sold then the nutritional quality of it becomes irrelevant. One particular problem in the U.K. is that rainbow trout

farmers are reluctant to change to a diet where a greater
proportion of the energy is provided by non-protein
sources and so is a cheaper diet in terms of actual fish
growth.   Despite the fact that the importance of lipids
in providing dietary energy in salmonid diets has been
recognised for many years, most UK trout farmers are using
grower diets with less than 10% oil.   In other parts of
Europe the higher energy diets have been accepted and most
or all feeds contain around 15% oil.   This illustrates
the fact that even when nutritional findings, economic
pressures and practical considerations all combine to
suggest a change in diet formulation, it is the customer
who often has the final say in whether that change is
implemented.

V. SUMMARY

Nutritional findings must be applied in the most
economically appropriate fashion. The formulation must
reflect the value of the fish and the cost of growth from
non-feed elements.

Since it is possible to measure the limiting factors in
rainbow trout nutrition, it is possible to use linear
programming techniques to reduce diet costs.   Such
techniques are not readily applicable to salmon or trout
fry diets since it would seem that palatability (which
cannot be measured) is a limiting factor in growth rate.

Practical and marketing considerations will always
influence the way in which nutritional findings can be
used.

REFERENCES

Adron, J.W., Grant, P.T. and Cowey, C.B. (1973). J. Fish
    Biol. 5, 625-636.
Adron, J.W. and Mackie, A.M. (1978). J. Fish Biol. 12,
    303-310.
Bolton, W. and Blair, R. (1974). "Poultry Nutrition",
    Ministry of Agriculture Fisheries & Food Reference book
    174, HMSO, London.
Lewis, M.R. (1979). "Fish Farming in Great Britain: an
    economic survey with special reference to rainbow
    trout", Misc. Study 67, Dept. of Agriculture, Econ. and
    Management. University of Reading.
Tacon, A.G.J. (1983). "The replacement of marine fish
    protein in salmonid diets, Part I" Report to Chief
    Scientist Group, MAFF, Lowestoft UK.   April 1980 to
    June 1983.

MINERAL NUTRITION: EFFECTS OF PHOSPHORUS IN
TROUT AND SALMON FEEDS ON WATER POLLUTION

H. GEORGE KETOLA

Tunison Laboratory of Fish Nutrition,
U.S. Fish and Wildlife Service, 28 Gracie Road,
Cortland, NY 13045, U.S.A.

I.   INTRODUCTION

This report demonstrates the effect of fish hatchery
diets on the pollution of effluent waters with
phosphorus. Interest in the problem began when the
Fisheries Division of the Michigan Department of Natural
Resources pointed out the need to reduce discharges of
phosphorus into the effluents from a coho salmon hatchery
in Michigan. The Water Quality Division in Michigan
reported that effluent discharges from the Platte River
Salmon Hatchery significantly increased the total amount
of phosphorus going into Platte Lake, thereby hastening
eutrophication of this 1018-hectare transitional
mesotrophic lake, which had an average depth of 9.1 meters
(Grant, 1979). The average concentration of phosphorus in
the river was 12 micrograms per liter above the hatchery
and 33 micrograms per liter below it.   Thus the hatchery
discharge increased phosphorus by 21 micrograms per liter
in the river as it flowed through the hatchery. The total
annual discharge of phosphorus was estimated to be 1500
kilograms. A later report (Kanaga and Evans, 1982)
estimated the annual discharge to be 1018 kilograms. Most,
if not all, of this phosphorus apparently came from the
fish feed. The Water Quality Division recommended that
the hatchery be permitted to discharge no more than about
640 kg of phosphorus per year. The Fisheries Division

NUTRITION AND FEEDING IN FISH
ISBN: 0 12 194055 1

considered that treatment of the effluent itself probably
could not meet this recommendation. Therefore they sought
possible ways to reduce the loss of dietary phosphorus
into the hatchery effluent. Estimates made from published
data on Atlantic salmon (Ketola, 1975), indicate that the
retention of dietary phosphorus in salmon tissues was, in
some cases, about 20%. Therefore up to 80% of dietary
phosphorus could pollute hatchery water. This suggested
the potential to markedly increase retention of phosphorus
and thereby reduce phosphorus pollution caused by fish
feeds.

II. METHODS

Three experiments were conducted with rainbow trout
(Salmo gairdneri) and coho salmon (Oncorhynchus kisutch)
to determine the influence of diet on pollution of
effluent water with phosphorus. Experiments 1 and 2 were
laboratory studies with trout. Experiment 3 was a
production-scale experiment at the Platte River Salmon
Hatchery conducted by Michigan Division of Fisheries.
This experiment was designed to meet scientific
requirements while following the general rearing practices
at the hatchery. Table I shows the composition of
experimental diets 3 and 5 that were formulated by
computer to contain low levels of phytin phosphorus and to
contain little or no excess phosphorus. Dietary phytin
phosphorus was minimized because it is absorbed poorly, if
at all, by trout and therefore represents a form likely to
pollute effluent water. Modifications of these diets
were also fed along with commercial diets. All diets
were analysed for phosphorus. The vitamin supplements
were those described by Ketola (1983) except that vitamin
E was supplemented at 350 IU/kg of diet, and all known
requirements for vitamins by salmonids were amply met. The
mineral supplements are shown in Table II and meet all
known requirements with the exception of phosphorus.
Supplemental phosphorus was supplied by dicalcium
phosphate dihydrate ($CaHPO_4 \cdot 2H_2O$).

Table III shows the experimental conditions for each of
the three studies: the average initial body weights
ranged from 2 to 5 grams per fish. Whereas there were 50
to 100 trout/jar in Experiments 1 and 2 (conducted in the
laboratory), there were 25 thousand coho salmon/raceway in
Experiment 3 (conducted in a hatchery). Diets were

Table I.   Composition of diets.

Ingredient	Diet 3	Diet 5
Soybean meal, 48%	22	42
Corn gluten meal, 60%	–	30
Alfalfa meal	7	–
Blood meal, ring	18	9.7
Casein	20	–
Marine oil	17	11
$CaHPO_4 \cdot 2H_2O$	3.6	3.8
Arginine·HCl, L	0.2	–
Phenylalanine, L	0.4	0.3
Lysine·HCl, L	–	0.4
Vitamins[1] & Minerals[2]	+	+

[1] Same vitamin supplements given in Ketola (1983) except that vitamin E was provided at 350 IU/kg of diet.

[2] Table 2

randomly assigned to triplicate lots of fish.   Duration of the experiments ranged from 8 to 12 weeks and water temperature ranged from 9 to 10°C.

Body weights were determined at the beginning and every 2 weeks throughout each experiment.   Feed was carefully and quantitatively fed to each lot of fish (at levels to minimize waste) according to body weights determined each weigh day.   Phosphorus was analyzed in the feed and in fasted trout carcass samples at the start and end of the studies.   Fasting was for 72 hours to ensure intestinal tracts were devoid of food phosphorus.   From these analyses, retention of dietary phosphorus in carcass samples was determined for each lot of fish.   Furthermore, at the end of Experiments 1 and 2, each lot of fish was fed a constant amount of feed for 10 days.   In these two

Table II. Minerals

Mineral (Source)	Mineral element (mg/kg diet)
Mn $(MnSO_4 \cdot H_2O)$	100
Zn $(ZnSO_4 \cdot 7H_2O)$	150
Cu $(CuSO_4 \cdot 5H_2O)$	15
Fe $(FeSO_4 \cdot 7H_2O)$	100
I (KIO_3)	5
Se (Na_2SeO_3)	0.1
Mo $(NaMoO_4 \cdot 2H_2O)$	3
Mg $(MgCO_3)$	1000
Na $(NaCl)$	1900
K (KCL)	2550

Table III. Conditions of Experiment

Experiment	1	2	3
Initial Body wt. (g/fish)	5	2	5
Fish/Tank	50	100	25,000
Tanks/Diet	3	3	3
Duration (wk)	12	12	8
Temp. (°C)	9	9	10
Species	RBT	RBT	COHO

RBT = rainbow trout, COHO = coho salmon

experiments, all solid waste (sludge) was recovered for
the last 72 hours of that 10-day period and analyzed for
phosphorus.   The sludge was recovered by use of sludge
traps having settling baffles.   Because of the constant
amounts of feed given for 10 days, the phosphorus
collected in the sludge represented the waste from a known
amount of feed phosphorus consumed.   Therefore it was
possible to calculate the amount of phosphorus pollution
of effluent water by subtracting the total phosphorus
retained in the carcass and that which settled out in the
solid sludge waste from the total phosphorus fed to the
fish.   This difference represented that portion of dietary
phosphorus that contributed to water pollution by ending
up dissolved or suspended in the effluent water.   Data on
pollution are expressed as grams of effluent phosphorus
per kilogram of weight gain and per kilogram of feed given.

In experiment 3, influence of diet on phosphorus
discharges was determined by analyses of concentrations of
phosphorus in the influent and effluent waters for each
raceway of salmon at 3, 5 and 7 weeks in the study.
Average increases in the concentrations of phosphorus
between the influents and effluents for the 3 periods were
used as the measure of pollution for each raceway.

Analyses of variance were conducted and individual
treatment differences were detected by Duncan's New
Multiple Range Test (Steel and Torrie, 1960).   The results
of the Duncan's Tests are shown by superscripts following
data values;   values not followed by the same superscript
are significantly different (P   0.05).   Pooled standard
errors of the means (Pooled SE) were calculated by the
formula:

$$\text{Pooled SE} = \sqrt{\text{Error Mean Square/Number of Replications}}$$

III.   RESULTS AND DISCUSSION

Results of the first experiment are shown in Table IV.
In this experiment, four diets were tested.   Diets 1 and 2
were commercial diets.   Diet 1 was a commercial European
diet advertized to reduce pollution.   Diet 2 was the diet
in use at the Platte River Salmon Hatchery where the
pollution problem was identified.   Diet 3 was the
low-phytin phosphorus diet shown in Table I, having
dicalcium phosphate dihydrate as a source of supplemental
phosphorus.   Diet 4 was the same as diet 3 except that it

Table IV.   Experiment 1

| Diet | Gain | F/G | Pollution (g P/kg of:) | |
(12 wk)	(g/fish)	(g/g)	Gain	Feed
1 (T-40) [1]	14.2[a]	0.9[a]	6.0	6.4
2 [1]	10.4[b]	1.2[b]	15.0	12.4
3	8.9[c]	1.3[c]	7.4	5.4
4 [2]	9.7[c]	1.2[bc]	5.7	4.5

[1] Commercial diets

[2] Diet 4 was the same as diet 3 except that $CaHPO_4 \cdot 2H_2O$ was replaced by
defluorinated rock phosphate

[a,b,c,] Duncan's Test (P < 0.05)

was supplemented with defluorinated rock phosphate (DRP)
instead of dicalcium phosphate dihydrate.   Defluorinated
rock phosphate was selected because it is readily absorbed
by domestic animals but dissolved only slightly in water –
a possibly beneficial property in reducing water pollution.

When diets were fed to rainbow trout in the laboratory
Diet 1 supported significantly better growth and feed
conversion than any other diet. Hatchery diet 2 supported
growth 76% as well as did diet 1. Experimental diets 3
and 4 supported growth 86 and 93% as well as hatchery diet
2, respectively;   these differences were significant.
Chemical determinations of the fate of dietary phosphorus
in this experiment showed that, whereas feeding 1 kilogram
of diet 2 generated 12.4 grams of phosphorus in the
effluent water diets 1, 3, and 4 generated only 6.4, 5.4
and 4.5 grams of phosphorus, respectively.   Similar
differences resulted when pollution values were calculated
on the basis of gain in fish weight.   Defluorinated rock
phosphate tended to reduce pollution more than did
dicalcium phosphate.   Though marked reductions in
effluent pollution were achieved with diets 1, 3 and 4,
these diets were all costly.   Therefore Experiment 2 was
conducted to test a new less-costly diet (diet 5).

The results of Experiment 2 are shown in Table V.   In
this experiment, five diets were fed.   Diet 4 was the

Table V. Experiment 2

| Diet (12 wk) | Gain (g/fish) | F/G (g/g) | Pollution (g P/kg of:) | |
			Gain	Feed
4	7.9^a	1.5^a	6.3	4.2
5	7.5^a	1.5^a	11.3	7.4
6^1	7.4^b	1.5^a	6.8	4.4
7^2	7.6^{ab}	1.5^a	7.2	4.8
OMP^3	8.8^c	1.8^b	13.3	7.4
Pooled SE	0.151	0.018	- -	- -

[1] Diet 6 was the same as diet 5 except that $CaHPO_4 \cdot 2H_2O$ was replaced by defluorinated rock phosphate

[2] Diet 7 was the same as diet 6 except that it contained no supplemental phenylalanine

[3] OMP (Oregon Moist Pellet), control

[a,b,c] Duncan's Test (P < 0.05)

same as diet 4 from the first experiment. It contained
very little phytin phosphorus and contained defluorinated
rock phosphate as the source of phosphorus. Diet 5, the
new less-costly diet (Table I) was formulated to be
moderately low in phytin phosphorus and contained
supplemental dicalcium phosphate dihydrate as the source
of phosphorus.   Diet 6 was the same as diet 5 except that
it contained defluorinated rock phosphate as a source of
phosphorus. Diet 7 was the same as diet 6 except that it
contained no supplemental phenylalanine (in an attempt to
reduce cost of the feed).   The OMP diet was a
commercially prepared Oregon Moist Pellet diet that was

being fed at the Platte River Salmon Hatchery at the time
of this experiment. The OMP diet contained 30% moisture
in contrast to the other diets which contained only about
7% moisture. It was fed at a higher level to equalize
dry matter intakes. Growth results showed that the OMP
diet produced significantly greater gains than did the
other experimental feeds but it also resulted in the
highest degree of phosphorus pollution of effluent water.
Weight gains of trout fed diets 4 to 7 were between 81 and
89% as good as for OMP and were acceptable for hatchery
performance. The new, less-costly diet 5 produced
considerable pollution but not when modified by replacing
dicalcium phosphate with defluorinated rock phosphate with
or without deletion of supplemental phenylalanine (diets 6
and 7, respectively). Diet 7 was the most favourable
diet cost-wise, and it had low pollution properties.

Table VI. Experiment 3

Diet (8 wk)	Gain (g/fish)	F/G (g/g)	P Pollution (µg P increase/L)
7 (DRP) [1]	6.2[a]	1.02[a]	10[a]
8 (DRP) [1]	5.8[a]	1.11[a]	15[a]
9 (BONE) [1]	5.2[a]	1.21[a]	15[a]
OMP[2]	7.7[b]	1.14[a]	33[b]

[1] Diets 7, 8 and 9 are modifications of diet 5 and contain defluorinated
rock phosphate (DRP) or bone meal at levels to provide 0.7, 0.65, and
0.7% P, respectively

[2] Oregon Moist Pellet, 3/32" pellets, control

[a,b] Duncan's Test (P < 0.05)

The third experiment was a large-scale hatchery study
conducted under as normal hatchery conditions as possible
under controlled conditions. The results in Table VI show
the effects of diets 7 to 9 on coho salmon growth and
water pollution in comparison with the standard hatchery

diet (OMP) fed at equal levels of dry matter. Diet 8 was the same as diet 7 except that the level of defluorinated rock phosphate was reduced by about 10%.   Diet 9 was the same as diet 7 except that defluorinated rock phosphate was replaced by enough cattle bone meal to supply phosphorus equal to that in diet 7. Growth of salmon fed OMP was significantly better than that for diets 7, 8 and 9; however, pollution was 2 to 3 times higher in those fed OMP. There were no significant (P > 0.05) differences between diets 7, 8 and 9 in terms of growth and pollution.

IV.   CONCLUSIONS

In summary, this research shows that dietary changes can markedly reduce phosphorus pollution of effluent waters of hatcheries. A commercial European diet designed to reduce pollution was highly effective but costly - at least in the United States. A new, low-cost experimental diet (#7) was formulated to contain only a modest level of phosphorus supplied mainly by defluorinated rock phosphate. This diet 7 supported significantly slower, but adequate, growth and reduced phosphorus pollution by more than 50%.

REFERENCES

Grant, J. (1979). Water Quality and Phosphorus Loading Analysis of Platte Lake 1970-1978. Publication #4833-9792, 68 pp. Water Quality Division, Michigan Department of Natural Resources, State of Michigan.

Kanaga, D. and Evans, E.D. (1982). The effect of the Platte River Anadromous Fish Hatchery on the fish, benthic macroinvertebrates and nutrients in Platte Lake. Water Quality Division, Michigan Department of Natural Resources, State of Michigan.

Ketola, H.G. (1975). Trans. American Fish. Soc. 104, 548-551.

Ketola, H.G. (1983). J. Animal Sci., 56, 101-107.

Steel, R.G.D. and Torrie, J.H. (1960). "Principles and Procedures of Statistics, with Special Reference to the Biological Sciences". pp 107-109. McGraw-Hill Book Co., Inc., New York.

INDEX